FROMMER'S
EasyGuide
TO
AUSTRALIA

By
Lee Mylne

EasyGuides are ✦ Quick To Read ✦ Light To Carry
✦ For Expert Advice ✦ In All Price Ranges

FrommerMedia LLC

Published by
FROMMERMEDIA LLC

ISBN 978-1-62887-007-7 (paper), 978-1-62887-037-4 (e-book)

Editorial Director: Pauline Frommer
Editor: Alexis Lipsitz Flippin
Production Editor: Donna Wright
Indexer: Kelly Henthorne
Cartographer: Roberta Stockwell
Cover Design: Howard Grossman

For information on our other products or services, see www.frommers.com.

FrommerMedia LLC also publishes its books in a variety of electronic formats. Some content that appears in print may not be available in electronic formats.

Manufactured in the United States of America

5 4 3 2 1

CONTENTS

LIST OF MAPS

For Sophie and Jess

ACKNOWLEDGMENTS

Many people—friends and strangers, too numerous to mention individually here—have shared their knowledge and insider tips about travel in Australia with me in both personal and professional capacities. Many of their suggestions, over the years, made it into this book, and I thank them all. In particular I would like to thank Marc Llewellyn for the groundwork done on some of the material that I drew on for inclusion in the Sydney chapter. I am also indebted to Lee Atkinson, Kris Madden, and Julie Hampson for their support and company while traveling to research this book.

ABOUT THE AUTHOR

Lee Mylne has been a journalist all her working life, specializing in travel writing for the past two decades. Based in Brisbane, she has traveled to every state and territory of Australia by almost every means of transport available. She writes for a range of Australian consumer and trade publications, and is a life member and past president of the Australian Society of Travel Writers. Her books include a number of Frommer's travel guides.

ABOUT THE FROMMER TRAVEL GUIDES

For most of the past 50 years, Frommer's has been the leading series of travel guides in North America, accounting for as many as 24% of all guidebooks sold. I think I know why.

Though we hope our books are entertaining, we nevertheless deal with travel in a serious fashion. Our guidebooks have never looked on such journeys as a mere recreation, but as a far more important human function, a time of learning and introspection, an essential part of a civilized life. We stress the culture, lifestyle, history and beliefs of the destinations we cover, and urge our readers to seek out people and new ideas as the chief rewards of travel.

We have never shied from controversy. We have, from the beginning, encouraged our authors to be intensely judgmental, critical—both pro and con—in their comments, and wholly independent. Our only clients are our readers, and we have triggered the ire of countless prominent sorts, from a tourist newspaper we called "practically worthless" (it unsuccessfully sued us) to the many rip-offs we've condemned.

And because we believe that travel should be available to everyone regardless of their incomes, we have always been cost-conscious at every level of expenditure. Though we have broadened our recommendations beyond the budget category, we insist that every lodging we include be sensibly priced. We use every form of media to assist our readers, and are particularly proud of our feisty daily website, the award-winning Frommers.com.

I have high hopes for the future of Frommer's. May these guidebooks, in all the years ahead, continue to reflect the joy of travel and the freedom that travel represents. May they always pursue a cost-conscious path, so that people of all incomes can enjoy the rewards of travel. And may they create, for both the traveler and the persons among whom we travel, a community of friends, where all human beings live in harmony and peace.

Arthur Frommer

THE BEST OF AUSTRALIA

Australia is like nowhere else you've been. It has truly unique wildlife, some of the world's best natural scenery, the most brilliant scuba diving and snorkeling, the best beaches, the oldest rainforest (110 million years and counting), the oldest human civilization (some archaeologists say 40,000 years, some say 120,000), the best wines, the best weather, the most innovative East-meets-West-meets-someplace-else cuisine—all bathed in sunlight that brings everything up in Technicolor. Prepare yourself for a lifetime of memories.

Scarcely a visitor lands on these shores without having the **Great Barrier Reef** at the top of their to-do list. So they should, because it really is a glorious natural masterpiece. Also high on most lists is **Uluru,** a sacred monolith that—rightly—attracts hundreds of thousands of tourists. And it's not just "The Rock" you should see; the vast Australian desert all around it is equally unmissable. The third attraction on most visitors' lists is **Sydney,** Australia's glittering harborside city.

Of course, there is much more to Australia than just these highlights. For those who have more time, Tasmania, South Australia, Western Australia, and the Top End of the Northern Territory have much to offer too. But we know you can't do everything or go everywhere, so in this book, I'll be introducing you to these three iconic attractions, as well as the places that are their gateways—Brisbane, Cairns, the coastal cities of Queensland that give you access to the Reef, and Alice Springs in the Red Centre—as well as Australia's other major city, Melbourne, in Victoria.

AUSTRALIA'S best AUTHENTIC EXPERIENCES

o **Seeing the Great Barrier Reef (QLD):** It's a glorious 2,000km-long (1,240-mile) underwater coral fairyland with electric colors and bizarre fish life—and it comes complete with warm water and year-round sunshine. When you're not snorkeling over coral and giant clams almost as big as you, scuba diving, calling at tropical towns, or lying on deserted

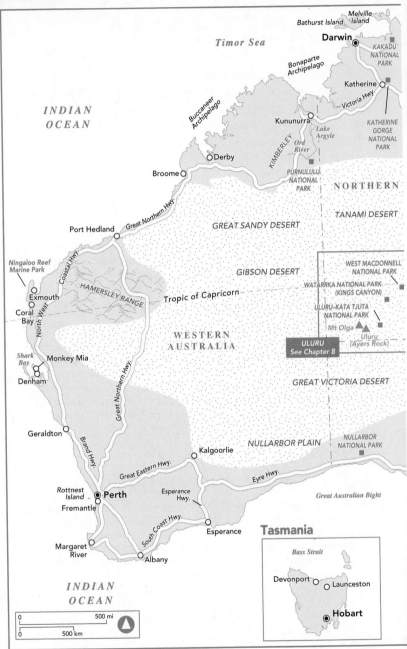

A Note on Abbreviations

In the listings below and throughout the book, **NSW** stands for New South Wales, **QLD** for Queensland, **NT** for the Northern Territory, and **VIC** for Victoria.

island beaches, you'll be trying out the sun lounges or enjoying the first-rate food. See p. 148.

o **Experiencing Sydney (NSW):** Sydney is more than just the magnificent Harbour Bridge and Opera House. No other city has beaches in such abundance, and few have such a magnificently scenic harbor. Our advice is to board a ferry, walk from one side of the bridge to the other, and try to spend a week here, because you're going to need it. See p. 35.

o **Exploring the Wet Tropics Rainforest (QLD):** Folks who come from such skyscraper cities as New York City and London can't get over the moisture-dripping ferns, the neon-blue butterflies, and the primeval peace of this World Heritage rainforest stretching north, south, and west from Cairns. Hike it, four-wheel-drive it, or glide over the treetops in the Skyrail gondola. See p. 152.

o **Bareboat Sailing (QLD):** "Bareboat" means unskippered—that's right, even if you think port is an after-dinner drink, you can charter a yacht, pay for a day's instruction from a skipper, and then take over the helm yourself and explore the 74 island gems of the Whitsundays. It's easy. Anchor in deserted bays, snorkel over dazzling reefs, fish for coral trout, and feel the wind in your sails. See p. 185.

o **Exploring Kata Tjuta (the Olgas) & Uluru (NT):** This sacred, mysterious, and utterly unforgettable landscape may well be the highlight of your time in Australia. Uluru and Kata Tjuta demand at least 3 days to see everything there is to offer. See p. 209.

o **Taking an Aboriginal Culture Tour:** Seeing the landscape through the eyes of Australia's indigenous people, hearing the Creation stories of their ancestors, and learning more about Aboriginal culture will give you a different perspective on Australia, no matter which part of it you are in. See p. 161.

AUSTRALIA'S best RESTAURANTS

o **Donovans** (Melbourne, VIC; ℰ 03/9534 8221): A glass in hand while the sun goes down over St. Kilda beach, watched from the veranda at Donovans, is a perfect way to end the day. A former 1920s bathing pavilion has been transformed into a welcoming beach-house-style restaurant, complete with views across the sand and a seafood-rich menu. See p. 105.

o **e'cco bistro** (Brisbane, QLD; ℰ 07/3831 8344): Simple food elegantly done—accompanied by an extensive wine list—has won this small but stylish bistro a stack of awards, and you'll soon see why. Booking ahead is essential. See p. 137.

o **Flower Drum** (Melbourne, VIC; ℰ 03/9662 3655): Praise pours in for this upscale eatery serving exquisite Cantonese food. The service impeccable. See p. 101.

o **Guillaume at Bennelong** (Sydney, NSW; ℰ 02/9241 1999): With amazing views of the Sydney Harbour Bridge, great food, and a position inside the Sydney Opera House, how could you go wrong with dinner at Guillaume? See p. 53.

o **Icebergs Dining Room and Bar** (Sydney, NSW; ℰ 02/9365 9000): Come here for exquisite food and one of the best ocean views in the Southern Hemisphere. Not surprisingly, seafood features highly on the menu. Probably the best place to have lunch in Sydney. See p. 61.

- **MoVida** (Melbourne, VIC; *Ⓒ* **03/9663 3038**): This little corner of Spain is relaxed and fun, with seriously good food and good wine. Melbournians flock here for the tapas and *raciones*. If it's full, try one of the two sister restaurants, **MoVida Next Door** and **MoVida Aqui.** See p. 102.

- **Quay** (Sydney, NSW; *Ⓒ* **02/9251 5600**): Sydney's best seafood restaurant offers perhaps the loveliest view in town. Gaze through the large windows toward the Opera House, the city skyline, the North Shore suburbs, and the Harbour Bridge. See p. 56.

- **Red Ochre Grill** (Alice Springs, NT; *Ⓒ* **08/8952 9614**): "Gourmet bush tucker" might sound like a contradiction, but this restaurant (part of an upscale chain) pulls it off. The kitchen combines native ingredients and international techniques to exceptionally good effect. See p. 202.

- **Salsa Bar & Grill** (Port Douglas, QLD; *Ⓒ* **07/4099 4922**): The animated atmosphere and attractive surroundings set the scene for an excellent dining experience. Appetizers and main courses run the gamut from simple fare to sophisticated tropical creations; desserts are fantastic. Ensure you book as far ahead as possible. See p. 172.

- **Tetsuya's** (Sydney, NSW; *Ⓒ* **02/9267 2900**): Chef Tetsuya Wakuda is arguably Sydney's most famous chef, and his *nouveau* Japanese creations are imaginative enough to guarantee that this hip eatery is a constant number one in Australia, and ranks among the top restaurants in the world. See p. 57.

AUSTRALIA'S best HOTELS

- **Sir Stamford at Circular Quay** (Sydney, NSW; *Ⓒ* **02/9252 4600**): Plush and luxurious, but relaxed rather than stuffy despite the clubby feel. That's why I count this as one of Sydney's best hotels. And it's in a great location, a short walk from Circular Quay and the Opera House, and just across the road from the Royal Botanic Gardens. See p. 45.

- **Reef House Boutique Hotel & Spa** (Palm Cove, QLD; *Ⓒ* **07/4080 2000**): Airy rooms look onto tropical gardens, waterfalls cascade into the pools, mosquito nets drape over the beds, and you could swear pith-helmeted colonial officers will be back any minute to finish their gin-and-tonics in the Brigadier Bar. Idyllic Palm Cove Beach is just across the road. See p. 155.

- **qualia** (Hamilton Island, Whitsundays, QLD; *Ⓒ* **07/4946 9999**): This is one of Australia's most glamorous island resorts, an exclusive adults-only enclave away from the hurly-burly of the main island accommodations. Each private pavilion has its own plunge pool, and there's a decadent day spa. See p. 187.

- **Longitude 131°** (Uluru, Red Centre, NT; *Ⓒ* **08/8957 7131**): The luxury option at the Ayers Rock resort scene, Longitude 131° is an African-style safari camp set in the sand dunes, with great views of Uluru. It's very exclusive and very expensive, but you experience the Outback in style. See p. 213.

- **The Russell** (The Rocks, Sydney NSW; *Ⓒ* **02/9241 3543**): This B&B, wonderfully positioned in the city's old quarter, is the coziest place to stay in Sydney. It has creaky floorboards, a ramshackle feel, brightly painted corridors, and rooms with immense character. See p. 48.

- **Marae** (near Port Douglas, QLD; ✆ **07/4098 4900**): Lush bushland full of butterflies and birds is the setting for this gorgeous B&B in a contemporary timber Queenslander house. Owners John and Pam Burden promise a warm welcome and a wonderful breakfast. See p. 173.
- **The Olsen** (Melbourne, VIC; ✆ **03/9040 1222**): With a giant mural by one of Australia's greatest living artists, John Olsen, and a stunning suspended swimming pool, this flagship of the Art Series Hotels is worth a splurge. Or try its sister hotels, the Cullen or the Blackman. See p. 95.

THE best PLACES TO VIEW WILDLIFE

- **Lone Pine Koala Sanctuary (QLD):** Cuddle a koala (and have your photo taken doing it) at this park in Brisbane, the world's first and largest koala sanctuary. Apart from some 130 koalas, lots of other Aussie wildlife—including wombats, Tasmanian devils, 'roos (which you can hand-feed), and colorful parakeets—are on show. See p. 140.
- **Hartley's Crocodile Adventures (QLD):** Cruise a beautiful lagoon surrounded by paperbark trees to spot crocodiles in their natural setting, then watch the daily "croc attack" show at Australia's original croc show. There are also snakes, koalas, cassowaries, and other animals to see at this family run wildlife park just north of Cairns. See p. 162.
- **Australian Butterfly Sanctuary (QLD):** Walk through the biggest butterfly "aviary" in Australia, in Kuranda, near Cairns, and you'll spot some of the most gorgeous butterflies on the continent, including the electric-blue Ulysses. See many species of butterfly feed, lay eggs, and mate; and inspect caterpillars and pupae. Wearing pink, red, or white encourages the butterflies to land on you. See p. 167.
- **Heron Island (QLD):** You'll spot wonderful wildlife on this "jewel in the reef" off Gladstone any time of year, but the best time to visit is November to March, when the life cycle of giant green loggerhead and hawksbill turtles is in full swing. From November to January, the turtles come ashore to lay their eggs. From late January to March, the hatchlings emerge and head for the water. You can see it all by strolling down to the beach, or join a university researcher to get the full story. See p. 189. Mon Repos Conservation Park, near Bundaberg in Queensland (p. 191), is another good turtle-watching site.
- **Moonlit Sanctuary (VIC):** For the chance to see many of Australia's nocturnal animals, including some (such as the eastern quoll, the red-bellied pedmelon, and the southern bettong) that are now extinct in the wild, take a guided night tour at this sanctuary on the Mornington Peninsula. See p. 119.

THE best DIVING & SNORKELING

- **Port Douglas (QLD):** Among the fabulous dive sites off Port Douglas, north of Cairns, are Split-Bommie, with its delicate fan corals and schools of fusiliers; Barracuda Pass, with its coral gardens and giant clams; and the swim-through coral spires of the Cathedrals. Snorkelers can glide over the coral and reef fish life of Agincourt Reef. See p. 168.

- **Cairns (QLD):** Moore, Norman, Hardy, Saxon, and Arlington reefs and Michaelmas and Upolu cays—all about 90 minutes off Cairns—offer great snorkeling and end-less dive sites. Explore on a day trip from Cairns, or join a live-aboard adventure. See p. 152.

- **The Whitsunday Islands (QLD):** These 74 breathtaking islands offer countless dive sites both among the islands and on the Outer Great Barrier Reef, 90 minutes away. Bait Reef on the Outer Reef is popular for its drop-offs. Snorkelers can explore not just the Outer Reef but also patch reefs among the islands and rarely visited fringing reefs around many islands. See p. 180.

- **Heron Island (QLD):** Easily the number-one snorkel and dive site in Australia—if you stayed in the water for a week, you couldn't snorkel all the acres of coral stretching from shore. Take your pick of 22 dive sites: the Coral Cascades, with football trout and anemones; the Blue Pools, favored by octopus, turtles, and sharks; Heron Bommie, with its rays, eels, and Spanish dancers; and more. Absolute magic. See p. 189.

- **Lady Elliot Island (QLD):** Gorgeous coral lagoons, perfect for snorkeling, line this coral cay island off the town of Bundaberg. Boats take you farther out to snorkel above manta rays, plate coral, and big fish. Divers can swim through the blowhole, 16m (52 ft.) down, and see gorgonian fans, soft and hard corals, sharks, barracudas, and reef fish. See p. 192.

THE best OF OUTDOORS

- **Blue Mountains (NSW):** Many bushwalks in the Blue Mountains National Park offer awesome views of valleys, waterfalls, cliffs, and forest. All are easy to reach from Sydney. See p. 81.

- **Four Mile Beach (QLD):** The sea is turquoise, the sun is warm, the palms sway, and the low-rise hotels starting to line this country beach in Port Douglas can't spoil the feeling that it is a million miles from anywhere. But isn't there always a serpent in paradise? In this case, the "serpents" are north Queensland's seasonal potentially deadly marine stingers. Come from June through September to avoid them, or con-fine your swimming to the stinger net the rest of the year. See p. 171.

- **Larapinta Trail (NT):** You can start from Alice Springs in the Red Centre and walk the entire 250km (155-mile) semidesert trail, which winds through the stark crimson McDonnell Ranges. You don't have to walk the entire length—plenty of day-length and multiday sections are possible. This one's for the cooler months only (Apr–Oct). See p. 205.

- **The MacDonnell Ranges (NT):** The Aborigines say these red rocky hills were formed by the Aboriginal "Caterpillar Dreaming" that wriggled from the earth here. To the west of Alice Springs are dramatic gorges, idyllic (and icily cold) water holes, and cute wallabies. To the east are Aboriginal rock carvings and the Ross River Homestead, where you can crack a cattle whip, throw a boomerang, feast on damper and billy tea, and ride a horse or camel in the bush. See p. 206.

- **Surfing:** No visit to Oz could really be considered complete without checking out one of the iconic Aussie activities—surfing. It's not just the rush of the waves that pulls people in, it's the ethos and everything that goes with surfing. Every state has its special spots where the surf can be especially challenging.

o **Uluru–Kata Tjuta National Park (NT):** Don't go home until you've felt the powerful heartbeat of the desert. Uluru will enthrall you with its eerie beauty. Nearby Kata Tjuta is equally interesting, so make the time to wander through the Valley of the Winds. Hike around Uluru's base, burn around it on a Harley-Davidson, saunter up to it on a camel . . . but don't climb it. See p. 209.

o **Whitehaven Beach (QLD):** It's not a surf beach, but this 6km (3¾-mile) stretch of white silica sand on uninhabited Whitsunday Island is pristine and peaceful. Bring a book, curl up under the rainforest lining its edge, and fantasize that the cruise boat is going to leave without you. See p. 185.

SUGGESTED ITINERARIES

Australia's size and its distance from Northern Hemisphere destinations are the two most daunting things about planning a visit. It's a long way to come for just a week, but if that's all you can spare, you still want to see as much as possible. While my inclination is to immerse myself in one spot, I know that not everyone can do that. Seeing as much as possible is often a priority, so here are some ideas on how to do just that.

A week or two in Australia is just enough time to scrape the surface of this vast, complex and fascinating place.

If you're a first-time visitor, with only 1 or 2 weeks, you may find these two itineraries most helpful: **"Australia in 1 Week"** or **"Australia in 2 Weeks."** These itineraries can be adapted to suit your needs; for example, you could substitute the Cairns section of "Australia in 1 Week" for the Uluru/Red Centre suggestions in "Australia in 2 Weeks," flying from Sydney to Uluru.

If you're traveling as a family, the **"Australia for Families"** itinerary is designed to give you some ideas on keeping the young ones occupied (while still being interesting for parents!).

Getting around this continent, where major attractions are thousands of miles apart, can be daunting and time-consuming. Flying is the only way to cover long distances efficiently, but unfortunately it can also be expensive. Remember to build flying time into your itineraries, and don't try to pack in too much on the days you fly—even domestic flights can be draining, some clocking in at around 3 hours. See "Getting There & Getting Around," in chapter 9, for information on air passes and getting the best rate on Australia's domestic carriers.

My best advice: If the pace gets too hectic, just chill out and reorder your sightseeing priorities. Take time to meet the locals and ask their advice on what you should see as well.

AUSTRALIA IN 1 WEEK

Australia is so vast that in 1 week, you'll only be able to get to a small corner of it—perhaps one city or a few of its natural wonders. It will be memorable, nevertheless, and careful planning will maximize your time and allow you to see some of the major sights.

Use the following itinerary to make the most of a week in Australia, but make sure you don't exhaust yourself trying to cram everything in.

Australia in 1 or 2 Weeks

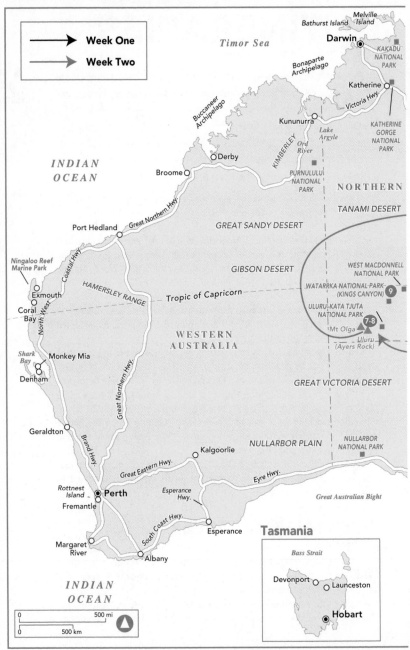

Week One

Week Two

Timor Sea

Darwin

Bathurst Island

Melville Island

KAKADU NATIONAL PARK

Katherine

Victoria Hwy.

KATHERINE GORGE NATIONAL PARK

Bonaparte Archipelago

Kununurra

Lake Argyle

Ord River

KIMBERLEY

PURNULULU NATIONAL PARK

Buccaneer Archipelago

Derby

Broome

INDIAN OCEAN

GREAT SANDY DESERT

NORTHERN

TANAMI DESERT

Port Hedland

Great Northern Hwy.

Coastal Hwy.

North West

GIBSON DESERT

WEST MACDONNELL NATIONAL PARK

WATARRKA NATIONAL PARK (KINGS CANYON) 9

ULURU-KATA TJUTA NATIONAL PARK 7-8

Mt Olga

Uluru (Ayers Rock)

Ningaloo Reef Marine Park

Exmouth

Coral Bay

HAMERSLEY RANGE

Tropic of Capricorn

WESTERN AUSTRALIA

Shark Bay

Monkey Mia

Denham

Great Northern Hwy.

GREAT VICTORIA DESERT

Geraldton

Brand Hwy.

NULLARBOR PLAIN

NULLARBOR NATIONAL PARK

Kalgoorlie

Great Eastern Hwy.

Eyre Hwy.

Great Australian Bight

Rottnest Island

Perth

Fremantle

Esperance Hwy.

South Coast Hwy.

Esperance

Tasmania

Bass Strait

Margaret River

Albany

INDIAN OCEAN

Devonport

Launceston

Hobart

0   500 mi
0   500 km

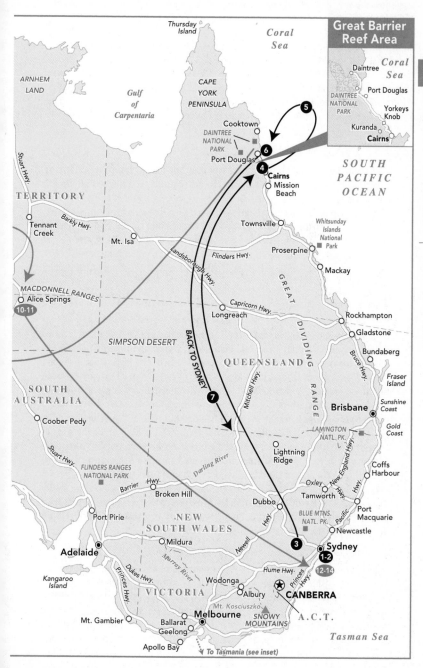

Great Barrier
Reef Area

Coral
Sea

Daintree

Port Douglas

DAINTREE
NATIONAL
PARK

Yorkeys
Knob

Kuranda

Cairns

Thursday
Island

Coral
Sea

ARNHEM
LAND

Gulf
of
Carpentaria

CAPE
YORK
PENINSULA

Cooktown

DAINTREE
NATIONAL
PARK

Port Douglas

Cairns

Mission
Beach

SOUTH
PACIFIC
OCEAN

Stuart Hwy.

TERRITORY

Tennant
Creek

Barkly Hwy.

Mt. Isa

Landsborough Hwy.

Townsville

Flinders Hwy.

Proserpine

Whitsunday
Islands
National
Park

Mackay

MACDONNELL RANGES

Alice
Springs

Capricorn Hwy.

Longreach

GREAT

Rockhampton

Gladstone

SIMPSON DESERT

QUEENSLAND

DIVIDING

Bundaberg

Fraser
Island

SOUTH
AUSTRALIA

Coober Pedy

BACK TO SYDNEY

Mitchell Hwy.

RANGE

Brisbane

Bruce Hwy.

Sunshine
Coast

LAMINGTON
NATL. PK.

Gold
Coast

Stuart Hwy.

FLINDERS RANGES
NATIONAL PARK

Barrier Hwy.

Broken Hill

Darling River

Lightning
Ridge

Coffs
Harbour

New England Hwy.

Oxley
Hwy.

Tamworth

Pacific Hwy.

Port Pirie

NEW
SOUTH
WALES

Mildura

Dubbo

Newell Hwy.

Hwy.

BLUE MTNS.
NATL. PK.

Port
Macquarie

Newcastle

Adelaide

Murray River

Sydney

Kangaroo
Island

Dukes Hwy.

Princes Hwy.

VICTORIA

Wodonga

Albury

Hume Hwy.

Princes Hwy.

CANBERRA

A.C.T.

Mt. Gambier

Ballarat

Geelong

Melbourne

Mt. Kosciuszko

SNOWY
MOUNTAINS

Tasman Sea

Apollo Bay

To Tasmania (see inset)

11

Australians are a laid-back lot, generally, and in some places the pace is relaxed. And that's just the way to enjoy it. One week provides barely enough time to see the best of Sydney, which for most people is the entry point to Australia.

If you have only a week and want to head farther afield, there are two main choices, depending on your interests. The **Great Barrier Reef** is a must for divers, but don't forget that you should allow time on either side of your reef trip for flying. There are no such problems with Australia's other icon, **Uluru,** in the heart of the **Red Centre.** This triangle of highlights is something of a cliché, but it still gives you a complete Australian experience. Realistically, you will have to choose between the Reef and the Rock, or forego scuba diving while you are in Queensland.

Day 1: Arrive in Sydney ★★★

Check into your hotel and spend whatever time you have upon arrival recovering from the almost-guaranteed jet lag. If you arrive in the morning and have a full day ahead of you, try to stay up. Hit the nearest cafe for a shot of caffeine to keep you going. Head to **Circular Quay,** and from there get a fantastic view of **Sydney Harbour Bridge** ★★★ (p. 66) before strolling to the **Sydney Opera House** ★★★ (p. 67) and soaking up some history at **The Rocks** ★★★. If you have time, take the ferry from Circular Quay to Manly beach and round off a fairly easy day with fish and chips. Then head to bed for some much-needed sleep.

Day 2: Explore Sydney

Start with a ride to the top of the **Sydney Tower** ★ to experience Sydney's highest open-air attraction, **Skywalk** (p. 72), a breathtaking 260m (853 ft.) above Sydney. Harnessed onto a moving, glass-floored viewing platform that extends out over the edge of the tower, you can view all of Sydney's landmarks, including the Sydney Harbour Bridge, the Sydney Opera House, Sydney Harbour, and even the Blue Mountains beyond. Don't worry, it's not actually as scary as it sounds. For an introduction to Australia's wildlife, head to **Taronga Zoo** ★★★ (p. 73) or the **Sydney Aquarium** ★★ (p. 70). If you have time to spare, another great choice is **Featherdale Wildlife Park** ★★★ (p. 72), but keep in mind it's about an hour and a half from the city center. If you enjoy museums, put the **Australian Museum** ★★ (p. 71), the **Australian National Maritime Museum** ★★ (p. 69) at Darling Harbour, and the interactive **Powerhouse Museum** ★★★ (p. 70) on your list for the day. For an insight into Sydney's beginnings as a convict settlement, visit the **Hyde Park Barracks Museum** ★★ (p. 71), a convict-built prison. Finish off your day with a twilight (or later on weekends) **BridgeClimb** ★★★ (p. 66) up the Sydney Harbour Bridge.

Day 3: The Blue Mountains ★★★

Take the train from Central Station to **Katoomba** (p. 81) for a day, exploring the beauty of the Blue Mountains—only 2 hours from Sydney. Once there, jump on the **Blue Mountains Explorer** bus (p. 82), which allows you to hop on and off wherever you please. There are also many day-tour operators running to the Blue Mountains from Sydney. Whichever mode of transport you use, don't miss the spectacular **Three Sisters** (p. 83) rock formations, best viewed from Echo Point

Road at Katoomba. Make sure you also spend some time at **Scenic World** (p. 84), where you can ride the world's steepest railway into a valley full of ancient rainforest, and come back up on a cable car—among other adventures that kids especially will enjoy. At the end of the day, head back to Sydney and have dinner somewhere with a view of the harbor.

Day 4: Cairns, Gateway to the Great Barrier Reef

Take the earliest flight you can from Sydney to Cairns—flight time is 3 hours—and check into a hotel in the city, which on such a tight schedule will make getting to the major attractions quicker and easier than staying on the northern beaches, out of town. Explore the city a little, and see some wildlife—including a massive saltwater crocodile—in the bizarre setting of the **Cairns Wildlife Dome** ★★ (p. 160), atop the Hotel Sofitel Reef Casino. You will have the rest of the day to head out to visit the **Tjapukai Aboriginal Cultural Park** ★ (p. 161). If you are not going to the Red Centre, this is a great place to learn about Aboriginal culture and life, albeit in a theme-park kind of way. You could spend several hours here, or save the visit for the evening, when **Tjapukai by Night** tours offer a different look at traditional ceremonies, including dinner and a fire-and-water outdoor show.

Day 5: A Day Trip to the Reef ★★★

Day trips to the Great Barrier Reef leave from the **Reef Fleet Terminal.** The trip to the outer reef takes about 2 hours, and once there, you will spend your day on a pontoon with about 300 people. Experienced divers may prefer to take a day trip with one of several dive charter companies that take smaller groups and visit two or three reefs. The pontoons of the big operators also offer the chance to take a scenic flight—a truly spectacular experience. Divers must spend another 24 hours in Cairns before flying. If you are content to snorkel, ride the glass-bottom boats, and soak up the sun, you will be able to fly the next day. After returning to Cairns, take a stroll along the **Esplanade** and eat at one of the busy cafes and restaurants that line the strip.

Day 6: Kuranda, a Rainforest Village ★★

Waiting out the day after diving (you can't fly for 24 hr. after you've been on a dive) can be spent discovering another aspect to Australia—its rainforests. Take a trip to the mountain village of **Kuranda** aboard the steam train along the **Kuranda Scenic Railway** ★★★ (p. 166), past waterfalls and gorges. In Kuranda, explore the markets and the nature parks, and maybe take a **Kuranda Riverboat Tour** ★★ (p. 168), which runs about 45 minutes. Return on the **Skyrail** ★★★ cableway (p. 160), which carries you over the rainforest (you can get to ground level at a couple of stations on the way) to the edge of Cairns. The views are sensational. This is a big day out!

Day 7: Cairns to Sydney

In the morning, head to the airport for your flight to Sydney. Unless you are lucky enough to have an international flight directly out of Cairns, you will spend most of your last day in Australia returning to Sydney. With the time you have left in Sydney, treat yourself to dinner at a restaurant overlooking the harbor, with its bridge and Opera House illuminated. It's a sight you'll carry home with you.

AUSTRALIA IN 2 WEEKS

With 2 weeks, your visit to Australia will be much more relaxed and you'll get a greater sense of the diversity of Australia's landscape, wildlife, and people. You will be able to explore the country's trio of icons—Sydney, the Great Barrier Reef, and Uluru—in more depth, and maybe even have time to go outside those areas, especially if you limit your icons to two instead of three.

Days 1–6: Sydney to Cairns

Follow the itinerary as outlined in "Australia in 1 Week," above.

Day 7: Cairns to Uluru

Leave Cairns as early as you can. Your flight to Ayers Rock Airport will take around 3 hours. Make sure you book a direct flight, not one that goes via Sydney! Try to get a window seat for the spectacular views as you fly over the Outback. If you take the early flight, you can be in **Uluru** by around 10am, which gives you the entire day to take in the enormity of this fabulous monolith. Take the shuttle from **Ayers Rock Resort** (the only place to stay, albeit one with many accommodations choices; p. 212) to the Rock. Spend some time in the impressive and interesting **Uluru–Kata Tjuta Cultural Centre** (p. 210), near the base of Uluru, and explore the area on one of the many walking trails or tours. End the day by watching the sun set over Uluru—an unforgettable sight. After doing all that in a day, you'll be ready for a quiet dinner at whatever hotel you've chosen.

If you decide to **climb Uluru** (remembering that the traditional Aboriginal owners would prefer you didn't), make sure you don't do it at the hottest time of day. A climb should take you between 2 and 4 hours, depending on your fitness.

Day 8: Exploring Uluru ★★★

Sunrise is one of those magic times at Uluru, so make the effort to get up early. This is also a great time to do the 9.6km (6-mile) **Base Walk** circumnavigating Uluru (p. 215), which takes 2 to 3 hours. There are a range of other ways to experience Uluru, including camel rides, Harley-Davidson tours, and helicopter joy flights, but walking up close to the Rock beats them all.

You will also have time today to head to **Kata Tjuta** (also called "The Olgas"; p. 209), where you'll see there's much more to the Red Centre than just one rock. Kata Tjuta is about 48km (30 miles) west of Uluru, but plenty of tour operators go there if you don't have your own wheels.

End your day in the desert with the **Sounds of Silence** ★★ dinner (p. 213), run by Ayers Rock Resort. Sip champagne as the sun sets over Uluru to the eerie music of the didgeridoo, and then tuck into kangaroo, barramundi, and other native foods. But it's not the food you're here for—it's the silence and the stars. A short stargazing session with an astronomer ends a memorable evening.

Day 9: Uluru to Kings Canyon

Hire a four-wheel-drive vehicle and tackle the long Outback drive from Uluru to Alice Springs, stopping for a night at **Kings Canyon Resort** (www.kingscanyon resort.com.au). It is 306km (190 miles) from Uluru to Kings Canyon (also known as **Watarrka National Park**), which offers another unbeatable look at Outback Australia. You can spend the afternoon walking up the side of the canyon and around the rim. Parts of it are very steep, and the whole hike will take you around 4 hours, but it's well worth the effort. A gentler walk is the short and shady canyon floor walk.

Day 10: Kings Canyon to Alice Springs

Get an early start for Alice Springs, and take the unpaved but interesting **Mereenie Loop Road,** which threads through the **Glen Helen Gorge** or the historic **Hermannsburg** mission settlement (p. 208). Whichever road you take, the scenery is like nowhere else. You will probably spend most of the day driving to Alice, making a few stops along the way.

On arrival, check into a hotel and head out to one of the local restaurants, several of which offer sophisticated versions of "bush tucker," including kangaroo, emu, and crocodile dishes.

Day 11: Alice Springs

If you can stand another early start, take a **dawn balloon flight** over the desert (p. 205), usually followed by a champagne breakfast. If you don't head back to bed immediately for a few hours of catch-up sleep, there are plenty of attractions to discover, including the **Alice Springs Desert Park** ★★★ (p. 202), for a look at some unusual Australian creatures; the **School of the Air** ★★ (p. 204); and the **Royal Flying Doctor Service** ★★ base (p. 204). In the afternoon, drop into the **Mbantua Aboriginal Art Gallery** (p. 206) to see some of the best Aboriginal art from the outlying communities in the desert region called Utopia, famed for its paintings. Alternatively, visit the **Alice Springs Telegraph Station Historical Reserve** ★★ (p. 203), set in an oasis just outside town, for a look at early settler life. Finish the day with a **sunset camel ride** (p. 205) down the dry Todd River bed and have dinner at the camel farm.

Day 12: Alice Springs to Sydney

Direct flights from Alice Springs to Sydney leave in the early afternoon, so you'll have all morning to explore more of the town and perhaps buy some Aboriginal art. (This is one of the best places to get it.)

On arrival in Sydney, after an almost 3-hour flight, check into your hotel and spend the night discovering the city's nightlife.

Day 13: A Day at Bondi Beach

For sands of a different hue from those you've experienced in recent days, take the bus to Sydney's most famous beach, **Bondi** (p. 76), and spend it lazing on the sand or—in summer, at least—taking a dip in the surf. Take a public bus or the Bondi Explorer from Circular Quay, which gives you a choice of harborside bays and coastal beaches. The scenic cliff-top walk to **Bronte Beach** is worth doing, or you can continue farther to **Coogee.**

Day 14: Sydney

Your final day in Australia can be spent on last-minute shopping and seeing those Sydney sights that you haven't yet had time for. Cap it all off with a slap-up seafood dinner somewhere with a fantastic view of the Harbour Bridge.

AUSTRALIA FOR FAMILIES

Australia is a wonderful destination for kids—and not just because of the kangaroos and koalas. Our suggestion is to explore Sydney for 2 days with family in tow, then head up to the beautiful Blue Mountains on a day trip to ride the cable car and the world's steepest railway. The climax comes with a few days of exploring the Barrier Reef and the rainforest around Port Douglas.

Days 1 & 2: Sydney

First off, head to Circular Quay to see the **Sydney Opera House** ★★★. A tour inside might be a bit much for younger kids, but you can walk around a fair bit of it and take the obligatory photos of Australia's most famous landmark. To stretch your legs, head from here into the **Royal Botanic Gardens** (p. 77) to spot long-beaked ibises wandering around the grass and hundreds of fruit bats squabbling among the treetops. Walk back past the Opera House and the ferries to **The Rocks,** where you can take a quick stroll through the historic streets, stopping for a look at some of the trendy shops or the Market on Saturdays.

There are plenty of places to eat lunch at Circular Quay, where you can sit outside and watch the world go by. After lunch, take a ferry to **Taronga Zoo** ★★★, where a cable car zips you up the hill to the main entrance. All the kids' favorite animals are here, from kangaroos and koalas to platypuses, located in a nocturnal house. A farmyard section edges onto a playground, with lots of water features to give your kids a sprinkle on a hot day.

On **Day 2,** head to the city center for an elevator ride up to the top of **Sydney Tower** ★ (p. 72), where you can look right across Sydney as far as the Blue Mountains in the distance. Entry includes admission to the 4D Cinema Experience. It's a short walk from here to Darling Harbour, where you can cap off the morning with a visit to **Sydney Aquarium** ★★. The sharks that swim right above your head are huge, but the real attraction is the Barrier Reef section, where tens of thousands of colorful fish swim by in enormous tanks to the sounds of classical music.

Eat lunch at one of the many cheap eateries at Darling Harbour before taking the ferry from near the Aquarium back to Circular Quay.

If it's a hot day, or you simply want to hit the beach, you have two main choices: From Circular Quay, you can take a half-hour ferry ride or a 15-minute high-speed JetCat trip to **Manly** (p. 39). Here you can laze the afternoon away and even rent a surfboard or body board. Or hop a bus to **Bondi Beach** (p. 76), where you can reward your efforts with gelati or a late-afternoon pizza from Pompei's (p. 61).

Day 3: The Blue Mountains

You could easily spend a couple more days with the kids having fun in Sydney, but you shouldn't miss a trip to the mountains. If you go, prepare for a long day; pack plenty of snacks and a few favorite toys. Several companies run tour buses to the area, stopping off at an animal park along the way. The best one to visit is **Featherdale Wildlife Park** ★★★ (p. 72), where you can get up close to more kangaroos, koalas, and Tasmanian devils. The tour also stops at **Scenic World** ★ (p. 84), where you can take the short ride on the Scenic Railway. It's very steep, so hold on tight. At the bottom you'll find yourselves among an ancient tree fern forest—it's truly remarkable. A short walk takes you to the **Skyway,** a cable car that travels 300m (984 ft.) above the Jamison Valley.

Elsewhere in the mountains there are fabulous views across craggy bluffs and deep bowls of gum trees. See chapter 4 for details.

Days 4, 5 & 6: The Reef & the Rainforest

Now it's time to head north to the Tropics. You'll need to fly, of course; otherwise it would take you several days to drive up the coast. The flight from Sydney to Cairns takes 3 hours. As a family, you might prefer to base yourselves in **Port Douglas** (see p. 168) rather than Cairns—the Port Douglas beach is huge and uncrowded and some of the best Barrier Reef trips originate from here. "Port," as the locals call it, is about an hour's drive from Cairns, so your first day will be largely taken with getting there.

After all that traveling, take the rest of the day to relax on beautiful Four Mile Beach, but remember to swim inside the nets off the sand; the "stingers" (box jellyfish) around here can cause life-threatening stings, especially where kids are concerned.

On **Day 5,** it's time to visit the **Reef.** Thankfully, once on the Reef itself, the dangerous jellyfish are very uncommon. Cruise boats take around 90 minutes to get from Port Douglas to the outer reef; but once there, you are in for some amazing snorkeling. Expect to see numerous species of corals and fish, and even an occasional turtle. A good seafood lunch is generally served on board, so you won't go hungry!

Day 6 will be another nature experience, this time meeting some of the giants of the north. In the morning, head out to **Mossman Gorge** ★★★ (p. 171), a 15- to 20-minute drive from Port Douglas, for some Aboriginal culture in the rainforest with **Ngadiku Dreamtime Walks,** guided by a member of the local KuKu-Yalanji tribe. On your way back to Cairns stop off at **Hartley's Crocodile Adventures** ★★★ (p. 162) to see crocs in their natural habitat. After the 3pm "croc attack" show, you'll have time for a leisurely drive back to Cairns to get ready for your departure. See chapter 7 for detailed information on these attractions.

Day 7: Fly Back to Sydney

If you have time to kill before you leave Sydney, take the kids by ferry to **Luna Park** ★, just across from Circular Quay, or walk there across the Harbour Bridge. Although this fun park is small, with a few rides suitable for younger kids, it does boast a magnificent view across to the Harbour Bridge and Opera House, which look glorious after the sun's gone down.

AUSTRALIA IN CONTEXT

When most people think of Australia, they conjure up images of bounding kangaroos, dusty red deserts, and golden sandy beaches. The Sydney Opera House is right up there too. They imagine drawling accents and slouch hats, suntanned lifesavers, and men who wrestle crocodiles for the fun of it. It's all that—and more (apart from the crocodile wrestling)! This huge continent is truly remarkable, offering everything from rolling green hills, dense ancient rainforests, historic towns, vast areas of sparsely inhabited ochre-red Outback, giant coral reefs and deserted beaches, unique animals and plants, cosmopolitan modern cities, and intriguing Aboriginal culture for visitors to explore.

Most people visiting Australia for the first time head to Sydney or Melbourne. They explore the Red Centre and the giant rock Uluru; or they take to the warm waters and dive or snorkel on the Great Barrier Reef. But it's also often the places that come to them by chance, or deeper research, that remain locked in their memory forever. Who could forget holding a koala in your arms, or feeding a kangaroo from the palm of your hand? Or traveling ochre-red dirt tracks and seeing emus running alongside your 4WD? This book will concentrate on those areas that are the most traveled, the ones on every visitor's wish-list, while at the same time taking you to some of the lesser-known treasures of each city and sharing some of my personal favorite places and experiences. Of course, no travel experience is complete without a little background information, which is where this chapter comes in.

AUSTRALIA TODAY

Perhaps it's to do with the weather, or the wide-open spaces, or the quality of the light, but Australians are generally an optimistic, positive lot—and to me, that's a big part of its appeal. Phrases like "It's a lucky country, mate" and "She'll be right" (meaning everything will be okay) may have become clichés, but they sum up the attitude held by most Australians. The food is good and there's plenty of it; the education system is mostly good (and mostly free, unless you choose to pay for a private school or you happen to be saddled with student loans to cover university fees); gun ownership is heavily restricted; the public health-care system is universal and largely free or inexpensive; and the government—whichever persuasion it is—is generally stable. It's a great place to live—even though it can sometimes feel a long, long way away from everywhere else.

Of course, nothing is always clear-cut. The country has plenty of socially disadvantaged areas, and many of Australia's indigenous people in particular are struggling on the fringes of mainstream society.

As a nation, Australia is also facing tough challenges in balancing the benefits of industry with caring for the environment. Australia makes a massive amount of revenue from mining, supplying China with a significant proportion of its iron and other metals, as well as supplying the rest of the world with everything from uranium and coal to natural gas. This inevitably means the ruin of some once-pristine landscapes. Australia also has one of the world's highest per capita levels of greenhouse gas emissions (nearly twice the OECD average and more than four times the world average) and suffers from severe droughts and dramatic weather events that most experts believe are the result of human-induced climate change.

Australia is also one of the world's fastest-growing industrialized nations. Today the population stands at just under 23 million, a figure driven in recent years by immigration, with around 236,000 people settling here in 2012.

One thing Australia realized early on was the importance of tourism to its economy. Millions visit every year. You'll find Australians helpful and friendly, and services, tours, and food and drink to rival any in the world. Factor in the landscape, the indigenous culture, the sunshine, the unique wildlife, and some of the world's best cities, and, all in all, you've got a fascinating, accessible destination of amazing diversity and variety.

LOOKING BACK AT AUSTRALIA

The Beginning

In the beginning, there was the Dreamtime. Australia's indigenous people have lived on this land for up to 40,000 years or more. Their "Dreamtime" stories explain how they see the creation story and what followed. In scientific terms, a supercontinent split into two and over millions of years continental drift carried the great landmasses apart. Australia was part of what we call Gondwanaland, which also divided into South America, Africa, India, Papua New Guinea, and Antarctica. Giant marsupials evolved to roam the continent of Australia. The last of these creatures are believed to have died out around 20,000 years ago, possibly helped toward extinction by drought, or by Aboriginal hunters, who lived alongside them for thousands of years.

Early European Explorers

The existence of a great southern land had been on the minds of Europeans since the Greek astronomer Ptolemy drew a map of the world in A.D. 150 showing a large landmass in the south, which he believed existed to balance out the land in the Northern Hemisphere. He called it Terra Australia Incognita—the "Unknown Southland."

Portuguese ships reached Australia as early as 1536 and charted part of its coastline. In 1606, William Jansz was sent by the Dutch East India Company to open up a new route to the Spice Islands, and to find New Guinea. He landed on the north coast of Queensland instead and fought with local Aborigines. Between 1616 and 1640, many more Dutch ships made contact with Australia as they hugged the west coast of what they called "New Holland," after sailing with the westerly winds from the Cape of Good Hope.

THE ancient art OF AUSTRALIA

A history of the Aboriginal people lies partly in the **rock paintings** they have left behind all over Australia. In the tropical north, for example, a wide-ranging body of prehistoric art decorates sandstone gorges near the tiny township of Laura on the rugged Cape York Peninsula. Depictions on rock-shelter sites range from spirit figures of men and women to eels, fish, wide-winged brolga birds, crocodiles, kangaroos, snakes, and stenciled hands. One wall, the "Magnificent Gallery," stretches more than 40m (131 ft.) and is adorned with hundreds of Quinkan figures—Quinkans being the Aboriginal spirits associated with this region.

Much Aboriginal rock art is preserved in national parks. Examples readily accessible on day trips from major Australian cities include Ku-Ring-Gai Chase National Park, and the Royal National Park near Sydney. Then there's the Grampians National Park west of Melbourne, and the fabulous hand stencils at Mutawintji National park near Broken Hill in New South Wales. There are also ancient paintings near Uluru in Australia's Red Centre.

In Queensland, Carnarvon National Park (about 400km/249 miles west of Brisbane) offers a breathtaking display of early indigenous paintings.

In 1642, the Dutch East India Company, through the governor general of the Indies, Anthony Van Diemen, sent Abel Tasman to search for and map the great Southland. During two voyages, he charted the northern Australian coastline and discovered Tasmania, which he named Van Diemen's Land.

The Arrival of the British

In 1766, the Royal Society hired James Cook to travel to the Pacific Ocean to observe and record the transit of Venus across the sun. In 1770 Cook charted the east coast of Australia in his ship the HMS *Endeavour.* He claimed the land for Britain and named it New South Wales. On April 29, Captain Cook landed at Botany Bay, which he named after the discovery of scores of plants hitherto unknown to science. Turning northward, he passed an entrance to a possible harbor that appeared to offer safe anchorage and named it Port Jackson, after the secretary to the admiralty, George Jackson. Back in Britain, King George III viewed Australia as a potential colony and repository of Britain's overflowing prison population, which could no longer be transported to the United States of America following the War of Independence.

The First Fleet left England in May 1787, made up of 11 store and transport ships (none of them bigger than the passenger ferries that ply modern-day Sydney Harbour from Circular Quay to Manly) led by Arthur Phillip. Aboard were 1,480 people, including 759 convicts. Phillip's flagship, the *Supply,* reached Botany Bay in January 1788, but Phillip decided the soil was poor and the surroundings too swampy. On January 26, now celebrated as Australia Day, he settled for Port Jackson (Sydney Harbour) instead.

The convicts were immediately put to work clearing land, planting crops, and constructing buildings. Phillip decided to give some convicts pardons for good behavior and service, and even granted small land parcels to those who were really industrious.

When gold was discovered in Victoria in 1852 and in Western Australia 12 years later, hundreds of thousands of immigrants from Europe, America, and China flooded the country in search of fortune. By 1860, more than a million non-Aboriginal people were living in Australia.

The last 10,000 convicts were transported to Western Australia between 1850 and 1868, bringing the total shipped to Australia to 168,000. Some early colonial architecture, built and designed by those convicts, still remains in Sydney. Be on the lookout for buildings designed by the colonial architect Francis Greenway. Between 1816 and 1818, while still a prisoner, Greenway was responsible for the Macquarie Lighthouse on South Head, at the entrance to Sydney Harbour, and also Hyde Park Barracks and St. James Church in the city center.

Federation & the Great Wars

On January 1, 1901, the six states that made up Australia proclaimed themselves to be part of one nation, and the Commonwealth of Australia was formed. In the same ceremony, the first governor general was sworn in as the representative of the Queen, who remained head of state.

In 1914, Australia joined Britain in World War I. In April of the following year, the Australian and New Zealand Army Corps (ANZAC) formed a beachhead on the peninsula of Gallipoli in Turkey. The Turkish troops had been warned, and 8 months of fighting ended with 8,587 Australian dead and more than 19,000 wounded. That day, April 25, is commemorated each year as Anzac Day.

Australians fought in World War II in North Africa, Greece, and the Middle East. In March 1942, Japanese aircraft bombed Broome in Western Australia and Darwin in the Northern Territory. In May 1942, Japanese midget submarines entered Sydney Harbour and torpedoed a ferry before ultimately being destroyed. Later that year, Australian volunteers fought an incredibly brave retreat through the jungles of Papua New Guinea on the Kokoda Track against superior Japanese forces.

Recent Times

Following World War II, mass immigration to Australia, primarily from Europe, boosted the non-Aboriginal population. "White" Australia was always used to distinguish the Anglo-Saxon population from that of the indigenous people of Australia, and until 1974 there existed a "White Australia Policy"—a result of conflict between European settlers and Chinese immigrants in the gold fields in the 1850s. This policy severely restricted the immigration of people who lacked European ancestry. In 1974, the left-of-Center Whitlam Labor government put an end to the White Australia policy that had largely restricted black and Asian immigration since 1901. In 1986, an act of both British and Australian Parliament once

A Moment in Time

In 1964, a group of 20 nomadic women and children became the last Aboriginal people to make "first contact" with Europeans. They were living in the Great Sandy Desert, south of Broome, in Western Australia. When they first saw two officers from the Weapons Research Establishment, who were checking land destined for a series of rocket tests, the Aborigines presumed the white-skinned creatures were ghosts.

THE ABORIGINAL "stolen generations"

When Captain James Cook landed at Botany Bay in 1770 determined to claim the land for the British Empire, at least 300,000 **Aborigines** were living on the continent. Despite varying estimates of how long Aboriginal people have inhabited Australia (some believe it is since the beginning of time), there is scientific evidence that people were walking the continent at least 60,000 years ago.

At the time of the arrival of Europeans, there were at least 600 different tribal communities, each linked to their ancestral land by **"sacred sites"** (certain features of the land, such as hills or rock formations). They were hunter-gatherers, spending about 20 hours a week harvesting the resources of the land, the rivers, and the ocean. The rest of their time was taken up by complex social and belief systems, as well as by life's practicalities such as making utensils and weapons.

The basis of Aboriginal spirituality rests in the **Dreamtime** stories, which recount how ancient spirits created the

and for all severed any remaining ties to the United Kingdom. Australia had begun the march to complete independence.

Waves of immigration have brought in millions of people since the end of World War II. Results from the last census, conducted in 2006, show that 25 percent of the population was born overseas. Of those, 7% were born in Northern Europe (including the U.K.), 7% were born in Asia, and 4% were born in Southern Europe. In 2009 immigrant numbers from China topped those from the U.K. for the first time. New waves of immigration have recently come from countries such as Iraq and Somalia. So what's the typical Australian like? Well, he's hardly Crocodile Dundee.

AUSTRALIA IN POPULAR CULTURE

Movies

Australia has produced its fair share of movies good and bad. Some of the better ones are listed here.

- **Walkabout** (1971): The hauntingly beautiful and disturbing movie set in the Australian desert stars Jenny Agutter and the Aboriginal actor David Gulpilul. A white girl and her brother get hopelessly lost and survive with help from a doomed Aboriginal hero.
- **Picnic at Hanging Rock** (1974): This Peter Weir movie is about a group of schoolgirls and a teacher who go missing at an eerie rock formation north of Melbourne. It's set at the beginning of the 20th century, when bonnets and teapots were the norm.
- **Mad Max** (1979): Mel Gibson fights to the death in the Outback, which presents the ideal setting for a post-apocalyptic world. The movie was so popular that it spawned two sequels: "The Road Warrior" (1981) and "Mad Max: Beyond Thunderdome" (1985).

- **Gallipoli** (1981): Peter Weir's brilliant movie tries to capture the reality of the World War I military disaster that saw Australian and New Zealand troops fighting against overwhelming odds on the Turkish coastline.
- **The Man from Snowy River** (1982): Kirk Douglas, Tom Burlinson, and Sigrid Thornton star in this startling Australian movie that showcases the mountainous wilderness of Australia, where wild horses roam.
- **Crocodile Dundee** (1986): Paul Hogan shot to worldwide fame as a "typical" crocodile-wrestling Outback hero. He wears the same hat and a few more wrinkles in "Crocodile Dundee II" (1988) and "Crocodile Dundee in L.A." (2001).
- **Shine** (1991): This portrayal of the real-life classical pianist David Helfgott, who rose to international prominence in the 1950s and 1960s before having a nervous breakdown, is remarkable. Oscar-winner Geoffrey Rush gives a powerful performance as the adult Helfgott; Sir John Gielgud plays Helfgott's teacher.
- **Strictly Ballroom** (1992): A boy, played by Paul Mercurio, becomes a champion ballroom dancer in this whimsical, playful movie with, thankfully, not too much dancing.
- **Muriel's Wedding** (1994): This classic Australian comedy tells the tale of Muriel Heslop (Toni Collette), a young woman who dreams of getting married and moving far away from her boring life in Porpoise Spit. Fabulous characters, great catchphrases, and Abba music abound.
- **The Adventures of Priscilla, Queen of the Desert** (1994): A transsexual takes to traveling through the desert in a big pink bus with two drag queens. They sing Abba classics and dress the part, kind of. Where else but Australia . . . .
- **The Dish** (2000): This comedy about Australia's role in the Apollo 11 mission in 1969 was set around a group of characters operating the Parkes/Canberra radio telescope.
- **Rabbit Proof Fence** (2002): This fictionalized tale addresses the real-life experience of plucking Aboriginal children from their homes in order to put them in white foster families or—as is the case in this true story—to train three girls to work as domestic servants.
- **Australia** (2008): An English aristocrat in the 1930s, played by Nicole Kidman, arrives in northern Australia. After an epic journey across the country with a rough-hewn cattle drover played by Hugh Jackman, she is caught in the bombing of Darwin during World War II.
- **Samson and Delilah** (2009): This confronting movie depicts two indigenous Australian 14-year-olds living in a remote Aboriginal community who steal a car and escape their difficult lives by heading off to Alice Springs.
- **Animal Kingdom** (2010): Jacki Weaver's role as a crime family matriarch in this gripping drama set in Melbourne won her multiple awards, including an Oscar nomination for Best Supporting Actress.
- **Red Dog** (2011): A tearjerker family flick about a kelpie looking for his master in a Western Australian Outback mining town. Adapted from the novel by Louis de Bernières and based on a true story.

Music

Aboriginal music has been around for tens of thousands of years. Most well-known is the sound of the **didgeridoo,** made from a hollowed-out tree limb. Listen carefully and you might hear animal sounds, including the flapping of wings and the thumping of feet on the ground. You might hear the sounds of wind, or of thunder, or trees creaking, or water running. It just goes to show how connected the Aboriginal people were, and still are in many cases, to the landscape they lived in. For contemporary fusions of indigenous and Western music, look for music by Yothu Yindi, Christine Anu and Geoffrey Gurrumul Yunupingu (who sings only in his own language).

As far as Australian rock 'n' roll goes, you might know a few of the following names. The big star in the '50s was Johnny O'Keefe, but he soon gave way to the likes of the Easybeats. Running into the 1970s, we find the Bee Gees, AC/DC, Sherbet, John-Paul Young, and the Little River Band. Others that made a name for themselves included the solo stars Helen Reddy, Olivia Newton-John, and Peter Allen. The 1980s saw Men at Work, Crowded House, The Go-Betweens, Hunters and Collectors, Kylie Minogue, and Midnight Oil. INXS, Silverchair, and Savage Garden took us into the 1990s, which Kylie managed to stitch up, too. Jet and the Vines were both Australian rock groups that saw considerable international success in the 21st century, along with, you guessed it, Kylie Minogue. For songs with a contemporary Australian voice, go no further than Paul Kelly. In recent years, the best-known Australian singer in the U.S. has probably been Gotye, who won three Grammy awards in 2013.

Australia's Literature

Australian literature has come a long way since the days when the bush poets A. B. "Banjo" Paterson and Henry Lawson penned their odes to a way of life now largely lost. The best known of these is Paterson's epic *The Man from Snowy River,* which first hit the bestseller list in 1895 and was made into a film. But the literary scene has always been lively, and Australia has a wealth of classics, many of them with the Outback at their heart.

Miles Franklin wrote *My Brilliant Career,* the story of a young woman faced with the dilemma of choosing between marriage and a career, in 1901 (made into a film starring Judy Davis in 1979); *We of the Never Never* (1902), by Mrs. Aeneas Gunn, tells the story of a young woman who leaves the comfort of her Melbourne home to live on a cattle station in the Northern Territory; Colleen McCullough's *The Thorn Birds* (1977) is a romantic epic about forbidden love between a Catholic priest and a young woman (made into a television miniseries in 1983); and *Walkabout* (1959), by James V. Marshall, explores the relationship between an Aborigine and two lost children in the bush. It was made into a powerful film by Peter Weir in 1971.

A good historical account of Australia's early days is Geoffrey Blainey's *The Tyranny of Distance,* first published in 1966. Robert Hughes' *The Fatal Shore: The Epic of Australia's Founding* (1987) is a best-selling nonfiction study of the country's European history.

For a contemporary, if somewhat dark, take on the settlement and development of Sydney, delve into John Birmingham's *Leviathan* (1999). From an Aboriginal perspective, *Follow the Rabbit-Proof Fence* (1997), by Doris Pilkington, tells the true story of three young girls from the "stolen generation," who ran away from a mission school to return to their families. (A movie version was released in 2002; see "Australia in Popular Culture: Movies," previously.)

Modern novelists include David Malouf, Elizabeth Jolley, Helen Garner, Sue Woolfe, and Peter Carey, whose *True History of the Kelly Gang* (2001), a fictionalized autobiography of the outlaw Ned Kelly, won the Booker Prize in 2001. West Australian

Tim Winton evokes his part of the continent in stunning prose; his latest work, *Breath* (2008), is no exception. The multi-award-winning *The Light Between Oceans,* by Australian novelist M. L. Stedman is set in a Western Australian lighthouse. Stay tuned for the movie!

Outsiders who have tackled Australia include Jan Morris and Bill Bryson. Morris' *Sydney* was published in 1992, and Bryson's *In a Sunburned Country* (2001), while not always a favorite with Australians, may appeal to American readers.

EATING & DRINKING IN AUSTRALIA

For a long time, the typical Aussie home-cooked meal consisted of English-style "meat and three veg," and a Sunday roast. Spaghetti was something foreigners ate, and zucchini and eggplant (aubergine) were considered exotic. Then came mass immigration and all sorts of food that people only read about in *National Geographic.*

The first big wave of Italian immigrants in the 1950s caused a national scandal. The great Aussie dream was to have a quarter-acre block of land with a hills hoist (a circular revolving clothesline) in the backyard. When Italians started hanging freshly made pasta out to dry on this Aussie icon, it caused an uproar, and some clamored for the new arrivals to be shipped back. As Australia matured, southern European cuisine became increasingly popular, until olive oil was sizzling in frying pans the way only lard had previously done.

In the 1980s, waves of Asian immigrants hit Australia's shores. Suddenly, everyone was cooking with woks. These days, a fusion of spices from the East and ingredients and styles from the Mediterranean make up what's become known as Modern Australian cuisine.

Still, some of the old ways remain. Everyone knows that Aussies like a barbecue, usually referred to as a "barbie." Most Aussies aren't really that adventurous when it comes to throwing things on the hot plate and are usually content with some cheap sausages and a steak washed down by a few beers.

Seafood is popular, as you would expect, and a typical Christmas Day meal usually includes prawns and/or fish.

In the big cities, you'll find every kind of cuisine, including Thai, Vietnamese, Italian, Spanish, Middle Eastern, and Indian. Even the smallest country town usually has a Chinese restaurant (of varying quality). Melbourne is proud of its coffee culture, but American readers should note that the bottomless cup of coffee is rare.

Many restaurants allow you to bring your own wine (referred to simply as BYO) but some may charge a corkage fee of a few dollars (even when there's a screw-cap and no cork).

While you might see kangaroo, crocodile, and emu on the menu at some restaurants, Australians tend not to indulge in their local wildlife that much, preferring to stick to introduced species instead.

Beer & Wine

If you order a beer in a pub or bar, you should be aware that the standard glass size differs from state to state. Thus, in Sydney you can order a schooner or a smaller midi. In trendy places you might be offered an English pint or a half-pint. In Melbourne and

Brisbane a midi is called a pot, while in Darwin it's called a handle, and in Hobart a ten. It can be confusing! You can get smaller glasses, too, though thankfully they're becoming rare. These could either be called a pony, a seven, a butcher, a six, or a bobbie, depending on which city you're in. If in doubt, just mime a big one or a small one, and you'll get your meaning across.

As far as wine goes, Australia has come a long way since the first grape vines arrived on the First Fleet in 1788. Today, more than 550 major companies and small winemakers produce wine commercially in Australia. There are dozens of recognized wine-growing regions, but the most well known include the Hunter Valley in New South Wales; the Barossa Valley, McClaren Vale, Coonawarra, Adelaide Hills, and the Clare Valley in South Australia; the Yarra Valley in Victoria; and Margaret River in Western Australia.

Aboriginal Foods

In the past couple of decades, many Australian chefs have woken to the variety and tastes of "bush tucker," as native Aussie food is tagged. Now it's all the rage in the most fashionable restaurants, where wattleseed, lemon myrtle, and other native tastes have a place in one or two dishes on the menu. Below is a list of some of those foods you may encounter.

- **Bunya nut:** Crunchy nut of the bunya pine, about the size of a macadamia.
- **Bush tomato:** Dry, small, darkish fruit; more like a raisin in look and taste.
- **Native cranberry:** Small berry that tastes a bit like an apple.
- **Illawarra plum:** Dark berry with a strong, rich, tangy taste.
- **Kangaroo:** A strong meat with a gamey flavor. Tender when correctly prepared, tough when not. Excellent smoked.
- **Lemon aspen:** Citrusy, light-yellow fruit with a sharp, tangy flavor.
- **Lemon myrtle:** Gum leaves with a fresh lemon tang; often used to flavor white meat.
- **Lillipilli:** Delicious juicy, sweet pink berry.
- **Quandong:** A tart, tangy native peach.
- **Rosella:** Spiky petals of a red flower with a rich berry flavor.
- **Wattleseed:** Roasted ground acacia seeds that taste a little like bitter coffee. Sometimes used in cakes.
- **Wild lime:** Smaller and sourer than regular lime.

One ingredient you will not see on menus is **witchetty grubs;** most people are too squeamish to eat these fat, juicy slimy white creatures. They live in the soil or in dead tree trunks and are a common source of protein for some Aborigines. You eat them alive, not cooked. If you are offered one in the Outback, you can either freak out (as most locals would do)—or enjoy its pleasantly nutty taste as a reward for your bravery.

WHEN TO GO

When it is winter in the Northern Hemisphere, Australia is basking in the Southern Hemisphere's summer, and vice versa. Midwinter in Australia is July and August, and the hottest months are November through March. Remember, unlike in the Northern Hemisphere, the farther south you go in Australia, the colder it gets.

...vel Seasons

...alia are lowest from mid-April to late August—the best time to visit
... and the Great Barrier Reef.

...ON The peak travel season in the most popular parts of Australia is the
...er. In much of the country—particularly the northern half—the most pleas-
...o travel is April through September, when daytime temperatures are 66°F to
...(19°C–31°C) and it rarely rains. June, July, and August are the busiest months in
...ese parts; you'll need to book accommodations and tours well in advance, and you
will pay higher rates then, too.

On the other hand, Australia's summer is a nice time to visit the southern states, and
even in winter, temperatures rarely dip below freezing.

Generally, the best months to visit Australia are September and October, when it's
often still warm enough to hit the beach in the southern states, it's cool enough to tour
Uluru, and the humidity and rains have not come to Cairns (although it will be very
hot by Oct).

LOW SEASON October through March (summer) is just too hot, too humid, or too
wet—or all three—to tour the Red Centre. North Queensland, including Cairns, suffers
an intensely hot, humid wet season from November or December through March or
April. So if you decide to travel at this time—and lots of people do—be prepared to
take the heat, the inconvenience of potential flooding, and the slight chance of encoun-
tering cyclones.

Australian National Public Holidays

On national public holidays, services such as banking, postal needs, and purchase of
alcohol might be limited or unavailable. There may also be additional holidays as
declared by individual states and territories, such as Melbourne Cup Day: Based on the
country's most famous thoroughbred horse race, Melbourne Cup Day is celebrated the
first Tuesday of November, and the race is nicknamed "the race that stops the nation."

- **New Year's Day,** January 1. Expect the usual fireworks and festivities to begin the
  night of December 31 to ring in the New Year.
- **Australia Day,** January 26. This national day recognizes the First Fleet's arrival in
  1788, when 11 ships made their way from England to establish a colony here in
  Australia.
- **Good Friday,** the Friday before Easter. The Christian commemoration of Jesus'
  crucifixion and his death. In Australia, Good Friday is observed the first Friday after
  the full moon (on or after Mar 21).
- **Easter Monday,** day after Easter Sunday. The Christian commemoration of Jesus'
  resurrection from the dead.

Steer Clear of the Vacation Rush

Try to avoid Australia from Boxing Day (Dec 26) to the end of January, when Aussies take their summer vacations. In popular seaside holiday spots, hotel rooms, and airline seats get scarce as hen's teeth, and it's a rare airline or hotel that will discount full rates by even a dollar.

- **Anzac Day,** April 25. ANZAC (Australian and New Zealand Army Corps) Day recognizes those who have served the nation in times of war.
- **Christmas Day,** December 25. When Christians celebrate Jesus' birth. *Note:* If Christmas is on a weekend day, the next Monday is termed a public holiday.
- **Boxing Day,** December 26. Originally a British tradition involving giftgiving, Boxing Day is now an Australian holiday, and some sports kick off their seasons on this date. If Boxing Day falls on a Saturday, the next Monday is deemed a public holiday. If it falls on a Sunday, the next Tuesday is the holiday.

Australia Calendar of Events

For an exhaustive list of events beyond those listed here, check http://events.frommers.com, where you'll find a searchable, up-to-the-minute roster of what's happening in cities all over the world.

JANUARY

Sydney Festival: Highlights of Sydney's visual and performing-arts festival are free jazz or classical music concerts held outdoors on two Saturday nights near the Royal Botanic Gardens. (Take a picnic and arrive by 4pm to get a spot on the grass.) The festival involves about 100 events featuring 1,000 artists at 20 venues. Call (ⓒ **02/8248 6500** or go to **www.sydneyfestival.org.au.** Three weeks from early January.

The Australian Open: The Asia/Pacific Grand Slam is played every year at the Melbourne Park National Tennis Centre. Tickets go on sale in October through **Ticketek** (ⓒ **1300/888 104** in Australia or 02/8736 2711; www.ticketek.com.au). For more information check out **www.australianopen. com.** Last 2 weeks of January.

Australia Day: Australia's answer to the Fourth of July marks the landing of the First Fleet of convicts at Sydney Cove in 1788. Every town puts on some kind of celebration; in Sydney, there are ferry races and tall ships on the harbor, food and wine stalls in Hyde Park, open days at museums and other attractions, and fireworks in the evening. **www.australiaday.com.au.** January 26.

FEBRUARY

Sydney Gay & Lesbian Mardi Gras: A month of events, culminating in a spectacular parade of costumed dancers and decorated floats, watched by several hundred thousand onlookers. Contact Sydney Gay & Lesbian Mardi Gras ((ⓒ **02/9383 0900;** www.mardigras.org.au).

MARCH

Formula 1 Australian Grand Prix, Melbourne: The first Grand Prix of the year, on the international FIA Formula 1 World Championship circuit, is battled out on one of its fastest circuits, in Melbourne. For tickets, contact Ticketek (ⓒ **13 19 31** in Australia), or order online at **www.grandprix.com. au.** Four days in the second week of March.

APRIL

Anzac Day, nationwide: April 25 is Australia's national day of mourning for servicemen and women who have died in wars and conflict. Commemorative services are held even in the smallest towns, some at dawn and some later, with major cities holding street parades for returned servicemen and women. Huge crowds turn out. Details of all services in Australia can be found at **www. dva.gov.au/anzac.**

Melbourne International Comedy Festival: Venues all over the city participate in this festival of laughs, which attracts top Australian and international talent. (ⓒ **1300/660 013**; www.comedyfestival.com.au). First 3 weeks in April.

JUNE

Sydney Film Festival: World and Australian premieres of Aussie and international movies take place in the State Theatre and other venues over 12 days. Contact the Sydney Film Festival (☎ 02/9690 5333; www.sff.org.au). First and second week in June.

JULY

Melbourne International Film Festival: About 350 films—new releases, shorts, and avant-garde movies—from 50 countries play at venues around the city during this annual festival (☎ 03/9662 3722; www.miff.com.au). Late July through early August.

AUGUST

Henley-on-Todd Regatta, Alice Springs: Sounds sophisticated, doesn't it? It's actually a harum-scarum race down the dry bed of the Todd River in homemade "boats," made from anything you care to name—an old four-wheel-drive chassis, say, or beer cans lashed together. The only rule is the vessel has to look *vaguely* like a boat. Contact the organizers at ☎ 0418/897 027 (mobile phone) or **www.henleyontodd.com.au.** Third Saturday in August.

SEPTEMBER

Melbourne Fringe Festival: During the Fringe Festival (☎ 03/9660 9600; www.melbournefringe.com.au), the city's streets, pubs, theaters, and restaurants play host to everyone from jugglers and fire-eaters to musicians and independent productions covering all art forms. Three weeks in late September/early October.

Brisbane Festival: A highlight of this arts festival (☎ 03/9660 9600; www.brisbanefestival.com.au) is Riverfire, a spectacular pyrotechnics display best seen from the riverbank. The festival program includes music, theatre, dance, comedy, opera, circus and much more. Three weeks in September.

NOVEMBER

Melbourne Cup, Flemington: They say the entire nation stops to watch this horse race. That's about right. If you're not actually at the A$3.5-million race, you're glued to the TV—or, well, you're probably not an Australian. Women wear hats to the office, files on desks all over the country make way for a late chicken and champagne lunch, and don't even think about flagging a cab at the 3pm race time. For tickets, contact Ticketek (☎ 132 849 in Australia; www.ticketek.com.au); for information, visit **www.vrc.net.au.** First Tuesday in November.

DECEMBER

Sydney-to-Hobart Yacht Race: Find a clifftop spot near the Heads to watch the glorious show of spinnakers, as 100 or so yachts leave Sydney Harbour for this grueling world-class event. The organizer is the Sydney-based Cruising Yacht Club of Australia (☎ 02/8292 7800; www.cyca.com.au). Starts December 26.

New Year's Eve, Sydney: Watching the Sydney Harbour Bridge light up with fireworks is a treat. The main show is at 9pm, not midnight, so young kids don't miss out. Pack a picnic and snag a Harbour-side spot by 4pm, or even earlier at the best vantage point—Mrs. Macquarie's Chair in the Royal Botanic Gardens. December 31.

THE LAY OF THE LAND

People who have never visited Australia wonder why such a huge country has a population of just 22 million people. But the truth is, much of Australia is uninhabitable, and about 90 percent of the population lives on only 2.6 percent of the continent, mainly clustered around the coast. Climatic and physical land conditions ensure that the only relatively decent rainfall occurs along a thin strip of land around Australia's coast. Compounding that is the fact that Australia falls victim to long droughts. Most of Australia is harsh Outback, characterized by saltbush plains, arid brown crags, shifting sand deserts, and salt-lake country. People survive where they can in this arid land because of one thing—the Great Artesian Basin. This saucer-shaped geological formation comprises about a fifth of Australia's landmass, stretching over much of inland New South Wales, Queensland, South Australia, and the Northern Territory. Beneath it are massive underground water supplies stored during Jurassic and Cretaceous times (some 66–208 million years ago), when the area was much like the Amazon basin is today. Bore holes bring water to the surface and allow sheep, cattle, and humans a respite from the dryness.

As for the climate, as you might expect with a continent the size of Australia, it can differ immensely. The average rainfall in central Australia ranges from between just 200 to 250mm (8–10 in.) a year. Summer daytime temperatures range from between 90° and 104°F (32°–40°C). In winter, temperatures range from around 64° to 75°F (18°–24°C). Summer in the Southern Hemisphere roughly stretches from early November to the end of February, though it can be hot for a couple of months on either side of these dates, depending where you are.

Parts of the Northern Territory and far northern Queensland are classified as tropical, and as such suffer from very wet summers—often referred to simply as "the Wet." Flooding can be a real fact of life up here. The rest of the year is called "the Dry," for obvious reasons.

Most of Queensland and northern New South Wales are subtropical. This means warm summers and cool winters. Sydney falls into the "temperate" zone, with generally moderate temperatures and no prolonged periods of extreme hot or cold conditions. Parts of central Victoria can get snow in winter, while the Australian Alps, which run through southern central NSW and northeastern Victoria, have good snow cover in winter.

The Queensland coast is blessed with one of the greatest natural attractions in the world. The Great Barrier Reef stretches 2,000km (1,240 miles) from off Gladstone in Queensland to the Gulf of Papua, near Papua New Guinea. It's relatively new, not more than 8,000 years old, although many fear that rising seawater, caused by global warming, will cause its demise. As it is, the invasive Crown of Thorns starfish and a bleaching process believed to be the result of excessive nutrients flowing into the sea from Australia's farming land are already causing significant damage. The Reef is covered in chapter 7.

Australia's other great natural formation is, of course, Uluru—which is sometimes (but not commonly) still called by the name Europeans gave it, Ayers Rock. (see p. 209).

Australia's Wildlife

Australia's isolation from the rest of the world over millions of years has led to the evolution of forms of life found nowhere else. Probably the strangest of all is the **platypus.** This monotreme, or egg-laying marsupial, has webbed feet, a ducklike bill, and a tail like a beaver's. It lays eggs, and the young suckle from their mother. When a specimen was first brought back to Europe, skeptical scientists insisted it was a fake—a concoction of several different animals sewn together. It is unlikely you will see this shy, nocturnal creature in the wild, but several wildlife parks have them.

Australia is also famous for **kangaroos** and **koalas.** There are 45 kinds of kangaroos and wallabies, ranging in scale from small rat-size kangaroos to the man-size red kangaroos. The koala is a fluffy marsupial (not a bear!) whose nearest relative is the wombat. It eats gum (eucalyptus) leaves and sleeps about 20 hours a day. There's just one koala species, although those found in Victoria are much larger than those in more northern climes.

The animal you're most likely to come across in your trip is the **possum,** named by Captain James Cook after the North American opossum, which he thought they resembled. (In fact, they are from entirely different families of the animal kingdom.) The brush-tailed possum is commonly found in suburban gardens, including those in Sydney.

Then there's the **wombat.** There are four species of this bulky burrower in Australia, but the common wombat is, well, most common.

The **dingo** is a wild dog, varying in color from yellow to a russet red, mainly seen in the Outback. Because dingoes can breed with escaped "pet" dogs, full-blooded dingoes are becoming increasingly rare.

Commonly seen birds in Australia include the fairy penguin or **Little Penguin** along the coast, **black swans, parrots** and **cockatoos,** and **honeyeaters.**

DANGEROUS NATIVES

Snakes are common throughout Australia, but you will rarely see one. The most dangerous land snake is the taipan, which hides in the grasslands in northern Australia—one bite contains enough venom to kill up to 200 sheep. If by the remotest chance you are bitten, immediately demobilize the limb, wrapping it tightly (but not tight enough to restrict the blood flow) with a cloth or bandage, and call ℂ **000** for an ambulance. Antivenin should be available at the nearest hospital.

One creature that scares the living daylights out of anyone who visits coastal Australia is the **shark,** particularly the great white (though these marauders of the sea are uncommon, and mostly found in colder waters, such as those off South Australia). Shark attacks are very rare, particularly when you consider how many people go swimming. Some years there are none, other years (2011, for example) there have been up to four in a year, but the average is around one a year, according to the Australian Shark Attack File kept at Sydney's Taronga Zoo. You are more likely to get hit by a car on your way to the beach than get taken by a shark. Certainly, more people drown in Australian waters than are victims of shark attack.

There are two types of **crocodile** in Australia: the relatively harmless freshwater croc, which grows to 3m (10 ft.), and the dangerous estuarine (or saltwater) crocodile, which reaches 5 to 7m (16–23 ft.). Freshwater crocs eat fish; estuarine crocs aren't so picky. Never swim in or stand on the bank of any river, swamp, beach, or pool in northern Australia unless you know for certain it's croc-free.

Spiders are common all over Australia, with the funnel web spider and the red-back spider being the most aggressive. Funnel webs live in holes in the ground (they spin their webs around a hole's entrance) and stand on their back legs when they're about to attack. Red-backs have a habit of resting under toilet seats and in car trunks, generally outside the main cities. Caution is a good policy.

If you go bushwalking, check your body carefully. **Ticks** are common, especially in eastern Australia, and can cause severe itching and fever. If you find one on you, pull it out with tweezers, taking care not to leave the head behind.

Fish to avoid are **stingrays** (Australian television star and crocodile hunter Steve Irwin was killed by a stingray barb through the heart), as well as **porcupine fish, stonefish,** and **lionfish.** Never touch an **octopus** if it has blue rings on it, or a **cone shell,** and be wary of the painful and sometimes deadly tentacles of the **box jellyfish** along the northern Queensland coast in summer. This jellyfish is responsible for more deaths in Australia than snakes, sharks, and saltwater crocodiles.

Closely related to the box jellyfish is the **Irukandji,** which also inhabits northern Australian waters. This deadly jellyfish is only 2.5 centimeters (1 in.) in diameter, which makes it very hard to spot in the water.

If you brush past a jellyfish, or think you have, pour vinegar over the affected site immediately—authorities leave bottles of vinegar on beaches for this purpose. Vinegar deactivates the stinging cells that haven't already affected you, but doesn't affect the ones that already have. If you are in the tropics and you believe you may have been stung by a box jellyfish or an Irukandji, seek medical attention immediately.

In Sydney, you might come across **"stingers,"** also called "blue bottles." These long-tentacled blue jellyfish can inflict a nasty stinging burn that can last for hours. Sometimes you'll see warning signs on patrolled beaches. The best remedy if you are severely stung is to wash the affected area with fresh water and have a very hot bath or shower (preferably with someone else, just for the sympathy).

Threats to the Landscape

Australia is suffering from climate change, water shortages, and serious threats to wildlife and ecosystems. Australia is one of the highest per capita polluters in the world, thanks largely to its reliance on mining and coal-fired power generation.

Meanwhile, the Great Barrier Reef is being damaged by coral bleaching, which occurs when water temperatures rise. Corals can recover, but if the heat persists, or if bleaching happens too frequently, they can die. Nutrient-rich sediment washed out to sea from farmland doesn't help matters much, as hard-hit corals become colonized by nutrient-loving algae. The runoff can also contain pesticides and herbicides, which damage the reef further and make it more vulnerable to the introduced crown-of-thorns starfish, which likes snacking on coral.

As for Australia's native animals and birds—well, history hasn't been too kind to them. At least 23 species of birds, 4 frog species, and 27 mammal species have become extinct since European settlement in Australia. Habitat destruction and introduced species have been the main causes of extinctions.

Threatened with extinction today are 19 species of fish, 15 species of frogs, 14 species of reptiles, 46 species of birds, 36 species of mammals, and 513 species of plants. Many more are classified as vulnerable.

RESPONSIBLE TRAVEL

Sustainable travel—and its close cousin, responsible travel—are important issues in Australia, and you'll find plenty of places that claim to be ecofriendly. So how do you find the places that will truly help you make as little impact as possible on our fragile environment, while still enjoying your holiday? When planning your trip, look for Australian tourism operators who have their tour, attraction, or accommodations accredited under **Ecotourism Australia**'s Eco Certification Program (www.eco tourism.org.au). The **Eco Certification** logo is carried by those businesses that are recognized as being tours, attractions, cruises, or accommodations that are environmentally, socially, and economically sustainable. The program assures travelers that these products are backed by a strong, well-managed commitment to sustainable practices and provide high-quality nature-based tourism experiences. The website allows you to search for companies that are accredited. Ecotourism Australia also publishes the online **Green Travel Guide,** which carries a list of all accredited businesses.

RESOURCES FOR responsible TRAVEL

In addition to the resources for Australia listed above, the following websites provide valuable wide-ranging information on sustainable travel.

o **Sustainable Travel International** (www.sustainabletravel.org) promotes ethical tourism practices.

o **Carbonfund** (www.carbonfund. org), **TerraPass** (www.terrapass. org), and **Cool Climate** (http:// coolclimate.berkeley.edu) provide info on "carbon offsetting," or offsetting the greenhouse gas emitted during flights.

o **Greenhotels** (www.greenhotels. com) recommends green-rated member hotels around the world that fulfill the company's stringent environmental requirements.

For general info on volunteer travel, visit **www.goabroad.com/volunteer-abroad** and **www.idealist.org**.

Like people in developed nations everywhere, Australians are becoming more and more aware of their environmental responsibilities. Recycling is common practice, with local government areas providing bins for general household refuse, for paper and glass, and for vegetative material such as prunings.

Because of frequent and prolonged droughts, people have become more aware of where their water is coming from too, and you might be very surprised at how water conscious the average Australian is these days.

That said, what we gain on one hand we often lose on the other. Gas-guzzling four-wheel-drives are popular, four-wheelers zip around the Outback and on some beaches, and air travel within Australia is generally necessary.

If you are keen to offset the large carbon footprint created by your flight to Australia, use public transport where you can, turn electronic gadgets off at the wall when you aren't using them, and recycle batteries if possible. Don't throw cigarette butts on the ground—as well as risking a possible hefty fine, your butt might end up polluting Australia's waterways.

There are hundreds of tourism operators and hotels who use the eco-friendly banner when promoting themselves. Choose a hotel designed to reduce its environmental impact with its use of non-toxic cleaners and renewable energy sources. The hotels may be reducing their emissions further by utilizing local food, energy-efficient lighting, and eco-friendly forms of transport. Most hotels now offer you the choice of using the same towels for more than one night—and of course, you should, because laundry makes up around 40 percent of an average hotel's energy use. Some accommodations offer you the same choice regarding your bed linens if you're staying more than one night.

Choose tours that are eco-friendly, environmentally sustainable, and preferably employ local guides. Choose a sailing boat rather than a giant motor cruiser to discover the Barrier Reef or the Whitsunday Islands in Queensland, for example, or an Aboriginal guided walking tour above a large coach excursion.

If you are looking for a way of "giving something back" on your holiday, several organizations offer the opportunity to do some volunteer work in Australia, such as helping to save endangered wildlife. Often there is a fee involved, to cover transportation, accommodations, meals, and so on.

If you wish to work with sick or injured native animals, then you can work in a volunteer capacity at the **Currumbin Wildlife Sanctuary** (ℭ **07/5534 1266;** www. cws.org.au), on the Gold Coast, just south of Brisbane in Queensland.

The Australian Wildlife Conservancy (ℭ **08/9380 9633;** www.australianwildlife. org) offers the occasional option for volunteering on animal projects.

Real Gap Experience (ℭ **1800/985-4852** in the United States or 1300/844 270 in Australia; www.realgap.com) offers you the chance to volunteer in Australia, including in a koala sanctuary.

The various **official state tourism websites,** such as visitvictoria.com, visitnsw. com, and queenslandholidays.com.au, can also recommend responsible local travel companies and green hotel/lodge options. Go to "Visitor Information," for each destination to find the appropriate visitor's bureau.

See **frommers.com/planning** for more tips on responsible travel.

SYDNEY

Warm-natured, sun-kissed, and naturally good looking, Sydney is rather like its lucky, lucky residents. Situated on one of the world's most striking harbors, where the twin icons of the Sydney Opera House and Harbour Bridge steal the limelight, the relaxed Australian capital is surprisingly close to nature. Within minutes you can be riding the waves on Bondi Beach, bushwalking in Manly or gazing out across Botany Bay, where the first salt-encrusted Europeans arrived in the 18th century. You can understand why they never wanted to leave.

For that "I'm in Sydney!" feeling, nothing beats the first glimpse of the white-sailed Opera House and the iconic Harbour Bridge, which you can climb for a bird's-eye view of the sparkling harbor. Move on to the Royal Botanical Gardens' tropical greenery and the Museum of Contemporary Art's cutting-edge exhibitions. With 70 beaches close by—from the fizzing surf of famous Bondi Beach to Manly's coastal walks and pine-flanked bays—it's no wonder Sydneysiders look so bronzed and relaxed.

Don't let the knockout views of Sydney Harbour distract you from your shopping in The Rocks' specialty shops and galleries, crammed with one-off gifts, quirky fashion, and hand-painted ceramics. Sydneysiders shop for designer styles under the soaring glass arches of the Queen Victoria Building. There's also the city's very own Oxford Street and the fashionable Surry Hills and Paddington suburbs. Combine a morning looking for vintage clothes and swimwear at Bondi Market with time out on the beach.

Dine on a different cuisine every night in multicultural Sydney—whether late-night noodles in Chinatown, tasty tapas in the Spanish Quarter or authentic Thai curries on bohemian King Street. BYO restaurants and sensible prices make eating out affordable in all but the very top places—French-Japanese Tetsuya's, for instance. Head to Circular Quay's sleek waterfront restaurants for the Opera House view and Australia's distinctive modern cuisine—a fusion of Australian, Mediterranean, and spicy Asian flavors.

There's so much to do in Sydney that you could easily spend a week here and still not see it all.

ESSENTIALS

Arriving

BY PLANE Sydney International Airport is 8km (5 miles) from the city center. Shuttle buses link the international and domestic terminals. Single tickets cost A$5.50. The journey takes up to 10 minutes and operates every 30 minutes from 6am to 9pm (more often in the morning peak period). Bus stops are on arrivals levels, at T1 Bus Bay 21 (near the McDonald's), and at T2 on the first roadway in the centre of the terminal. In both terminals, you'll find luggage carts, wheelchairs, a post office (daily 6am–8:30pm), mailboxes, currency exchange, duty-free shops, restaurants, bars, stores, showers, luggage lockers, a baggage-held service for larger items, ATMs, and tourist-information desks. You can rent mobile phones in the international terminal. Smarte Carte (at the southern end of the arrivals level) has luggage storage for A\$12 a day for a small bag and A\$15 for a suitcase. Luggage trolleys are free to use in the international arrival terminal but cost A\$4 outside departure terminals (you'll need coins).

Airport Link (www.airportlink.com.au) trains connect the international and domestic airports to the city stations of Central, Museum, St. James, Circular Quay, Wynyard, and Town Hall. You'll need to change trains for other Sydney stations. Unfortunately, the line has no dedicated luggage areas and because it's also a commuter train to the city from the suburbs, it gets very crowded during rush hours (around 7–9am and 4–6:30pm). If you have lots of luggage, it's probably best to take a taxi. The train takes 10 minutes to reach the Central Railway Station and continues to Circular Quay. Trains leave every 10 minutes and cost A\$17 one-way for adults and A\$12 for children from the international terminal. Round-trip tickets are only available if you want to return to the airport on the same day.

Sydney Airporter coaches (© 02/9666 9988; www.kst.com.au) travel to the city center from bus stops outside the terminals every 15 minutes. This service will drop you off (and pick you up) at hotels in the city, Kings Cross, and Darling Harbour. Pickups from hotels require at least 3 hours advance notice, and you can book online. Tickets cost A\$15 adults and A\$10 children 4 to 11 one-way and A\$28 adults and A\$18 round-trip.

A **taxi** from the airport to the city center costs about A\$50. An expressway, the Eastern Distributor, is the fastest way to reach the city from the airport. There's a A\$5 toll from the airport to the city (the taxi driver pays the toll and adds the cost to your fare), but there is no toll to the airport. A 10% credit-card charge applies, and the Sydney airport charges a A\$3.75 fee to catch a taxi from there.

BY TRAIN **Central Station** (© 13 15 00 for **Sydney Trains**, or 13 22 32 for NSW TrainLink interstate trains) is the main city and interstate train station. It's at the top of George Street in downtown Sydney. All interstate trains depart from here, and it's a major Sydney Trains hub. Many city buses leave from neighboring Railway Square for such places as Town Hall and Circular Quay.

BY BUS **Greyhound** coaches operate from the **Sydney Coach Terminal** (© 02/9281 9366), on Eddy Avenue (Bay 13 at Central Station).

Taxi Savvy

Taxi queues can be long, and drivers may try to cash in by insisting you share a cab with other passengers in line at the airport. Here's the scam: After dropping off the other passengers, the cabdriver will attempt to charge you the full price of the journey, despite the fact that the other passengers paid for their sections. You certainly won't save any money sharing a cab if this happens, and your journey will be a long one. If you are first in line in the taxi stand, the law states that you can refuse to share the cab. Taxi drivers appreciate a tip, but there is no compulsion to do so. If you've had good service, a 10% tip is enough.

BY CRUISE SHIP   Ships dock at the **Overseas Passenger Terminal** in The Rocks, opposite the Sydney Opera House, or the White Bay Cruise Terminal in the suburb of Rozelle, about 5km (3 miles) from the city center.

BY CAR   Drivers enter Sydney from the north on the Pacific Highway, from the south on the M5 and Princes Highway, and from the west on the Great Western Highway.

Visitor Information

The Sydney Visitor Centre, corner of Argyle and Playfair streets, The Rocks (✆ **1800/ 067 676** in Australia, or 02/8273 0000; www.sydneyvisitorcentre.com), is a good place to pick up maps, brochures, Youth Hostel Association (YHA) cards, and general tourist information. There's also the **Sydney Visitor Centre Darling Harbour,** at Palm Grove (between Cockle Bay Wharf and Harbourside), Darling Harbour. Both are open from 9:30am to 5:30pm daily. In Manly, find the **Manly Visitor Information Centre** (✆ **02/9976 1430**) at Manly Wharf (where the ferries come in). It's open Monday to Friday from 9am to 5pm and on weekends between 10am and 4pm.

Elsewhere, **City Host information kiosks,** on George Street (next to Sydney Town Hall), at Circular Quay (corner of Pitt and Alfred sts.), and at Kings Cross (corner of Darlinghurst Rd. and Springfield Ave.) provide maps, brochures, and advice and are open daily (except Christmas Day) 9am to 5pm. Another kiosk at Dixon Street (near Goulburn St.) is open open from 11am to 7pm.

A good website for events, entertainment, dining, and shopping is **CitySearch Sydney** (www.sydney.citysearch.com.au). Another is **www.sydney.com.**

City Layout

Sydney is one of the largest cities in the world, covering more than 1,730 sq. km (675 sq. miles) from the sea to the foothills of the Blue Mountains. Thankfully, the city center, or Central Business District (CBD), is compact. The jewel in Sydney's crown is its magnificent harbor, which empties into the South Pacific Ocean through head-lands known as North Head and South Head. On the southern side of the harbor are the high-rises of the city center; the Sydney Opera House; a string of beaches, includ-ing Bondi; and the inner suburbs. The Sydney Harbour Bridge and a tunnel connect the city center to the high-rises of the North Sydney business district and the affluent suburbs and ocean beaches beyond.

MAIN ARTERIES & STREETS   The city's main thoroughfare, **George Street,** runs up from **Circular Quay,** past Wynyard train station and Town Hall, to Central Station. Other main streets running parallel to George include Pitt, Elizabeth, and Macquarie streets. **Macquarie Street** runs up from the Sydney Opera House, past the Royal Botanic Gardens and Hyde Park. **Martin Place** is a pedestrian thoroughfare between Macquarie and George streets. It's about halfway between Circular Quay and Town Hall—in the heart of the city center. The easy-to-spot Sydney Tower, facing onto pedestrian-only **Pitt Street Mall** on Pitt Street, is the main city-center landmark. Next to Circular Quay and across from the Opera House is **The Rocks,** a cluster of small streets that was once part of a historic larger slum and is now a tourist attraction. Roads meet at **Town Hall** from Kings Cross in one direction and Darling Harbour in the other. From Circular Quay to The Rocks, it's a 5- to 10-minute stroll, to Wynyard a 10-minute walk, and to Town Hall a 20-minute stroll. From Town Hall to the near side of Darling Harbour it's about a 10-minute walk.

Neighborhoods in Brief

SOUTH OF SYDNEY HARBOUR

CIRCULAR QUAY   This transport hub for ferries, buses, and trains is tucked between the Harbour Bridge and the Sydney Opera House. The Quay, as it's called, is a good spot for a stroll, and its outdoor restaurants and street performers are popular. The Rocks, the Royal Botanic Gardens, the Contemporary Art Museum, and the start of the main shopping area (centered on Pitt and George sts.) are a short walk away. To get there by public tranport, take a train, ferry, or city bus to Circular Quay.

THE ROCKS   This small historic area, a short stroll west of Circular Quay, is packed with colonial stone buildings, intriguing back streets, boutiques, pubs, tourist stores, restaurants, and hotels. It's the most exclusive place to stay in the city because of its beauty and its proximity to the Opera House and harbor. Shops are geared toward Sydney's yuppies and wealthy tourists—don't expect bargains. On weekends, a portion of George Street is blocked off for The Rocks Market, with stalls selling souvenirs and crafts. A foodies' market operates on Fridays. To reach the area on public transport, take any bus for Circular Quay or The Rocks (on George St.) or a train or ferry to Circular Quay. Check out www.therocks.com for event info.

TOWN HALL   In the heart of the city, this area is home to the main department stores and two Sydney landmarks, the Town Hall and a historic shopping mall called the Queen Victoria Building (QVB). Also in this area are Sydney Tower and the boutique-style chain stores of Pitt Street Mall. Farther up George Street are movie houses, the entrance to Sydney's Spanish district (around Liverpool St.), and Chinatown. Take any bus from Circular Quay on George Street or a train to the Town Hall stop.

DARLING HARBOUR   Designed as a tourist precinct, Darling Harbour features Sydney's main convention, exhibition, and entertainment centers; a waterfront promenade;

the Sydney Aquarium; an IMAX theatre; the Australian Maritime Museum; the Powerhouse Museum; the Star City casino; a food court; and plenty of shops. Nearby are the restaurants of Cockle Bay and King Street Wharf. To reach Darling Harbour by public transport, take a ferry from Circular Quay (Wharf 5) or the light rail from Central Station. It's a short walk from Town Hall.

KINGS CROSS & THE SUBURBS BEYOND   "The Cross," as it's known, is the city's red-light district—and it's also home to some of Sydney's best-known nightclubs and restaurants. The area has plenty of backpacker hostels, a few bars, and some upscale hotels. The main drag, Darlinghurst Road, is short but crammed with strip joints, prostitutes, drunks, and such. It's certainly colorful. Also here are cheap Internet centers. There's a heavy police presence and usually plenty of "ordinary" people around, but do take care. Beyond the strip clubs and glitter, the neighborhoods of Elizabeth Bay, Double Bay, and Rose Bay hug the waterfront. To get here, take a train to Kings Cross. From the next stop, Edgecliff, it's a short walk to Double Bay and a longer one to Rose Bay along the coast.

PADDINGTON/OXFORD STREET   This central-city neighborhood, centered on trendy Oxford Street, is known for its expensive terrace houses, off-the-wall boutiques and bookshops, and restaurants, pubs, and nightclubs. It's also the heart of Sydney's large gay community and has a liberal scattering of gay bars and dance spots. To reach the area by public transport, take bus no. 380 or 382 from Circular Quay (on Elizabeth St.); no. 378 from Railway Square, Central Station; or no. 355, 378 or 380 from Bondi Junction. The lower end of Oxford Street is a short walk from Museum Station (take the Liverpool St. exit).

DARLINGHURST   Between grungy Kings Cross and upscale Oxford Street, this extroverted, grimy, terraced area is home to some of Sydney's best cafes—though it's probably not wise to wander around here at night alone. Take the train to Kings Cross and head right from the exit.

CENTRAL The congested, polluted crossroads around Central Station, the city's main train station, has little to recommend it. Buses run from here to Circular Quay, and it's a 20-minute walk to Town Hall. The Sydney Central YHA (youth hostel) is here.

GLEBE Young professionals and students come to this central-city neighborhood for the cafes, restaurants, pubs, and shops along the main thoroughfare, Glebe Point Road. All this, plus a location 15 minutes from the city and 30 minutes from Circular Quay, makes it a good place for budget-conscious travelers. To reach Glebe, take bus no. 370, 431, 433, 439 or 470 from Circular Quay.

BONDI & THE SOUTHERN BEACHES Some of Sydney's most glamorous surf beaches—Bondi, Bronte, and Coogee—lie along the South Pacific coast, southeast of the city center. Bondi has a wide sweep of beach (crowded in summer), some interesting restaurants and bars, plenty of attitude, and beautiful bodies—but no train station. To reach Bondi, take bus no. 333 to Bondi Beach from Circular Quay—it takes about 40 minutes. You need to buy a ticket at a newsdealer or 7-Eleven store beforehand. A Travelten bus ticket (See "Getting Around," below) is a good option if you are staying in Bondi. Bus no. 378 from Railway Square, Central Station, goes to Bronte, and bus no. 373 travels to Coogee from Circular Quay.

WATSONS BAY Watsons Bay is known for The Gap—a section of dramatic sea cliffs—as well as several good restaurants and a good beer garden. It's a terrific spot to spend a sunny afternoon. To reach it, take bus no. 324 from Circular Quay. There's limited ferry service daily from Circular Quay (Wharf 4), starting at 10:20am on weekdays, 9:30am on weekends and holidays.

NORTH OF SYDNEY HARBOUR

NORTH SYDNEY You can see the giant smiling clown face of Luna Park from Circular Quay, but North Sydney—across the Harbour Bridge—has little in the way of tourist attractions. It's predominantly a business area. Chatswood (take a train from Central or Wynyard station) has some good suburban-type shopping; and Milsons Point has a decent pub, the Kirribilli Hotel.

THE NORTH SHORE Ferries and buses provide access to these wealthy neighborhoods across the Harbour Bridge. Gorgeous Balmoral Beach, Taronga Zoo, and upscale boutiques are the attractions in Mosman. Take a ferry from Circular Quay (Wharf 2) to Taronga Zoo (10 min.) and a bus to Balmoral Beach (another 10 min.).

MANLY Half an hour from Circular Quay by ferry, Manly is famous for its ocean beach—it gives Bondi a run for its money—and scores of cheap food outlets. A privately operated fast-ferry service also runs from Circular Quay to Manly.

WEST OF THE CITY CENTER

BALMAIN A short ferry ride from Circular Quay, Balmain was once Sydney's main shipbuilding area. In the last few decades, the area has become trendy and expensive. The neighborhood has a village feel to it, abounds with restaurants and pubs, and stages a popular Saturday market at the local church. Take bus no. 441 or 442 from Town Hall or George Street, or a ferry from Circular Quay, and then a short bus ride (or walk) up the hill to the main shopping area.

GETTING AROUND
By Public Transportation

State Transit operates the city's buses and the ferry network; **Sydney Trains** runs the urban and suburban trains; and **Sydney** Ferries runs the public passenger ferries. Some private bus lines operate buses in the outer suburbs. In addition, a light rail line runs between Central Station and Wentworth Park in Pyrmont. **Infoline** (*©* **13 15 00; www.131500.info**) is a one-stop search engine for bus, train, and ferry timetables. Public transit fares are subject to change, so the prices below should act only as a guide. At press time, a new electronic ticketing system, the Opal Card, was in trial phase.

MONEY-SAVING TRANSIT PASSES Several passes are available for visitors who will be using public transportation frequently. All work out to be much cheaper than buying individual tickets. Child fares are for kids between 4 and 15 years old.

A **MyMulti Day Pass** ticket allows unlimited travel on buses, trains, and ferries for 24 hours. It costs A$22 for adults and A$11 for kids.

Your family can enjoy a fun day out with unlimited travel on Sydney's buses, trains, and ferries every Sunday with the **Family Funday Sunday** pass (A$2.50 per person). The ticket can only be purchased on Sundays. A minimum of one adult and one child related by family must travel together. Buy your ticket from bus drivers (excluding PrePay services), train stations, ferry ticket offices, and 7-Eleven convenience stores.

BY PUBLIC BUS Buses are frequent and reliable and cover a wide area of metropolitan Sydney. The minimum fare (which covers most short hops in the city) is A$2.20 for a 4km (2½-mile) "section." The farther you go, the cheaper each section is. For example, the 44km (27-mile) trip to Palm Beach, way past Manly, costs A$4.60. Sections are marked on bus-stand signs, but if you're confused or in doubt, ask the bus driver.

A **Mybus ticket** offers 10 bus rides for a discounted price. Tickets cost A$18 for trips within the city center, and A$29 or A$37 for trips farther out. Most buses bound for the northern suburbs, including night buses to Manly and the bus to Taronga Zoo, leave from Wynyard Park on Carrington Street, behind the Wynyard train station on George Street. Buses to the southern beaches, such as Bondi and Bronte, and the western and eastern suburbs leave from Circular Quay. Buses to Balmain leave from behind the QVB.

Buses run from 4:30am to around midnight during the week, less frequently on weekends and holidays. Some night buses to outer suburbs run throughout the night. You can buy single tickets onboard.

BY SIGHTSEEING BUS Bright red open-top **Sydney Explorer** buses operate daily, traveling a circuit that takes in 26 places of interest. These include the Sydney Opera House, the Royal Botanic Gardens, the State Library, Mrs. Macquarie's Chair, the Art Gallery of New South Wales, Kings Cross, Elizabeth Bay House, the QVB, Sydney Tower, the Australian Museum, Chinatown, Darling Harbour, and The Rocks. Bus stops are identified by a distinctive red sign. The interval between services is about 15 to 20 minutes, and you can board the bus at any stop along the route. The first departure from Alfred St., (near the corner of Pitt St.), at Circular Quay is at 8:30am and the last service will return you to Circular Quay at 7:30pm.

The **Bondi Explorer** operates every day, traveling a 30km (19-mile) circuit around the eastern harborside bays and coastal beaches. The 11 stops along the way include Chinatown, Sydney Tower, Double Bay, Rose Bay, Bondi Beach, North Bondi, and Paddington's Oxford Street. The interval between the hop-on-hop-off services is around 30 minutes. The first departure is from Central Station (Stop A at Eddy

Avenue) at 9:30am. Tickets cost A$40 for adults, A$25 for children 5 to 16, and A$110 for a family of four for 24 hours, or A$60 adults, A$40 children and A$170 families for 48 hours. If you stay on the bus, the full circuit of each tour will take around 90 minutes. When planning your itinerary, remember that some attractions, such as museums, close at 5pm. Buy tickets onboard the bus. Call ✆ **02/9567 8400** for details or check out www.theaustralianexplorer.com.au.

BY FERRY The best way to get a taste of a city that revolves around its harbor is to jump aboard a ferry. The main ferry terminal is at Circular Quay. For ferry information, call ✆ **13 15 00,** check out **www.131500.info,** or visit the ferry information office opposite Wharf 4. One-way trips within the inner harbor (virtually everywhere except Manly) cost A$5.80 for adults and A$2.90 for children ages 4 to 15. Kids under 4 travel free. If you are a family, the first child pays the normal child fare and other kids travel free.

The **FerryTen ticket** costs A$46 for adults and is good for 10 trips within the inner harbor (not Manly). Kids tickets are half price. Buy tickets at newsdealers, bus depots, or the Circular Quay ferry terminal.

The ferry to Manly takes 30 minutes and costs A$7.20 for adults and A$3.60 for children. It leaves from Wharf 3. A Manly FerryTen ticket costs A$58 for adults and A$29 for kids. Ferries run from 6am to midnight. There is also a privately run fast ferry that runs to Manly from Circular Quay, which takes 18 minutes. The **Manly Fast Ferry** (✆ **02/9583 1199;** www.manlyfastferry.com.au) uses its own ticketing system and turnstiles, and departs from Wharf 6 at Circular Quay. Tickets cost A$9 adults and $6 kids, one way. The first ferry leaves Circular Quay at 6:40am and the last at 7:30pm; the last fast ferry departs Manly at 7:50pm. Ferries operate every 25 minutes or so. The fast ferry also goes to Darling Harbour and Watson's Bay.

BY TRAIN Sydney's publicly owned train system is a good news/bad news way to get around. The good news is that it can be a cheap and relatively efficient way to see the city; the bad news is that the system is limited. Many tourist areas—including Manly, Bondi Beach, and Darling Harbour—are not connected to the network. Though trains tend to run regularly, the timetable is unreliable. And many carriages aren't air-conditioned, so it can be really hot in summer.

Single tickets within the city center cost A$3.60 for adults and A$1.80 for children. Round-trip tickets cost twice as much. After 9am on weekdays, and on weekends, it costs A$4.80 for adults and A$2.40 for children for a return ticket. The **Family Fare** deal means when at least one fare-paying adult travels with children or grandchildren, the first child travels for a child fare and the other children travel free. Weekly tickets are also available. Information is available from **Infoline** (✆ **13 15 00** in Australia or **www.131500.info**).

BY METRO LIGHT RAIL A system of trams runs on a route that traverses a 3.6km (2¼-mile) track between Central Station and Wentworth Park in Pyrmont. It provides good access to Chinatown, Paddy's Markets, Darling Harbour, the Star City casino, and the Sydney Fish Markets. The trams run every 10 minutes. The one-way fare is A$3.50 to A$4.50 for adults and A$2.30 to A$3.50 for children 4 to 15, depending on distance. Two-way tickets are also available. A day pass costs A$9 for adults, A$6.50 for children, and A$20 for a family of five. Contact **Metro Light Rail** (✆ **02/8584 5288;** www.metrotransport.com.au) for details.

By Taxi

Several taxi companies serve the city center and suburbs. All journeys are metered. If you cross either way on the Harbour Bridge or through the Harbour Tunnel, it will cost a few extra dollars (depending on the time of day). An extra 10% will be added if you pay by credit card.

Taxis line up at stands in the city, such as those opposite Circular Quay and Central Station. They are also frequently found in front of hotels. A yellow light on top of the cab means it's vacant. Cabs can be hard to get on Friday and Saturday nights and between 2 and 3pm every day, when cabbies are changing shifts after 12 hours on the road. Passengers must wear seatbelts in the front and back seats. The **Taxi Complaints Hotline** (✆ **1800/648 478** in Australia) deals with problem taxi drivers. Taxis are licensed to carry four people. The main taxi companies are: **Taxis Combined Services** (✆ **13 33 00;** www.taxiscombined.com.au); **Silver Service Fleet** (✆ **13 31 00;** www.silverservice.com.au); **RSL Cabs** (✆ **13 15 81;** www.rslcabs.com.au); **Legion Cabs** (✆ **13 14 51;** www.legioncabs.com.au); **Premier Cabs** (✆ **13 10 17;** www.premiercabs.com.au); and **St. George Cabs** (✆ **13 21 66;** www.stgeorgecabs.com.au).

By Water Taxi

Water Taxis operate 24 hours a day and are a quick, convenient way to get to waterfront restaurants, harbor attractions, and some suburbs. They can also be chartered for private cruises. Fares for a direct transfer are based on an initial flag-fall for the hire of the vessel and then a charge per person traveling. Fares for a harbor jaunt are usually around A$15 per person. On most transfers, the more people traveling, the lower the fare per person. The main operators are **Yellow Water Taxis** (✆ **1300/138 840** in Australia or 02/9299 0199) and **Water Taxis Combined** (✆ **02/9555 8888;** http://watertaxis.com.au).

By Car

Traffic restrictions, parking, and congestion can make getting around by car frustrating, but if you plan to visit some of the outer suburbs or take excursions elsewhere in New South Wales, then renting a car will give you more flexibility. The **National Roads and Motorists' Association (NRMA)** is the New South Wales auto club; for emergency breakdown service, call ✆ **13 11 11.**

Tolls apply for some roads, including the Cross City Tunnel and Sydney Harbour Bridge; increasingly you must go through automatic toll booths using a prepaid electronic tag called an **E-Tag.** If you are hiring a car, you may be provided with an E-Tag, but make sure you ask about how you pay. Drivers without E-Tags have 2 days to pay; call the **Roads and Traffic Authority** at ✆ **13 18 65** within 2 days for details on your payment options.

Car-rental agencies in Sydney include **Avis,** 200 William St., Kings Cross (✆ **13 63 33** in Australia or (02) 9246 4600); **Budget,** 93 William St., Kings Cross (✆ **13 27 27** in Australia or 02/8255 9600); **Europcar,** 100 William St., Kings Cross (✆ **13 13 90** in Australia or (02) 8255 9070); **Hertz,** corner of William and Riley streets, Kings Cross (✆ **13 30 39** in Australia or 02/9360 6621); and **Thrifty,** 75 William St., Kings Cross (✆ **13 61 39** in Australian or **02/8374 6177**). All also have desks at the airport. One of the best-value operations is **Bayswater Car Rental,** 180 William St., Kings

SYDNEY | Getting Around

Cross (© **02/9360 3622;** www.bayswatercarrental.com.au), which has small cars from around A$30 a day, sometimes less. A good option is to compare prices and book discounted vehicles through **Vroom, Vroom, Vroom** (www.vroomvroomvroom. com.au).

[Fast FACTS] SYDNEY

ATMs/Banks Banking hours are Monday through Friday from 9am to 5pm. Many banks, especially in the city center, are open from around 9:30am to 12:30pm on Saturday. Most major bank branches offer currency-exchange services.

Business Hours General office hours are Monday through Friday from 9am to 5pm. Shopping hours are usually from 8:30am to 5:30pm daily (9am–5pm Sat), and most stores stay open until 9pm on Thursday. Most city-center stores are open from around 10am to 4pm on Sunday.

Dentists CBD Dental Practice, Level 2, The Country Centre, 74 Castlereagh St., (© **02/9221 2453;** www.cbddental.com. au), offers same-day emergency treatment. It's open Monday through Friday 8am to 6pm (by appointment). The **Sydney Dental Hospital** is on 2 Chalmers St., Surry Hills (© **02/9293 3333**).

Doctors & Hospitals St. Vincent's Hospital is at Victoria and Burton streets in Darlinghurst, near Kings Cross (© **02/8382 1111**).The **Park Medical Centre,** Shop 4, 27 Park St.

(© **02/9264 4488**), in the city center near Town Hall, is open Monday through Friday 8am to 6pm. The **Travellers' Medical & Vaccination Centre,** Level 7, the Dymocks Building, 428 George St., in the city center (© **1300 658 844** or 02/9221 7133; www.travel-doctor.com.au), administers travel-related vaccinations and medications. It's open Monday to Friday 9am to 5pm (until 6pm Tuesday and 8pm Thursday) and 9am to 1pm Saturday. Appointments essential.

Embassies & Consulates All foreign embassies are based in Canberra. The following consulates are in Sydney: **Canada,** Level 5, 111 Harrington St., The Rocks (© **02/9364 3000**); **New Zealand,** 55 Hunter St. (© **02/9223 0144**); **United Kingdom,** Level 16, Gateway Building, 1 Macquarie Place, Circular Quay (© **02/9247 7521**); and **United States,** Level 59, MLC Centre, 19–29 Martin Place (© **02/9373 9200**).

Emergencies Dial © **000** to call the police, the fire service, or an ambulance. Call the **NRMA** for car breakdowns (© **13 11 11**). Call the **Poisons Information Centre** (© **13 11**

26); the **Rape Crisis Centre** (© **1800 424 017** in Australia); or the **Lifeline** 24-hour counseling service (© **13 11 14**).

Internet Access Sydney has many Internet and e-mail centers, particularly in and around Kings Cross, Bondi, and Manly.

Mail & Postage The **General Post Office (GPO)** is at 1 Martin Place (© **13 13 18** in Australia or **02/9244 3711**). It's open Monday through Friday 8:15am to 5:30pm and Saturday 10am to 2pm. For the nearest post office, call © **13 13 18** or find it online at **www.auspost.com.au.**

Newspapers & Magazines The **Sydney Morning Herald** is available throughout metropolitan Sydney. The equally prestigious daily **The Australian** is available nationwide. The metropolitan **Daily Telegraph** is a more casual read and publishes a couple of editions a day. The *International Herald Tribune* and other U.S. and U.K. newspapers can be found at Circular Quay newspaper stands and most newsdealers. **Time Out Sydney** is published monthly as a guide to everything that's on in and around the city (find the online version at www.timeout.com/Sydney).

Pharmacies (Chemist Shops) Most suburbs have pharmacies that are open late. For after-hours referral, contact the **Emergency Prescription Service** (✆ **1300/ 882 294**).

Police In an emergency, dial ✆ **000.** Make nonemergency police inquiries through the **City Central** police station (✆ **02/9265 6499** or 13 14 44).

Safety Sydney is generally a safe city, but as anywhere else, it's good to keep your wits about you and your wallet hidden. Be wary in Kings Cross and Redfern and around Central Station and the cinema strip on George Street near Town Hall station in the evening—the latter is a hangout for local gangs. Other places of concern are the back lanes of Darlinghurst, around the naval base at Woolloomooloo, and along the Bondi restaurant strip when sunburned drunken tourists spill out after midnight. If traveling by train at night, ride in the carriages next to the guard's van, marked with a blue light on the outside.

WHERE TO STAY

DECIDING WHERE TO STAY The best location for lodging in Sydney is in The Rocks and around Circular Quay—a short stroll from the Sydney Opera House, the Harbour Bridge, the Royal Botanic Gardens, and the ferry terminals.

Hotels around Darling Harbour offer good access to the local facilities, including museums, the Sydney Aquarium, and the Star City casino. Most Darling Harbour hotels are a 10- to 15-minute walk, or a short light rail trip, from Town Hall and the central shopping district in and around Sydney Tower and Pitt Street Mall.

More hotels are grouped around Kings Cross, Sydney's red-light district. Some of the hotels here are among the city's best, and it's also where you'll find a range of cheaper lodgings and backpacker hostels. Kings Cross can sometimes be unnerving (and noisy), especially on Friday and Saturday nights when the area's strip joints and nightclubs are jumping, but it's close to excellent restaurants and cafes around the Kings Cross, Darlinghurst, and Oxford Street areas.

If you want to stay near the beach, check out the options in Manly and Bondi, though you should consider their distance from the city center and the lack of trains to these areas. A taxi to Manly from the city will cost around A$55 and to Bondi around A$35.

MAKING A DEAL The prices given below for expensive hotels are mostly the **rack rates,** the recommended retail price, which guests can pay at the busiest periods if they book at short notice or walk in off the street. Check out **www.lastminute.com. au** and **www.wotif.com** for discounted rates.

Apartment hotels are also worth considering because you can save a bundle by cooking your own meals; many also have free laundry facilities. Almost all hotels offer nonsmoking rooms; inquire when you make a reservation if it's important to you. Most moderately priced to expensive rooms will have tea- and coffee-making facilities and an iron and ironing board. Coffeemakers as such are rare in Australian hotels, which instead offer tea bags, instant coffee, small plastic milk cartons, and a kettle. Some smarter hotels have in-room espresso machine.

Check **www.yha.com.au** for a full list of its eight Sydney hostels (some are listed in this section).

Around the Rocks & Circular Quay

EXPENSIVE

Sir Stamford at Circular Quay ★★★   This is one of my favorite Sydney hotels. It's plush and luxurious, but like all really great hotels the staff is friendly and the atmosphere relaxed rather than stuffy. It has a clubby European atmosphere, but it's warm and welcoming. There's even a mascot "bear" called Morris who pops up in the most unexpected places (and can be with you for company, on request). The other wonderful thing is the location, a short walk from Circular Quay and the Opera House, and just across the road from the Royal Botanic Gardens. Rooms are large and luxurious, with good-size marble bathrooms. Most rooms have a small balcony. The rooms on the east side of the hotel have the best views across the Botanic Gardens. Most rooms are accessible to wheelchairs.

93 Macquarie St., Sydney, NSW 2000. www.stamford.com.au/sscq. © **02/9252 4600.** 105 units. A$237–A$487 double; A$387–A$2,000 suite. Parking A$35–A$45. Train, bus, or ferry: Circular Quay. **Amenities:** Restaurant; bar; babysitting; concierge; exercise room; solar-heated outdoor pool; room service; sauna; Wi-Fi free in the business center or for 30 min. in lobby (A$25/24 hr. in rooms).

The Langham ★★★   I love the opulence of this hotel, and I love staying here. This exclusive colonial-style property, a 10-minute walk uphill from The Rocks and 15 minutes from Circular Quay (or a stroll down to Wynyard train station), is a turn-of-the-20th-century beauty competing for top-hotel-in-Sydney honors. A name change in mid-2012—it was formerly the **Observatory Hotel**—has done nothing to change the feel of the place. It's outfitted with antiques, objets d'art, and the finest carpets, wallpapers, and draperies. It is also renowned for its personalized service. Rooms are plush and quiet, with huge bathrooms. Some rooms have city views; others look out over the harbor. The pool here is one of the best in Sydney. (Note the Southern Hemisphere constellations on the roof.) The day spa is also one of the most exclusive in the city, as is the hotel's restaurant, **Galileo.**

89–113 Kent St., Sydney, NSW 2000. www.sydney.langhamhotels.com.au. © **02/9256 2222.** 96 units. A$295–A$430 double; A$385–A$780 suite. Parking A$30. Bus: 339, 431, or 433. **Amenities:** Restaurant; bar; concierge; health club; chemical-free heated indoor pool; 24-hr. room service; sauna; floodlit tennis court; free Wi-Fi in lobby (A$10/1 hr. or A$20/24 hr. in room).

MODERATE

The Lord Nelson Brewery Hotel★★★   Book a room upstairs in one of Sydney's oldest pubs (established in 1841) to be part of the city's living history. This attractive, three-story sandstone building is a busy pub on the ground floor, with hotel rooms on the second and the third. The simple but stylishly outfitted rooms are compact, and some have walls made from convict-hewn sandstone blocks. The creaky floorboards, narrow corridors, wood fire and boutique brewery in the bar all add to the Lord Nelson's colonial atmosphere without detracting from its essentially modern style. The smallest (and cheapest) of the rooms has a bathroom across the corridor; all the others have ensuites.

19 Kent St. (at Argyle St.), The Rocks, Sydney, NSW 2000. www.lordnelsonbrewery.com. © **02/9251 4044.** 8 units. A$180 double with external bathroom; A$200 double with bathroom. Extra person A$50. Rates include continental breakfast. No parking available. **Amenities:** 2 restaurants; bar; free Wi-Fi.

Central Sydney Hotels

Adina Apartment Hotel Sydney Central 12
Adina Apartment Hotel Sydney Harbourside 8
Arts Hotel Sydney 14
The Australian Hotel 4
Hotel 59 17
The Hughenden 15
Kirketon Hotel Sydney 18
The Langham 2
The Lord Nelson Brewery Hotel 1
Railway Square YHA 13
The Russell 5
Sir Stamford at Circular Quay 6
Sydney Central YHA 11
Sydney Harbour – The Rocks YHA 3
Travelodge Hotel Sydney 10
Vibe Hotel Rushcutters 16
Westin Sydney 7
Wool Brokers Arms 9

Port Jackson

Port Jackson

North Sydney
Bondi Junction
Sydney
MAIN map detail

Walsh Bay

Sydney Harbour Bridge

Dawes Point
Pier One

DAWES POINT

Sydney Theatre Dance Company

Harbour Control Tower

Merriman St.

MILLERS POINT

To Balmain

Darling Harbour

King Street Wharf

Bennelong Point

Sydney Opera House

Sydney Harbour Tunnel

Sydney Cove

Circular Quay

Overseas Passenger Terminal
Circular Quay West

Ferry Wharves

Circular Quay E

To Milsons Point
To Kirribilli
To Taronga Zoo

THE ROCKS

Hickson Rd.
Bradfield Hwy
Cumberland St.
George St.
Cahill Expressway
Argyle St.
Windmill St.
Towns Pl.
Trinity Ave.
Observatory Park
Observatory
Toll Gates
National Trust
Kent St.
Jenkins St.
Hickson Rd.

Dawes Point Park

Farm Cove

Main Pond

Royal Botanic Gardens

Tropical Centre

Conservatorium of Music

Government House

Mrs Macquaries Rd.

Visitors Centre

Art Gallery of New South Wales

Cahill Expressway

State Library of NSW

Parliament House

Hospital Rd.

Macquarie St.

Phillip St.
Phillip Ln.
Bent St.
Bligh St.
Hunter St.
Young St.
Albert St.
Bridge St.
Spring St.
Elizabeth St.
O'Connell St.

Martin Place
Martin Pl.

Pitt St.

Stock Exchange

Alfred St.
Reiby Pl.
Dalley St.
Bond St.

Tank Park

Jamison St.

George St.

Carrington St.

Barrack Street Mall

Gloucester St.
Grosvenor St.
Margaret St.
Erskine St.
Sussex St.
Shelley St.
Lime St.

Wynyard

Western Distributor

Maritime Centre

Sydney Passenger Terminal

POTTS POINT

Macleay St.
Wylde St.
Challis Ave.
Cowper Wharf Rd.

To Watsons Bay

Boy Charlton Pool

Woolloomooloo Bay

Lincoln Crescent
Bland St.

Farm Cove

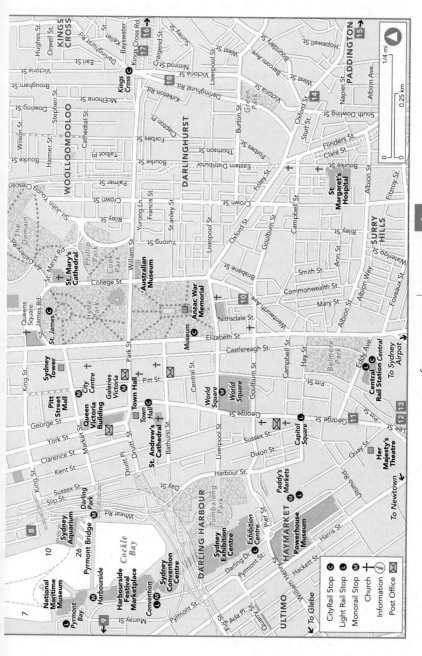

47

The Russell ★★★ This is the coziest place to stay in The Rocks and perhaps in all of Sydney. It's more than 120 years old, and it shows its age wonderfully in the creaks of the floorboards. There are no harbor views, but all the rooms have immense character and are furnished in period style. Some have shared bathrooms (and all rooms have bathrobes in them). The hotel also has single rooms for solo travelers, and guests have access to a sitting room, with a small library and a balcony overlooking Circular Quay. The rooftop garden is another perfect spot for wonderful views of the harbor, with tables and chairs and sun umbrellas. This is a real find.

143A George St., The Rocks, Sydney, NSW 2000. www.therussell.com.au. © **02/9241 3543.** 29 units, 19 with bathroom. A$159 single; A$169–A$209 double without bathroom; A$259–A$299 double with bathroom. Extra person A$30. Rates include continental breakfast. No parking. Train or ferry: Circular Quay. **Amenities:** Restaurant; lounge; Wi-Fi (A$5/24 hr.).

INEXPENSIVE

Sydney Harbour–The Rocks YHA★★ The Sydney Harbour YHA offers basic, clean, and new (it opened in 2010) rooms at a very reasonable price for this sought-after part of the city's prime tourist district. Some rooms have harbor views (if you crane your neck). All are air-conditioned, and even the dorms have private bathrooms. There are also some thoughtful design features, including an electric socket inside each of the dorm-room lockers, so you can securely charge your iPod/laptop/camera. It has a very large common area, and the roof terrace is an excellent place to hang out, particularly because of the fabulous views of the Opera House and the Sydney Harbour Bridge. *Note:* You do have to lug your luggage up a lot of steps to get to the building. There are also a couple of other inner-city YHA hostels worth considering (see p. 49).

110 Cumberland St., The Rocks, Sydney, NSW 2000. www.yha.com.au. © **02/8272 0900.** A$42–A$54 dorm; A$142–A$176 double; A$175–A$196 family room (4 people). Parking (1 block away) A$40 per day. Train or ferry: Circular Quay. **Amenities:** Self-catering kitchen and dining area; Internet cafe; coffee bar; lounge; convenience store; Wi-Fi (A$9.95/24 hr.).

The Australian Hotel ★ Rooms here are above one of Sydney's most historic pubs, but despite that, they are not noisy. Carry your bags up the narrow stairs and you'll find a charming—if somewhat frayed around the edges—little haven overlooking the action on the street. Each room has a double, queen, or twin beds, and the nine rooms share five bathrooms. The guest lounge, overlooking the street, has a TV, books, and magazines and nice little touches like free tea and coffee available all day, bowls of fruit, and a decanter of port. A second, quieter lounge is down another hallway. The Australian is clean, comfortable, and a bargain.

100 Cumberland St. (entry off Gloucester St.), The Rocks, Sydney, NSW 2000. www.australian heritagehotel.com. © **02/9247 2229.** 9 units. A$135 double. Rates include continental breakfast. Train or ferry: Circular Quay. No parking. **Amenities:** Restaurant; bar; Wi-Fi.

In the City Center

EXPENSIVE

Adina Apartment Hotel Sydney Central ★★ This heritage-listed building (built in 1821 and once the parcels post office for Central Station next door), has been converted to elegant and roomy studio rooms and apartments. My pick is the one-bedroom Premier apartments, which are on the higher levels of the hotel; some are corner rooms, which have wonderful round windows with view of the Central Station clock-tower. There's no restaurant, but meals are available in the great atmospheric cafe **Mezbah** (© **02/9555 7067;** www.mezbah.com.au) at the back of the hotel, with a charge-back to your room.

2 Lee St., Haymarket, NSW 2000. www.adinahotels.com.au. © **02/9274 0000.** 98 units. A$200–A$520 studio; A$250–A$636 1-bedroom apt; A$330–A$571 2-bedroom apt. Extra person A$50. Crib A$5. Limited free parking. **Amenities:** Gym; Jacuzzi; outdoor heated pool; Wi-Fi (A$30/24 hr.).

Westin Sydney ★★★ One of Sydney's most celebrated five-star hotels, the Westin is located in the center of the city, in the Martin Place pedestrian mall. Integrated into Sydney's original 19th-century General Post Office, the Westin has a charm that's modern and classic all at once. The large rooms have wonderfully comfortable beds and floor-to-ceiling windows. The hotel is home to several bars, restaurants, and clothing shops. Just steps from the central shopping streets and the QVB, and a 10- to 15-minute walk from both the Sydney Opera House and Darling Harbour, the hotel features an impressive seven-story atrium, a wonderful two-level health club, and an exclusive day spa.

1 Martin Place, Sydney, NSW 2000. www.starwoodhotels.com. © **02/8223 1111.** 416 units. A$350–A$480 double. Parking A$25. Train: Martin Place. **Amenities:** Cafe; bar; babysitting; health club; day spa; Wi-Fi (A$20/per day).

MODERATE

Travelodge Hotel Sydney ★ This business-oriented hotel is cheap for Sydney, comfortable, and reasonably well located, making it a good option for travelers who just want to unpack and explore. The Ikea-like rooms all include a kitchenette with a microwave and a queen- or twin-size bed. From here it's a short walk to Oxford Street, Town Hall, and Hyde Park.

27–33 Wentworth Ave., Sydney, NSW 2000. www.travelodge.com.au. © **1300/886 886** in Australia, or 02/8267 1700. 406 units. A$110–A$385 double. Parking (around corner) A$25. Train: Museum. **Amenities:** Restaurant; babysitting; Wi-Fi in executive rooms (A$20/24 hr.).

INEXPENSIVE

Sydney Central YHA ★★ This multiple-award-winning hostel is one of the biggest and busiest in the world. It is very popular, so you need to book as far ahead as possible. The rooms are clean and basic, and come dorm-style for four, six, or eight people or as doubles (with private bathrooms). There are also family rooms. In the basement is a bar with pool tables and occasional entertainment. There's also an entertainment room with more pool tables and e-mail facilities, TV rooms on every floor, and a cinema. The YHA is accessible to travelers with disabilities.

The **Railway Square YHA** is at the corner of Upper Carriage Lane and Lee Street, or enter via the Henry Dean Plaza (© **02/9281 9666**). The historic 1904 building adjoining "Platform Zero" at Central Railway Station has 64 beds in four- to eight-bed dorm rooms and 10 double rooms. Some dorm rooms are in old railway carriages. It has a sauna, pool, Internet cafe, tour desk, indoor and outdoor communal areas, and a self-catering kitchen. Rates here are slightly cheaper than at Sydney Central.

11 Rawson Place (at Pitt St., outside Central Station), Sydney, NSW 2000. www.yha.com.au. © **02/9281 9000.** 150 units. A$37–A$43 dorm bed; A$108–A$126 double/twin; A$152–A$170 family room. Parking A$25. Train: Central. **Amenities:** Restaurant; bar; small heated outdoor pool; sauna; Wi-Fi (A$10/24 hr.).

In Darling Harbour

Adina Apartment Hotel Sydney Harbourside ★★ This impressive hotel offers modern, very comfortable studio rooms and apartments at competitive prices. It's a short walk from the Sydney Aquarium and close to all of the Darling Harbour, Cockle Bay, and Town Hall attractions and shops. Studio and one-bedroom apartments have designer furniture, large windows, and balconies (some with good harbor views). Studio units have a kitchenette, and one-bedrooms have fully equipped kitchens. You'll pay higher prices for water views. Ask about package and weekend rates.

55 Shelley St. (at King St.), King St. Wharf, Sydney, NSW 2000. www.adinahotels.com.au. ℰ **02/9249 7000.** 114 units. A$225–A$255 studio; A$270–A$340 apt. Train: Town Hall. **Amenities:** Concierge; exercise room; small heated indoor pool; Wi-Fi (A$6/30 min.; A$24.95/24 hr.).

Wool Brokers Arms ★ You'll find this friendly circa-1886 heritage building on the far side of Darling Harbour, next to the prominent Novotel hotel and hidden behind a monstrous aboveground parking garage. It's on a noisy road, so unless you're used to traffic, avoid the rooms at the front. Rooms are simply furnished, with a fridge and TV, and by the time you read this phones and Internet access should be installed. Room no. 3 is one of the nicer ones. Family rooms have a king-size bed, bunks, and two singles through an open doorway. The hotel has 19 shared bathrooms. Check the website for a range of discounts.

22 Allen St., Pyrmont, Sydney, NSW 2009. www.woolbrokershotel.com.au. ℰ **02/9552 4773.** 26 units. A$80 single; A$95 double; A$130 double with bathroom; A$135 triple; A$212–A$254 family room for 4–8. Continental breakfast A$7.50. Parking A$13 (across the street). Bus: 501 Light Rail: Convention Centre. **Amenities:** Internet kiosk; guest laundry.

In Kings Cross & Suburbs Nearby

Hotel 59 ★ This popular and friendly B&B is well worth considering if you want to be near the Kings Cross action but far enough away to get some peace and quiet. It has two rooms for single travelers and three family rooms that can sleep two adults and two children. All rooms are well kept and comfortable, with private bathrooms, and are a good value. Each has a TV. The cafe below serves breakfast, which is included in the rate. A flight of stairs and the lack of an elevator might make this unsuitable for travelers with disabilities.

59 Bayswater Rd., Kings Cross, NSW 2011. www.hotel59.com.au. ℰ **02/9360 5900.** 9 units. A$99 single; A$130 standard double; A$140 family room. Extra person A$25; extra child 2–12 A$15. Rates include breakfast. No parking. Train: Kings Cross. **Amenities:** Cafe; TV lounge.

Kirketon Hotel Sydney ★ Popular among hip, fashionable types, this slightly offbeat boutique hotel in Darlinghurst offers rooms with modernist furniture and custom-made fittings, including mirrored headboards and sleek bathrooms hidden away behind mirrored doors. Standard rooms are quite compact and come with a double bed. Premium rooms have a queen-size bed. Superior and Executive rooms are quite large, with a king-size bed, and some have a small balcony overlooking the main road. For a quiet night, however, definitely ask for a room away from the main road.

229 Darlinghurst Rd., Darlinghurst, NSW 2010. www.8hotels.com/kirketon. ℰ **1800/332 920** in Australia or 02/9332 2011. 40 rooms. A$145–A$385 double. Parking A$25. **Amenities:** Restaurant; bar; free Wi-Fi.

Vibe Hotel Rushcutters ★★ Compared with other hotels in its price bracket, this flagship Vibe Hotel on the far side of Kings Cross really is a bargain, especially when you book online. Standard rooms are a reasonable size, and I love the rooms' brightly accented and colorful—well, yes—vibe. All rooms have king-size beds (which split into twins if necessary), and families can get connecting rooms. The hotel has a good cafe, called **Curve,** a heated rooftop swimming pool, and a good gym.

100 Bayswater Rd., Rushcutters Bay, NSW 2011. www.vibehotels.com.au. ✆ **02/8353 8988.** 245 units. A$175–A$199 double, A$250–A$330 suite. Parking A$30. Train: Kings Cross. **Amenities:** Restaurant; bar; concierge; gym; heated outdoor pool; Wi-Fi (A$12.50/1 hr.; A$24.95/24 hr.).

Around Oxford Street & Darlinghurst

Arts Hotel Sydney ★ This hotel (formerly called Sullivans Hotel) is right in the heart of the action in one of Sydney's most popular shopping, entertainment, restaurant, and gay pub and club areas. About half of the hotel's guests come from overseas, and it's popular with Americans during Mardi Gras. All rooms are simple, compact, and very motel-like (and shower-only), but are fine for a few nights. Standard rooms have two single beds, and the garden rooms have queen-size beds and pleasant garden views.

21 Oxford St., Paddington, NSW 2021. www.artshotel.com.au. ✆ **02/9361 0211.** 64 units. A$140–A$180 double. Limited free parking. Bus: 378 from Central Station or 380 from Circular Quay. **Amenities:** Breakfast cafe; bikes; fitness room; small heated outdoor pool; free Wi-Fi (garden rooms and public areas only).

The Hughenden ★★ I love this boutique hotel, part of which is set in an 1870s mansion house. It's warm and comfortable, with lots of sitting areas, including a wonderful library/den full of books. Hardly surprising, I suppose, given that one of the owners is children's book author Susanne Gervay, which also means the guests are often writers and artists too! You might also run into cricket buffs, given the proximity to the Sydney Cricket Ground. Wander through to enjoy the artwork, as well as the architecture, including lovely black marble fireplaces. It's in a great location, at the top end of Oxford Street and just across the road from Centennial Park. Eight new suites are located in a terrace house across the street.

14 Queen St., Woollahra, NSW 2025. www.thehughenden.com.au. ✆ **02/9363 4863.** 45 units. A$158–A$368 double; AA268–A$458 suite. Limited secured parking ($30 per night). Bus: 378. **Amenities:** Restaurant; bar; guest lounge; free Wi-Fi (free broadband in Terrace suites).

In Bondi

Bondi Beach is a good place to stay if you want to be close to the surf and sand, and for the budget-conscious there are two good backpacker hostels. **Surfside Backpackers,** 35a Hall St. (✆ **02/9365 4900;** www.surfsidebackpackers.com.au), offers four- to eight-person dorm rooms from A$27 in winter and A$38 in summer, and single, double and family rooms in a separate building (at higher rates). **Noah's,** 2 Campbell Parade (✆ **1800/226 662** in Australia; www.noahsbondibeach.com), has a great ambience and offers modern four- to eight-person dorm rooms for A$25 to A$27, as well as doubles for A$70 to A$80. Ask about weekly rates. Rates are more expensive in the summer peak season of December/January.

Ravesi's on Bondi Beach ★★ Right on Australia's most famous golden sands, this boutique property offers modern minimalist rooms with white marble bathrooms—all very chic. Side View double rooms are spacious and modern, but the Beach Front King rooms have the best views of the ocean. All rooms have Juliet balconies. The four split-level suites each have a white marble bathroom downstairs, and a bedroom, lounge area, and private outdoor terrace on the second level.

Corner of Hall St. and Campbell Parade, Bondi Beach, NSW 2026. www.ravesis.com.au. ℰ **02/9365 4422.** 12 units. A$269–A$499 double; A$299–A$399 suite. No parking. Bus: 333. **Amenities:** Restaurant; bar; room service; free Wi-Fi.

In Manly

If you decide to stay in Manly for a few days, consider buying a multiple-ride ferry ticket, which will save you a bit of money. And be warned that ferries from the city stop running at midnight. If you get stranded, you'll be facing an expensive taxi ride back.

Manly has several backpacker hostels that are worth checking out. The best is **Manly Backpackers Beachside,** 28 Ragland St. (ℰ **1800/662 500** in Australia or 02/9977 3411; www.manlybackpackers.com.au), which offers dorm beds from A$25 to A$50, doubles from A$70 to A$190, depending on the time of year (the more expensive prices are for the peak summer period).

Manly Paradise Motel and Beach Plaza Apartments ★ Rooms here are big, and some have glimpses of the sea. The traffic can make it a little noisy in your room during the day, but you'll probably be on the beach then, anyway. Motel rooms come with a queen, double, or twin beds. The apartments are magnificently roomy, offering everything you need, including a washing machine and dryer, a full kitchen with dishwasher, and two bathrooms (one with a tub). The sea views from the main front balcony are heart-stopping, and there's a pool on the rooftop.

54 N. Steyne, Manly, NSW 2095. www.manlyparadise.com.au. ℰ **1800/815 789** in Australia, or 02/9977 5799. 40 units. A$120–A$230 double motel unit; A$210–A$310 1-bedroom unit; A$310–A$475 2-bedroom apt; A$395–A$650 3-bedroom apt. Higher prices in summer (btw. around Dec 8 and Jan 31). Extra person A$25. Parking A$15 for motel rooms, free for apts. Ferry: Manly. **Amenities:** Indoor heated pool.

At the Airport

Formule 1 Sydney Airport ★ If all you want is somewhere clean to crash before an early flight, this no-frills hotel will be fine. It has almost no facilities, but it's next to a couple of fast-food joints, and the hotel does breakfast at A$9 per person extra. Rooms are air-conditioned and have TVs. You can reach the airport via the Airport Shuttle, which costs A$6 one way (or walk there in 10 min.).

5 Ross Smith Ave., Mascot, Sydney, NSW 2020. www.formule1.com.au. ℰ **02/8339 1840.** 200 units. A$99–A$119 double/triple. Limited parking A$10 per day. **Amenities:** Breakfast room; Wi-Fi.

Stamford Plaza Sydney Airport ★★ At the other end of the scale, this is Sydney's best airport hotel (just 7 min. from the terminals by the A$6 airport shuttle). It has the largest rooms, each with a king-size or two double beds, access to airport information, and a good-size bathroom with tub. Suites and deluxe rooms have views of the airport. The windows are reinforced to keep out the aircraft noise!

Corner of O'Riordan and Robey sts., Mascot, Sydney, NSW 2020. www.stamford.com.au/ssa. ℰ **02/9317 2200.** 314 units. A$175–A$250 double; from A$370 suite. Extra person A$25. Children 16 and under stay free in parent's room. Self-parking A$20 per day, valet parking A$25. **Amenities:**

2 restaurants; bar; babysitting; concierge; executive rooms; gym; Jacuzzi; outdoor rooftop pool; room service; sauna; Wi-Fi (A55¢/per minute; A$29/24 hr.).

WHERE TO EAT

Sydney is a gourmet paradise, with some of the world's best chefs. Asian and Mediterranean cooking have had a major influence on Australian cuisine, with spices and herbs finding their way into most dishes. Immigration has brought with it almost every type of cuisine, from African to Tibetan, Russian to Vietnamese.

Sydney is a great place to try the Australian style of contemporary cuisine, which emphasizes fresh ingredients and a creative blend of European styles with Asian influences. And because there's no doubt in my mind that a really great meal will stick in your mind long after your visit to Australia is over, I've included some of Australia's top restaurants in these listings. The prices may be high but are almost always well worth it, especially if you are looking for an experience rather than just a meal.

Breakfast is big in Australia, a favorite time of day to meet friends and linger over a hearty repast (albeit often a late one). As for coffee, Australians favor a range of Italian-style creations. Ask for a latte if you just want coffee with milk.

And remember that in Australia, the first course is called the entree and the second course the main.

Circular Quay, City Center & The Rocks
EXPENSIVE

Guillaume at Bennelong ★★★ FRENCH   If you go to Bondi, you have to swim in the Pacific; if you see the Harbour Bridge, you have to walk across it; if you visit the Opera House, you must eat at Guillaume at Bennelong. The restaurant is as uniquely designed as the building itself, with tall glass windows that furrow around in an arch and grab the harbor and Circular Quay by the throat. Renowned French chef

---

What to Know About Dining in Sydney

Most moderate and inexpensive restaurants in Sydney are **BYO**, as in "bring your own" bottle (wine only), though some places also have extensive wine and beer lists. More moderately priced restaurants are also introducing corkage fees, which mean you pay anywhere from A$2 to A$8 per person for the privilege of having the waiter open your bottle of wine. Very expensive restaurants are usually fully licensed and don't allow you to BYO.

Sydney's **cheap eats** congregate in center-city areas such as Crown Street in Darlinghurst, and Glebe Point Road in Glebe. There are also inexpensive joints scattered among the more upscale restaurants in Kings Cross and along trendy Oxford Street.

Some restaurants add a surcharge on public holidays and Sundays, usually around 5% or 10% per person. Restaurants argue that it's difficult to get staff to work on these days, so they need to provide a cash incentive. In Australia, waiters rely on their wages rather than tips.

Smoking is banned in all Sydney restaurants, except at some with sidewalk tables or courtyards. Always ask before lighting up.

Central Sydney Restaurants

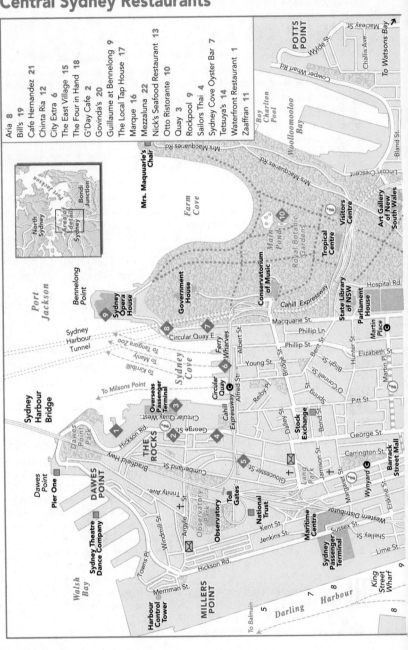

Aria **8**
Bill's **19**
Cafe Hernandez **21**
Chinta Ria **12**
City Extra **6**
The East Village **15**
The Four in Hand **18**
G'Day Cafe **2**
Govinda's **20**
Guillaume at Bennelong **9**
The Local Tap House **17**
Marque **16**
Mezzaluna **22**
Nick's Seafood Restaurant **13**
Otto Ristorante **10**
Quay **3**
Rockpool **9**
Sailors Thai **4**
Sydney Cove Oyster Bar **7**
Tetsuya's **14**
Waterfront Restaurant **1**
Zaaffran **11**

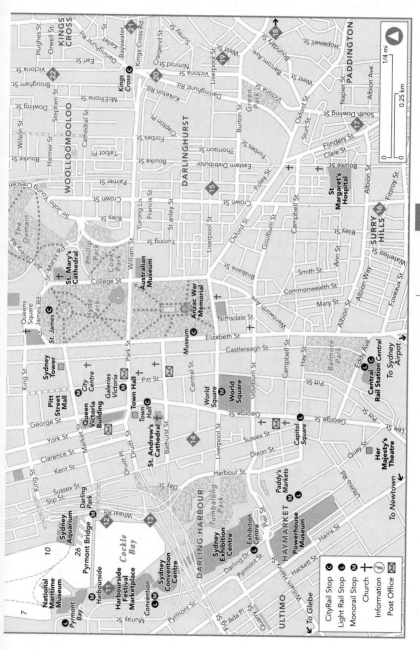

Legend:
- ☉ CityRail Stop
- ☉ Light Rail Stop
- Ⓜ Monorail Stop
- ✝ Church
- ⓘ Information
- ☒ Post Office

1/4 mi
0.25 km

Guillaume Brahimi has designed menus where the price is immaterial. The à la carte menu has one price for four courses; there's also a pre-theater menu and a *degustation* (tasting) menu. Offerings might include partridge with chestnut, peas, foie gras, and truffle, or barramundi with carrot, ginger, and coriander. Many would rather miss the first half of the opera they've paid a fortune to see than leave before dessert. The best bar in town is upstairs, where you can see over the water to the bridge and up to the other "sails." A tapas menu is available in the bar until 11:30pm.

In the Sydney Opera House, Bennelong Point. ℃ **02/9241 1999.** www.guillaumeatbennelong. com.au. A la carte (4 courses) A$150; tapas A$35–A$55 (4–8 dishes); pre-theater menu A$72 for 2 courses, A$89 for 3 courses; 8-course degustation menu A$195 (with matching wines A$285). Thurs–Fri noon–3pm; Tues–Sat 5:30pm–late. Train, bus, or ferry: Circular Quay.

Aria ★★★ CONTEMPORARY   With front-row views of the Harbour Bridge and the Sydney Opera House, Aria stands in one of the most enviable spots in the city. The windows overlooking the water are huge, the atmosphere is elegant and buzzy, and many of the tables have an intimate relationship with the stunning view. The food, created by Matthew Moran, one of Australia's great chefs, is imaginative and mouth-watering. Some examples: roasted lamb loin with crushed borlotti beans, eggplant, and nettle pesto; or roasted venison loin glaze crépinette with red cabbage, quince, and macadamia nuts. For lunch on weekdays, a set menu offers one, two, or three courses (A$46, A$74, or A$89). A supper menu is available from 10pm for those craving after-theater snacks. Reservations are essential.

1 Macquarie St., East Circular Quay. ℃ **02/9252 2555.** www.ariarestaurant.com.au. Main courses A$46–A$58. 4-course tasting menu A$120, A$170 including matching wines; 7-course tasting men A$160, A$250 including wines. Mon–Fri noon–2:30pm; pretheater daily 5:30–7pm; Mon–Sat 7–11:30pm; Sun 6–10pm. Train, bus, or ferry: Circular Quay.

Quay ★★★ CONTEMPORARY   You need to book as far in advance as possible for this wonderful, award-winning experience. At the time of writing, Quay was booked out 6 months in advance for Friday, Saturday, and Sunday nights for tables of two and four. It's hardly surprising. With its enviable location on top of the cruise-ship terminal, Quay offers another of the loveliest views in the city, and chef Peter Gilmore's menu is a revelation of French, Italian, and Australian ideas. Selections from the four-course dinner might include red claw yabbies with garlic-scented custard and yabby velvet; or squab and abalone with rare cultivated greens, fresh Jersey milk curd, anchovy, and seaweed broth, followed by pasture-raised veal with bitter chocolate black pudding, green walnuts, slow-cooked wallaby tail, salsify, smoked bone marrow, and chestnut mushrooms.

Upper level, Overseas Passenger Terminal, Circular Quay West, The Rocks. ℃ **02/9251 5600.** www.quay.com.au. Lunch: 3 courses A$130, 4 courses $150. Dinner: 4-course menu (5 choices per course) A$175. Tasting menu with 8 tasting plates (with the option of matching wines) from A$225. Tues–Fri noon–2:30pm; daily 6–10pm. Train, bus, or ferry: Circular Quay.

Rockpool ★★★ CONTEMPORARY   Rockpool is an institution known for its inventive food. Along with the bar, the kitchen—with its busy chefs and copper pots and pans—is very much at the center of things. At the helm is Neil Perry, one of Australia's most high-profile chefs. Now open for lunch on Fridays only, serving a "classics" menu (A$65) of three courses—but no choices—is a great way to find out what the fuss is about. It's a true Sydney dining experience—if you can afford it.

Reservations are essential. Also making waves in Sydney for its fish dishes, rotisserie meats, prime steaks, and pastas is sister restaurant **Rockpool Bar & Grill,** 66 Hunter St. (✆ **02/8078 1900**).

107 George St., The Rocks. ✆ **02/9252 1888.** www.rockpool.com. 6-course tasting menu A$180 per person; 2-course dinner A$100, 3 courses A$135, 4 courses A$155; lunch main courses A$45; lunch classics menu A$65. Tues–Sat 6–11pm; Fri lunch noon–3pm. Train, bus, or ferry: Circular Quay.

Sydney Cove Oyster Bar ★★ SEAFOOD   Just before you reach the Sydney Opera House, you'll notice a couple of small shedlike buildings with tables and chairs set up to take in the stunning views of the harbor and the Harbour Bridge. This is where you'll find some of the best oysters in town. You'll pay A$20 for a half-dozen oysters and A$34 for a dozen. Main courses, such as barbecued swordfish steak, pasta, or aged sirloin steak, are also on the menu. Share a dozen oysters and follow up with more shellfish or a seafood hotpot and a bottle of crisp white wine or sparkling champagne on a sunny day, and it's a perfect lunchtime spot.

No. 1 Eastern Esplanade, Circular Quay East. ✆ **02/9247 2937.** www.sydneycoveoysterbar.com. Main courses A$34–A$46. Mon–Fri 11am–late; Sat–Sun 8am–late. Train, bus, or ferry: Circular Quay.

Tetsuya's ★★★ JAPANESE/FRENCH FUSION   This is one of the world's best restaurants—it's that simple. To have a chance of getting a table, you need to book when reservations become available, 4 weeks in advance, and reconfirm a few days before. If you can, ask for a table right next to the floor-to-ceiling windows with intimate views across a Japanese-inspired courtyard of maples and waterfalls. The service is impeccable and the food truly inspired—many diners consider it a once-in-a-lifetime experience. Chef Tetsuya Wakuda's signature dish, a confit of Tasmanian ocean trout served with konbu seaweed, celery, and apple, is always on the menu.

529 Kent St., Sydney. ✆ **02/9267 2900.** www.tetsuyas.com. 10-course degustation menu A$210 per person. Sat noon–3pm and 6:30pm–10pm; Tues–Sat 6–10pm. Valet parking A$20. Train: Town Hall.

Best Pub Grub

You can get some really good food with a glass of wine or a schooner of beer on the side in several city pubs. Among the best is **The Four in Hand,** 105 Sutherland St., Paddington (✆ **02/9326 2254;** www.fourinhand.com.au), which has a great restaurant and also does good bar meals, including slow-roasted lamb shoulder and confit pork belly, with all main courses less than A$25. **Harts Pub,** corner of Essex and Gloucester streets, The Rocks (✆ **02/9251 6030;** www.hartspub.com.au), has a great range of craft beers and gourmet and pub grub offerings for A$18 to A$25. In Darlinghurst (Kings Cross), head to **The Local Taphouse,** 122 Flinders St. (✆ **02/9360 0088;** www.thelocal.com.au), where you can delve into a massive beer list and graze from the extensive menu; on Sundays, a roast's on offer from 1pm. Another gem in Darlinghurst is **The East Village,** 234 Palmer St., Darlinghurst (✆ **02/9331 5457;** www.theeastvillage.com.au), serving hand-rolled gnocchi, shepherd's pie, and more, with main courses from around A$15 to A$30.

Marque ★★★ FRENCH   The 2012 winner of the *Australian Gourmet Traveller's* Australian Restaurant of the Year—among its many other awards—Marque is seriously sophisticated, offering a set menu featuring classic French dishes. Politicians, actors, and food critics all rave about the place. Chef Mark Best has not been called a "culinary wizard" for nothing. Expect some real highlights here, at prices to match. A good way to discover what the fuss is about is the Friday set-price lunch menu, a very reasonable A$45 for three courses. Reservations are essential here.

4–5/355 Crown St., Surry Hills. *02/9332 2225*. www.marquerestaurant.com.au. 8-course degustation meal A$160, plus A$85 matching wines. Fri noon–2:30pm; Mon–Fri 6:30–10:30pm; Sat 6pm–10:30pm.

MODERATE

City Extra ★ ITALIAN/AUSTRALIAN   Because this place stays open around the clock, it's convenient if you get hungry at a ridiculous hour. It's also nicely situated, right next to the ferry terminals. The food can be variable in quality; if in doubt stick to the burgers. It's always busy, and service can be a mixed bag too, but the plastic chairs and outdoor tables make it a pleasant enough spot for a quick bite at any time of the day or night. It has a kids' menu, and free Wi-Fi.

Shop E4, Circular Quay. *02/9241 1422*. www.cityextra.com.au. Reservations not accepted. Main courses A$18–A$35. Daily 24 hr. Train, bus, or ferry: Circular Quay.

Sailors Thai ★★★ THAI   With a reputation as hot as the chilies in its jungle curry, the Sailors Thai "canteen" (the upper level of this establishment) attracts casual lunchtime crowds who come to eat great-tasting noodles, green papaya salad, a green curry of slow-cooked beef, and more . . . all at one long table with about 40 chairs. Four other tables on the balcony overlook the cruise-ship terminal and the quay. Downstairs, the upmarket "dining room" restaurant serves inventive food that's a far cry from your average Thai-restaurant fare, such as Berkshire pork belly wok-tossed with dry red curry and snake beans. Book well in advance for the restaurant (no bookings taken for the canteen).

106 George St., The Rocks. *02/9251 2466*. www.sailorsthai.com.au. Main courses A$14–A$29 in canteen, A$34–A$45 in restaurant. Canteen daily noon–4pm and 5:30–10pm. Restaurant Fri noon–2:30pm; Mon–Sat 6–10pm. Train, bus, or ferry: Circular Quay.

Waterfront Restaurant ★ CONTEMPORARY   You can't help but notice the mast, rigging, and sails that mark this restaurant in a converted stone warehouse. It's one of four in a row next to the water below the main spread of The Rocks, and it's popular at lunchtime, when businesspeople snap up the best seats outside in the sunshine. At night, with the colors of the city washing over the harbor, it can be magical. You get a choice of mains such as steaks, mud crab, fish filets, and prawns. The seafood platter, at A$185 for two, includes lobsters, Balmain bugs (small, odd-looking crayfish), prawns, blue swimmer crab, oysters, mussels, fish, and smoked salmon. The food is simple and fresh, at prices that reflect the glorious location and views.

In Campbell's Storehouse, 27 Circular Quay West, The Rocks. *02/9247 3666*. www.waterfrontrestaurant.com.au. Main courses A$24–A$50. Daily noon–10:30pm. Train, bus, or ferry: Circular Quay.

INEXPENSIVE

G'Day Café ★ CAFE Tourists flock here—especially for breakfast—but both the food and service can be inconsistent. On a good day, however, the food is simple but satisfying and about half the price you'll pay at many other places in the heart of the The Rocks tourist precinct. The interior is uninspiring, but the cafe has a leafy court-yard at the back. Among the offerings are focaccia sandwiches, hearty soups, salads, burgers, lasagna, chili con carne, and beef curry.

83 George St., The Rocks. *℃* **02/9241 3644.** Main courses A$3–A$10. Sun–Thurs 5am–midnight; Fri–Sat 5am–3am. Train, bus, or ferry: Circular Quay.

Darling Harbour
MODERATE

Nick's Seafood Restaurant ★ SEAFOOD This nice indoor and alfresco eatery overlooking the water on the same side as Darling Harbour (to the left of Sydney Aquarium if you're looking at the boats) offers good cocktails and plenty of seafood. The best seats are outside in the sunshine, where you can watch the world go by over a bottle of wine. A seafood platter for two (A$160) arrives piled with crab, prawns, mussels, fish, oysters, and lobster. A kids' menu for under 12s (A$15) offers either pasta, chicken, calamari, or fish with French fries and a soft drink, followed by ice cream. Nick's has another equally pleasant eatery on the other side of the Aquarium called **Nick's Bar & Grill,** and a sister establishment, **I'm Angus Steakhouse**—also at Cockle Bay Wharf—does good steaks, a great Guinness pie, and some seafood. The food and prices at all three places are similar, and they share the same phone number for bookings.

The Promenade, Cockle Bay Wharf (on the city side of Darling Harbour). *℃* **1300/989 989.** www. nicks-seafood.com.au. Main courses A$32–A$48. Mon–Sat 11:30am–3pm and 5:30–10pm (to 11pm Sat), Sun 11:30am–10pm. Ferry: Darling Harbour.

Zaaffran ★★ INDIAN Forget the dark interiors and exotic murals you usually find in an Indian restaurant; here are white surfaces, a glass-fronted wine cellar, and magnificent views of the water and the Sydney skyline from the far side of Darling Harbour. An outdoor terrace provides the best views. Chef Vikrant Kapoor, formerly the chef de cuisine at Raffles in Singapore, has revolutionized classic Indian cuisine on the menu here. Expect such delights as chicken *biryani,* baked in a pastry case and served with mint yogurt, or tiger prawns in coconut cream and a tomato broth, not to mention plenty of interesting vegetarian options.

Level 2, Harbourside Centre, 10 Darling Drive, Darling Harbour. *℃* **02/9211 8900.** www.zaaffran. com.au. Main courses A$19–A$33. Daily noon–2:30pm and Sun–Thurs 6–9:30pm, Fri–Sat 6–10:15pm. Ferry: Darling Harbour.

INEXPENSIVE

Chinta Ria ★★★ MALAYSIAN Cockle Bay's star attraction for those who appreciate good food and a fun ambience without paying a fortune, Chinta Ria is on the roof of the three-story complex. A round building dominated by a giant golden Buddha in the center, it serves cheap and delicious "hawker-style" Malaysian food. The food is good, but the atmosphere is even more memorable. Service can be slow, but who cares in such an interesting space, with plenty of nooks, crannies, and society folk to look at. There are seats outside (some within range of the noise of the highway, but it's still pleasant on a sunny day). The chicken laksa is very good, and I am always a fan of gado-gado (a vegetarian dish with spicy peanut sauce).

Cockle Bay Wharf Complex. ✆ **02/9264 3211.** www.chintaria.com. Main courses A$16–A$29. Daily noon–2:30pm and 6–11pm (10:30pm on Sun). Ferry: Darling Harbour.

Woolloomooloo Wharf

Otto Ristorante ★★ ITALIAN   Recognized as one of Sydney's premier restaurants, Otto is all lush designer appointments and dim lighting, making it popular with local celebrities and socialites. Hence the price of the food, perhaps. Outside it's all light and breezy, with nice views of a boardwalk and some harbor water. Menu possibilities include hand-rolled porcini pasta, with wild boar ragù, mushrooms, and reggiano; or pan-fried potato gnocchi with a Parmesan puree, black truffles, brioche crumbs, and rocket.

6 Cowper Wharf Rd., Woolloomooloo. ✆ **02/9368 7488.** www.ottoristorante.com.au. Main courses A$27–A$45. Daily noon–10:30pm. Bus: 311 from Circular Quay (or take a water taxi).

Kings Cross & Darlinghurst

MODERATE

Mezzaluna ★★ ITALIAN   Exquisite food, flawless service, and an almost unbeatable view across the city's western skyline have all helped Mezzaluna position itself firmly among Sydney's top waterside eateries. A spacious, candlelit place with white walls and polished wooden floorboards, the main dining room opens onto a huge all-weather terrace kept warm in winter by giant overhead fan heaters. The menu often features a fabulous risotto as well as other delights such as chicken involtino filled with prosciutto and San Daniele provolone cheese, and served with mashed potatoes. A "sunset menu" offers one course for A$25, two for A$40, or three for A$50. Whatever you choose, you really can't go wrong.

123 Victoria St., Potts Point. ✆ **02/9357 1988.** www.mezzaluna.com.au. Main courses A$24–A$32. Fri noon–3pm; Mon–Sat 6–11pm. Train: Kings Cross.

INEXPENSIVE

Bill's ★★★ CAFE   Strewn with flowers and magazines, this bright and airy place serves nouveau cafe–style food. It's so popular you might have trouble finding a seat. The signature breakfast dishes—including ricotta hotcakes with honeycomb butter and banana, and sweet corn fritters with roast tomatoes, spinach, and bacon—are the stuff of legend. In fact, some of my friends think Bill's serves the best breakfast in Sydney. Bill's has two more locations: in Surry Hills and Woollahra.

433 Liverpool St., Darlinghurst. ✆ **02/9360 9631.** www.bills.com.au. Main courses A$15–A$26. Mon–Sat 7:30am–3pm, Sun 8:30am–3pm. Train: Kings Cross.

Café Hernandez ★★ CAFE   The walls of the tiny, cluttered cafe are crammed with eccentric fake masterpieces, and the aroma of 20 types of coffee roasted and ground on the premises permeates the air. It's almost a religious experience for discerning central-city coffee addicts—and even better, it never closes! The Spanish espresso is a treat. Light meals are served: sandwiches, wraps, focaccias, and tortillas.

60 Kings Cross Rd., Potts Point. ℂ **02/9331 2343.** www.cafehernandez.com.au. Main courses A$3–A10. Daily 24 hr. Train: Kings Cross).

Govinda's ★★ VEGETARIAN   Simple vegetarian food—usually curries of some kind—coupled with a happy vibe and very cheap prices make this place a winner. Based in the Hare Krishna center, Govinda's serves buffet-style meals in a basic room of black-lacquer tables. The menu changes nightly but always includes a delicious Indian dahl soup, vegetable curry, penne pasta, lentil pie or potato au gratin, cauliflower pakoras, potato wedges, rice, poppadums, and salads. It's BYO, doctrine-free, and very bohemian. After the meal, there's a movie (albeit on a different floor). Movies start at 7pm, and you watch them prostrate on large futon-style chairs. It's hugely popular, so make a booking.

112 Darlinghurst Rd., Darlinghurst. ℂ **02/9380 5155.** www.govindas.com.au. Dinner A$20. Movie A$10. Wed–Sun 5:45–11pm. Train: Kings Cross.

In Bondi Beach
EXPENSIVE

Icebergs Dining Room & Bar ★★★ MEDITERRANEAN   The restaurant at the Bondi Icebergs Club, a revamped old swimming club complex, overlooks Bondi Beach and is a truly fabulous place to hang out. From its corner position on the cliffs, the Icebergs Bar looks directly across the beach and water, with floor-to-roof windows offering what is probably the best view in Sydney. The bar features lots of cushions and has a casual bar menu. The dining-room menu is Italian, with seafood featuring as well.

1 Notts Ave., Bondi Beach. ℂ **02/9365 9000.** www.idrb.com. Reservations essential. Main courses A$23–A$44. Tues–Sat noon–3pm and 6:30pm–midnight; Sun noon–3pm and 6:30–10pm. Bus: 333.

Ravesi's ★★ CONTEMPORARY   On a corner beside a run of surf shops, Ravesi's is a kind of fish tank—with the water on the outside. Downstairs, it's all glass windows and bar stools, the perfect place to watch the street life go by. On weekend nights, the place is packed. Upstairs is a fine casual restaurant with seating both inside and out on the balcony overlooking the beach, not to mention a nice wine bar. Menu choices include dishes like grilled barramundi with mustard basil mash, creamed spinach, and roast beets jus; or braised lamb shanks (two!) with rosemary, raisins, pine nuts, port wine, and garlic beans.

Corner of Campbell Parade and Hall St., Bondi Beach. ℂ **02/9365 4422.** www.ravesis.com.au. Main courses A$32–A$36. Mon–Fri noon–2:30pm and 6pm–late; Sat noon–4pm and 6pm–late; Sun noon–3:30pm (closed for dinner). Bus: 333.

INEXPENSIVE

Pompei's ★ ITALIAN   The recipe is simple: Use good ingredients, like an organic tomato sauce, and you'll get good pizzas. In fact, some people think these are the best pizzas in Sydney. The pizzas have a huge range of interesting toppings, but Pompei's also offers a variety of other fare, including sandwiches and panini (until 4pm). Don't miss the homemade gelato, the best in Sydney by far—try chocolate, tiramisu, or hazelnut. The water views and outside tables are another plus. When it's busy, it can be a little cramped inside, and service can vary.

126–130 Roscoe St. at Gould St., Bondi Beach. © **02/9365 1233.** www.pompeis.com.au. Reservations recommended. Pizza A$21–A$24. Pasta A$18–A$30. Tues–Thurs gelato bar 12:30–11pm, trattoria & pizzeria 4:30–11pm; Fri–Sun both open 11:30am–11pm. Bus: 380 or 333 from the city.

In Manly

Manly is 30 minutes from Circular Quay by ferry. The takeout shops that line **the Corso,** as well as the **pedestrian mall** that runs between the ferry terminal and the main Manly Beach, offer everything from Turkish kabobs to Japanese noodles. You'll find better restaurants along the seafront (though there's a road between them and the beach).

Ashiana ★★ INDIAN   You'll be hard-pressed to find a better moderately priced Indian restaurant in the Sydney area. Tucked away up a staircase next to the Steyne Hotel (just off the Corso near the main beach), Ashiana has won prizes for its traditional spicy cooking. Portions are large and filling. The signature dish is a magnificent butter chicken, while I have heard the *malai kofta* (cheese and potato dumplings in mild, creamy sauce) described as "the best this side of Bombay".

Corner of Sydney Rd. and the Corso, Manly. © **02/9977 3466.** www.ashianaindianrestaurant.com.au. Main courses A$14–A$23. Daily 6:30–10:30pm. Ferry: Manly.

EXPLORING SYDNEY

The only problem with visiting Sydney is fitting in everything you want to do and see. Of course, you won't want to miss the iconic attractions: the **Opera House** and the **Harbour Bridge.**

You should also check out the native wildlife in **Taronga Zoo** and the **Sydney Aquarium,** stroll around the tourist precinct of **Darling Harbour,** and get a dose of Down Under culture at the **Australian Museum.** If it's hot, take your "cozzie" (swimsuit) and towel to **Bondi Beach** or **Manly.**

Sydney Harbour & The Rocks

Officially called Port Jackson, **Sydney Harbour** is the focal point of Sydney and one of the features—along with the beaches and easy access to surrounding national parks—that makes this city so special. It's entered through the **Heads,** two bush-topped outcrops (you'll see them if you take a ferry to Manly), beyond which the harbor laps at some 240km (149 miles) of shoreline before stretching out into the Parramatta River. Visitors are often awestruck by the harbor's beauty, especially at night, when the sails of the Opera House and the girders of the Harbour Bridge are lit up, and the waters are swirling with the reflection of lights from the abutting high-rises—reds, greens, blues, yellows, and oranges. During the day, it buzzes with green-and-yellow ferries pulling in and out of busy Circular Quay, sleek tourist craft, fully rigged tall ships, giant container vessels making their way to and from the wharves of Darling Harbour, and hundreds of white-sailed yachts.

The greenery along the harbor's edges is a surprising feature, thanks to the **Sydney Harbour National Park,** a haven for native trees and plants, and a feeding and breeding ground for lorikeets and other nectar-eating bird life. In the center of the harbor is a series of islands; the most impressive is the tiny isle supporting **Fort Denison,** which once housed convicts and acted as part of the city's defense.

The Rocks neighborhood is compact and close to the ferry terminals at Circular Quay. Sydney's historic district is hilly and crosscut with alleyways. Some of Australia's oldest pubs are here, as well as boutique restaurants, stores, and hotels. Pick up a walking map from the visitor center and make sure to get off the main streets to see the original working-class houses that survived development. Today, there are 96 heritage buildings in The Rocks. The oldest house is Cadmans Cottage, built in 1815, while the Dawes Point Battery, built in 1791, is the oldest remaining European structure. On Observatory Hill you'll find the three remaining walls of Fort Phillip, built in 1804.

Luna Park ★ The huge smiling clown face and the fairground attractions, which are visible from Circular Quay, make up one of Australia's most iconic attractions. It's small but fun for kids, with traditional theme-park amusements rather than high-tech rides. It has a carousel, dodge-'em cars, a Ferris wheel, and the like. Several rides are suitable for small children, too. You buy tickets at booths inside the park. The best way to get here is either to walk over the Sydney Harbour Bridge from The Rocks or to catch a train from the city center to Milsons Point. Leave some time to take a walk along the foreshore of Sydney Harbour, right beneath the Bridge. Hours tend to vary, so check online before setting out.

1 Olympic Dr., Milsons Point. ℂ **02/9922 6644,** or 02/9033 7676 for information. www.lunaparksydney.com. Free admission. Unlimited ride pass A$25–A$30 small child; A$35–A$40 big kids and A$45-A$50 adults (measured by height, not age!). More expensive prices during school holidays. Mon 11am–4pm; Fri-Sat 11am–10pm; Sun 10am–6pm; closed Tues–Thurs. In school holidays: Sun–Thurs 10am–6pm; Fri–Sat 10am–10pm. Ferry or train: Milsons Point.

Museum of Contemporary Art (MCA) ★★★ After being closed for nearly 2 years for a A$53 million redevelopment, the MCA reopened in 2012 with a major focus on its permanent Australian collection. Two new MCA Collection Galleries (Level 2 and Level 1 South) feature the works of more than 150 Australian artists acquired since the founding of the MCA in 1989. This imposing sandstone museum, set back from the water on The Rocks side of Circular Quay, also offers a changing program of exhibitions by Australian and international artists, and is worth at least an hour (probably more!) of your time. Free guided tours are conducted daily at 11am and 1pm, with extra tours on Thursdays at 7pm, and on weekends at 3pm. The **MCA Café and Sculpture Terrace** (ℂ **02/9250 8443**) has good views of the harbor and Opera House. It's open daily from 10am to 4pm (to 9pm Thurs).

140 George St., The Rocks. ℂ**02/9245 2400.** www.mca.com.au. Free admission. Daily 10am–5pm (to 9pm on Thurs). Train, bus, or ferry: Circular Quay.

The Rocks Discovery Museum ★★ Drop in to this small but interesting museum at lunchtime on Fridays for free half-hour talks on a range of topics—mostly about arts and culture—by guest speakers. On the third Friday of each month, the speaker is an Aboriginal Australian. Housed in a restored 1850s sandstone warehouse, this museum is dedicated to telling the story of The Rocks from pre-European days to the present. Learn about the area's traditional landowners; the establishment of the English colony; the sailors, whalers, and traders who called the area home; and the 1970s union-led protests that preserved this unique part of Sydney.

Kendall Lane (off Argyle St.), The Rocks. ℂ **02/9240 8680.** www.therocks.com. Free admission. Daily 10am–5pm. Closed Good Friday and Christmas Day. Train: Circular Quay or Wynyard.

Central Sydney Attractions

Art Gallery of New South Wales 15
Australian Museum 16
Australian National Maritime Museum 10
Hyde Park Barracks Museum 14
Museum of Contemporary Art 6
Museum of Sydney 7
Powerhouse Museum 12
The Rocks Discovery Museum 3
Royal Botanic Gardens 8
Sealife Sydney Aquarium 11
Susannah Place Museum 5
Sydney Harbour Bridge 1
Sydney Jewish Museum 17
Sydney Observatory 4
Sydney Opera House 2
Sydney Tower 13
Wildlife Sydney Zoo 9

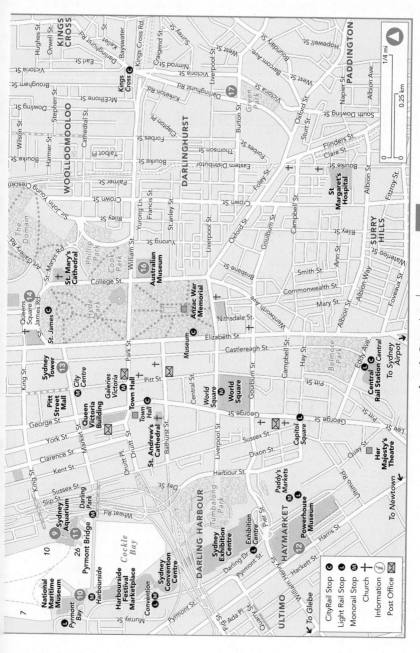

Susannah Place Museum ★★ Entry to this small museum is now by guided tour only, but don't let that put you off—it may even enhance your visit. Contained in a terrace of four houses built in 1844, this museum is a real highlight of The Rocks area. It provides visitors with the opportunity to explore domestic working-class life from 1844 to 1990. The modest interiors and rear yards illustrate the restrictions of 19th-century inner-city life. The layers of paint, wallpapers, and floor coverings that have survived provide a valuable insight into the tastes of the working class. There's also a delightful little shop selling cordials, postcards, old-fashioned candies, and knickknacks.

58–64 Gloucester St., The Rocks. ℗ **02/9241 1893.** www.hht.net.au. Entry by guided tour only, A$8 adults, A$4 children, A$17 family of 4 (entry to shop free). Daily 2–5pm (last tour at 4pm); closed Good Friday and Christmas Day. Bus, ferry, or train: Circular Quay.

Sydney Harbour Bridge ★★★ One thing few tourists do—which is a shame—is to walk across the Harbour Bridge. The bridge, completed in 1932, is 1,150m (3,772 ft.) long and spans 503m (1,650 ft.) from the south shore to the north. It accommodates pedestrian walkways, two railway lines, and an eight-lane road. The 30-minute walk from one end to the other offers excellent harbor views. From the other side, you can take a train from Milsons Point back to the city.

As you walk across, stop off at the **Pylon Lookout** (℗ 02/9240 1100; www.pylon lookout.com.au) at the southeastern pylon. Admission is A$11 for adults, A$6.50 for children aged 5 to 12. There are four levels inside the pylon, with displays about the bridge's history. On level two, there are observation balconies on both sides, and when you get to the top, 89m (292 ft.) above the water, you get panoramic views of Sydney Harbour, the ferry terminals of Circular Quay, and beyond. The Pylon Lookout is open daily from 10am to 5pm (closed Christmas Day).

Another very popular way of enjoying the wonderful views from the Bridge is to climb to the top. The Sydney BridgeClimb is an exhilarating achievement, and one you won't forget. **BridgeClimb,** 3 Cumberland St., The Rocks (℗ **02/8274 7777;** www. bridgeclimb.com), offers three climbs. The **Bridge Climb** takes you along the outer arch of the bridge on catwalks and ladders all the way to the summit. The **Discovery Climb** takes climbers into the heart of the bridge. You traverse the suspension arch and then wind your way through a tangle of hatchways and girders suspended above the traffic. You also climb between the arches to the summit. Both experiences take 3½ hours from check-in to completion. An **Express Climb** is the same as the standard Bridge Climb but with fewer people and a quicker preparation, which allows you to discover the wonders of the bridge in just 2 hours and 15 minutes. Climbers wear "Bridge Suits" and are harnessed to a safety line. You will also be given an alcohol breathalyzer test and are not allowed to carry anything, including cameras (the guide will take photos of you at a couple of stops along the way and at the summit). Daytime climbs cost A$235 for adults and A$148 for children ages 10 to 15 on weekdays, A$10 more on weekends. Twilight climbs cost A$298 for adults (A$308 on weekend) and A$208 for kids (anytime). Night climbs cost A$198 for adults and A$148 for kids (rug up, it can be cold up there!). A dawn climb costs A$308 for adults and A$208 for kids. Children under 10 are not allowed to climb. Prices are slightly higher in the peak time between Christmas and early January. The **Sydney Harbour Bridge Visitor Centre,** where you set out from, has good displays featuring Sydney's famous icon. It's open daily 8am to 6pm.

Sydney Observatory ★★ The city's only major observatory offers visitors a chance to see the southern skies through modern and historic telescopes. The best time to visit is during the night on a guided tour, when you can take a close-up look at the stars and planets. During the day, the 3D theatre, in which you seem to zoom through the stars, is worth seeing. It runs at 2:30, 3:30, and 4pm Mondays to Fridays, and 11am, noon, and 2:30 and 3:30pm on weekends and daily during school holidays. Ninety-minute night tours start at 6:15pm and 8:15pm April to September; 8:15pm October and November, and February and March; and 8:30pm December and January. Schedules are subject to change, so check the times when you book your tour. The planetarium and hands-on exhibits are also interesting. Daytime admission to the gardens and the exhibitions is free, but doesn't include the telescope towers, telescope viewings, and 3D theatre. For A$300 you can also name a star after yourself or someone you love!

Observatory Hill, Watson Rd., The Rocks. ℂ **02/9921 3485.** www.sydneyobservatory.com.au. Daytime A$8 adults, A$6 children 4–15, A$22 family of 4. Guided night tours (reservations required) A$18 adults, A$12 children, A$50 families. Daily 10am–5pm (until noon on Dec 31). Closed Good Friday, Christmas Day, and Boxing Day (Dec 26). Train, bus, or ferry: Circular Quay.

Sydney Opera House ★★★ Only a handful of buildings around the world are as architecturally and culturally significant as the Sydney Opera House. But what sets it apart from some other famous buildings is that this white-sailed construction caught midbillow over the waters of Sydney Cove is a working building housing a full-scale performing-arts complex with four major performance spaces. The biggest and grandest is the 2,690-seat **Concert Hall.** Come here to experience chamber music, symphonies, dance, choral performances, and even rock 'n' roll. The **Joan Sutherland Theatre** is smaller, seating 1,547, and books opera, ballet, and dance. The **Drama Theatre,** seating 544, and the **Playhouse,** seating 398, specialize in plays and smaller-scale performances.

The history of the building is as intriguing as the design. The New South Wales Government raised the construction money with a lottery. Danish architect Jørn Utzon won an international competition to design it. Following a disagreement, Utzon returned home without ever seeing his finished project. The project was budgeted at A$7 million, but by its completion in 1973 it had cost a staggering A$102 million, most raised through a series of lotteries. After a A$152-million upgrade over the past couple of years, the Opera House has never looked better.

Guided tours of the Opera House last about an hour and are conducted daily from 9am to 5pm, except on Good Friday and Christmas Day. If you don't get to see everything, it's because the Opera House is a working venue. There's almost always some performance, practice, or setting up to be done. Reservations are essential, and tour sizes are limited, so be prepared to wait. Backstage tours include about 200 stairs, and are not available for children under 12. Tours for people with limited mobility are run daily at noon.

The Tourism Services Department at the Sydney Opera House can book **combination packages,** including dinner and a show; a tour, dinner, and a show; or a champagne-interval performance. Prices vary depending on shows and dining venues. Visitors from overseas can buy tickets by credit card and pick them up at the box office on arrival, or contact a local tour company specializing in Australia. Advance

4

purchases are a good idea, because performances are very popular and it's worth doing to ensure a good seat.

The Opera House is where you will see performances by the **Australian Ballet** (which is based in Melbourne) during its Sydney season, from mid-March until the end of April. A second Sydney season runs November through December (📞 **02/9253 5300;** www.australianballet.com.au). **Opera Australia** (📞 **02/9319 1088** bookings; www.opera-australia.org.au) performs at the Joan Sutherland Theatre from January through March and June through September. **Sydney Symphony Orchestra** (📞 **02/ 8215 4600** box office; www.sydneysymphony.com) performs throughout the year in the Opera House's Concert Hall. The main symphony season runs March through November, and there's a summer season in February.

Free performances take place outside on the Opera House boardwalks on Sunday afternoons and during festival times. The artists range from musicians and performance artists to school groups.

Bennelong Point. 📞 **02/9250 7250** for guided tours and information, or 02/9250 7777 box office. www.sydneyoperahouse.com. Box office Mon–Sat 9am–8:30pm; Sun 2 hr. before performance. Tours A$35 for adults, A$25 for kids, and A$90 for a family of 4. Book online for discounts. Tours daily 9am–5pm (every 30 min.), subject to theater availability. Backstage Tour A$155 starts daily at 7am, for 2 hr., with breakfast. Train, bus, or ferry: Circular Quay. Parking: Mon–Fri daytime A$12 per hour; weekend daytime flat rate A$15 (leave before 5pm); evening A$35 flat rate.

SYDNEY HARBOUR ON THE CHEAP

The best way to see Sydney Harbour is from the water. Several companies operate tourist craft (see "Harbor Cruises," later in this chapter), but it's easy enough just to hop on a regular passenger ferry (see "Getting Around," earlier in this chapter). The best ferry excursions are to the beachside suburb of **Manly** (return after dusk to see the lights ablaze around The Rocks and Circular Quay); to **Watsons Bay,** where you can have lunch and wander along the cliffs; to **Darling Harbour,** for all the area's entertainment and the fact that you travel right under the Harbour Bridge; and to **Mosman Bay,** just for the ride and to see the grand houses that overlook exclusive harbor inlets.

FAST ACTION ON SYDNEY HARBOUR

For a thrill ride, you can board a 420-horsepower jet boat, which zooms about on three high-speed waterway tours at speeds of up to 40 knots (about 80kmph/50 mph), with huge 240-degree turns and instant stops. **Harbour Jet** (📞 **1300/887 373** in Australia or 02/9280 4662; www.harbourjet.com) offers a 35-minute Jet Blast Adventure costing A$65 for adults, A$45 for kids under 15, and A$198 for a family. It leaves at noon, 2:15, and 4pm daily. A 50-minute Sydney Harbour Adventure costs A$80 for adults, A$55 for kids, and A$243 for a family. It leaves at 10:30am, 1:15, and 3pm daily. An 80-minute Middle Harbour Adventure cruise costs A$95 for adults, A$70 for kids, and A$297 for a family. It leaves at 9am daily. Rides are fast and furious and pump with rock music. The boat leaves from the Convention Centre Jetty at Darling Harbour.

Another option is **Oz Jet Boat** (📞 **02/9808 3700;** www.ozjetboating.com), which departs every hour from the Eastern Pontoon at Circular Quay (on the walkway to the Opera House). These large red boats are a bit more powerful than the blue Harbour Jet ones, but you might not notice the difference. This company offers a 30-minute Thrill Ride for A$75 for adults, A$45 for kids under 16, and A$195 for a family of four. It

SEEING SYDNEY HARBOUR THROUGH
aboriginal EYES

The *Deerubbun*, a former Australian navy torpedo recovery vessel, makes quite an impression as it pulls up to the dock near the Opera House concourse with speakers blaring out a recording of clapsticks and didgeridoos. The boat, which is owned by the Tribal Warrior Association (an Aboriginal-operated nonprofit organization that aims to provide maritime training programs for Aboriginal youths) offers an Aboriginal perspective of the famous waterway, and every visitor to Sydney should do this trip. The boat putters past the Royal Botanic Gardens, and the guide tells stories of the early Europeans and their hopeless farms, and the smallpox epidemic of 1789. Mixed in with the observations of the landscape are tales of the first Aboriginal tour guides, who took early settlers inland from the harbor, stories of soldiers, statesmen, and farmers who came into contact with the Aborigines, and much more. Tourists disembark at Clark Island to see cave shelters with roofs stained black from ancient fireplaces, convict engravings, and a natural fish trap. Two Aboriginal guides, their bodies plastered in ghostly white ochre, beat a rhythm with hardwood sticks and growl through a didgeridoo as they beckon tourists to the Welcoming Ceremony. Then comes a repertoire of haunting songs, music, and dance. **Aboriginal Cultural Cruises ★★★** depart either at 1pm or 3pm, depending on the time of year, from the Eastern Pontoon at Circular Quay (near the Sydney Opera House). The cost is A$60 adults and A$40 children 5 to 14. For more information or to book, call Ⓒ **02/9699 3491** or visit www.tribalwarrior.org.

leaves every hour from 11am to 4pm daily (5pm in summer). Kids must be at least 1.2 meters tall.

Darling Harbour

Many tourists head to Darling Harbour for the cheap eateries and a few interesting shops, but Sydney's dedicated tourist precinct has much more to offer. See **www. darlingharbour.com** for current events.

Australian National Maritime Museum ★★   Australia owes almost everything to the sea, so it's not surprising that there's a museum dedicated to seafarers and ships, from Aboriginal vessels to submarines. In 2012, another 300 names were added to the museum's migrant Welcome Wall which celebrates the arrival of waves of migrants as part of Australia's maritime history. There are now more than 25,000 names from 206 countries on the wall. The museum's "Big Ticket" gives access to everything, including the Australian navy destroyer *Vampire*, an Oberon Class submarine, and a replica of the *Endeavour*, the ship Captain James Cook commanded when he laid claim to Australia, and the tall ship *James Craig*, as well as all the galleries, exhibitions and the Cape Bowling Green lighthouse, and the Kids on Deck program (Sundays and school holidays). You'll find ships' logs and things to pull and tug at and clamber over—kids love it! Allow 2 hours.

2 Murray St., Darling Harbour. ☏ **02/9298 3777.** www.anmm.gov.au. Admission to galleries and exhibitions A$7 adults, A$3.50 children 5–15, A$17.50 families. Admission to galleries, exhibitions, ships and Kids on Deck A$25 adults, A$15 children, A$65 families. Free admission to galleries and exhibitions on the first Thurs of the month (except during school holidays). Daily 9:30am–5pm (until 6pm in Jan). Closed Christmas Day. Ferry: Darling Harbour.

Powerhouse Museum ★★★   Sydney's most interactive museum is also one of the largest in the Southern Hemisphere. At press time for this book, the museum was undergoing a renovation to create a new gallery for international exhibitions, a new public forecourt, a cafe, and gift shop. Inside, you'll find displays, sound effects, and gadgets relating to the sciences, transportation, human achievement, decorative art, and social history, much of it with relevance or connections to Sydney and Australian exploration. You could easily spent 2 or 3 hours discovering everything here. There's plenty to keep kids interested as well.

> ### Deals on Sightseeing
>
> Several major Sydney attractions offer discounts if you buy passes for entry to more than one of them. If you plan to visit the Sydney Tower, Sealife Sydney Aquarium, Manly Sealife Sanctuary, Wildlife World, or the new Madame Tussaud's Wax Museum, it would be worth checking out their websites. Passes can be used for two, three, four, or five attractions. Once you've entered your first attraction, you've got 3 months to visit the remaining three attractions on the pass, and you can make considerable savings.

500 Harris St., Ultimo (near Darling Harbour). ☏ **02/9217 0111.** www.powerhouse museum.com. Admission A$12 adults, A$6 children 4–15, A$30 families of 4. Daily 10am–5pm. Closed Christmas Day. Ferry: Darling Harbour.

Sealife Sydney Aquarium ★★   Sharks, crocodiles, penguins, dugongs (sea cows), and platypus are just some of the marine life that you will see at this top aquarium. The main attractions are the underwater walkways through two enormous tanks—one full of giant rays and gray nurse sharks and the other where you can see the seals. The sharks are fed at 11am and the Fairy Penguins at 3pm daily. Other exhibits include a magnificent section on the Great Barrier Reef, where thousands of colorful fish school around coral outcrops. A touch pool allows you to stroke baby sharks. You can take a 15- to 20-minute behind-the-scenes tour of the Great Barrier Reef oceanarium in a glass-bottom boat, which leaves every 30 minutes from noon to 4:30pm and costs A$10 adults, half-price kids. You can also take the boat at shark-feeding time for about 30 minutes; the cost is A$15 per person. Try to visit during the week, when it's less crowded. Allow around 2 hours.

Aquarium Pier, Darling Harbour. ☏ **02/8251 7800.** www.sydneyaquarium.com.au. Admission A$38 adults, A$24 children 4–15, A$120 families of 4. Tickets cheaper if booked online. Family tickets only available online. Daily 9am–8pm (last entry 7pm). Train: Town Hall. Ferry: Darling Harbour.

Other Top Attractions

Art Gallery of New South Wales ★★★   This beautiful gallery, established in 1871, has a fine collection of international and Australian art that you should take time to see. Contemporary works are displayed in light-filled galleries with views of Sydney and the harbour, while colonial and 19th-century Australian art and European Old Masters are housed in the Grand Courts. There are also dedicated galleries for Asian and Aboriginal and Torres Strait Islander art. The gallery hosts more than 30 temporary exhibitions each year, including the annual Archibald Prize for portraiture (late March to early June), in which you'll see plenty of famous Australian faces. Enter from the Domain parklands (across the road from the Royal Botanic Gardens) onto the third floor (ground level) of the museum. Allow at least 1 hour, probably more if you are interested in any of the many free tours on offer.

Art Gallery Rd., The Domain. *©* **1800/679 278** in Australia or 02/9225 1744. www.artgallery.nsw. gov.au. Free admission to most galleries. Prices vary for special exhibitions. Daily 10am–5pm; Wed 10am–9pm. Closed Good Friday and Christmas Day. Tours of collection highlights daily 11am. Tours of Aboriginal galleries daily 11am. Bus: 441. Train: St. James.

Australian Museum ★★ "Behind-the-Scenes" tours of Sydney's premier natural-history museum give a special look at this interesting place. Run daily at 11am, they allow a glimpse of areas such as the taxidermy lab where you might see a specimen of the now-extinct Tasmanian Tiger. You must be 12 years or over to take the tour, but family tours are also run on the first Saturday and Sunday of each month for ages 8 and up. Displays are presented thematically, one of the best being the Aboriginal section with its traditional clothing, weapons, and everyday implements. There are plenty of stuffed Australian mammals and birds, an insect display, and a mineral collection.

6 College St. *©* **02/9320 6000.** www.austmus.gov.au. Admission A$12 adults, A$6 children 5–15, A$30 families of 4. Special exhibits extra. Behind-the-Scenes tours A$88 per person; family Behind-the-Scenes tours A$50 for one adult/one child, A$20 extra adult, A$15 extra child. Daily 9:30am–5pm. Closed Christmas Day. Train: Museum, St. James, or Town Hall.

Elizabeth Bay House★ Perched on a headland with some of the best harbor views in Sydney, this colonial mansion was built in 1835 and was considered "the finest house in the colony." You can tour the house and get a feeling for the history of that fledgling settlement.

7 Onslow Ave., Elizabeth Bay. *©* **02/9356 3022.** www.hht.net.au. Admission A$8 adults, A$4 children, A$17 families. Fri–Sun 111am–4pm and on Australia Day (Jan 26). Closed Good Friday and Christmas Day. Bus: 311 from Circular Quay. Train: Kings Cross.

Hyde Park Barracks Museum ★★ If you don't know the terms "Lags and Swells," you will after meeting some convict characters at this museum, where a new touch-screen interactive program now brings to life some of the 50 convicts who passed through the Hyde Park Barracks between 1819 and 1848. These Georgian-style barracks, designed by the convict Francis Greenway (an architect), were built by convicts and inhabited by prisoners. These days they house relics from those days, including log books, settlement artifacts, and a room full of ships' hammocks in which you can lie and listen to fragments of prisoner conversation. If you are interested in Sydney's early beginnings, I highly recommend a visit. There are also new free audio tours available. Allow at least 1 hour.

Queens Sq., 10 Macquarie St. *©* **02/8239 2311.** www.hht.net.au. Admission A$10 adults, A$5 children, A$20 families. Daily 10am–5pm. Train: St. James or Martin Place.

Museum of Sydney ★ Changes to the forecourt of this museum means there's now reason to linger . . . for a game of outdoor chess, perhaps, or just to lounge in a chair on the grassy areas. A visit to the Museum of Sydney will make you think! In a postmodern building near Circular Quay, encompassing the remnants of Sydney's first Government House, the museum is certainly not what you might expect. No stuffy and conventional showcase of history, this museum houses a collection of first-settler and Aboriginal objects and multimedia displays that invite you to discover Sydney's past for yourself. Some of it is underfoot, in the archaeological digs exposed through "windows" in the paths. A forest of poles filled with hair, oyster shells, and crab claws in the courtyard, called *Edge of Trees,* represents first contact between Aborigines and the British. Modern . . . yes. And very interesting.

37 Phillip St., (at Bridge St.). © **02/9251 5988.** www.hht.net.au. Admission A$10 adults, A$5 children 14 and under, A$20 families. Daily 10am–5pm. Closed Good Friday and Christmas Day. Train, bus, or ferry: Circular Quay.

Sydney Jewish Museum ★★★ Volunteer guides, many of whom are Holocaust survivors, are on hand on every floor of this important museum to answer questions and talk to visitors. Some of the exhibits are harrowing, including documents and objects relating to the Holocaust. Other exhibits include soundscapes, audiovisual displays, and interactive media. It has a museum shop, a resource center, a small theater, and a kosher cafe. Allow 1 to 2 hours.

148 Darlinghurst Rd. (at Burton St.), Darlinghurst. © **02/9360 7999.** www.sydneyjewishmuseum. com.au. Admission A$10 adults, A$7 children, A$22 families. Guided tours run Mon, Wed, Fri, and Sun at noon for about 45 min. Sun–Thurs 10am–4pm; Fri 10am–2pm. Closed Sat and Jewish holy days. Train: Kings Cross.

Sydney Tower ★ The Sydney Tower is hard to miss—it resembles a giant steel pole skewering a golden marshmallow. Standing 309m (984 ft.) tall, the tower offers stupendous 360-degree views across Sydney and as far as the Blue Mountains. At the top is a revolving restaurant and bar. The indoor viewing platform on the top floor is called the Sydney Tower Eye. Don't be too concerned if you feel the building tremble slightly, especially in a strong wind—apparently it's built to do that! The ticket price includes admission to a new 4D cinema, where you can watch a film about Sydney with footage of the harbor, coastline, famous landmarks, and events. The **Sydney Tower Skywalk** is a heart-stopping experience definitely not for people who are scared of heights. You don a special suit, walk out onto a glass-floored platform 260m (853 ft.) above the city floor and walk around the building. The views are breathtaking (even between your feet!). You are harnessed to a safety rail with a sliding harness, so there's no chance of falling off, and well-informed guides offer a helping hand to the nervous. Each Skywalk lasts about 90 minutes. Cameras aren't allowed for safety reasons, but the guide will take group or individual shots that you can buy. Children under 8 aren't allowed on the Skywalk.

100 Market St. (another entrance on Pitt St. Mall). © **02/9333 9222.** www.sydneytowereye.com. au. Admission A$25 adults, A$15 children 4–15, A$55 families. Daily 9am–10:30pm (last entry 9:30pm). Closed Christmas Day. Skywalk A$69 for adults, A$45 for kids 8–15. Daily 9am–10pm (last Skywalk departs 8:45pm). Train: St. James or Town Hall.

Kangaroos, Koalas & Other Aussie Wildlife

See p. 70 for Sealife Sydney Aquarium.

Featherdale Wildlife Park ★★★ If you have time to visit only one wildlife park in Sydney, make it this one. The selection of Australian animals is excellent, and, most important, the animals are very well cared for. You could easily spend a couple of hours here, despite the park's compact size. You'll have the chance to hand-feed friendly kangaroos and wallabies and get a photo taken next to a koala. The **Reptilian Pavilion** houses 30 native species of reptiles in 26 realistic exhibits. If you are heading to the Blue Mountains (see p. 81) on a bus tour, you are well advised to choose one that stops off here. Allow 1½ hours to get here by public transport or 45 minutes by car from the city center.

217 Kildare Rd., Doonside. © **02/9622 1644.** www.featherdale.com.au. Admission A$28 adults, A$16 children 3–15, A$79 families of 4. Daily 9am–5pm. Closed Christmas Day. Train: Blacktown station; then bus no. 725.

Koala Park Sanctuary ★   In all, around 55 koalas roam within the park's leafy boundaries (it's set in 4 hectares/10 acres of rainforest). Free koala cuddling sessions take place at 10:20 and 11:45am, and 2 and 3pm daily. There are wombats, dingoes, kangaroos, wallabies, emus, and native birds here, too. The sanctuary also has live sheep shearing at 10:30am and 2:30pm each day. Allow 1½ hours to get here by public transport from the city center or about 30 minutes to drive.

84 Castle Hill Rd., West Pennant Hills. © **02/9484 3141.** www.koalaparksanctuary.com.au. Admission A$26 adults, A$15 children. Daily 9am–5pm. Closed Christmas Day. Train: Pennant Hills station via North Strathfield (45 min.). Cross over railway line and join Glenorie Bus routes 651 to 655. The bus takes about 10 min. to Koala Park.

Manly Sealife Sanctuary ★★★   Penguin Cove is the newest attraction at this marine sanctuary (a sister attraction to Sydney Aquarium), showing off a colony of Little Penguins and explaining their importance to the shores of Manly. Talks and feeding demonstrations are offered every day, and you can get "hands-on" in the interactive rockpool, which kids love. There's a good display of Barrier Reef fish, as well as giant sharks. If you're braver than me, you can take the plunge with **Shark Dive Xtreme,** diving into the tank to swim with large grey nurse sharks, turtles, and stingrays. It costs from A$195 for qualified divers, A$270 for nonqualified divers (including an Introduction to Scuba Diving course). Bookings are essential, and you'll save on ticket prices by booking online.

West Esplanade, Manly. © **02/8251 7878.** www.manlysealifesanctuary.com.au. Admission A$24 adults, A12 children 4–15, A$40-A$60 families (cheaper if bought online). Daily 10am–5:30pm. Closed Christmas Day. Ferry: Manly.

Wildlife Sydney Zoo ★★   Not to be confused with Taronga Zoo (Sydney's premier outdoor zoo; see below), this inner-city attraction has a big collection of Australian creatures, including kangaroos, a cassowary, snakes, wallabies, Tasmanian Devils, birds, and butterflies. You'll find koalas lazing around in the rooftop garden. The new Wild Discovery Zone was designed especially for kids, with hands-on animal encounters. You walk through eight themed Australian habitats, each with its own inhabitants. No elephants or giraffes here, but it might not matter!

Aquarium Pier, Darling Harbour. © **02/9333 9288.** www.wildlifesydney.com.au. Admission A$38 adults, A$24 kids 3–15, A$120 family (cheaper if booked online). Daily 9am–6pm (last entry 5pm); 9am–8pm (last entry 7pm) early Oct–late Mar; 9am–5pm Christmas Day and New Year's Eve (last entry 4pm). Ferry: Darling Harbour.

Taronga Zoo ★★★   Taronga has the best views of any zoo in the world. Set on a hill, it looks out over Sydney Harbour, the Opera House, and the Harbour Bridge. It's easiest on the legs to explore the zoo from the top down (admission includes a trip on the cable car from the ferry pier to the main entrance). The big attractions are the fabulous chimpanzee exhibit, the gorilla enclosure, and the Nocturnal Houses, where you can see some of Australia's unique marsupials, including the platypus and the cute bilby, out and about. There's an interesting reptile display, a couple of impressive Komodo dragons, a scattering of indigenous beasties—including a few koalas, echidnas, kangaroos, dingoes, and wombats—and lots more. Animals are fed at various times during the day. A 2-hour "Aboriginal Discovery Tour" is offered on Monday, Wednesday, and Friday at 9:45am; it costs A$99 adults and A$69 children, including zoo entry for the day (to book, call 𝒞 **02/9978 4782**). Despite the quite steep entry price, the zoo can get crowded on weekends, so it's a good idea to plan your visit for a weekday or early in the morning on weekends. Allow around 3 hours.

Bradley's Head Rd., Mosman. 𝒞 **02/9969 2777.** www.taronga.org.au. Admission A$44 adults, A$22 children 4–15, A$112 family of 4. Daily 9am–5pm (until 9pm Jan; until 4:30pm in winter, May–Aug). Ferry: Taronga Zoo. Lower zoo entrance is at ferry terminal.

4 ORGANIZED TOURS

For details on the **Sydney Explorer** and **Bondi Explorer** sightseeing buses, see "Getting Around," p. 39.

Harbor Cruises

The best thing about Sydney is the harbor, and you shouldn't leave without taking a cruise. **Captain Cook Cruises,** departing Jetty 6, Circular Quay (𝒞 **02/9206 1111;** www.captaincook.com.au), offers several harbor excursions on its sleek vessels, with commentary along the way. Two-hour morning or afternoon "Coffee Cruises" cost A$55, and there's a range of dining cruises as well. The 1-hour, 15-minute "Harbour Highlights Cruise," which costs A$30 for adults and runs five times a day from Circular Quay, is popular. Whale-watching cruises are run from May to November, costing A$88 adults. Check the website for special deals. Captain Cook Cruises has ticket booths at Jetty 6, Circular Quay (open 8:30am–7pm daily), and at Pier 26, Aquarium Wharf, Darling Harbour (open 11am–4pm daily). You will also find other cruise operators here, including **Matilda Cruises** (𝒞 **02/8270 5188;** www.matilda.com.au), which offers a similar range of cruises at similar prices. Matilda offers a "Zoo Express," including zoo entry, from both Darling Harbour and Circular Quay. It costs A$52 for adults and A$26 for kids, round-trip.

Yellow Water Taxis (𝒞 **1300/138 840** in Australia or 02/9299 0199; www.yellowwatertaxis.com) offers a 15-minute mini-tour by small water taxi from its bases at King Street Wharf in Darling Harbour and Circular Quay Jetty 1. This tour is good for a quick look at Sydney's famous harbor and a great way to travel to or from Darling Harbour and Circular Quay. The tours depart every 20 minutes from 10am until sunset and cost A$15 for adults, A$10 for children (4–12 years of age), and A$40 for a family. A 45-minute Harbour Highlights Tour includes hop-on, hop-off options at Darling Harbour, Luna Park, Taronga Zoo, and the Sydney Opera House. This tour costs A$40 for adults, A$20 for kids, and A$100 for a family.

It's a good idea to check websites or pop into a ticket office at Darling Harbour or Circular Quay, because cruise options, departure times, and prices change frequently.

Walking Tours

If you want to learn more about Sydney's early history, book an excellent guided tour with **The Rocks Walking Tours**, based at Clocktower Square, corner of Argyle and Harrington streets (𝄐 **02/9247 6678;** www.rockswalkingtours.com.au). Walks leave daily at 10:30am and 1:30pm. The 1½-hour tour costs A$25 for adults, A$12 for children ages 5 to 16, A$62 for families of four.

Motorcycle Tours

Blue Thunder Motorcycle Tours (𝄐 **1300/258 384** in Australia; www.bluethunder downunder.com.au) runs Harley-Davidson tours of Sydney, the Blue Mountains, and further. A 1-hour ride (you sit on the back of the bike) around the city or Manly costs A$130. A 1½-hour ride through the city and out to Bondi costs A$155. A 3-hour trip to the northern beaches or down the south coast through the Royal National Park costs A$240. Full-day trips including lunch and snacks cover the Hunter Valley, Bathurst, or the Blue Mountains.

If you love motorbikes and want to rent one on your own for a self-guided or guided tour, contact **Bikescape** (𝄐 **1300/736 869** in Australia or 02/9569 4111; www.bikes cape.com.au).

OUTDOOR ACTIVITIES

Hitting the Beach

One of the big bonuses of visiting Sydney in the summer (Dec–Feb) is that you get to experience the beaches in their full glory. Most major city beaches, such as Manly and Bondi, have lifeguards on patrol, especially during the summer. They check the water conditions and are on the lookout for **"rips"**—strong currents that can pull a swimmer far out. Always swim in the area between the red and yellow flags that mark the patrolled area. Fiberglass surfboards must be used outside the flags. (Expect a warning from the loudspeakers and a fine if you fail to do this.)

WHAT ABOUT SHARKS & OTHER NASTIES? One of the first things visitors ask before they hit the water in Australia is: "Are there sharks?" The answer is yes, but fortunately they are rarely spotted inshore—you are far more likely to spy a migrating whale. In reality, the chance of a shark attack is very small. Some beaches—such as the small beach next to the Manly ferry wharf—have permanent shark nets, while others rely on portable nets that are moved from beach to beach. Shark attacks are most likely in early morning and at dusk—avoid swimming at these times!

More common off Sydney's beaches are **"blue bottles"**—small blue jellyfish, often called "stingers" in Australia (and Portuguese man-o'-war elsewhere). You'll often find these creatures (which are not the same as the stingers in north Queensland) washed up on the beach. Be on the lookout for warning signs erected on the shoreline. Minute stinging cells that touch your skin can cause minor itching. You might be hit by the full force of a blue bottle if it wraps its tentacles around you, which causes a severe burning sensation almost immediately. Wearing a T-shirt in the water reduces the risk somewhat. If you are stung, rinse the area liberally with seawater or fresh water to remove any tentacles stuck in your skin. To combat intense pain, take a hot shower.

Plenty of tourists get into real trouble on Sydney's beaches each year by being caught in a rip tide—a fast current that moves away from the shore (but that will not pull you under the water). If this happens, the most important thing to do is not to panic. If you can't stand up and are being pulled out to sea, try and attract attention by raising a hand in the air. Whatever you do, don't try to battle it out with the rip by trying to swim against it back to shore. You will quickly become exhausted; this is how people drown. Keep calm, and swim parallel to the beach. If you run out of energy, float on your back. If you swim parallel to the beach you will be pulled a little farther out to sea—it won't take you far out—but before long you should be out of the rip and able to swim back to the beach. Never swim outside of the area marked by yellow and red flags on a beach patrolled by lifeguards. If there are no lifeguards around, it's safest not to swim.

In the unlikely event that you experience breathing difficulties or disorientation, seek medical attention immediately.

SOUTH OF SYDNEY HARBOUR

Sydney's most famous beach is **Bondi.** The beach, sadly, is cut off from the cafe and restaurant strip that caters to beachgoers by a busy road that pedestrians have to cross to reach the sand. On summer weekend evenings, it's popular with souped-up cars driven by young men strutting their stuff. To reach Bondi Beach, take the train to Bondi Junction, and then transfer to bus no. 380 or 333 (a 15-min. bus journey). The 333 bus takes about 40 minutes from Circular Quay.

If you're facing the water at Bondi, to your right is a scenic cliff-top trail that takes you to **Bronte Beach** (a 20-min. walk) via gorgeous little **Tamarama,** nicknamed "Glamourama" for its trendy sun worshippers. This beach is known for its dangerous rips and is often closed to swimming. Bronte has better swimming. To go straight to Bronte, catch bus no. 378 from Circular Quay or pick up the bus at the Bondi Junction train station.

Clovelly Beach, farther along the coast, is blessed with a large rock pool carved into a rock platform that's sheltered from the force of the Tasman Sea. This beach is accessible for visitors in wheelchairs on a series of ramps. To reach Clovelly, take bus no. 339 from Circular Quay.

The cliff walk from Bondi will eventually bring you to **Coogee,** which has a pleasant strip of sand with a couple of hostels and hotels nearby. To reach Coogee, take bus no. 373 or 374 from Circular Quay.

NORTH OF SYDNEY HARBOUR

On the North Shore you'll find **Manly,** a long curve of golden sand edged with Norfolk Island pines. The best way to reach Manly is on a ferry from Circular Quay. Follow the crowds through the pedestrian Corso to the main ocean beach, ignoring the two small beaches on either side of the ferry terminal—this is not your destination!

Facing the ocean, head to your right along the beachfront and follow the coastal path to small and sheltered **Shelly Beach,** a nice area for snorkeling and swimming. This is one of Sydney's nicest walks. Follow the path up the hill to the car park. Here, a track cuts up into the bush and leads toward a firewall, which marks the entrance to the Sydney Harbour National Park and offers spectacular ocean views across to Manly and the northern beaches.

The best harbor beach is at **Balmoral,** a wealthy suburb with some good cafes and restaurants. Reach Balmoral on the ferry to Taronga Zoo and then a 10-minute ride on a connecting bus from the ferry wharf, or catch the bus from the stop outside the zoo's top entrance.

Surfing

Bondi Beach and **Tamarama** are the best surf beaches on the south side of Sydney Harbour. **Manly, Narrabeen, Bilgola, Collaroy, Long Reef,** and **Palm** beaches are the most popular on the north side. Most beach suburbs have surf shops where you can rent a board. At Bondi Beach, **Lets Go Surfing,** 128 Ramsgate Ave. (© **02/9365 1800;** www.letsgosurfing.com.au), rents surfboards for A$20 for 1 hour or A$40 all day. There are discounts for all-week hires, and you can also hire wet suits for A$5 to A$10. Let's Go also offer surfing lessons, both group and individual. A 2-hour session in a small group costs between A$89 and A$99; 1-hour private lessons cost A$140.

In Manly, **Manly Surf Guide** (© **0412/417 431** mobile phone; www.manly surfguide.com) rents (and delivers) surfboards. **Manly Surf School** (© **02/9977 6977;** www.manlysurfschool.com) offers 2-hour small-group surf classes for A$70 adults, A$55 kids. The more lessons you take, the cheaper it is. For A$99 you get a full day's outing that includes pickup from the city, lessons, and surfing at various places on the northern beaches. If you're already proficient, you might want to consider a 1-day trip with **Waves Surf School** (© **1800/616 667** in Australia or 02/9641 2358; www.waves surfschool.com.au) to the Royal National Park. Trips cost A$95, including lunch. Waves Surf School also offers a 2-day surfing trip to Seal Rocks, north of Sydney, for A$239, as well as 4- and 5-day trips farther afield.

Parks & Gardens

If you have time to spend in one of Sydney's green spaces, make it the **Royal Botanic Gardens** (© **02/9231 8111;** www.rgbsyd.nsw.gov.au), next to the Sydney Opera House. Open daily (7am–dusk), these lovely, informal gardens were laid out in 1816 on the site of a farm that supplied food for the colony. The gardens have a scattering of duck ponds and open spaces, with several areas dedicated to particular plant species. These include the rose garden, the cacti and succulent display, and the central palm and rainforest groves. Try to spot the thousands of large fruit bats, which chatter and bicker among the rainforest trees. Free guided walks are run daily at 10:30am and take about 90 minutes. **Mrs. Macquarie's Chair,** along the coast path, offers superb views of the Opera House and the Harbour Bridge. The "chair" bears the name of Elizabeth Macquarie (1788–1835), the wife of Governor Lachlan Macquarie. The sandstone building dominating the gardens nearest the Opera House is **Government House.** The gardens are open daily (10am–4pm), and the house is open Friday through Sunday (10:30am–3pm). Entrance is free, but you'll need a ticket from the gatehouse to tour the house. Note that the house is sometimes closed for official functions.

In the center of the city is **Hyde Park,** a favorite with lunching businesspeople. Here you will find the **Anzac Memorial** to Australian and New Zealand troops killed in action and the **Archibald Fountain,** complete with spitting turtles and sculptures of Diana and Apollo.

Another Sydney favorite is giant **Centennial Park** (✆ **02/9339 6699;** www.centennial parklands.com.au). The park has five main entrances, but the easiest one from the city is at the top of Oxford Street. The park opened in 1888 to celebrate the centenary of European settlement and today encompasses huge areas of lawn, several lakes, picnic areas with barbecues, cycling and running paths, and a cafe. It's open from sunrise to sunset.

Biking

The best place to cycle in Sydney is Centennial Park. Rent bikes from **Centennial Park Cycles,** 50 Clovelly Rd., Randwick (✆ **02/9398 5027;** www.cyclehire.com.au), which is 200m (656 ft.) from the Musgrave Avenue entrance. Mountain bikes cost A$15 for the first hour, A$20 for 2 hours, A$40 for 4 hours, and A$50 for a full day. Extra days cost just A$10 each.

Bonza Bike Tours (✆ **02/9247 8800;** www.bonzabiketours.com), at 55 Harrington St., The Rocks, runs regular bike tours of the city, and also hires out bikes. A half-day city tour costs A$119 for adults, A$99 for kids, A$349 for families, including a bike and helmet. Its also offers a tour of Manly and another that takes you across Sydney Harbour Bridge. Bike hire alone costs A$20 an hour, A$35 a half-day, or A$50 a day.

Kayaking

Natural Wanders (✆ **02/9899 1001;** www.naturalwanders.com.au) takes paddlers out on Sydney Harbour. Tours start from Lavender Bay, near Luna Park, and this is the only kayaking company that takes you under Sydney Harbour Bridge. Group tours run on weekends only, but if you'd like a private tour, owner Patrick Dibben will take you during the week too. There's no minimum number for group tours, though, so you may still be in a group of only two or three. If you choose a private tour, you will be the one to decide where you want to paddle and for how long. Group tours cost A$65 per person for a 2-hour paddle. A 3½-hour paddle costs A$90 and takes you from Lavender Bay west, across the Harbour and south to explore Balmain, then north to land at Berry Island before returning to Lavender Bay (about 10–12km/6–7 miles). Private tours cost A$150 for one person or A$120 each if there are two or more of you. These tours usually go under Sydney Harbour Bridge and past the Opera House and stop on a beautiful beach in a bushland setting before returning. All tours start at 6:30am on weekdays and 8am at weekends. You must be 15 years or older, have a good level of fitness, and be able to swim!

Swimming

With all that ocean, why bother with a pool? Well, Sydney has some great pools that you might want to try just for their settings. The **Bondi Icebergs Club,** 1 Notts Ave. (✆ **02/9130 4804;** www.icebergs.com.au), at Bondi Beach, has an Olympic-size ocean tidal pool built into the rocks with the ocean lapping into it. It also has a children's pool. Entrance costs A$5.50 for adults, A$3.50 for kids, or A$15 for a family of five. Spectators pay A$3. Towel hire is A$3.50. The Icebergs Club is open from 11am till late Monday to Friday and from 9am on weekends. *Be warned:* This is a true ocean pool, so the water is sometimes very cold (hence the name of the club!).

Another good pool with fabulous views across Sydney Harbour is the **Andrew (Boy) Charlton Swimming Pool,** the Domain, Mrs. Macquaries Road, near the Royal Botanical Gardens (② 02/9358 6686; www.abcpool.org). This is an outdoor pool, and it also has a learner's pool and a toddler's pool. Entry is A$6.20 for adults and A$4.70 for kids. It's open 6am to 7pm daily September to April.

Yachting

Sydney by Sail (② 02/9280 1110; www.sydneybysail.com.au) offers day sails on Sydney Harbour. It's based at Darling Harbour. A skippered, 3-hour afternoon sail leaving at 1pm costs A$165 for adults and A$85 for kids under 14, or A$420 or a family of four. You can help sail, or just relax!

SHOPPING

You'll find plenty of places to keep your credit cards in action in Sydney. Most shops of interest to the visitor are in **The Rocks** and along **George and Pitt streets** (including the shops below the Sydney Tower and along Pitt Street Mall). Other precincts worth checking out are **Mosman,** on the North Shore; **Double Bay,** in the eastern suburbs, for boutique shopping; **Chatswood,** for its shopping centers; and various **weekend markets** (see p. 80).

Don't miss the **Queen Victoria Building (QVB),** on the corner of Market and George streets. This Victorian shopping arcade is one of the most ornate in Australia and has around 200 boutiques—mostly men's and women's fashion—on four levels. Here you'll find fashion-statement stores featuring the best of Australian design, including Oroton, Country Road, and the fabulous woman's clothing designer Lisa Ho. The arcade is open 24 hours, but the shops do business Monday through Saturday from 9am to 6pm (Thurs to 9pm) and Sunday from 11am to 5pm.

The **Strand Arcade** (between Pitt Street Mall and George St.) was built in 1892 and is interesting for its architecture and small boutiques, food stores, and cafes, and the Downtown Duty Free store on the basement level. Labels to look for include Third Millennium, Allanah Hill, and Wayne Cooper.

On **Pitt Street Mall** you'll find a few shops and a Westfield Shopping Centre full of fashion boutiques. **Oxford Street** runs from the city to Bondi Junction through Paddington and Darlinghurst and is home to countless stylish clothing stores. You could spend anywhere from 2 hours to an entire day making your way from one end to the other. Detour down William Street, once you get to Paddington, to visit the headquarters of celebrated international Australian designer **Collette Dinnigan** and the trendy boutiques Belinda and Corner Store (cutting-edge designs), and Pelle and Di Nuovo (luxury recycled goods).

For Aboriginal artifacts and crafts, head to **Original & Authentic Aboriginal Art** (② 02/9251 4222) at 79 George St., The Rocks, which has quality Aboriginal art from some of Australia's best-known painters. Artists include Paddy Fordham Wainburranga, whose paintings hang in the White House in Washington, D.C., and Janet Forrester Nangala, whose work has been exhibited in the Australian National Gallery in Canberra.

The two big department store names in Sydney shopping are David Jones and Myer. **David Jones** (② 02/9266 5544; www.davidjones.com.au) is the city's largest

SYDNEY'S markets

Sydney has many good markets worth a look for quirky gifts or souvenirs and to soak up the local vibe, especially on weekends.

Closest to the city is **The Rocks Market** (www.therocks.com), held every Saturday and Sunday (with a smaller "foodies" market on Fri). This touristy market has more than 100 vendors selling everything from crafts, housewares, and posters to jewelry and curios. George Street in The Rocks is closed to traffic from 10am to 4pm to make it easier to stroll around.

Paddy's Markets (www.paddysmarkets.com.au) are a Sydney institution, with hundreds of stalls selling everything from cheap clothes and plants to chickens. It's open Wednesday to Sunday, 9am to 5pm. Above Paddy's Markets is **Market City,** which has three floors of fashion stalls, food courts, and specialty shops, and a huge Asian-European supermarket. Paddy's is at the corner of Thomas and Hay sts., Haymarket, near Chinatown.

Balmain Market (www.balmainmarket.com.au), held from 8:30am to 4pm every Saturday, has about 140 vendors selling crafts, jewelry, and knickknacks. Take the ferry to Balmain (Darling St.); the market is a 10-minute walk up Darling Street, on the grounds of St. Andrew's Church.

Bondi Markets (www.bondimarkets.com.au) is a nice place to stroll around on Sunday and discover upcoming young Australian designers. This market specializes in clothing and jewelry, new, secondhand, and retro. It's open Sunday from 9am to 5pm at the Bondi Beach School, Campbell Parade.

Paddington Markets (www.paddingtonmarkets.com.au) is a Saturday-only market where you'll find everything from essential oils and designer clothes to New Age jewelry and Mexican hammocks. Expect things to be busy from 10am to 4pm. Take bus no. 380 or 389 from Circular Quay and follow the crowds. It's held in the grounds of St. John's Church, Oxford St., on the corner of Newcome St.

department store, selling everything from fashion to designer furniture. You'll find the women's section on the corner of Elizabeth and Market streets, and the men's section on the corner of Castlereagh and Market streets. The food section offers expensive delicacies. **Myer** (© **02/9238 9111;** www.myer.com.au) is similar, but the building is newer and flashier. It's on the corner of George and Market streets.

Nearer to Circular Quay is **Chifley Plaza,** home to a selection of the world's most famous and stylish international brands. For really trendy clothing, walk up Oxford Street to **Paddington** or head to **Surry Hills,** and for alternative clothes, go to **Newtown.**

If you are looking for trendy surf- and swimwear, the main drags at Bondi Beach and Manly Beach offer plenty of choices.

For gifts and souvenirs, the shops at **Taronga Zoo,** the **Sydney Sealife Aquarium,** and the **Australian Museum** are all good sources for gifts and souvenirs. Many shops around **The Rocks** are worth browsing, too.

A DAY TRIP TO THE BLUE MOUNTAINS

Katoomba: 114km (71 miles) W of Sydney; Leura: 107km (66 miles) W of Sydney; 3km (2 miles) E of Katoomba; Blackheath: 114km (71 miles) W of Sydney; 14km (8¾ miles) NW of Katoomba; Wentworth Falls: 103km (64 miles) W of Sydney; 7km (4½ miles) E of Katoomba.

The **Blue Mountains** offer breathtaking views, rugged tablelands, sheer cliffs, deep, inaccessible valleys, enormous chasms, colorful parrots, cascading waterfalls, historic villages, and stupendous walking trails. In 2000, UNESCO classified it as a World Heritage Site. Although the Blue Mountains are where Sydneysiders now go to escape the humidity and crowds of the city, in the early days of the colony the mountains kept at bay those who wanted to explore the interior. In 1813, three explorers—Gregory Blaxland, William Charles Wentworth, and William Lawson—managed to conquer the cliffs, valleys, and dense forests and cross the mountains to the plains beyond. There they found land the colony urgently needed for grazing and farming. The **Great Western Highway** and **Bells Line of Road** are the access roads through the region today—winding and steep in places, they are surrounded by the Blue Mountains and Wollemi national parks.

This area is known for its spectacular scenery, particularly the cliff-top views into valleys of gum trees and across to craggy outcrops that tower from the valley floor. It's colder up here than in the city, and clouds can sweep in and fill the canyons with mist in minutes, while waterfalls cascade down sheer drops, spraying the dripping fern trees that cling to the gullies. A day tour may only scratch the surface but should give you a glimpse into why Sydneysiders love it.

There are four main towns in the Blue Mountains. **Katoomba** (pop. 11,200) is the largest and the focal point of the Blue Mountains National Park. It's an easy 1½- to 2-hour trip from Sydney by train, bus, or car.

Leura is known for its gardens, its attractive old buildings (many holiday homes for Sydneysiders), and its cafes and restaurants. Just outside Leura is the **Sublime Point Lookout,** which has spectacular views of the **Three Sisters** in Katoomba (see box on p. 83). From the southern end of Leura Mall, a cliff drive takes you all the way back to **Echo Point** in Katoomba; along the way you'll enjoy stunning views across the Jamison Valley.

The pretty town of **Wentworth Falls** has numerous crafts and antiques shops, but the area is principally known for its 281m (922-ft.) waterfall, situated in **Falls Reserve.** On the far side of the falls is the **National Pass Walk**—one of the best in the Blue Mountains. It's cut into a cliff face with overhanging rock faces on one side and sheer drops on the other. The views over the Jamison Valley are spectacular. The track takes you down to the base of the falls to the **Valley of the Waters.** Climbing up out of the valley is quite a bit more difficult, but just as rewarding.

Blackheath is the highest town in the Blue Mountains at 1,049m (3,441 ft.). Take the **Cliff Walk** from **Evans Lookout** to **Govetts Leap,** where there are magnificent

Color Me Blue

The Blue Mountains derive their name from the ever-present blue haze that is caused by light striking the droplets of eucalyptus oil that evaporate from the leaves of the dense surrounding forest.

views over the **Grose Valley** and **Bridal Veil Falls.** The 1½-hour trek passes through banksia, gum, and wattle forests, with wonderful views of mountain peaks and valleys.

The Blue Mountains are also one of Australia's best-known adventure playgrounds. Rock climbing, caving, abseiling (rappelling), bushwalking, mountain biking, horseback riding, and canoeing are practiced here year-round.

Essentials

GETTING THERE   By car from central Sydney, take Parramatta Road and turn off onto the M4 motorway (around 2 hr. to Katoomba). Another route is via the Harbour Bridge to North Sydney, along the Warringah Freeway (following signs to the M2). Then take the M2 to the end and follow signs to the M4 and the Blue Mountains. This takes around 1½ hours.

Frequent rail service connects Sydney to Katoomba and Blackheath from Central Station; contact **Sydney Trains** (© **13 15 00;** www.sydneytrains.info) for details. The train trip takes around 2 hours. Trains leave almost hourly. An adult same-day round-trip ticket costs around A$12 off-peak and A$17 during commuter hours. A child's ticket is about A$6. The **Blue Mountains ExplorerLink** ticket includes return train travel to Katoomba and a pass for the Explorer Bus (see "Getting Around," below) for either 1 or 3 days. The 1-day pass from Central Station is A$50 for adults and half-price for kids, but you can get on the train at other stations too (and the price may vary).

VISITOR INFORMATION   You can pick up maps, walking guides, and other information and book accommodations at **Blue Mountains Tourism,** Echo Point Road, Katoomba, (© **1300/653 408** in Australia; www.visitbluemountains.com.au). The information center is an attraction itself, with glass windows overlooking a gum forest, and cockatoos and lorikeets feeding on seed dispensers. It's open from 9am to 5pm daily (closed Christmas Day).

The **Blue Mountains Heritage Centre,** end of Govetts Leap Road, Blackheath (© **02/4787 8877;** www.nationalparks.nsw.gov.au), is run by the National Parks and Wildlife Service and offers detailed information about the Blue Mountains National Park. It's open daily from 9am to 4:30pm (closed Christmas Day).

Another good website is **www. bluemts.com.au.**

> ### Timing Is Everything: When to Visit
>
> If you can, try to visit the Blue Mountains on **weekdays,** when most Sydney-siders are at work and prices are lower. Note that the colder winter months (June–Aug) are the busiest season.

GETTING AROUND   The best way to get around the Blue Mountains without a car is the **Blue Mountains Explorer** bus (© **1300/300 915** in Australia or 02/4782 1866; www.explorer bus.com.au). You can buy a combined train/bus pass (see Blue Mountains ExplorerLink above). The double-decker "hop-on, hop-off" bus leaves from outside the Katoomba train station about every 30 minutes between 9:45am and 4:05pm and stops at 29 attractions, resorts, galleries, and tearooms in and around Katoomba and Leura. Tickets cost A$38 for adults, A$19 for children, and A$95 for a family; other passes include rides on the Scenic Railway and the Skyway (see "Exploring the Blue Mountains," below).

A similar but cheaper option is **Trolley Tours** (© **1800/801 577** in Australia or 02/4748 7999; www.trolleytours.com.au), a kind of tram on wheels with commentary.

An all-day pass costs A$25 and includes stops at 29 various attractions around Katoomba and Leura. The trolley leaves from outside the Carrington Hotel on Katoomba Street once an hour from 9:45am until 4:45pm.

Tours

Many private bus operators offer day trips from Sydney, but it's important to shop around. Some offer a guided coach tour, during which you just stretch your legs occasionally, while others let you get your circulation going with a couple of longish bushwalks. Remember, this will be a long day, leaving at 7am or 8am and returning to the city at about 6pm.

Trips with **Oz Trek Adventure Tours** (℗ **1300/661 234** in Australia, or 02/9666 4262; www.oztrek.com.au) include all the major Blue Mountain sites, and time for a bushwalk; it costs A$59 per person. **Sydney Tours-R-Us** (℗ **02/9498 4084;** www.sydneytoursrus.com) runs minicoaches to the Blue Mountains, stopping off at the Telstra Stadium (where the Sydney Olympics were held) on the way. Then you see all the major sights in the mountains and come home via ferry from Parramatta to Circular Quay. The trip costs A$110 for adults and A$85 for kids ages 4 to 12 (not including lunch). **Wonderbus Tours** (℗ **02/9637 4466;** www.wonderbus.com.au) offers a Blue Mountains tour for A$165 for adults and A$113 for kids 3 to 12, including all entry fees and lunch. You also come back by ferry. All these tours include a stop at Featherdale Wildlife Park (see p. 72).

Blue Mountains Walkabout (℗ **0408/443 822** mobile; www.bluemountains walkabout.com) is owned and operated by Aboriginal man Evan Yanna Muru. This guided walk follows a traditional walkabout song line for about 8km (5 miles), exploring part of the Blue Mountains wilderness for a full day (about 3½ hr. walking and 4 hr. of relaxation and activities). You'll see ancient art, ceremonial sites, and artifacts, and hear Dreamtime stories. Also included is ochre-bark and body painting, bushtucker tastings, wildlife viewing, sandstone cave exploring, and bathing in a crystal-clear billabong (pool) below a waterfall. You should be reasonably fit. Bring wet-weather gear, good boots or walking shoes, lots of water, and lunch. The trek costs A$95 per person (no kids under 7). The walk begins in the Blue Mountains on Faulconbridge Railway Station platform at 10:35am weekdays and 10:45am weekends and public holidays. Take the train from Central Station in Sydney (see "Getting There," p. 82).

The Legend of the Three Sisters

The Aboriginal Dreamtime legend has it that three sisters, Meehni, Wimlah, and Gunnedoo, lived in the Jamison Valley as members of the Katoomba tribe. These beautiful young women had fallen in love with three brothers from the Nepean tribe, yet tribal law forbade them to marry. The brothers were not happy to accept this law and so decided to use force to capture the three sisters, which caused a major tribal battle. As the lives of the three sisters were in danger, a witch doctor from the Katoomba tribe took it upon himself to turn the three sisters into stone to protect them from any harm. He had intended to reverse the spell later, but was killed in the battle and the sisters were doomed to remain in their magnificent rock formation forever.

Exploring the Blue Mountains

Almost every other activity in the Blue Mountains costs money, but bushwalking (hiking) is the exception. There are some 50 walking trails, ranging from routes you can cover in 15 minutes to the 3-day **Six Foot Track.** The staff at the national park and tourist offices will be happy to point you in the right direction.

The most visited and photographed attractions in the Blue Mountains are the rock formations known as the **Three Sisters.** For the best vantage point, head to **Echo Point Road,** across from the Blue Mountains Tourism office. Or try Evans Lookout, Govetts Leap, and Hargreaves Lookout, all at Blackheath.

Four-attractions-in-one are offered at **Scenic World** (✆ **1300/759 929** in Australia or 02/4780 0200; www.scenicworld.com.au). The **Scenic Railway,** the world's steepest, consists of a carriage on rails that is lowered 415m (1,361 ft.) into the Jamison Valley at a maximum incline of 52 degrees. It's *very* steep and quite a thrill. The trip takes only a few minutes; at the bottom is the 2.4km **Scenic Walkway,** a boardwalk through forests of ancient tree ferns. Another way to get down is on the **Scenic Cableway,** not to be confused with the **Scenic Skyway,** a different form of cable car that travels 270m (885 ft.) above—and across—the Jamison Valley, between two cliffs. A ticket that includes all four attractions costs A$35 adults, A$18 children 4 to 12, and A$88 families of up to 7 (you can't buy separate tickets for any of the attractions). Scenic World is open 9am to 5pm daily. You'll find it on Violet Street (corner of Cliff Dr.), Katoomba.

If you are driving back to Sydney, take the Bells Line of Road through Bilpin and stop off at the wonderful **Blue Mountains Botanic Garden** (✆ **02/4567 3000;** www.mounttomahbotanicgarden.com.au) at Mount Tomah. (You can't miss the large sign on your right about 10 min. before you get to Bilpin.) It is an adjunct of the Royal Botanic Gardens in Sydney and well worth a stop.

> ### Seeing the Blue Mountains from the Back of a Harley
>
> A thrilling way to see the Blue Mountains is on the back of a chauffeur-driven Harley-Davidson motorcycle. **Wild Ride Australia** (✆ **1300/783 338,** or 0410/418 740 mobile; www.wildride.com.au) will take you on a 1-hour exhilarating ride to see some of the sights around Katoomba. Rides cost A$130.

Where to Eat

Katoomba Street has many ethnic dining choices, whether you're hungry for Greek, Chinese, or Thai. Restaurants in the Blue Mountains are generally more expensive than equivalent places in Sydney. In addition to the ones below, try the **Elephant Bean,** at 159 Katoomba Rd. (✆ **02/4782 4620**), for hearty soups, burgers, muffins, and good coffee.

Conservation Hut Café ★ CAFE   This pleasant cafe is in the national park on top of a cliff overlooking the Jamison Valley. It's a good place for a bit of lunch on the balcony after the Valley of the Waters walk, which leaves from outside. In addition to lighter meals like soup or a vegetable stack, dishes may include a Thai-style chicken curry or roast pork loin. It has vegetarian and great breakfast/brunch options, too. There's a nice log fire inside in winter. Children are welcome.

Fletcher St., Wentworth Falls. ✆**02/4757 3827.** www.conservationhut.com.au. Lunch items A$14–A$29; dinner mains A$23–A$30. Sun–Thurs 9am–5pm; Fri–Sat 9am–late; daily 10am–5pm in winter.

Paragon Café ★★ CAFE   The Paragon has been a Blue Mountains institution since it opened for business in 1916. It's worth stopping here—even if it's just for morning or afternoon tea—to see the wonderful richly detailed Art Deco interior. As well as delicious food—try the homemade soups or light lunches (or a steak if you're here for dinner on a Saturday night)—you may also come away with Paragon's handmade chocolates!

65 Katoomba St., Katoomba. ℂ **02/4782 2928.** Main courses A$10–A$24. Mon–Thurs 11am–3pm; Fri 11am–9pm, Sat 10am–11pm, Sun 10am–4pm.

MELBOURNE

It's rare to find anyone who lives in Melbourne who doesn't adore it. I've lived there, and I love it too, and I hope this chapter explains to you the many reasons why. Victoria's capital, Melbourne (pronounced *Mel*-bun), is a cultural melting pot. For a start, more people of Greek descent live here than in any other city except Athens, Greece. Multitudes of Chinese, Italian, Vietnamese, and Lebanese immigrants have all left their mark. Almost a third of Melburnians were born overseas or have parents who were born overseas. With such a diverse population—and with trams rattling through the streets and stately European-style architecture surrounding you—it is sometimes easy to think you are somewhere else.

Melbourne's roots can be traced back to the 1850s, when gold was found in the surrounding hills. British settlers took up residence and prided themselves on coming freely to their city, rather than having been forced here in convict chains. The city grew wealthy and remained a conservative bastion until World War II, when another wave of immigration, mainly from southern Europe, made it a more relaxed place.

With elegant tree-lined boulevards and a raging cafe culture, Victoria's capital maintains a distinctly European feel. Expect wonderful architecture both old and new and green spaces like the Royal Botanic Gardens. Wander down atmospheric laneways, often adorned with street art. This cosmopolitan city is also Australia's culture capital, with vibrant dining, shopping, and nightlife scenes.

In fact, Melbourne, which has a population of more than 3 million, is at the head of the pack when it comes to shopping, restaurants, fashion, music, nightlife, and cafe culture. It frequently beats other state capitals in bids for major concerts, plays, exhibitions, and sporting events. Oh, and everyone wears black.

ESSENTIALS

Arriving

BY PLANE   **Qantas** (℃ **13 13 13** in Australia; www.qantas.com.au) and **Virgin Australia** (℃ **13 67 89** in Australia; www.virginaustralia.com.au) both fly to Melbourne from all state capitals and some regional centers. Qantas's discount arm, **Jetstar** (℃ **13 15 38** in Australia; www.jetstar.com. au) flies to and from Sydney, Brisbane, Cairns, Townsville, Hamilton Island, the Sunshine Coast and Gold Coast, and varies other cities around the country. Jetstar also flies between **Avalon Airport,** about a 50-minute drive outside Melbourne's city center, and Sydney and Brisbane. Low-cost carrier **Tigerair** (℡ **03/9335 3033;** www.tigerairways.com) also has its hub in Melbourne, and from there flies to Sydney, Alice Springs, Cairns, Brisbane, and the Gold and Sunshine Coasts in Queensland, and several other cities.

Melbourne Airport's international and domestic terminals (www.melair.com.au) are all under one roof at Tullamarine, 22km (14 miles) northwest of the city center (often referred to as Tullamarine Airport). Tigerair has a separate terminal next door, distinguished by the tiger-striped water-tower landmark outside it. Travelers' information desks are on the ground floor of both the international and domestic terminals, open from 6am until the last flight. The international terminal has snack bars, a restaurant, currency-exchange facilities, and duty-free shops. ATMs are available at both terminals. Showers are on the first floor of the international area. Baggage carts are free in the international baggage claim hall but cost A$4 in the parking lot, departure lounge, or domestic terminal. Baggage storage is available in the international terminal and costs from A$12 to A$25 per day, depending on size. The storage desk is open from 5am to 12:30am daily, and you need photo ID. There are three airport hotels: **Parkroyal Melbourne Airport** (℡ **03/8347 2000**), **Holiday Inn Melbourne Airport** (℡ **03/9933 5111**) and **Ibis Budget Melbourne Airport** (℡ **03/8336 1811**), all within 5 minutes' walk of the terminals.

Avis (℡ **13 63 33** in Australia, or 03/9338 1800), **Budget** (℡ **13 27 27** in Australia or 039241 6366), **Europcar** (℡ **1300/131 390** in Australia or 03/9241 6800), **Hertz** (℡ **13 30 39** in Australia or 03/9338 4044), **Thrifty** (℡ **1300/367 227** in Australia or 03/9241 6100) and **Redspot** (℡ **1300/668 810** in Australia or 02/8303 2222) all have airport rental desks. The Tullamarine freeway to and from the airport joins with the CityLink, an electronic toll-way system. Drivers need a CityLink pass. Check with your car-rental company.

The distinctive red **Skybus** (℡ **03/9600 1711;** www.skybus.com.au) runs between the airport and Melbourne's Southern Cross station in Spencer Street every 10 to 15 minutes throughout the day and every 30 to 60 minutes overnight, 24 hours a day, every day. Buy tickets from Skybus desks outside the baggage claim areas or at the information desk in the international terminal. A free Skybus hotel shuttle will pick you up at your hotel to connect with the larger airport-bound bus at Southern Cross railway station in the city center, but you must book this. It operates from 6am to 10:30pm weekdays and 7:30am to 5:30pm weekends. One-way tickets cost A$17 for adults, and A$28 gets you a two-way journey. Kids aged 4 to 14 cost A$6.50 each way. Family tickets cost A$24 to A$38A for up to six people or A$40 to A$65 round-trip. The trip takes about 20 minutes from the airport to Southern Cross station, but allow longer for your return journey.

Sita Coaches (℡ **03/9689 7999;** www.sitacoaches.com.au) operates a transfer service to Avalon Airport for Jetstar flights. One-way fares from Avalon Airport are A$22 for adults and A$10 for children 4 to 14 to Southern Cross station, more to other CBD locations and other suburbs.

A **taxi** to the city center takes about 30 minutes and costs around A$55.

BY TRAIN Interstate trains arrive at **Southern Cross Railway Station,** Spencer and Little Collins streets (5 blocks from Swanston St., in the city center). You may often hear locals refer to it as Spencer Street Station. Taxis and buses connect with the city.

The **Sydney–Melbourne** *XPT* travels between Australia's two largest cities daily; trip time is 11 hours. For more information, contact **NSW Trainlink** (𝒞 **13 22 32** in Australia; www.nswtrainlink.info). **V/Line** (𝒞 **13 61 96** in Australia or 03/9697 2076; www.vline.com.au) services also connect Melbourne with country Victoria destinations and other capital cities.

BY BUS   Several bus companies connect Melbourne with other capitals and regional areas of Victoria. Among the biggest are **Greyhound Australia** (𝒞 **1300/473 946** in Australia, or 03/9642 8562; www.greyhound.com.au). Coaches serve Melbourne's **Transit Centre,** 58 Franklin St., two blocks north of the Southern Cross Railway station on Spencer Street. Trams and taxis serve the station; **V/Line buses** (𝒞 **13 61 96** in Australia; www.vline.com.au), which travel all over Victoria, depart from the Spencer Street Coach Terminal.

BY CAR   You can drive from Sydney to Melbourne along the Hume Highway (a straight trip of about 9½ hr.). Another route is along the coastal Princes Highway, for which you will need a minimum of 2 days, with stops. For information on all aspects of road travel in Victoria, contact the **Royal Automotive Club of Victoria** (𝒞 **13 13 29** in Australia or 03/8792 4006; www.racv.com.au).

Visitor Information

The first stop on any visitor's itinerary should be the **Melbourne Visitor Centre,** Federation Square, Swanston and Flinders streets (𝒞 **03/9658 9658;** www.thats melbourne.com.au). The center serves as a one-stop shop for tourism information, accommodations and tour bookings, event ticketing, public transport information, and ticket sales. Also here are an ATM, Internet terminals, and interactive multimedia providing information on Melbourne and Victoria. The center is open daily from 9am to 6pm (except Christmas Day). The **Melbourne Greeter Service** also operates from the Melbourne Visitor Centre. This service connects visitors to enthusiastic local volunteers who offer free one-on-one, half-day orientation tours of the city at 9:30am daily. Book at least 24 hours in advance (𝒞 **03/9658 9658** on weekdays, 03/9658 9942 on weekends). The Melbourne Visitor Centre also operates a staffed information booth in Bourke Street Mall, between Swanston and Elizabeth streets, open daily 9am to 5pm. In the central city area (mainly along Swanston St.), also look for **Melbourne's City Ambassadors**—people, usually volunteers, who give tourist information and directions. They'll be wearing bright red shirts and caps.

Good websites about the city include **CitySearch Melbourne, http://melbourne. citysearch.com.au;** as well as the official City of Melbourne site, **www.melbourne. vic.gov.au;** and the official tourism site for the city, **www.visitmelbourne.com.** Also worth a look is the locally run site **www.onlymelbourne.com.au.**

City Layout

Melbourne is on the Yarra River and stretches inland from Port Philip Bay, which lies to its south. On a map, you'll see a distinct central oblong area surrounded by Flinders Street to the south, Latrobe Street to the north, Spring Street to the east, and Spencer Street to the west. Cutting north to south through its center are the two main shopping thoroughfares, Swanston Street and Elizabeth Street. Cross streets between these major thoroughfares include Bourke Street Mall, a pedestrian-only shopping promenade. If you continue south along Swanston Street and over the river, it turns into

St. Kilda Road, which runs to the coast. Melbourne's various urban "villages," including South Yarra, Richmond, Carlton, and Fitzroy, surround the city center. The seaside suburb of St. Kilda is known for its diverse restaurants.

Neighborhoods in Brief

At more than 7,695sq. km (2,971 sq. miles), Melbourne is one of the biggest cities in the world by area, with a population of about 3½ million. Below are the neighborhoods of most interest to visitors.

CITY CENTER Made up of a grid of streets north of the Yarra River, the city center is bordered by Flinders, Latrobe, Spring, and Spencer streets. There's good shopping and charming cafes, and in recent years an active nightlife has sprung up with the opening of a swath of funky bars and restaurants playing live and recorded music to suit all ages. The gateway to the city is the Flinders Street Station, with its dome and clock tower, flanked by the Federation Square precinct.

CHINATOWN This colorful section centers on Little Bourke Street between Swanston and Exhibition streets. The area marks Australia's oldest permanent Chinese settlement, dating from the 1850s, when a few boardinghouses catered to Chinese prospectors lured by gold rushes. Plenty of cheap restaurants crowd its alleyways. Tram: Any to the city.

CARLTON North of the center, Carlton is a rambling suburb famous for Italian restaurants along Lygon Street with outdoor seating—though the quality of the food varies. It's the home of Melbourne University, so there's a healthy student scene. From Bourke Street Mall, it's a 15-minute walk to the restaurants. Tram: 1 or 22 from Swanston Street.

FITZROY A ruggedly bohemian place 2km (1¼ miles) north of the city center, Fitzroy is raw and funky, filled with students and artists and popular for people-watching. Fitzroy revolves around Brunswick Street, with its cheap restaurants, busy cafes, late-night bookshops, art galleries, and pubs. Around the corner, on Johnston Street, is a growing Spanish quarter with tapas bars, flamenco restaurants, and Spanish clubs. Tram: 11 from Collins Street.

RICHMOND One of Melbourne's earliest settlements is a multicultural quarter noted for its historic streets and back lanes. Victoria Street is reminiscent of Ho Chi Minh City, with Vietnamese sights, sounds, aromas, and restaurants everywhere. Bridge Road is a discount-fashion precinct. Tram: 48 or 75 from Flinders Street to Bridge Road; 70 from Batman Avenue at Princes Bridge to Swan Street; 109 from Bourke Street to Victoria Street.

SOUTHGATE & SOUTHBANK This flashy entertainment district on the banks of the Yarra River opposite Flinders Street station (linked by pedestrian bridges) is home to the Crown Casino, Australia's largest gaming venue. Southbank has a myriad of restaurants, bars, cafes, nightclubs, cinemas, and designer shops. On the city side of the river is the Melbourne Aquarium. All are a 10-minute stroll from Flinders Street Station. Tram: 8 from Swanston Street.

DOCKLANDS Near the city center, at the rear of the Spencer Street station, this industrial area has become the biggest development in Melbourne. NewQuay on the waterfront has a diverse range of restaurants, shops, and cinemas. This is also where you'll find Melbourne's celebration of the dominance of Australian Rules football, the 52,000-seat Etihad Stadium. Docklands is accessible by the free City Circle Tram.

ST. KILDA Hip and bohemian in a shabby-chic sort of way, this bayside suburb (6km/3¾ miles south of the city center) has Melbourne's highest concentration of restaurants, ranging from glitzy to cheap, as well as some superb cake shops and delis. Historically it was Melbourne's red-light district. The Esplanade hugs a beach with a vintage pier and a lively arts-and-crafts market on Sundays. Acland Street houses many restaurants. Check out Luna Park, one of the world's oldest fun parks, built in 1912, and ride the wooden roller coaster. Tram: 10 or 12 from Collins Street; 15 or 16 from Swanston Street; 96 from Bourke Street.

SOUTH YARRA/PRAHRAN This posh part of town abounds with boutiques, cinemas, nightclubs, and galleries. Chapel Street is famous for its upscale eateries and designer-fashion houses, while Commercial Road is popular with the gay and lesbian community. Off Chapel Street in Prahran is Greville Street, a bohemian enclave of retro boutiques and music outlets. Every Sunday from noon to 5pm, the Greville Street Market offers arts, crafts, old clothes, and jewelry. Tram: 8 or 72 from Swanston Street.

SOUTH MELBOURNE One of the city's oldest working-class districts, South Melbourne is known for its historic buildings, old-fashioned pubs and hotels, and markets. Tram: 12 from Collins Street; 1 from Swanston Street.

THE RIVER DISTRICT The muddy-looking Yarra River runs southeast past the Royal Botanic Gardens and near other attractions such as the Arts Centre, the National Gallery of Victoria, the Sidney Myer Music Bowl, the Melbourne Cricket Ground, and Birrarung Marr parkland. It is accessible by the free City Circle Tram.

WILLIAMSTOWN A lack of extensive development has left this waterfront suburb with a rich architectural heritage. It centers on Ferguson Street and Nelson Place—both reminiscent of old England. On the Strand overlooking the sea is a line of bistros and restaurants and a World War II warship museum. Ferry: From Southgate, the World Trade Center, or St. Kilda Pier.

GETTING AROUND
By Public Transportation

Trams are the major form of transport in the city; you will probably only use a train or bus if you are going into the suburbs. Melbourne's transport system uses an electronic ticketing system called **myki,** a reusable smart card that stores either a **myki pass** (travel days) or **myki money** (dollar value) to pay for your travel. You "touch on" and "touch off" at an electronic machine on board the tram or bus, or as you enter the train station. When your myki balance gets low or your pass runs out, you just top up your card. **Myki money** is a dollar amount (minimum A$10), and when you touch on and touch off as you travel, the system calculates the best available fare for the journey. With myki money you aren't restricted to zones, as you pay for what you use. A 2-hour trip in Zone 1, which will allow you to travel on all trams and trains within the city and close surrounding suburbs mentioned in this chapter from 5:30am to midnight (when transportation stops), will cost you A$3.50 or a daily fare of A$7. The maximum daily myki money fare is $12, for travel in Zones 1 and 2, but on a Saturday, Sunday, or public holiday, you will pay the off-peak rate of $3.50 per day. A **7-day myki pass** will cost $35 to travel in Zone 1. You can get cards at Flinders Street or Southern Cross stations or at the MetShop (see below) and top them up through the Public Transport Victoria website (www.ptv.vic.gov.au) or at the call center (© **1800/800 007**); or top up as little as A$1 at myki machines in train stations and at selected tram platforms and bus interchanges.

You can pick up a free route map from the Melbourne Visitor Centre, Federation Square, or from the **PTV Hub** at Southern Cross station (© **1800/800 007** in Australia;

www.ptv.vic.gov.au), which is open Monday through Friday from 7am to 7pm, and weekends and public holidays (except Christmas Day) 9am to 6pm. There's another hub at 750 Collins St., Docklands, open from 8am to 6pm weekdays only (except public holidays).

BY TRAM Melbourne has the oldest tram network in the world. Trams are an essential part of the city, a major cultural icon, and a great non-smoggy way of getting around. Several hundred trams run over 325km (202 miles) of track.

Trams stop at numbered tram-stop signs, sometimes in the middle of the road (so beware of oncoming traffic!). To get off the tram, press the button near the handrails or pull the cord above your head.

The **City Circle Tram** is the best way to get around the center of Melbourne—and it's free. The burgundy-and-cream trams travel a circular route between all the major central attractions, and past shopping malls and arcades. The trams run, in both directions, every 12 minutes between 10am and 6pm (and until 9pm Thurs–Sat), except on Good Friday and Christmas Day. The trams run along all the major thoroughfares including Flinders and Spencer streets. Burgundy signs mark City Circle Tram stops.

BY BUS The free **Melbourne City Tourist Shuttle** operates buses that pick up and drop off at 13 stops around the city, including Federation Square, the Melbourne Museum, Queen Victoria Market, Immigration Museum, Southbank Arts Precinct, the Shrine of Remembrance and Botanic Gardens, Chinatown, and many other attractions. You can hop on and off during the day. The entire loop takes about 90 minutes nonstop, and there's a commentary. The bus runs every 30 minutes from 9:30am until 4:30pm daily (except Christmas Day, and with limited service on some public holidays).

By Taxi

Cabs are plentiful in the city, but it may be difficult to hail one in the city center late on Friday and Saturday night. From 10pm to 5am, anywhere in Victoria, you must prepay your fare. The driver estimates the fare at the start of the journey, gives you a receipt, and then adjusts it according to the meter reading plus any fees such as road tolls, at the end of your trip. Taxi companies include **Silver Top** (✆ **13 10 08** in Australia), **Embassy** (✆ **13 17 55** in Australia), and **Yellow Cabs** (✆ **13 22 27** in Australia).

By Car

Driving in Melbourne can be challenging. Roads can be confusing, there are trams everywhere, and there is a rule about turning right from the left lane at major intersections in the downtown center and in South Melbourne (which leaves the left lane free for trams and through traffic). Here, you must wait for the lights to turn amber before turning. Also, you must always stop behind a tram if it stops, because passengers usually step directly into the road. Add to this the general lack of parking and expensive hotel valet parking, and you'll know why it's better to avoid driving and get on a tram instead. For road rules, pick up a copy of the Victorian Road Traffic handbook from bookshops or from a **Vic Roads** office (✆ **13 11 71** in Australia for the nearest office).

Major car-rental companies, all with offices at Tullamarine Airport, include **Avis,** Shop 2, 8 Franklin St. (✆ **03/9204 3933**); **Budget,** Shop 3, 8 Franklin St. (✆ **03/9203**

4844); **Europcar,** 89 Franklin St. (✆ **03/8633 0000**); **Hertz,** 97 Franklin St. (✆ **13 30 39** in Australia, or 03/9663 4205); and **Thrifty,** 390 Elizabeth St. (✆ **1300/367 227** in Australia or 03/8661 6000).

[Fast FACTS] MELBOURNE

ATMs/Banks Banks are open Monday through Thursday from 9:30am to 4pm, and Friday from 9:30am to 5pm.

Business Hours In general, stores are open Monday through Wednesday and Saturday from 9am to 5:30pm, Thursday from 9am to 6pm, Friday from 9am to 9pm, and Sunday from 10am to 5pm. The larger department stores stay open on Thursday until 6pm and Friday until 9pm.

Dentists The **Royal Dental Hospital of Melbourne** (✆ **03/9341 1000**), at 720 Swanston St., Carlton, offers emergency services 9am to 9:15pm daily.

Doctors & Hospitals The "casualty" department at the **Royal Melbourne Hospital,** 300 Grattan St., Parkville (✆ **03/9342 7000**), responds to emergencies. The **Traveller's Medical & Vaccination Centre,** Second Floor, 393 Little Bourke St. (✆ **03/9935 8100;** www.travel doctor.com.au), offers full

vaccination and travel medical services.

Embassies & Consulates The following English-speaking countries have consulates in Melbourne: **United States,** Level 6, 553 St. Kilda Rd. (✆ **03/9526 5900**); **United Kingdom,** Level 17, 90 Collins St. (✆ **03/9652 1600**); and **New Zealand,** Level 4, 45 William St. (✆ **03/9678 0201**).

Emergencies In an emergency, call ✆ **000** for police, ambulance, or the fire department.

Internet Access The **State Library of Victoria,** 328 Swanston St. (✆ **03/ 8864 7000;** www.slv.vic.gov. au), has free wireless Internet in all areas of the library and powerpoints in all reading rooms. There are many Internet cafes along Elizabeth Street, between Flinders and Latrobe streets, and around Flinders Lane and Little Bourke Street in Chinatown. Most are open from early until well into the night.

Mail & Postage The **General Post Office (GPO)** at 250 Elizabeth St. (✆ **13 13 18** in Australia) is open Monday through Friday 8:30am to 5:30pm and on Saturday 9am to 5pm.

Newspapers & Magazines Melbourne's daily newspapers are *The Age* and the *Herald-Sun.* Both have Sunday versions as well.

Pharmacies (Chemist Shops) The **Mulqueeny Pharmacy,** 99 Swanston St. (✆ **03/9654 8569**), is open Monday through Friday from 8am to 8pm, Saturday from 9am to 6pm, and Sunday 11am to 6pm. The **Mulqueeny Midnight Pharmacy,** 416 High St., Prahran (✆ **03/9510 6130**), is open every day of the year until midnight.

Safety St. Kilda might be coming up in the world, but walking there alone at night still isn't wise. Parks and gardens can also be risky at night, as can the area around the King Street nightclubs.

WHERE TO STAY

Getting a room is easy enough on weekends, when business travelers are back home. You need to book well in advance, however, during the city's hallmark events (say, the weekend before the Melbourne Cup, and during the Grand Prix and the Australian Open). Hostels in the St. Kilda area tend to fill up quickly in December and January.

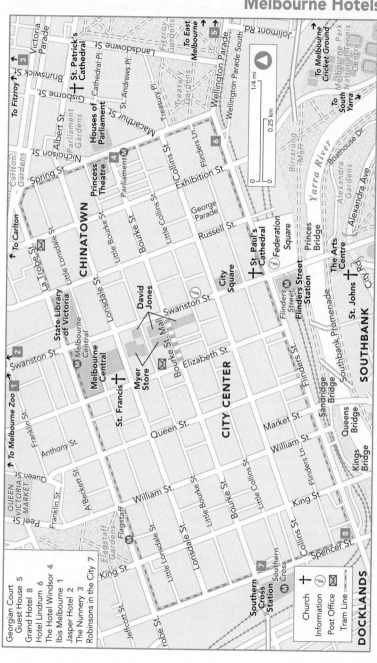

Georgian Court Guest House 5
Grand Hotel 8
Hotel Lindrum 6
The Hotel Windsor 4
Ibis Melbourne 1
Jasper Hotel 2
The Nunnery 3
Robinsons in the City 7

Church
Information
Post Office
Tram Line

DOCKLANDS

Southern Cross Station
Southern Cross

CITY CENTER

CHINATOWN

SOUTHBANK

QUEEN VICTORIA MARKET

To Melbourne Zoo
To Fitzroy
To Carlton

St. Patrick's Cathedral
Houses of Parliament
Princess Theatre
State Library of Victoria
Melbourne Central
St. Francis
Myer Store
David Jones
St. Paul's Cathedral
Federation Square
City Square
St. Johns
The Arts Centre

Victoria Parade
Brunswick St.
Gisborne St.
Albert St.
Nicholson St.
Spring St.
Cathedral Pl.
St. Andrews Pl.
Landsdowne St.
Macarthur St.
Treasury Pl.
Wellington Parade South
Wellington Parade
Jolimont Rd.
To East Melbourne
To Melbourne Cricket Ground
To Melbourne Park National Tennis Centre
To South Yarra

Carlton Gardens
Parliament Gardens
Fitzroy Gardens
Treasury Gardens
Birrarung Marr
Yarra River
Alexandra Gardens
Boathouse Dr.
Alexandra Ave.

La Trobe St.
Little Lonsdale St.
Lonsdale St.
Little Bourke St.
Bourke St.
Little Collins St.
Collins St.
Flinders Ln.
Flinders St.
Exhibition St.
Russell St.
Swanston St.
Elizabeth St.
Bourke St. Mall
George Parade
Swanston St.
Franklin St.
Anthony St.
A'Beckett St.
Queen St.
William St.
Market St.
King St.
Spencer St.
Collins St.
Jeffcott St.
Trobe St.
Franklin St.
Peel St.
Flagstaff Gardens

Parliament
Melbourne Central
Flinders Street Station
Flinders St.

Princes Bridge
Sandridge Bridge
Queens Bridge
Kings Bridge
Southbank Promenade
Southern Cross
City Rd.

1/4 mi
0.25 km
0

You'll feel right in the heart of the action if you stay in the city center, which seems to buzz all day (and night). Otherwise, the inner-city suburbs are all exciting satellites, with good street life, restaurants, and pubs—and just a quick tram ride from the city center. Transportation from the airport to the suburbs is a little more expensive and complicated than to the city center, however.

The **Best of Victoria** booking service, Federation Square (📞 **1300/780 045** in Australia, or 03/9928 0000; www.bestof.com.au), opens daily 9am to 6pm, can help you book accommodations after you arrive in the city.

In the City Center

EXPENSIVE

Grand Hotel Melbourne ★★   This majestic heritage-listed six-story building, which was originally home to the Victorian railway administration, is striking for its remarkable scale and imposing Italianate facade. Building started in 1887, and it became a hotel in 1997. Suites have plush carpets and full kitchens with dishwashers; one-bedroom loft suites have European-style espresso machines and a second TV in the bedroom, and some have great views over the new Docklands area beyond—though rooms are whisper-quiet. All are similar but vary in size; some have balconies (mostly on the sixth floor). Many of the one- and two-bedroom suites are split-level, with bedrooms on the second floor.

33 Spencer St., Melbourne, VIC 3000. www.grandhotelmelbourne.com.au. 📞 **1300/361 455** in Australia, or 03/9611 4567. 94 units. A$229–A$259 studio; from A$239 1-bedroom suite; from A$329 2-bedroom suite. Extra person A$55. Free crib. Parking A$35. Tram: 48 or 75 from Flinders St. **Amenities:** Restaurant; bar; babysitting; concierge; golf course nearby; exercise room; Jacuzzi; heated indoor swimming pool (with retractable roof); room service; sauna; Wi-Fi (A$28/24 hr.).

Hotel Lindrum ★★   If you like your hotels stylish and contemporary, then this is the place for you. It's quite typical of the new wave of modern hotels that emphasize trendy interior design. Standard rooms, if you can call them that, have queen-size beds or two singles, lots of hardwood, soft lighting, and forest-green tones. Superior rooms have king-size beds and lovely polished wood floorboards, and deluxe rooms have wonderful views across to the Botanic Gardens through large bay windows. The hotel boasts a smart restaurant, a billiards room, and a bar with an open fire.

26 Flinders St., Melbourne, VIC 3000. www.hotellindrum.com.au. 📞 **03/9668 1111.** 59 units. A$235 standard double; A$265 superior room; A$305 deluxe room; A$330 suite. Parking off-site A$20. **Amenities:** Restaurant; bar; nearby health club; room service; free Wi-Fi.

The Hotel Windsor ★★   By the time you arrive at the Windsor, a long-awaited, controversial A$285-million redevelopment and restoration of one of Australia's grandest and most historic hotels will possibly be underway. Or not . . . depending on the progress of the applications, objections, and appeals that have been raging for several years now. The Windsor opened in 1883, an upper-crust establishment that has oozed sophistication and hosted the rich, famous, and glamorous. The hotel holds a special place in Australia's history as the setting for the drafting of the country's Constitution in 1898. The planned facelift, expected to take 2 years (once it starts), would add a 26-story tower (and 152 guest rooms) behind the heritage building. But some things won't ever change: The renowned "high tea" will continue to be served each afternoon, as it has been for 130 years. Many guest bedrooms have striking views of Parliament House and the Treasury Gardens.

MELBOURNE'S art hotels

Melbourne's Deague family has combined a passion for the arts and a desire to join the global boutique hotel trend by dedicating a series of hotels to well-known Australian artists. The flagship of the **Art Series Hotel Group** is **The Olsen,** at Chapel Street and Toorak Road, South Yarra (*© 03/9040 1222*), named for the man regarded as Australia's greatest living painter, John Olsen. It has 229 rooms and claims to have the world's largest glass-bottomed swimming pool, suspended over the street. Rates start from A$249 double per night for a studio suite. **The Cullen,** a 115-room boutique hotel and entertainment precinct at 164 Commercial Rd., Prahran (*© 03/9098 1555*), is named after the controversial artist Adam Cullen, and has a rooftop cocktail bar and two

restaurants. **The Blackman,** named for Sydney artist John Blackman and housed within the heritage-listed Airlie House (backed by a modern high-rise annex), at 452 St. Kilda Rd. (*© 03/9039 1444*), has 207 rooms.

Each hotel features a major artwork commissioned especially for the hotel foyer by the naming artist, including one from Adam Cullen's *Ned Kelly* series and Olsen's 6m (19-ft.) mural *The Yellow Sun and Yarra,* set in the spectacular glass lobby of the Olsen. Prints and a photographic history of each artist's life adorn walls of rooms and public spaces of the hotels while the architecture, interior design, linens, and stationery also reflect the artist's style. Visit **www.artseries hotels.com.au.**

103 Spring St., Melbourne, VIC 3000. www.thewindsor.com.au. *© 03/9633 6000.* 332 units. A$179–A$269 double; A$319–A$619 double suite. Valet parking A$40 per night. **Amenities:** Restaurant; 2 bars; babysitting; concierge; health club; room service; Wi-Fi (A$25/24 hr.).

MODERATE

Ibis Melbourne ★   A good deal, the Hotel Ibis is next door to a tram stop, close to the bus station, and a short walk from the central shopping areas. Rooms in the AAA–rated three-star hotel are spacious, immaculate, and bright, and the whole hotel was refurbished in 2012. All apartments come equipped with kitchenettes and bathtubs.

15–21 Therry St., Melbourne, VIC 3000. www.ibishotels.com.au. *© 03/9666 0000.* 250 units. A$144–A$189 double; A$234 1-bedroom apt; A$324 2-bedroom apt. Parking A$25. **Amenities:** Restaurant; bar; Wi-Fi (A$28/24 hr.).

Jasper Hotel ★★   Color your world—or at least your stay in Melbourne—the shades of jasper (the gemstone) when you stay at this redeveloped YWCA hotel. After a A$4.5-million revamp, the former Hotel Y is looking good. Facilities include computer stations, a laundry service, and free access to the nearby Melbourne City Baths health club and pool. Executive rooms have iPhone docking stations. The hotel also offers in-house massage and spa treatments and is home to a small art gallery featuring Melbourne artists, with exhibitions changing every few months.

489 Elizabeth St., Melbourne. www.jasperhotel.com.au. *© 1800 468 359* or (03) 8327 2777. 65 units. A$297–A$327 double including breakfast. Commercial carpark nearby. Tram: 19, 57, 59. Train: Melbourne Central. **Amenities:** Restaurant; room service; Wi-Fi ($20/24 hr.).

Robinsons in the City ★★★ Artfully created in what was once Melbourne's first commercial bakery, this lovely boutique hotel is tastefully elegant as well as being casual and comfortable, with lots of personal touches. Built around 1850, the building retains some original features, including the brick ovens that are now a feature of the breakfast room. All rooms have either queen- or king-size beds, and each guest room has its own private bathroom just across the hallway. There's a guest lounge with an extensive library, and a "butler's pantry" with a bar that operates on an honor system. Owner Paul Humphreys is passionate about Melbourne and happy to help you with your travel plans.

405 Spencer St. (at Batman St.), Melbourne, VIC 3003. www.robinsonsinthecity.com.au. ⓒ **03/9329 2552.** 6 units. A$175–A$255 double. Rates include full "farmhouse" breakfast. Ask about discount rates. Limited free off-street parking, which must be prebooked. **Amenities:** Guest lounge; iPod-docking stations; free Wi-Fi.

INEXPENSIVE

All Seasons Kingsgate Hotel ★ A 10-minute walk from the city, this interesting hotel resembles a terrace building from the outside, but inside it's a maze of corridors and rooms. It has a real B&B feel to it, and the staff is friendly. The least expensive economy rooms have two single beds, a wardrobe, and a hand basin; there's barely enough room to swing a backpack, and the bathroom is down the hallway. Standard rooms are light and spacious, with double or twin beds as well as ensuite bathrooms. The 15 or so family rooms have double beds and two singles. It has a 24-hour reception desk, free luggage-storage facilities, a guest laundry, and free use of the safety deposit boxes. Check the hotel's website for really good deals.

131 King St., Melbourne, VIC 3000. www.kingsgatehotel.com.au. ⓒ **1300/734 171** in Australia, or 03/9629 4171. 225 units, 104 with bathroom. A$82–A$209 double; A$164–A$245 family room (for 4). Parking at nearby Southern Cross Station, A$25 per exit. **Amenities:** 2 restaurants; bar; 30 min. free Wi-Fi in lobby; A$5/30 min. or A$20/3 hr. in rooms.

In East Melbourne

Georgian Court Guest House ★ The appearance of the comfortable Georgian Court, set on a beautiful tree-lined street, hasn't changed much since it was built in 1910. The sitting and dining rooms have high ceilings and offer old-world atmosphere. The guest rooms are simply furnished, and some are in need of a refurbishment; others have already been refreshed. Some have ensuite bathrooms; others have private bathrooms in the hallway. One room comes with a queen-size bed and a Jacuzzi. The Georgian Court is a 15-minute stroll through the Fitzroy and Treasury Gardens from the city center and is also close to the fashion shops of Bridge Road.

21 George St., East Melbourne, VIC 3002. www.georgiancourt.com.au. ⓒ **03/9415 8225.** 31 units. A$179 double; A$199 queen spa room; A$220 family room. Rates include breakfast. Free parking. Tram: 75 from Flinders St., or 48 from Spencer St. **Amenities:** Wi-Fi (A$8/hr.; A$20/day).

In Fitzroy

The Nunnery ★★ This former convent offers smart budget accommodations—and something a little more upmarket—a short tram ride from the city center, close to the restaurant and nightlife of Brunswick and Lygon streets in nearby Carlton. The informal, friendly 1860s main building has high ceilings, handmade light fittings, polished floorboards, marble fireplaces, and a hand-turned staircase. There's also a clever and rather irreverent play on its past in the decor. It's well suited to couples and families. The Guesthouse next door, built in the early 1900s, is also comfy, stylish, and decorated with tasteful furnishings and artwork. All rooms share bathrooms. The Nunnery, former home of the Daughters of Charity, also houses dorm rooms that have four, eight, or twelve beds. There are no elevators.

112–120 Nicholson St., Fitzroy, Melbourne, VIC 3065. www.nunnery.com.au. ⓒ 1800/032 635 in Australia, or 03/9419 8637. 30 units, none with bathroom. Guesthouse A$140 double, A$155 double family room, plus A$30 per extra adult or A$15 per extra child 5–12 years; Budget section A$32–A$36 per person bunk rooms, A$120–A$125 double, A$90 single private rooms. Free parking (reservation required). Tram: 96. **Amenities:** Kitchen; Wi-Fi (A$4/hour; A$15/day).

In Port Melbourne

La Maison de Babette ★
Owned and run by French-born artist Elisabeth "Babette" Shields, this large, delightful Victorian home is an affordable and welcoming B&B. The upstairs guest wing has three air-conditioned bedrooms (double, twin, and single) and a shared luxury bathroom; downstairs is the guest lounge with a fireplace, stacked bookshelves, and a TV. There's a courtyard garden with a barbecue at the back. It's less than 10 minutes from the city center. Elisabeth puts together a hearty French breakfast (the baguettes and croissants are fresh from one of Melbourne's best boulangeries). Advance bookings are essential.

4 Garton St. (corner of Bay St.), Port Melbourne. www.lamaisondebabette.com.au. ⓒ 03/9645 6067 or 0423/317 182 (mobile phone). 3 units. A$120 single, A$150 double. Rates include breakfast. 2-night minimum, 7-night maximum stay. Free on-street parking. Free pickup from airport-city shuttle. Tram: 109. **Amenities:** TV lounge, bikes; free Wi-Fi.

In St. Kilda

Hotel Barkly/St. Kilda Beach House ★
Be prepared for a pleasant surprise at this busy pub; the rooms upstairs are light, bright, and white, with red accents. They're clean, modern and attractive, much more so than you'd expect for somewhere that offers backpacker dorms. The best of the private rooms are the three large studios, which have wonderful views of St. Kilda and the bay. All rooms—even the dorms—have ensuite bathrooms. The dorms (six-, eight- and ten-beds) include female-only dorms, and family rooms that sleep four to six people. The huge rooftop bar is very popular, and there's a nightclub in the basement (which means it can be noisy on weekends and the night before public holidays!).

109 Barkly St. (at Grey St.), St. Kilda. www.stkildabeachhouse.com.au. ⓒ 1800 551 271 in Australia or (03) 9525 3332. 31 units. A$21–A$27 dorms, A$79–A$119 double, A$99–A$130 studio double. Dorm rates include continental breakfast. Tram: 16, 96. **Amenities:** Restaurant; bar; Wi-Fi (first 30 min. free, then $10/3 hr.).

Hotel Tolarno ★★
The quirky Hotel Tolarno is in the middle of St. Kilda's cafe and restaurant strip and just a short stroll from the beach. Rich red carpets bedeck the corridors throughout the retro-style (1950s and 1960s) building. In an earlier life, the building was owned by Melbourne artist Mirka Mora (after whom the hotel's restaurant is named), and the tradition continues today, with the walls hung with work by Melbourne artists. Rooms vary, but all are modern and colorful. The most popular, the deluxe doubles, are in the front of the building and have balconies overlooking the main street. They are larger than the standard rooms. Superior doubles come with a

St. Kilda Hotels & Restaurants

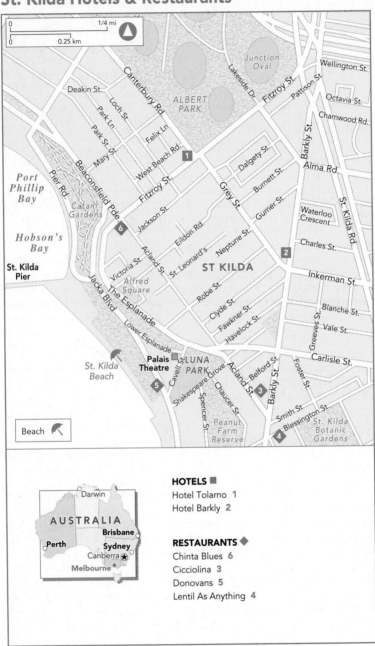

0   1/4 mi
0   0.25 km

Junction Oval

Wellington St.

Deakin St.

Canterbury Rd.

ALBERT PARK

Lakeside Dr.

Fitzroy St.

Pattison St.

Octavia St.

Loch St.

Charnwood Rd.

Park Ln.

Felix Ln.

Park St.

Mary St.

West Beach Rd.

Dalgery St.

Burnett St.

Barkly St.

Alma Rd.

1

Port Phillip Bay

Pier Rd.

Beaconsfield Pde.

Fitzroy St.

Grey St.

Gurner St.

St. Kilda Rd.

Catani Gardens

Jackson St.

Eildon Rd.

Neptune St.

Waterloo Crescent

Charles St.

Hobson's Bay

6

Victoria St.

Acland St.

St. Leonard's

ST KILDA

2

St. Kilda Pier

Alfred Square

Robe St.

Inkerman St.

Clyde St.

Blanche St.

The Esplanade

Jacka Blvd.

Fawkner St.

Greeves St.

Vale St.

Lower Esplanade

Havelock St.

Carlisle St.

St. Kilda Beach

Palais Theatre

LUNA PARK

Cavell St.

Acland St.

Belford St.

Barkly St.

Foster St.

5

Shakespeare Grove

Chaucer St.

3

Spencer St.

Smith St.

Blessington St.

St. Kilda Botanic Gardens

Beach

Peanut Farm Reserve

4

Darwin

AUSTRALIA

Brisbane

Perth

Sydney

Canberra

Melbourne

HOTELS ■
Hotel Tolarno 1
Hotel Barkly 2

RESTAURANTS ◆
Chinta Blues 6
Cicciolina 3
Donovans 5
Lentil As Anything 4

microwave, and two have Japanese baths. Suites come with a separate kitchen and lounge. Some suites have Jacuzzis, but none come with balconies.

42 Fitzroy St., St. Kilda, Melbourne, VIC 3182. www.hoteltolarno.com.au. ⓒ **03/9537 0200.** 36 units. A$155–A$195 double; A$230–A$280 suite; A$400 2-bedroom suite. Free on-street parking. Tram: 16 from Swanston St. or 96 from Flinders St. **Amenities:** Restaurant; bar; babysitting; bikes; concierge; room service; 4 lit tennis courts; free Wi-Fi.

In South Yarra & Toorak

Cotterville ★★★   You will love the courtyard gardens as much as the art and music that surround you in this beautifully restored terrace house. You will also likely become fast friends with your hosts and their two schnauzers. Owners Howard Neil and Jeremy Vincent are extremely knowledgeable about the city's arts scene—Jeremy works at the Arts Centre and Howard is a former theater and television director. You can join them for "happy hour" drinks at 5pm, and, for an extra A$50 per person (and advance notice), Howard will whip up a three-course gourmet dinner.

204 Williams Rd., Toorak, Melbourne, VIC 3142. www.cotterville.com. ⓒ **03/9826 9105** or 0409/900 807 mobile. 2 units with shared bathroom. A$130 single; A$160 double. Weekly rates available. Rates include breakfast. Free on-street parking. Train: Hawkesburn.

The Hatton ★★   This striking Italianate mansion was built as a hotel in 1902, and was meticulously restored and stylishly updated to become a sophisticated and contemporary boutique hotel in 2005. Many of the original features—rosettes, cornices, stained-glass windows, wide verandas, and high ceilings—have been retained, and the guest rooms have been fashioned from the original structure, making each an individual space. Clever combinations of old and new—antiques alongside specially commissioned modern art pieces—give it an unusual but welcoming atmosphere. A massive kauri pine counter dominates the front lounge, where you can read the papers or use the guest computer.

65 Park St., South Yarra, VIC 3141. www.hatton.com.au. ⓒ **03/9868 4800.** 20 units. A$215–A$240 double; A$350 suite. Extra person A$50. Crib A$30. Rates include continental breakfast. Free parking. Tram: No. 8 from Swanston St. **Amenities:** Bar; lounge; guest laundry; free Wi-Fi.

WHERE TO EAT

Melbourne's ethnically diverse population ensures a healthy selection of international cuisines. Chinatown, in the city center, is a fabulous hunting ground for Chinese, Malaysian, Thai, Indonesian, Japanese, and Vietnamese fare, often at bargain prices. Carlton has plenty of Italian restaurants, but some of the outdoor eateries on Lygon Street target unsuspecting tourists with overpriced and disappointing fare; avoid them. Richmond is crammed with Greek and Vietnamese restaurants, and Fitzroy has cheap Asian, Turkish, Mediterranean, and vegetarian food. To see and be seen, head to Chapel Street or Toorak Road in South Yarra, or travel to St. Kilda, where you can join the throng of Melburnians dining out along Fitzroy and Acland streets. Most of the cheaper places in Melbourne are strictly BYO (bring your own wine or beer). Smoking is banned by law in Melbourne cafes and restaurants, so don't even think about lighting up.

Melbourne Restaurants

Babka Bakery 4
Bamboo House 5
Becco 6
Brunetti 1
Chocolate Buddha 18
Flower Drum 9
Grossi Florentino 8
Hopetoun Tea Rooms 14
Il Bacaro 11
Il Solito Posto 12
Koko 19
Mario's 3
MoVida 17
MoVida Aqui 15
Nudel Bar 7
Shakahari 2
Sheni's Curries 13
Supper Inn 10
Young & Jackson 16

In the City Center

EXPENSIVE

Flower Drum ★★★ CANTONESE   Praise pours in from all quarters for this upscale restaurant just off Little Bourke Street, Chinatown's main drag. Take a slow elevator up to the restaurant, which has widely spaced tables (perfect for politicians and businesspeople to clinch their deals). Take note of the specials—the chefs are extremely creative and use the best ingredients they find in the markets each day. A smart idea is to put your menu selections into the hands of the waiter. The signature dish is Peking duck. King crab dumplings in soup is a great starter, and you can also order more unusual dishes, such as abalone (at a price: A$145 per 100 grams). The atmosphere is clubby and a bit old-fashioned, but the service is beyond reproach. But be prepared to pay for the privilege.

17 Market Lane. © **03/9662 3655.** www.flower-drum.com. Main courses A$18–A$55. Mon–Sat noon–3pm and 6–11pm; Sun 6–10:30pm.

Grossi Florentino ★★★ ITALIAN   Under the management of the Grossi family, this is probably the best Italian restaurant in Melbourne. It has a casual bistro downstairs, next to the Cellar Bar (where a bowl of pasta on the bar menu is less than A$20); upstairs is the fine-dining restaurant, with its chandeliers and murals reflecting the Florentine way of life. The food is not your traditional Italian, with such innovative dishes as roasted partridge with quince puree, glazed chestnuts, truffle reduction, parsnip, and partridge leg buckwheat risotto; about as old-world Italian as the dishes get is *risotto Venere*, risotto with Moreton Bay bugs (a local lobster) and a Parmesan Sabayon sauce. On the menu, too, are seafood and steak dishes. Save room for dessert: perhaps the chocolate soufflé with malt ice cream and chocolate syrup, or the cheese plate to share? On weekdays, a two-course lunch special for A$65 is available.

80 Bourke St. © **03/9662 1811.** www.grossiflorentino.com. Main courses A$39–A$56. Mon–Fri noon–3pm; Mon–Sat 6–11pm.

Koko ★★ JAPANESE   Though you'll find plenty of Japanese sushi and noodle bars around Chinatown, there's nothing quite like raw fish with a bit of panache. Koko's decor is contemporary-traditional, with a goldfish pond in the center of the main dining room and wonderful views over the city. There are separate teppanyaki grills and screened tatami rooms where you sit on the matted floor. Koka has a vast and changing seasonal menu that includes lots of seafood dishes (think grilled lobster with sea urchin sauce), or you can opt for a set menu to take the agony out of choosing. A large selection of different sakes aids digestion.

Level 3, Crown Towers, Southbank. © **03/9292 6886.** www.crownmelbourne.com.au/koko. Main courses A$36–A$60. Daily noon–2:30pm, Sun–Thurs 6–10pm, Fri–Sat 6–10:30pm.

MODERATE

Bamboo House ★★ CHINESE/CANTONESE   If Flower Drum (see above) is full or strains your budget, try this more budget-friendly place, esteemed by both the Chinese community and local business big shots. The service is a pleasure, and the food is definitely worth writing home about. The waiters will help you construct a feast from the myriad Cantonese and northern Chinese dishes. It's worth ordering ahead to get a taste of the signature dish, Szechuan tea-smoked duck. Other popular dishes include pan-fried beef dumplings and spring onion pancakes.

47 Little Bourke St. ⓒ **03/9662 1565.** www.bamboohouse.com.au. Main courses A$25–A$32. Mon–Fri noon–3pm (except public holidays); Mon–Sat 5:30–11pm; Sun 5:30–10pm.

Becco ★★ ITALIAN   Tucked away on a quiet lane, this favorite of Melburnians consistently lives up to its many awards and accolades. Here you find stylish service and stylish customers, all without pretension. The cuisine mixes Italian favors with Australian flair. Try the roast duck with grappa sauce, one of the tasty pasta dishes, or the specials, which your waiter will fill you in on. If you prefer something lighter, there's a bar menu of equally tempting dishes. On the upstairs level is the ultracool late-night bar, **Bellavista Social Club.**

11–25 Crossley St., near Bourke St. ⓒ **03/9663 3000.** www.becco.com.au. Main courses A$28–A$55. Mon–Sat noon–3pm and 6–11pm.

Chocolate Buddha ★★ JAPANESE   This place offers mostly organic produce, including some organic wines. Based generally on Japanese-inspired noodle, ramen, and soba dishes to which the kitchen adds meat, chicken, or seafood, it's casual yet satisfying dining. The best way to eat here is to order dishes to share. The food is creative, and the view across the square to the Yarra River and Southbank is a delight at dusk. It can get very crowded, so book ahead if you can.

Federation Sq., corner of Flinders and Swanson sts. ⓒ **03/9654 5688.** www.chocolatebuddha. com.au. Main courses A$14–A$25. Daily noon–11:30pm.

Il Bacaro ★★ ITALIAN   Walk into Il Bacaro and you'll experience a little piece of Venice. Dominated by a horseshoe-shaped bar, it's jam-packed with small tables and weaving waiters carrying interesting dishes such as Roman-style braised goat with tomato, green beans, potato, and truffled pecorino. The pasta dishes and the risotto of the day always go down well, as do the salad side dishes. It's often crowded at lunch with businesspeople digging into the excellent wine list.

168–170 Little Collins St. ⓒ **03/9654 6778.** www.ilbacaro.com.au. Main courses A$35–A$45. Mon–Sat noon–3pm; Mon–Thurs 6–10:30pm, Fri–Sat 6–11pm.

Il Solito Posto ★★ ITALIAN   This below-ground restaurant consists of two parts. The casual bistro or *caffeteria* has a blackboard menu offering good pastas, soups, and salads. Then there's the sharper and more upmarket trattoria, with an a la carte menu of northern Italian dishes offering the likes of slow-cooked lamb in chili, garlic, herbs, and tomato, with fresh peas, as well as steak, fish, and veal dishes. It's open for breakfast, lunch, and dinner. You'll find the coffee excellent, too.

113 Collins St., basement (enter through George Parade). ⓒ **03/9654 4466.** www.ilsolitoposto. com.au. Main courses A$25–A$32 in bistro, A$27–A$46 in trattoria. Mon–Fri 7:30am–1am; Sat 9am–1am.

MoVida ★★★ SPANISH   Barcelona-born chef and co-owner Frank Camorra has made MoVida one of the most talked-about restaurants in Melbourne. His restaurant reflects the spirit of Spain, relaxed and fun, with seriously good food and good wine. Melburnians flock here, and it's truly one of those places I was tempted to keep a secret (if that's possible due to the fact that everyone talks about how great it is). MoVida offers a choice of tapas (small individual dishes) or *raciones* (plates to share among two or more people, or a larger dish for one). Specials are available every night to keep the regulars happy. So successful is the first MoVida that there's also now **Next Door,** which is . . . you guessed it, next door. And if you have a large group, or you want to dine outdoors, there is **MoVida Aqui,** at level 1, 500 Bourke St. (entry off Little Bourke St.), which has a huge casual dining area and a terrace and serves the same great food. Be sure to book a table (but only if you are a group of six or less).

1 Hosier Lane. © **03/9663 3038** (for both restaurants). www.movida.com.au. Tapa A$3.50–A$6.50; *raciones* (main courses) A$8–A$30; banquet menu (10 dishes) A$75 per person. Daily noon–late.

Young & Jackson ★★ PUB   Melbourne's oldest and most famous pub is a great place to stop in for a drink in the bar or a meal in the stylish upstairs restaurant or bistro areas. It's a landmark on the corner opposite Federation Square and Flinders Street Station. Head upstairs to see the nude *Chloe,* the famous painting brought to Melbourne from Paris for the Great Exhibition in 1880 and which has a special place in the hearts of customers and Melburnians. The pub, which was built in 1853 and started selling beer in 1861, has a few years on *Chloe,* which was painted in Paris in 1875.

At the corner of Flinders and Swanston sts. © **03/9650 3884.** www.youngandjacksons.com.au. Main courses A$22–A$41. Bar meals available daily 10am–late. Restaurant opens daily noon–2:30pm, Sun–Thurs 5:30–9pm, Fri–Sat 5:30–9:30pm.

INEXPENSIVE

Hopetoun Tea Rooms ★ CAFE   The first cup of tea served in this Melbourne institution left the pot in 1892. The Hopetoun Tea Rooms is very genteel, with green-and-white Regency wallpaper and marble tables, but the fine china has gone by the wayside in favor of rather chunky cups, and the sugar comes in paper packets. It does a full lunch menu, but really you should come for tea or coffee and cakes (which are very good). Scones, croissants, pasta, and grilled food are also available. The clientele is a mix of little old ladies and students, with the odd tourist or businessman thrown into the mix. Traditional "High Tea" at A$50 per person can be taken between 10am and 3pm.

Block Arcade, 280–282 Collins St. © **03/9650 2777.** www.hopetountearooms.com.au. Main courses A$19–A$24; sandwiches A$13–A$19. Mon–Sat 8am–5pm; Sun 9am–5pm.

Nudel Bar ★ NOODLES   A favorite among city slickers, the Nudel Bar serves a variety of noodle dishes—from Italian to Asian—to diners at the crowded tables and bar. Examples include cold, spicy green-tea noodles and *mie goreng* (a Malaysian noodle dish with peanuts and, here, often chicken). The signature dish is macaroni and cheese, and the sticky rice pudding is a favorite for dessert. Reservations are recommended for Friday and Saturday nights.

76 Bourke St. © **03/9662 9100.** Main courses A$13–A$24. Tues–Sat 11am–10pm.

Sheni's Curries ★★ SRI LANKAN   This small, basic, very busy place seats only 30 and offers a range of authentic, excellent-value Sri Lankan curries. You can dine in or take your lunch special to go. Choose from three vegetable dishes and a selection of meat and seafood options. All meals come with rice, three types of chutney, and a pappadum; small serves are A$10, larger ones A$11. You can also buy extra items such as samosas and roti.

Shop 16, 161 Collins St. (corner of Flinders Lane and Russell St., opposite the entrance to the Grand Hyatt). © **03/9654 3535.** Main courses A$6–A$15. No credit cards. Mon–Fri 8am–9pm.

Supper Inn ★★ CANTONESE   Head here if you get the Chinese-food munchies late at night. It's a friendly place with a mixed crowd of locals and tourists chowing down on such dishes as steaming bowls of *congee* (rice-based porridge), barbecued suckling pig, mud crab, or stuffed scallops. Everything here is the real thing.

15 Celestial Ave. ℰ **03/9663 4759.** Main courses A$15–A$40. Daily 5:30pm–2:30am.

In Carlton

Brunetti ★★ ITALIAN Don't be daunted by the crowds around the cake counters—and there *will* be crowds! This is a real Italian/Melbourne experience. A move—just around the corner onto the main drag of Lygon Streeet—in mid-2012 has seen some changes, but the essence of Brunetti remains the same. New are the wood-fired pizza oven (imported from Italy) and an open kitchen so you can watch the chefs and a traditional *gelatieri* (ice-cream maker) in action. If you can get past the mouthwatering array of excellent cakes, the menu also offers authentic Italian cuisine, done very well. Or pop in for breakfast. On Sundays (and only Sundays) the lunch special (until it runs out) is always Nonna Angela's maccheroni, with pork meatballs. If you can't get to Carlton, there's the cafe-style **Brunetti City Square** at Swanston Street and Flinders Lane in the city, and another on level three of the city Myer store.

380 Lygon St., Carlton. ℰ **03/9347 2801.** www.brunetti.com.au. Main courses A$16–A$27. Sun–Thurs 6am–11pm; Fri–Sat 6am–midnight. Tram: 1, 15, 21, or 22 traveling north on Swanston St.

Shakahari ★ VEGETARIAN Good vegetarian food isn't just a meal without meat; it's a creation in its own right. At Shakahari you're assured a creative meal that's not at all bland. The large restaurant is quite low-key, and there's a lovely courtyard out the back. The signature satay dish—skewered, lightly fried vegetables and tofu pieces with a mildly spicy peanut sauce—is a perennial favorite. Also available are curries, croquettes, green papaya salad, a linguine dish, and a fragrant laksa. A second restaurant, **Shakahari Too,** is located in South Melbourne (ℰ **03/9682 2207**).

201–203 Faraday St., Carlton. ℰ **03/9347 3848.** www.shakahari.com.au. Main courses A$21–A$22. Mon–Sat noon–3pm; Sun–Thurs 6–9:30pm; Fri–Sat 6–10pm. Tram: 1, 15, 21, or 22 traveling north along Swanston St.

In Fitzroy

Marios ★★★ ITALIAN Opened in the 1980s by two Italian-Australian friends, both called Mario, this place has ambience, groovy decor, and impeccable service. There is little here you can fault, including the food. Offerings include a range of pastas (like gnocchi with pancetta, peas, basil, tomato and shaved Parmesan) and cakes, and breakfast is served all day. The art on the cafe walls, all by local artists, is always interesting—and for sale. The coffee is excellent (just don't ask for skim, decaf, or anything other that the real deal). You can also buy a jar of Mario's jam or marmalade to take home for A$8.

303 Brunswick St., Fitzroy. ℰ **03/9417 3343.** www.marioscafe.com.au. Reservations not accepted. Main courses A$15–A$30. No credit cards. Mon–Sat 7am–10:30pm; Sun 8am–10:30pm.

The Staff of Life

The aroma of fresh bread will draw you to **Babka Bakery,** a Russian-style cafe-bakery that is nearly always packed. Come for breakfast or a light lunch of eggs on fresh sourdough, or any of the bakery's quiches, tarts, and brioches. Or perhaps try the homemade borscht. It's at 358 Brunswick St., in Fitzroy (ℰ **03/9416 0091**), and is open Tuesday to Sunday 7am to 7pm.

With a novel approach that not surprisingly has become a hit, the vegetarian restaurant **Lentil as Anything** (www.lentilasanything.com) has a menu without prices. Here you eat—then pay "as you feel" for the meal and service (or for some people, what they can afford). The food is organic, with lots of noodles and vegetables and such things as tofu, curries, and stir-fries. Before you leave, you put your money in a box. The restaurant has three locations. The original is at 41 Blessington St., St. Kilda (📞 **0430/388 984** mobile phone), open noon to 4pm and 6pm to 9pm daily. A second outlet is at the Abbotsford Convent, 1 Saint Heliers St., Abbotsford (📞 **03/9419 6444**), open daily from 9am to 9pm; and the newest is in the old Barkly Hotel, 233 Barkly St., Footscray (📞 **0414/613 695** mobile phone), open noon to 3:30pm and 5pm to 9pm daily; cash only.

Seaside Dining in St. Kilda

Chinta Blues ★ MALAYSIAN   Head to this very popular eatery if you're looking for simple, satisfying food with a healthy touch of spice. The big sellers are laksa, *mie goreng* noodles, chicken curry, *sambal* spinach, and a chicken dish called "Ayam Blues." Lots of noodles, too. It's very busy, but there's usually not more than a 30-minute wait for a table. It does takeout as well.

6 Acland St., St. Kilda. 📞 **03/9534 9233**. www.chintablues.com.au. Reservations not accepted. Main courses A$13–A$25. Daily noon–2:30pm; Mon–Thurs 6–10:30pm; Fri–Sat 6–11pm; Sun 5:30–10pm. Tram: 16 from Swanston St. or 96 from Bourke St.

Cicciolina ★★★ CONTEMPORARY   It's difficult enough to get a table at this wonderful but understated place, which doesn't take bookings for dinner, without encouraging more people to line up. But I'd be depriving you of a terrific night out if I kept quiet. So if you're looking for somewhere that's intimate, crowded, well-run, and has superb but simple food, look no further than Cicciolina. Although you cannot book for dinner, there's a waitlist after 6pm—first come, first served. You may have to wait for an hour or so for a table (have a drink in the Back Bar, and they'll call you), but it will be worth it for delights such as a veal filet wrapped in pancetta, with a broadbean purée, roasted beetroot, and a turnip soufflé, or—my favorite—an elegantly simple spaghettini tossed with spinach, chili, and oil.

130 Acland St., St. Kilda. 📞 **03/9525 3333**. www.cicciolinastkilda.com.au. Main courses A$17–A$42. Daily noon–11pm (10pm on Sun). Bookings available for lunch only. Tram: 16 from Swanston St., or 94 or 96 from Bourke St.

Donovans ★★ CONTEMPORARY   Watching the sun go down over St. Kilda beach from the veranda at Donovans (with glass in hand) is a perfect way to end the day. Gail and Kevin Donovan have transformed a 1920s bathing pavilion into a welcoming restaurant designed to make you feel as if you're a guest in the Donovan home (or at least their beach house). Lots of cushions, a log fire, coffee-table books, and the sound of jazz and breakers on the beach complete the picture. If that's not enough, the menu includes a mind-boggling array of dishes, many big enough for two, and even a children's menu. Try the seafood linguine or perhaps slow-braised Wagyu beef cheek with creamy mash, baby vegetables and a golden-crust mushroom pie.

40 Jacka Blvd., St. Kilda. ℂ **03/9534 8221.** www.donovanshouse.com.au. Main courses A$36–A$57. Daily noon–10:30pm. Tram: 16, 94 or 96.

EXPLORING MELBOURNE

Visitors to Melbourne come to experience the contrasts of old-world architecture and the exciting feel of a truly multicultural city. This is a wonderfully compact city, with all the major attractions within easy reach of the city heart. Most visitors also venture to the bayside suburb of St. Kilda, an easy tram ride away.

Bennetts Lane Jazz Club ★   Often exceptional and always varied, this venue has a reputation as the best jazz club in Australia and is sought out by the best international players. The back-lane location may be a little hard to find, but that doesn't keep it from being packed out most nights. Get here early if you want a table; otherwise it's standing-room only or a perch on the steps at the back.

25 Bennetts Lane. ℂ **03/9663 2856.** www.bennettslane.com. Entry prices vary depending on the performer, but start at around A$15. Daily from 8:30pm (music starts at 9pm weeknights and 9:30pm on weekends).

Crown Casino ★   Australia's largest casino is a plush affair that's open 24 hours. You'll find all the usual roulette and blackjack tables and so on, as well as an array of gaming machines. This is also a major venue for international headline acts, and some 25 restaurants and 11 bars are on the premises, with more in the extended Southgate complex.

8 Whiteman St. (at Clarendon St.), Southbank. ℂ **03/9292 8888.** www.crownmelbourne.com.au. Daily 24 hr., except on Christmas Day, Good Friday and Anzac Day (Apr 25) when it is closed 4am–noon.

Eureka Skydeck 88 ★   The vertigo-challenging Eureka Skydeck 88 is the highest public vantage point in the Southern Hemisphere. On the 88th floor of the Eureka Tower, a viewing deck gives a 360-degree panorama of the city from 285m (935 ft.) above the ground. But there's more adrenaline-pumping action than just the view: A huge glass cube called the Edge is actually a 6-ton horizontal elevator, which emerges from inside the walls of Skydeck 88 carrying 12 passengers out over the tower's east side. As the opaque glass cube reaches its full extension, the reinforced, 45-millimeter-thick (1¾-in.) glass becomes clear, giving passengers uninterrupted views below, above, and to three sides. All this is accompanied by recorded sounds of creaking chains and breaking glass—just to scare you more! Actually, it's not as scary as it sounds, and the ride is only 4 minutes long. For an extra A$3.50 on your admission price, you can return at night for a look at the city all lit up.

Eureka Tower, Riverside Quay, South Bank. ℂ **03/9693 8888.** www.eurekaskydeck.com.au. Admission A$19 adults, A$10 children 4–16, A$42 family of 4; A$12 adults, A$8 children, A$29 families extra for the Edge. Daily 10am–10pm (last entry 9:30pm); 10am–5:30pm on Christmas Day and New Year's Eve (last entry 5pm).

Federation Square ★★   You have to get into Federation Square, physically, to appreciate it. The controversial design—Melburnians either love it or hate it (I fall into

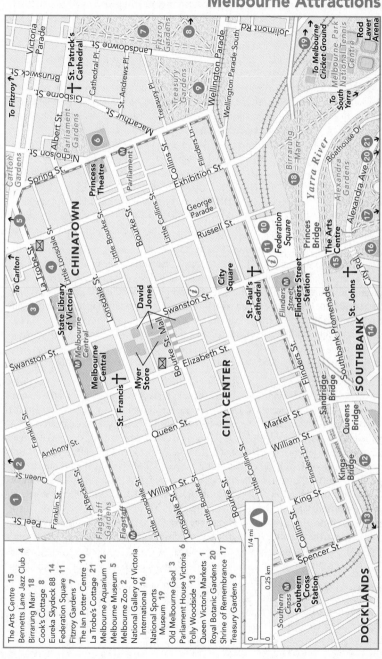

The Arts Centre **15**
Bennetts Lane Jazz Club **4**
Birrarung Marr **18**
Cook's Cottage **8**
Eureka Skydeck 88 **14**
Federation Square **11**
Fitzroy Gardens **7**
The Ian Potter Centre **10**
La Trobe's Cottage **21**
Melbourne Aquarium **12**
Melbourne Museum **5**
Melbourne Zoo **2**
National Gallery of Victoria International **16**
National Sports Museum **19**
Old Melbourne Gaol **3**
Parliament House Victoria **6**
Polly Woodside **13**
Queen Victoria Markets **1**
Royal Botanic Gardens **20**
Shrine of Remembrance **17**
Treasury Gardens **9**

the former category)—has given the city a gathering place, and you only have to visit on the weekends to see that it works. A conglomerate of attractions is centered on a large open piazza-style area cobbled with misshapen paving. Here you'll find the **Ian Potter Centre** (see below) and the **Australian Centre for the Moving Image (ACMI),** which has two state-of-the-art cinemas and large areas where visitors can view movies, videos, and digital media. It has a one-stop visitor center (see "Visitor Information," earlier in this chapter), and there are many cafes and coffee shops throughout the precinct. It's worth visiting "Fed Square" just to see the architecture, made up of strange geometrical designs, and the glass Atrium. Lots of events happen in the square's 450-seat amphitheater, including theatrical performances and free concerts. Other events take place on the plaza and along the banks of the Yarra River. Melbourne's biggest **book market** is held every Saturday from 11am to 5pm in the Atrium, with 5,000 titles, both new and secondhand. And you can get free Wi-Fi anywhere in the square. Free 50-minute guided tours are run Monday through Saturday at 11am.

Flinders St. (at St. Kilda Rd.). © **03/9655 1900.** www.fedsquare.com. Free admission; charges for some special events and exhibitions. Outdoor spaces open 24 hr. Tram: City Circle.

The Ian Potter Centre ★★★   This fascinating gallery, featuring 20 rooms dedicated to Australian art, opened in 2002 in the heart of Federation Square. Part of the National Gallery of Victoria (NGV), it contains the largest collection of Australian art in the country, including works by Sidney Nolan, Russell Drysdale, and Tom Roberts, as well as Aboriginal and Torres Strait Islanders. Some 20,000 objects are stored here, but only about 800 are on display at any one time. Aboriginal art and colonial art collections are the centerpieces of the gallery, but you will find modern paintings here, too. Temporary exhibitions include anything from ceramics to shoes.

Federation Sq. (corner of Flinders St. and St. Kilda Rd.). © **03/8660 2222.** www.ngv.vic.gov.au. Free admission. Tues–Sun 10am–5pm. Closed Mon (except public holidays), Good Friday, Christmas Day, and until 1pm on Anzac Day (Apr 25). Tram: City Circle. Bus: City Explorer.

Melbourne Aquarium ★   The Melbourne Aquarium's prize exhibit is an Antarctica display featuring King and Gentoo penguins playing in the pool (with underwater viewing) and sliding across the snow-covered ice. The 20 beguiling birds are Australia's only collection of sub-Antarctic penguins. The aquarium also features a reef exhibit, some jellyfish displays, and a 2.2-million-liter (581,000-gallon) Oceanarium walk-through tank with larger fish, sharks, and rays. Dive-feeding demonstrations are held at 11am and 2pm. You can also arrange to dive with the sharks (A$210 for qualified divers, A$299 for nondivers; must be 15 years or older). Bookings are essential; call © **03/9510 9081.**

Corner of Flinders and Kings St. © **03/9923 5999.** www.melbourneaquarium.com.au. Admission A$35 adults, A$22 children 3–15, A$92 families of 4 (cheaper if booked online). Daily 9:30am–6pm (last admission 5pm). Tram: City Circle.

Melbourne Museum ★★★   This museum is Australia's largest and one of the most interesting. For me, the highlight is Bunjilaka, the Aboriginal Cultural Centre, which gives an insight into the Victorian Koori people. This area of the museum has undergone a major redevelopment, reopening in late 2013 with even more to see and learn. Other highlights of the museum include a genuine blue-whale skeleton, an indoor rainforest, and a brilliant insect and butterfly collection with lots of real-life exhibits, including revolting cockroaches, ant colonies, and huge spiders (kids love these creepy-crawlies). Apart from that, there are interactive exhibits and science displays and social history, including a stuffed racehorse called Phar Lap. Check out the brightly colored **Children's Museum,** which will bring hours of enjoyment to the little ones. Allow 2 hours (more if you would like to also tour the 19th-century Royal Exhibition Building adjacent).

11 Nicholson St., Carlton. Ⓒ **13 11 02** in Victoria, 1300/130 152 in Australia or 03/8341 7777. http://museumvictoria.com.au. Admission A$10 adults, free for children 15 and under. Daily 10am–5pm. Closed Good Friday and Christmas Day. Tram: 86 or 96 or the free City Circle Tram.

Melbourne Zoo ★★   Built in 1862, this is the oldest zoo in the world and makes a great day out with kids. Some 3,000 animals reside here, including kangaroos, wallabies, echidnas, koalas, wombats, and platypuses. Rather than being locked in cages, most animals are in almost natural surroundings or well-tended gardens. Don't miss the butterfly house, with its thousands of colorful occupants flitting around; the free-flight aviary; the lowland gorilla exhibit; and the treetop orangutan exhibit. Allow at least 90 minutes if you just want to see the Australian natives, and around 4 hours for the entire zoo.

Elliott Ave., Parkville. Ⓒ **1300/966 784.** www.zoo.org.au. Admission A$27 adults, A$13 children 4–15, A$61–A$84 families (Mon–Fri, except school holidays). Entry is free for children on weekends, public holidays and school holidays. Daily 9am–5pm. Free parking. Tram: 55 going north on William St. to stop 25; 19 from Elizabeth St. to stop 16 (then a short walk to your left, following signposts). Train: Royal Park Station.

National Gallery of Victoria International ★★   The NGV International is a showcase for Australia's finest collections of international art. On display are Gainsboroughs and Constables, as well as paintings by Bonnard, Delacroix, Van Dyck, El Greco, Monet, Manet, Magritte, and Rembrandt. Architecturally, the building itself is a masterpiece, with high ceilings, fabulous lighting, and great open spaces.

180 St. Kilda Rd. Ⓒ **03/8620 2222.** www.ngv.vic.gov.au. Free admission to general collection; fees for some temporary exhibitions. Wed–Mon 10am–5pm. Closed Tues, Good Friday, Christmas Day, and until 1pm on Anzac Day (Apr 25). Tram: Any tram from Swanston St. to Victorian Arts Centre.

National Sports Museum ★★★   In a nation that's quite frankly sports-mad, you really can't miss this outstanding and interesting museum, located within the Melbourne Cricket Ground (MCG). It tells Australia's sporting story from its early beginnings to the present, celebrating memorable moments and achievements in just about every sport you can think of, from basketball and boxing to hockey, rugby, tennis, and everything in between. It also includes the Australian Cricket Hall of Fame, the Sport Australia Hall of Fame and Champions Racing Gallery. The huge collection includes Australia's first-ever Olympic gold medal, Ian Thorpe's swimsuit, and the Malvern Star bicycle that Hubert Opperman rode in his record-breaking 24-hour cycling marathon in Sydney in 1940. Recognition has been given to Australia's first Paralympic gold medalist and first female Paralympian in a new addition to the Paralympic display. There's lots of interactive areas, and even room for kids to bowl a ball or two. Allow 1 hour (more if you are a real sports fanatic).

During MCG major event days, including the AFL Grand Final, Day 1 of the Boxing Day Test, and Anzac Day football, access to the museum (at half-price) is restricted to patrons holding an event ticket. Opening hours on weekends when events are being held within the MCG arena vary, so check the website.

Tours of the MCG run every half-hour daily from 10am to 3pm. Tickets include admission to the museum. Tours leave from Gate 3 in the Olympic Stand on non-event days only.

Melbourne Cricket Ground, Brunton Ave., Richmond. ✆ **03/9657 8879**. www.nsm.org.au. Admission A$20 adults, A$10 children 5–15, or A$60 families of 6 for museum only; A$30 adults, A$15 children, or A$60 families for museum and MCG tour. Daily 10am–5pm (last admission 4:30pm). Closed Good Friday and Christmas Day. Bus: Melbourne City Tourist Shuttle. Tram: 75 or 70 from the city center. Train: Jolimont. Entry is through Gate 3 at the MCG.

Old Melbourne Gaol ★★★

This is number one on my list of favorite Melbourne attractions. Old Melbourne Gaol's **Crime & Justice Experience** is a fascinating way to spend a few hours. Start off at the spooky old prison, with its stone walls, tiny cells, and bizarre collection of death masks and artifacts of 19th-century prison life. Among the 135 hangings that took place here was that of notorious bushranger Ned Kelly, in 1880. The scaffold where he was hanged still stands, and his gun, as well as a replica suit of homemade armor (similar to those used by his gang), is on display. The jail closed in 1924, and profiles of former prisoners give a fascinating insight into what it was like to be locked up here. Each Saturday, performances of "The Real Ned Kelly Story—Such a Life" are held at 12:30 and 2pm (included in your ticket price).

Then move next door for a guided tour of the former **City Watch House** to find out first-hand what it might have been like to spend time here. The lockup, which operated from 1908 to 1994, is just across the road from the scene of one of Melbourne's most notorious crimes, the 1986 bombing of the Russell Street police station. There's role-playing involved for everyone, but be warned, it can be quite confronting for children. During holiday times, you can also visit the adjacent former Magistrate's Court and take part in a reenactment of Ned Kelly's trial.

New ghost tours have been introduced, giving the brave a chance to explore the gaol by night. Run every Tuesday at 7:30pm, the tours are an alternative to the equally chilling "hangman" tours run by candlelight every Monday, Wednesday, Friday, and Saturday night. Not for the fainthearted or children under 12. Tickets cost A$30 for ghost tours and A$38 for hangman's tours.

377 Russell St. ✆ **03/9663 7228**. www.oldmelbournegaol.com.au. Admission A$25 adults, A$14 children, A$55 families of 6. Ask about a combo pass including admission to Polly Woodside (see p. 111). Daily 9:30am–5pm. Closed Good Friday and Christmas Day. Tram: City Circle to corner of Russell and Latrobe sts.

Parliament House Victoria ★

Now the home of the Victorian Parliament, this monument to Victorian (as in Queen Victoria) architecture at the top of a run of sandstone steps was built in 1856. During the Australian Federation (1900–27), it was used as the national parliament. When the state government is in session—generally on Tuesday afternoon and all day Wednesday and Thursday between March and July, and again between August and November (there's a break between sessions)—you can view the proceedings from the public gallery. However, you should ring ahead or check the website, as sitting times do vary. During nonsitting times, both the opulent Upper House and the less ornate Lower House chambers are open to the public by guided tour. Free architecture tours are held at 2pm on the last Friday of each month (bookings essential).

Spring St. ✆ **03/9651 8568**. www.parliament.vic.gov.au. Mon–Fri 9am–5pm. Free guided tours Mon–Fri at 9:30, 10:30, 11:30am, 1:30, 2:30, and 3:45pm when Parliament is not in session. Bookings are not necessary.

Polly Woodside ★★ A new gallery with six exhibition zones is the latest on-shore adjunct to the historic tall ship *Polly Woodside*. Set in the original Dockside sheds, the exhibit includes interactive displays about life at sea, the crew, navigation, maritime language, and Melbourne's docks (you can even try your hand at loading coal onto a robot ship!). Beloved by generations of Melburnians, *Polly Woodside* has lots of fun activities and hands-on stuff for children. Launched in 1885 in Ireland, the ship sailed to all corners of the globe between 1885 and 1904, rounding the infamous Cape Horn 16 times. After World War II, the ship was towed back to Melbourne and worked as a coal supply ship for the next 20 years. Tours by a "first mate" are run throughout the day, and every first Sunday of the month is "Pirate Day" for kids.

2A Clarendon St., South Wharf. ℭ **03/9656 9804.** www.pollywoodside.com.au. Admission A$15 adults, A$8 children, A$42 family of 6. Ask about a combo pass including entry to the Old Melbourne Gaol (see p. 110). Daily 9:30am–5pm. Closed Christmas Day and Good Friday. Tram: 96, 109 or 112.

Queen Victoria Market ★ This Melbourne institution—the "Vic Market"—covers several blocks. Ignore the hundreds of stalls selling everything from live rabbits to bargain clothes. There's a lot of junk here, and the crowds can be awful. The best part of the markets are the indoor food section, particularly the interesting delicatessen section. The 2-hour **Foodies Dream Tour** of the market explores the market's food and heritage and is well worth doing. It departs Tuesday, Thursday, Friday, and Saturday at 10am and costs A$40 per person, including generous tastings. Bookings (ℭ **03/9320 5835**) are essential. **Night markets** are held every Wednesday from 5:30 to 10pm, from November to late February (except the last week of Dec).

Btw. Peel, Victoria, Elizabeth, and Therry sts. on the northern edge of the city center. ℭ **03/9320 5822.** www.qvm.com.au. Tues and Thurs 6am–2pm; Fri 6am–5pm; Sat 6am–3pm; Sun 9am–4pm. Closed public holidays. Tram: Any tram traveling north along William St. or Elizabeth St.

The Arts Centre ★★ The spire atop the Theatres Building of the Arts Centre, on the banks of the Yarra River, crowns the city's leading performing arts complex. Beneath it, the State Theatre, the Playhouse, and the Fairfax Studio present performances that are the focal point of culture in Melbourne. The **State Theatre,** seating 2,085 on three levels, can accommodate elaborate stagings of opera, ballet, musicals, and more. The **Playhouse** is a smaller venue that often books the Melbourne Theatre Company. The **Fairfax** is more intimate still and is often used for experimental theater or cabaret. Adjacent to the Theatres Building is **Hamer Hall,** home of the Melbourne Symphony Orchestra and often host to visiting orchestras. Many international stars have graced this stage, which is known for its excellent acoustics. After a 2-year closure and redevelopment, Hamer Hall has never looked better, and you can do a guided tour Tuesdays and Thursdays at 5:30pm or on Fridays at 11am for A$30.

Guided tours of other parts of The Arts Centre are also offered. Tour the Theatres Building Monday to Thursday and Saturdays, or do a backstage tour on Sunday at 11am. Tours cost A$20 adults and A$15 children (under 18). Buy tickets from the concierge in the foyer of the Theatres Building.

100 St. Kilda Rd. ℭ **1300/182 183** for tickets. www.artscentremelbourne.com.au. Ticket prices vary depending on the event. Box office 9am–9pm Mon–Sat in the Theatres Building.

Outlying Attractions

Healesville Sanctuary ★★★ The sanctuary is a great place to see native animals in almost-natural surroundings. Walk through the peppermint-scented gum forest, which rings with the chiming of bellbirds, and see wedge-tailed eagles, dingoes, koalas, wombats, reptiles, and more. The sanctuary opened in 1921 to preserve endangered species and educate the public and played a major role in saving and rehabilitating the hundreds of animals injured or displaced by the bushfires which devasted parts of Victoria in 2009. You can visit the Wildlife Health Centre (an animal rescue hospital) to see veterinarians caring for (and operating on) injured or orphaned wildlife. The sanctuary has a gift shop, a cafe serving light meals, and picnic grounds.

Badger Creek Rd., Healesville. © **03/5957 2800.** www.zoo.org.au. Admission A$27 adults, A$13 children ages 4–15, A$57–A$78 families. Daily 9am–5pm. Train from Flinders St. station to Lilydale; then bus no. 685 to Healesville and bus no. 686 toward Badger Creek, which will stop at the sanctuary.

Puffing Billy Railway ★★★   For almost a century, Puffing Billy steam railway has chugged over a 13km (8-mile) track from Belgrave to Emerald and Lakeside. Passengers ride on open carriages—often dangling their legs from the "windows"—and enjoy lovely views as the train passes through forests and fern gullies and over a National Trust–classified wooden trestle bridge. Trips take around an hour each way, and there's time to walk around the lake before the return journey. Special "Steam and Cuisine" fares are available daily. You can choose from a cheese platter and dessert for A$70 adults or A$63 children, or a three-course lunch (and perhaps a glass of wine) in a "first class" enclosed carriage with white tablecloths for A$92 adults, A$82 children (excluding drinks). On Friday and Saturday nights you can take the train to dinner at a historic packing shed for A$93. Trains do not run on days of total fire ban.

Belgrave Station, Belgrave. © **03/9757 0700.** www.puffingbilly.com.au. Round-trip fares A$26–A$59 adults, A$13–A$30 children 4–16, A$89–A$119 families of 6 (depending on how far you travel). Closed Christmas Day. Train from Flinders St. station in Melbourne to Belgrave; Puffing Billy station is a short walk away.

The Mansion at Werribee Park ★★★   I never tire of visiting this stately 60-room Italianate mansion, just a 30-minute drive along the Princes Freeway from Melbourne. Dubbed "the palace in the paddock," it was built in 1877 and is surrounded by 132 hectares (326 acres) of magnificent formal gardens and bushland. You can wander around the house alone, hire an audio tour, or take a guided tour. Guided tours run at 11:30am, 1:30, and 2:30pm weekdays or 11:30am and 2pm on weekends. It also has an interesting and extensive contemporary sculpture garden to wander in, which you shouldn't miss, and a cafe.

K Rd., Werribee. © **03/8734 5100.** www.parkweb.vic.gov.au. Admission A$8.10 adults, A$5.80 children 4–15, A$25 family of 4. Guided tours cost A$8.50 per person. Mon–Fri 10am–4pm; Sat–Sun and public holidays 10am–4pm (Apr–Sep), daily 10am–5pm (Oct–Mar). Train from Flinders St. station to Werribee; then bus no. 439 or a A$13 taxi ride. The **Werribee Park Shuttle** (© **03/9748 5094;** www.werribeeparkshuttle.com.au) leaves the National Gallery of Victoria, 180 St. Kilda Rd., daily at 9:30am and costs A$25 adults, A$20 children 10–14, A$15 children 4–10 (bookings essential).

Werribee Open Range Zoo ★   This zoo is part of Zoos Victoria, which also runs the Melbourne Zoo. It has a collection of Aussie animals, but the main focus is on the open range part of the zoo, where you will see giraffes, hippos, rhinoceros, lions, zebras, and more. The zoo also has one of the largest gorilla exhibits in the world, home to the silverback Motaba and his two sons. Access to the open-range part of the zoo is strictly by guided tour on a safari bus. The tour takes about an hour. On

Exploring Melbourne

MELBOURNE

busy days, it might pay to spend the extra money to take a small group tour in an open-sided jeep, as you'll get a better view and better photo opportunities. The zoo also has a walk-through section featuring African cats, including cheetahs, and monkeys. If you've been to Africa, you may find little to excite you, but kids love it, and it's crowded with families.

K Rd., Werribee. ℂ **1300/966 784** in Australia or 03/9731 9600. www.zoo.org.au/werribee. Admission A$27 adults, A$13 children 4–15, A$61–A$84 families (Mon–Fri, except school holidays). Entry is free for children on weekends, public holidays, and school holidays. Daily 9am–5pm (last entry at 3:30pm). Safari tours run hourly 10:30am–3:40pm. Take train from Flinders St. station to Werribee, then bus no. 439 or a A$13 taxi ride. The **Werribee Park Shuttle** (ℂ **03/9748 5094;** www.werribeeparkshuttle.com.au) leaves the National Gallery of Victoria, 180 St. Kilda Rd., daily at 9:30am and costs A$25 adults, A$20 children 10–14, A$15 children 4–10 (bookings essential).

Organized Tours

Melbourne River Cruises (ℂ **03/8610 2600;** www.melbcruises.com.au) offers a range of boat trips up and down the Yarra River, taking from 1 to 2 hours. It's a really interesting way to get a feel for the city, and the tours include commentaries. Tours from the city to Williamstown cost A$22 for adults, A$11 for kids 4 to 14, or A$50 for a family of four. Or you can take a 2-hour Melbourne Highlights tour for A$29 adults, A$16 kids, or A$75 families. Call ahead to confirm cruise departure times, as they change, and pick up tickets from the blue Melbourne River Cruises kiosks at the Federation Square riverfront (opposite Flinders St. Station) or on the river at Southgate (on the lower promenade at South Bank).

Real Melbourne Bike Tours (ℂ **0417/339 203** mobile phone; www.rentabike.net.au/biketours) can help you find your bearings and discover some of hidden Melbourne—the back streets and bluestone lanes, markets, cafes, arcades, and bike paths. Run by former journalist Murray Johnson, tours are fun and interesting. The cost is A$110 adults and A$79 children ages 12 to 18, including bike hire, helmet, guided tour, and coffee and cake and lunch along the way. There's even an option to ride an electric bike if you don't want to work up a sweat! Tours leave at 10am (or other times by arrangement) from Rentabike at Federation Square and return around 2pm. Tours can be customized to suit your needs. Bookings are essential.

Outdoor Activities

Birrarung Marr, along the Yarra River east of Federation Square on Batman Avenue (ℂ **03/9658 9658;** www.melbourne.vic.gov.au/parks), is Melbourne's newest major parkland. *Birrarung* means "river of mists" in the Woiwurrung language of the Wurundjeri people who originally inhabited the area; *marr* relates to the side of the river. The wide-open spaces and large, sculptured terraces were designed to

---

Half-Price Tickets

Buy tickets for entertainment events, including opera, dance, and drama, on the day of the performance from the **Half-Tix Desk** (ℂ **03/9650 9420** for daily listings; www.halftixmelbourne.com) in the Melbourne Town Hall on Swanston Street. The booth is open Monday from 10am to 2pm, Tuesday through Thursday 11am to 6pm, Friday 11am to 6:30pm, and Saturday 10am to 4pm (also selling for Sun shows). Tickets must be purchased in person and in cash. Available shows are displayed on the booth door and on the website.

host some of Melbourne's top events and festivals throughout the year, and the terraces provide views of the city, Southbank, King's Domain, and the Yarra River.

The **Royal Botanic Gardens,** 2km (1¼ miles) south of the city on Birdwood Avenue, off St. Kilda Road (✆ **03/9252 2300;** www.rbg.vic.gov.au), are the best gardens in Australia and well worth a few hours of wandering. More than 40 hectares (99 acres) are lush and blooming with some 12,000 plant species from all over the world. Don't miss a visit to the oldest part of the garden, the Tennyson Lawn, with its 120-year-old English elm trees. Other special corners include a fern gully, camellia gardens, an herb garden, rainforests packed with fruit bats, and ponds full of ducks and black swans. Take time to do a guided **Aboriginal Heritage Walk** through the ancestral lands of the Boonerwrung and Woiwurrung people. The 90-minute walk costs A\$25 adults, A\$10 children 6 to 17. It will make you look at the gardens in a different light. Bookings essential on ✆ **03/9252 2429.** The gardens are open daily from 7:30am to sunset. Admission is free. To get there, catch the no. 8 tram and get off at stop 21. Allow at least 2 hours.

Nearby, in King's Domain, take a look at Victoria's first Government House, **La Trobe's Cottage** (✆ **03/9656 9800**). It was built in England and transported to Australia brick by brick in 1836. It is open every Sunday from 2pm to 4pm from October to May, and on Australia Day (Jan 26) and some other public holidays. Admission is A\$5 adults, A\$3 children, and A\$10 for a family. The cottage is also open as part of Government House tours (bookings essential: ✆ **03/8663 7260**) on Mondays and Thursdays. On the other side of Birdwood Avenue is the **Shrine of Remembrance,** a memorial to the servicemen lost in Australia's wars. It's designed so that at 11am on Remembrance Day (Nov 11), a beam of sunlight hits the Stone of Remembrance in the Inner Shrine. Note the eternal flame in the forecourt. King's Domain is stop 12 on the no. 15 tram traveling south along St. Kilda Road.

In **Fitzroy Gardens,** off Wellington Parade, is **Cooks' Cottage** (✆ **03/9419 5766**), which was moved to Melbourne from Great Ayton, in Yorkshire, England, in 1934 to mark Victoria's centenary. The cottage was built by the parents of explorer Captain James Cook, and today it provides the opportunity to learn about Cook's voyages of discovery around the world. Inside, it's spartan and cramped, not unlike a ship's cabin. Admission is A\$5 for adults, A\$2.50 for children 5 to 15, and A\$14 for families. It's open daily from 9am to 5pm (except Christmas Day). Also east of the central business district are the **Treasury Gardens.** Look for the memorial to John F. Kennedy near the lake. To reach Treasury Gardens and Fitzroy Gardens, take tram no. 48 or 75 (or the City Circle) traveling east along Flinders Street. Get off at stop 14 for Treasury Gardens, stop 14A for Fitzroy Gardens.

Extensive bicycle paths wind through the city and suburbs. **Melbourne Bike Share,** Melbourne's public bike hire (✆ **1300 711 590;** www.melbournebikeshare.com.au), has 50 bike stations and 600 bikes at locations around the city. You can't miss the racks of bright blue bikes. You can pay for a bike with Visa or MasterCard (limit of two bikes per credit card). Your card swipe will also take a A\$50 security deposit, which will be refunded later. The first 30 minutes of usage are free, then you pay a fee of A\$2 for 30 minutes (up to your first hour), A\$7 for 90 minutes, and A\$10 for every half-hour after that. The daily rate makes the bike-share system one of the cheapest transport options in town, but only if you have the bike for less than about 2 hours. If you need a bike for longer than that, it's probably cheaper to hire a bike elsewhere. Bike helmets are compulsory by law, and you can buy one for A$5 at 7-Eleven stores in the city center (at press time, however, a free helmet scheme was being trialed, so helmets may be free by the time you arrive in Melbourne). You must be 16 years or older to use the bike-share system.

Melbourne Bike Share has developed a range of suggested bike tours that you can download from the website. You can also buy books and maps from **Bicycle Network Victoria,** Level 4, 246 Bourke St., Melbourne (*C* **1800/639 634** in Australia, or 03/9636 8888; www.bicyclenetwork.com.au); it is also worth checking out their web-site, which is a font of information.

SHOPPING

Ask almost any Melburnian to help you plan your time in the city, and he or she will advise you to shop until you drop. All Australia regards Melbourne as a shopping capital—it has everything from fashion houses to major department stores and unusual souvenir shops. So even if you're also visiting Sydney, save your money until you get to Melbourne, and then indulge!

Start at the magnificent city arcades, such as the **Block Arcade** (between Collins and Little Collins sts.), which has more than 30 shops, including the historic **Hope-toun Tea Rooms** (p. 103), and the **Royal Arcade** (stretching from Little Collins St. to the Bourke St. Mall). Then hit the courts and lanes around **Swanston Street** and the huge **Melbourne Central shopping complex** between Latrobe and Lonsdale streets.

Department store giants **David Jones** (*C* **03/9643 2222;** www.davidjones.com. au)—or DJs, as it's affectionately known—and **Myer** (*C* **03/9661 1111;** www.myer. com.au) both have stores in the city center. DJs spans 2 blocks separated into men's and women's stores and has a vast and tantalizing food hall. Myer is the grand dame of Melbourne's department stores and is in hot competition with David Jones. It has household goods, perfume, jewelry, and fashions, as well as a food section. Both stores are on the Bourke St. Mall.

High-fashion boutiques line the eastern stretch of **Collins Street,** between the Grand Hyatt and the Hotel Sofitel. Collins Street features most international labels, as well as shoe heaven **Miss Louise,** 205 Collins St. (*C* **03/9654 7730**). Nearby Flinders Lane has earned style status with the likes of **Christine,** 181 Flinders Lane (*C* **03/9654 2011**), where women are reputed to sometimes faint over the accessories. Down the road is **Little Collins Street,** another fashionista run with lots of local labels. **Alice Euphemia,** in Cathedral Arcade, 37 Swanston St. (*C* **03/9650 4300**), also stocks upcoming Australian and New Zealand designers.

Next, fan out across the city, taking in **Chapel Street** in South Yarra, for its Austra-lian fashions, and the **Jam Factory,** 500 Chapel St., South Yarra, a series of buildings with a range of shops and food outlets as well as 16 cinema screens. Get there on tram no. 8 or 72 from Swanston Street.

There's also **Toorak Road** in Toorak, for Gucci and other high-priced, high-fashion names; **Bridge Road** in Richmond, for budget and outlet fashion stores; **Lygon Street** in Carlton, for Italian fashion, footwear, and accessories; and **Brunswick Street** in Fitzroy, for a more alternative scene.

DAY TRIPS FROM MELBOURNE

Phillip Island: Penguins on Parade

139km (86 miles) S of Melbourne

Phillip Island's **penguin parade,** which happens every evening at dusk, is one of Australia's most popular animal attractions. There are other, less crowded places in Australia where watching homecoming penguins feels less staged, but at least the guides and boardwalks protect the little ones and their nesting holes from the throngs. Nevertheless, the commercialism of the penguin parade puts a lot of people off—busloads of tourists squashed into a sort of amphitheater hardly feels like being one with nature. But Phillip Island also offers nice beaches, good bushwalking, fishing, and Seal Rocks.

ESSENTIALS

GETTING THERE   Most visitors come to Phillip Island on a day trip from Melbourne and arrive in time for the penguin parade and dinner. Several tour companies run day trips. Among them are **Gray Line** (℗ **1300/858 687** in Australia; www.grayline.com or www.grayline.com.au), which operates a number of different tours, including the daily "penguin express" trips for those who are short of time. The express tour departs Melbourne at 3pm and returns at around 9pm. Tours cost A$126 for adults and A$63 for children, and can be booked online in U.S. dollars before arrival. Upgrades to premium seating at the penguin parade and various other options are available.

If you're driving yourself, Phillip Island is an easy 2-hour trip from Melbourne along the South Gippsland Highway and then the Bass Highway. A bridge connects the island to the mainland.

V/Line (℗ **13 61 96** in Australia; www.vline.com.au) runs a bus from Melbourne to Cowes, but does not take you to any of the attractions on Phillip Island. Once on the island, you need to hire a car, take a tour, or hire a push bike to get around. The parade is 15km (9½ miles) from the center of Cowes.

VISITOR INFORMATION   There are two information centers on the island. The **Phillip Island Information Centre** is at 895 Phillip Island Tourist Rd., Newhaven, just a few kilometers onto the island, and is open daily from 9am to 5pm (6pm in Dec and Jan) and closed Christmas Day. The **Cowes Visitor Information Centre** is at Thompson Avenue, Cowes and is open 9am to 5pm daily (except Christmas Day). The centers share the toll-free number ℗ **1300/366 422** in Australia and the website **www.visitphillipisland.com.**

EXPLORING PHILLIP ISLAND

Visitors approach the island from the east, passing through the town of **Newhaven.** The main town on the island, **Cowes** (pop. 2,400), is on the north coast. The penguin parade is on the far southwest coast.

A **ThreeParks Pass** gives discounted entry to the top attractions, the **Koala Conservation Centre** (see p. 117), the penguin parade, and **Churchill Island Heritage Farm** (℗ **03/5956 7214;** www.churchillisland.org.au). The pass costs A$38 adults, A$19 children ages 4 to 15, and A$96 for families of four; it can be purchased online (www.penguins.org.au) or at any of the attractions.

The trip to the west coast of Phillip Island's Summerland Peninsula ends in an interesting rock formation called the **Nobbies.** This strange-looking outcropping can be reached at low tide by a basalt causeway. You'll get some spectacular views of the coastline and two offshore islands from here. On the farthest of these islands is a population of up to **12,000 Australian fur seals,** the largest colony in Australia. Bring your binoculars. This area is also home to thousands of nesting silver gulls. The **Nobbies Centre** (℡ 03/5951 2800; www.penguins.org.au) is a marine interpretive center with information about the wildlife, binoculars for better viewing, and a cafe. Entry is free from 11am daily until an hour before sunset, when the area is closed to the public to protect the wildlife.

On the north coast of the island, you can explore **Rhyll Inlet,** an intertidal mangrove wetland inhabited by wading birds such as spoonbills, oystercatchers, herons, egrets, cormorants, and the rare bar-tailed godwit and whimbrel. Birders will also love **Swan Lake,** another breeding habitat for wetland birds.

Elsewhere, walking trails lead through heath and pink granite to **Cape Woolamai,** the island's highest point, where there are fabulous coastal views. From September through April, the cape is home to thousands of short-tailed shearwaters (also known as mutton birds).

PHILLIP ISLAND ATTRACTIONS

Koala Conservation Centre ★★   Koalas were introduced to Phillip Island in the 1880s, and at first they thrived in the predator-free environment. However, over-population, the introduction of foxes and dogs, and the clearing of land for farmland and roads have taken their toll. Though you can still see a few koalas in the wild, the best place to find them is at this sanctuary, set up for research and breeding purposes. Visitors can get quite close to them, especially on the elevated boardwalk, which lets you peek into their treetop homes. At around 4pm, the ordinarily sleepy koalas are on the move—but this is also the time when tour buses converge on the place, so it can get crowded.

Fiveways, Phillip Island Tourist Rd., Cowes. ℡ **03/5952 1610.** www.penguins.org.au. Admission A$11 adults, A$5.65 children 4–15, A$28 families of 4. Daily 10am–5pm (2–5pm on Christmas Day).

National Vietnam Veterans Museum ★★   Phillip Island may seem an unusual place to find a national museum, but it's definitely worth a stop. Dedicated to the Australian veterans of the Vietnam War, the collection includes about 6,000 artifacts, including the marbles used in Australia's conscription lottery, uniforms, vehicles, and weapons. Four new galleries have been developed at the NVVM over the past year or so: a Remembrance Gallery, and separate Air, Ground, and Naval Operations galleries. In a revamp of the whole museum, the mezzanine galleries have been rearranged to include exhibition space and a larger exhibit of the Vietnamese story. New interpretative panels have helped give visitors clearer explanations of what they are seeing. The big-ticket item is a Bell AH-IG HueyCobra helicopter gunship, one of only three in Australia, and the museum is also restoring a Canberra bomber, the only surviving example of its kind in the world. There's a moving audiovisual on Australia's involvement in the war from 1962 to 1972. You can have a coffee in the **Nui Dat Café** or buy books and memorabilia from the shop.

25 Veterans Dr., Newhaven. ℡ **03/5956 6400.** www.vietnamvetsmuseum.org. Admission A$12 adults, A$8 children 14 and under, A$30 families of 4. Wed–Mon 10am–5pm (daily during school holidays). Closed Tues, Good Friday, Christmas Eve, Christmas Day and Boxing Day (Dec 26).

Phillip Island Penguin Reserve ★★ The penguin parade takes place every night at dusk, when hundreds of Little Penguins appear at the water's edge, gather in the shallows, and waddle up the beach toward their burrows in the dunes. They're the smallest of the world's 17 species of penguins, standing just 33 centimeters (13 in.) high, and the only penguins that breed on the Australian mainland. **Photography is banned,** because it scares the penguins, as are smoking and touching the penguins. Wear a sweater or jacket, because it gets chilly after the sun goes down. A kiosk selling food opens an hour before the penguins turn up. Reservations for the parade are essential during busy holiday periods such as Easter and in summer.

For a better experience, the more exclusive small-group tours give you a better view of the penguins. **Penguins Plus** allows you to watch the parade from a boardwalk in the company of rangers, while the **Ultimate Penguin Tour** for groups of only 10 people (no children under 16) takes you to a secluded beach away from the main viewing area to watch penguins coming ashore. Another option is a ranger-guided tour, a few hours before the penguins appear, to see behind-the-scenes research.

Summerland Beach, Phillip Island Tourist Rd., Cowes. ℂ **03/5951 2820.** www.penguins.org.au. Admission A$23 adults, A$11 children 4–15, A$57 families of 4. Penguins Plus A$44 adult, A$22 child, A$110 families; VIP Tour (no children 15 and under) A$69; Ultimate Penguin Tour A$80; Penguin Research Tour (no children under 12) A$69 per person. Visitor center opens daily at 10am.

The Mornington Peninsula

80km (50 miles) S of Melbourne

The Mornington Peninsula, a scenic 40km (25-mile) stretch of windswept coastline and hinterland, is one of Melbourne's favorite day-trip and weekend-getaway destinations—and not just because it's a popular wine-producing region. The peninsula's fertile soil, temperate climate, and rolling hills produce excellent wine, particularly pinot noir, shiraz, and chardonnay. Many wineries offer cellar-door tastings; others have excellent restaurants.

ESSENTIALS

GETTING THERE From Melbourne, you can drive to the Mornington Peninsula in about an hour. There are two toll roads, but taking the toll-free Neapean Highway, and then the Point Nepean Road, is just as easy. Getting there by public transport is a time-consuming process, and does not solve the problem of how to get around once you are there.

VISITOR INFORMATION The **Peninsula Visitor Information Centre,** 359 Point Nepean Rd., Dromana (ℂ **1800/804 009** in Australia, or 03/5987 3078; www.visit morningtonpeninsula.org), has plenty of maps and information on the area and can also help book accommodations. It's open daily from 9am to 5pm, except Christmas Day and Good Friday, and from 1pm to 5pm on Anzac Day (Apr 25).

EXPLORING THE MORNINGTON PENINSULA

The coastline of the Mornington Peninsula is lined with good beaches and thick bush. The **Cape Shanck Coastal Park** stretches along the peninsula's Bass Strait foreshore from Portsea to Cape Shanck. It's home to gray kangaroos, southern brown bandicoots, echidnas, native rats, mice, reptiles, bats, and many forest and ocean birds. The park has numerous interconnecting walking tracks providing access to some remote beaches. You can get more information on this and all the other Victorian national parks from www.parkweb.vic.gov.au or by calling ℂ **13 19 63.**

Along the route to the south, stop at the **Mornington Peninsula Regional Gallery,** Dunns Road, Mornington (© **03/5975 4395;** http://mprg.mornpen.vic.gov.au), to check out the work of well-known Australian artists (Tues–Sun 10am–5pm; admission A\$4), or visit the summit at **Arthurs Seat State Park** for glorious views of the coastline. At Sorrento, take time out to spot pelicans on the jetty or visit the town's many galleries.

If you are traveling with kids, stop in at Australia's oldest maze, **Ashcombe Maze & Lavender Gardens,** 15 Shoreham Rd., Shoreham (© **03/5989 8387;** www.ashcombe maze.com.au). My kids loved it. In addition to the big hedge maze, there is also a rose maze made out of 1,200 rose bushes, and the gardens are huge. It also has a pleasant cafe with indoor and outdoor dining. The park is open daily from 8am to 5pm, except Christmas Day; admission is A\$19 for adults, A\$10 for children 4 to 15, and A\$52 to A\$66 for families.

For fabulous wildlife viewing, take a night tour of **Moonlit Sanctuary Wildlife Conservation Park,** 550 Tyabb Tooradin Rd., Pearcedale (© **03/5978 7935;** www. pearcedale-conservation-park.com.au), at the northern end of the peninsula. The sanctuary is open daily from 10am to 5pm (except Christmas Day), but the best way to see Australia's nocturnal animals is on a guided evening tour. The bushland tour will enable you to see animals such as the eastern quoll, the red-bellied pademelon, and the southern bettong, all of which are extinct in the wild on Australia's mainland. Night tours must be booked in advance. I highly recommend this—it's a wonderful way to see and interact with animals and birds you'd never see during daylight hours! Day admission is A\$17 adults, A\$8.50 children, and A\$45 families of four. Night-time admission and guided tour is A\$40 adults, A\$25 children 4 to 15, A\$15 children under 4, or A\$120 for a family of four.

WHERE TO EAT

The Portsea Hotel ★★   The large restaurant at this Tudor-style pub on the seafront is very popular, and the outdoor beer garden overlooking the sea is hard to beat on a sunny day. This sprawling old hotel—looking better than ever after a spruce-up—has a large terrace area at the back, so you can enjoy the sea views from a sheltered spot. On Sundays the popular carvery offers soup and a roast meal for A\$28. The bistro menu is huge, with the daily seafood special changing according to the local catch of the day. Other features are locally caught gummy shark (with chips) and Mt. Martha mussels. There's also a kids' menu. After dining, it's an easy walk down the stairs through the sand dunes to the beach below (keep your eye out for dolphins).

3746 Point Nepean Rd., Portsea, VIC 3944. © **03/5984 2213.** www.portseahotel.com.au. Main courses A\$16–A\$36. Daily noon–9pm (9:30pm Sat.).

The Macedon Ranges

Some of Victoria's finest gardens dot the hills and valleys of the Macedon Ranges, just an hour from Melbourne. In bygone times, the wealthy swapped the city's summer heat for the cooler climes of Macedon. Their legacy of "hill station" private gardens and impressive mansions, along with the region's 40 cool-climate wineries and gourmet foods, are enough reason to visit.

ESSENTIALS

GETTING THERE & GETTING AROUND   The Macedon Ranges are less than an hour's drive from Melbourne along the Calder Freeway, which is a continuation of the

Tullamarine Freeway. Follow the signs towards Bendigo until you reach Gisborne, and then move off the freeway. **V/Line** (✆ **13 61 96** in Australia; www.vline.com.au) trains from Melbourne to Bendigo pass through the Macedon Ranges, stopping at stations including Macedon, Woodend, Kyneton, and Malmsbury. Fares range from A\$14 round-trip to Macedon to A\$22 round-trip to Malmsbury.

VISITOR INFORMATION   There are two visitor information centers in the region: the **Woodend Visitor Centre,** 711 High St., Woodend (✆ **03/5427 2033**), and the **Kyneton Visitor Information Centre,** 127 High St., Kyneton (✆ **03/5422 6110**). Both share the same telephone information line (✆ **1800/244 711**) and are open daily 9am to 5pm (except Christmas Day and Good Friday). The website **www.visit macedonranges.com** is also a good source of information.

EXPLORING THE MACEDON RANGES

The best times to visit the Macedon Ranges for the gardens are April (autumn) and November (spring). During **Open Garden** months (www.opengarden.org.au), private gardens can be viewed by the public. Some homestead gardens open at other times too, including **Duneira** (✆ **03/5426 1490;** www.duneira.com.au) and **Tieve Tara** (✆ **0418/ 337 813** mobile phone; www.gardensoftievetara.com) at Mount Macedon; **Bringalbit,** near Kyneton (✆ **03/5423 7223;** www.bringalbit.com.au); and the Edna Walling garden at **Campaspe Country House,** Woodend (✆ **03/5427 2273;** www.campaspe house.com.au). It pays to call ahead to check times and access (the gardens are often closed in winter). Entry fees apply.

At **Hanging Rock Reserve**, South Rock Road, Woodend (✆ **1800/244 711**), the ghost of Miranda, the fictional schoolgirl who vanished at Hanging Rock in author Joan Lindsay's 1967 novel *Picnic at Hanging Rock,* is never far away. Peter Weir's 1975 film of the novel cemented its fame, but the natural beauty of the area overshadows its slightly spooky reputation. You can climb the rock, walk the tracks, and explore caves like the Black Hole of Calcutta and the Cathedral. You can take a guided tour (night tours are offered in summer). The Hanging Rock Discovery Centre explains the geology and history of the area and revisits the book and movie. The reserve is also home to lots of wildlife including koalas, kangaroos, sugar gliders, echidnas, and wallabies. It's open daily 9am to 5pm. Admission is A\$10 per car or A\$4 per pedestrian.

After the gold rush of the 1850s, Woodend became a resort town with guesthouses, private gardens, a racecourse, a golf club, and hotels. Reminders of those days can be found in the historical buildings and clock tower on High Street. Cafes, provedores, boutiques, and galleries abound. For example, stop in for a beer at the family-run **Holgate Brewhouse,** in the historic Keatings Hotel on High Street (✆ **03/5427 2510;** www.holgatebrewhouse.com). The brewery produces a range of draught beers, and you can buy "tastings" until you decide on your favorite. The beer is brewed using just four ingredients—malt, hops, yeast, and pure Macedon Ranges water. It's open daily noon till late (except Christmas Day).

The hamlet of **Malmsbury** has two main things worth stopping for on the Calder Highway. First, the **Malmsbury Botanic Gardens,** next to the Town Hall, were designed to take advantage of the Coliban River valley and a billabong that was transformed into a group of ornamental lakes. The 5-hectare (12-acre) gardens have a superb collection of mature trees; it's also a popular spot for barbecues, and at Apple Hole you'll find kids leaping into the river from a rope swing. At quiet times, you may even spot a platypus. But Malmsbury's most famous landmark may be the bluestone railway viaduct built by 4,000 men in 1859. At 25m (82 ft.) high, with five 18m (59-ft.) spans, it is one of Australia's longest stone bridges and is best viewed from the gardens. I also like to pop in to **Tin Shed Arts** (☎ 03/5423 2144), a spacious gallery on the highway that always has something interesting and unexpected. It hangs contemporary and traditional art from both local artists and well-known names from around Australia. You'll find paintings, mixed media, sculpture, and craftwork. It's open Thursday to Monday 10am to 5pm. The gallery is next door to the **Malmsbury Bakery** (☎ 03/5423 2369), a local institution where you'll find plenty of hot pies, bread, and snacks to tempt you. They share a website: www.malmsburybakeryandgallery.com.au.

In **Kyneton,** turn down **Piper Street** for antiques, homewares, cafes, a heritage pub, and much more. The **Kyneton Farmers' Market** is held at Saint Paul's Park in Piper Street on the second Saturday of the month from 8am to 1pm.

With more than 40 vineyards and 20 cellar doors in the region, wine buffs who want to sample the product should consider a tour. **Victoria Winery Tours** (☎ **1300/946 386;** www.winetours.com.au) runs small-group (minimum two people) day tours from Melbourne, visiting four or five wineries. Pickup in Melbourne is at 9am, returning by about 5:30pm. The cost is A$150 per person, including morning tea and lunch.

WHERE TO EAT

Pizza Verde ★★ PIZZA   If you like your pizza thin and crisp, made from organic or gluten-free flour and adorned with tasty organic toppings, then this 1950s-style diner is the place for you. Some unlikely combinations include the "green" pizza—topped with zucchini, ricotta, mint, garlic, and lemon (with optional chili)—or the potato-topped pizza with caramelized onions and pancetta. Some have the traditional tomato base, others an olive-oil base. There's also meatballs or a vegetable pasta for those who don't want pizza.

62 Piper St., Kyneton. ☎ **03/5422 7400.** www.pizzaverde.com. Main courses A$15–A$18. Thurs–Mon 5pm–late; Sat–Sun 11am–late.

Daylesford

108km (67 miles) NW of Melbourne

Daylesford can be a terrific day trip from Melbourne or can easily be combined with a trip to the Macedon Ranges (see p. 119). Part of "spa country," this village is a bit of a trendy getaway for Melburnians. Along the main street, you'll find small galleries, homewares shops, and some smart foodie outlets.

ESSENTIALS

GETTING THERE   From Melbourne, take the Citylink toll road (the M2) north towards Melbourne Airport. Take the Calder Highway turnoff towards Bendigo (M79), and continue until you see the turnoff to Daylesford (C792); then follow the signs. The road will take you through Woodend, Tylden, and Trentham. At Trentham take the C317 to Daylesford. When you arrive in Daylesford, turn right at the roundabout as signposted to get to Hepburn Springs.

VISITOR INFORMATION   The **Daylesford Regional Visitor Information Centre,** 98 Vincent St. (☎ 03/5321 6123; www.visitdaylesford.com), features an interpretive display about the area's mineral waters. It's open daily from 9am to 5pm, except Christmas Day.

EXPLORING DAYLESFORD

Australians have been heading to Hepburn Springs, on the edge of Daylesford, to "take the waters" since 1895, and the region now has about a dozen or so day spas. The original, and most famous, is **Hepburn Bathhouse & Spa** (© **03/5321 6000**; www. hepburnbathhouse.com). Not everyone likes the slick, modern, and rather cold new extension that has replaced the elegant old wooden building, but sink into the hot pools and it's easy to forget what the exterior looks like. There's traditional communal bathing in the Bathhouse and the Sanctuary, or you can book in to the Spa (in the original bathhouse building; reservations essential) for the usual range of therapies and treatments. The complex includes an aroma steam room, salt therapy pool, relaxation pool, and "spa couches" submerged in mineral water (which I didn't find very comfortable). The complex is on Mineral Springs Reserve Road and is open daily 9am to 6:30pm (except Christmas Day). Entry to the Bathhouse for 2 hours costs A$26 adults, A$19 children 2 to 16, and A$79 for a family of four Tuesday to Thursday; and A$39 adults, A$27 children, and A$109 families Friday to Monday and on public holidays. Entry to the Sanctuary is A$58 Tuesday to Thursday and A$83 Friday to Monday and public holidays. Towel hire is A$5. A 30-minute private mineral bath at The Spa costs from A$70 to A$77 depending on the day of the week.

On the hill behind Daylesford's main street is **The Convent** (© **03/5348 3211**; www.theconvent.com.au), a three-level historic 19th-century mansion, complete with twisting staircases. It is comprised of a restaurant, a gallery, gardens, a chapel, and shops, as well as a small museum that speaks to its origins as a private home, which later became the Holy Cross Convent and Boarding School for Girls. After years of dereliction, it reopened as a gallery in 1991, but the nuns' infirmary and one of the "cells," or bedrooms, were left unrestored. You'll find it on the corner of Hill and Daly streets. It's open daily 10am to 4pm (3pm on New Year's Eve), closed Good Friday, Christmas Day, and Boxing Day (Dec 26). Admission is A$5 per person. Take time to wander through the lovely gardens, with their sculptures and bench seats.

Just outside Daylesford is **Lavandula** (© **03/5476 4393**; www.lavandula.com.au), a Swiss-Italian lavender farm that has a rustic trattoria-style cafe and a cobblestone courtyard with a cluster of farmhouse buildings. Swiss immigrants ran a dairy farm here in the 1860s, but today you can see the process of lavender farming and buy lavender products. The restored stone farmhouse is a picturesque backdrop to gardens where you can picnic, play boules (like bocce), or just relax and admire the scenery. The lavender is in full bloom in December, with harvesting in January. Lavandula is at 350 Hepburn-Newstead Rd., Shepherds Flat, about 10 minutes' drive north of Daylesford. It is open daily from 10:30am to 5:30pm September to May (except Dec 24–26) and on weekends, public holidays, and school holidays only in June, July, and August. The cafe is closed during August. Admission is A$3.50 adults, A$1 school-age children.

WHERE TO EAT

The Lake House ★★★ Treat yourself to one of Australia's best restaurants while you're in Daylesford. The Lake House is set on the edge Lake Daylesford, on 2.4 hectares (6 acres) of beautiful gardens, and is the creation of Alla and Allan Wolf-Tasker. Alla is the executive chef, and Allan's vibrant artworks adorn the walls of the light-filled restaurant overlooking the lake (and adjoining the accommodation, if you can't tear yourself away). The restaurant is renowned for its commitment to local and seasonal produce, and the menu changes daily. If—like me—you are tempted by tastes not often on offer at city restaurants, you will relish the offerings on the lunch menu: for example, smoked Skipton eel with pancetta, shallot confit, beetroot remoulade, and mustard crème fraiche; or rabbit cassoulet. Walk it off on the track around the lake!

King St., Daylesford, VIC 3460. ℗ **03/5348 3329.** www.lakehouse.com.au. Lunch from A$76 for two to four courses; dinner from A$80; 8-course tasting menu A$140. Daily noon–2:30pm and 6–9:30pm.

Ballarat

113km (70 miles) W of Melbourne

History buffs will love Ballarat. Victoria's largest inland city (pop. 90,000) is synonymous with two major events in Australia's past: the gold rush of the 1850s and the birth of Australian democracy in the early 20th century. It all started with gold; in 1851 two prospectors found gold nuggets scattered on the ground at a place known as, ironically, Poverty Point. Within a year, 20,000 people had drifted into the area, and Australia's El Dorado gold rush had begun.

In 1858, the second-largest chunk of gold discovered in Australia (the Welcome Nugget) was found, but by the early 1860s, most of the easy diggings were gone. Larger operators continued digging until 1918, but by then Ballarat had developed enough industry to survive without mining. Today, you can still see the gold rush's effects in the impressive buildings, built from the miners' fortunes, lining Ballarat's streets.

ESSENTIALS

GETTING THERE   From Melbourne, Ballarat is a 1½-hour drive on the Great Western Highway. **V/Line** (℗ **13 61 96** in Victoria, or 03/8608 5011; www.vline.com.au) runs trains between the cities every day; the trip takes about 90 minutes. The return fare is A$30 for adults and A$15 for children. Ask about off-peak and family-saver fares.

Several companies offer day trips from Melbourne. They include **AAT Kings** (℗ **1300/228 546** in Australia; www.aatkings.com). A full-day tour costs A$149 for adults and A$75 for children.

VISITOR INFORMATION   The **Ballarat Visitor Information Centre** is at 43 Lydiard St. (℗ **1800/446 633** in Australia, or 03/5320 5741; www.visitballarat.com.au), opposite the Art Gallery of Ballarat. It is open daily from 9am to 5pm (except Christmas Day).

EXPLORING BALLARAT

Art Gallery of Ballarat ★★★   This excellent gallery, founded in 1884, is Australia's oldest regional gallery and houses a fine collection of Australian art, including paintings from the Heidelberg School and a stunning collection of 20th-century modernists. It also hosts interesting contemporary exhibitions on popular themes. Free guided tours are run at 2pm Wednesday to Sunday.

40 Lydiard St. N. ℗ **03/5320 5858.** www.balgal.com. Free admission. Daily 9am–5pm. Closed Christmas Day and Boxing Day (Dec. 26).

Ballarat Botanical Gardens ★★★   These delightful gardens are well worth visiting. The gold-rich citizens of Ballarat bestowed magnificent gifts on the gardens

A eureka MOMENT

The story that is central to Ballarat's history, and many of its attractions, is that of the **Eureka Uprising** in 1854. The story goes like this: After gold was discovered, the government introduced gold licenses, charging miners even if they came up empty-handed. The miners had to buy a license every month, and corrupt gold-field police (many of whom were former convicts) instituted a vicious campaign to extract the money. When license checks intensified in 1854, resentment flared. Prospectors began demanding political reforms, such as the right to vote, parliamentary elections, and secret ballots. The situation exploded when the Eureka Hotel's owner murdered a miner but was set free by the government. The hotel was burned down in revenge, and more than 20,000 prospectors joined together, burned their licenses in a huge bonfire, and built a stockade over which they raised a flag. Troops arrived at the "Eureka Stockade" the next month, but only 150 miners remained. The stockade was attacked at dawn, with 24 miners killed and 30 wounded. The uprising forced the government to act: The licenses were replaced with "miners' rights" and cheaper fees, and the vote was introduced to Victoria. It was a definitive moment in Australia's history, and the Eureka flag (p. 125) is still a potent (and often controversial) symbol of nationalism.

from its early days, including the collection of 12 marble statues that now stand in the conservatory, the elegant Statuary Pavilion and its contents—including the wonderful *Flight from Pompeii*—and a statue of William Wallace near the gardens' entrance. Other highlights include Prime Ministers Avenue, lined with bronze busts of Australia's 27 PMs, and the striking Australian Ex-Prisoners of War Memorial at the southwestern end of the gardens. One of the greatest attractions is an avenue of 70 giant redwoods, planted about 130 years ago. The gardens' cafe overlooks Lake Wendouree.

Wendouree Parade. ☏ **03/5320 5135.** www.ballarat.vic.gov.au. Free admission. Conservatory daily 9am–5pm. Bus: 16.

Blood on the Southern Cross ★★★   This breathtaking sound-and-light show re-creates the Eureka Uprising, one of the most important events in Australia's history. You will be outdoors, so bring something warm to wear, because it can get chilly at night. It's stirring stuff, and the reenactment does the story justice. The show runs 90 minutes and is full of surprises.

Sovereign Hill, Bradshaw St. ☏ **03/5337 1199.** www.sovereignhill.com.au. Reservations required. Admission A$57 adults, A$31 children 5–15, A$154 families of 4. Package with daytime entry to Sovereign Hill (see beloΣ) A$104 adults, A$52 children, A$272 families. Ask about package with dinner and overnight accommodations. 2 shows nightly (times vary seasonally).

The Gold Museum ★   A 4.4kg gold nugget—known as "Goldasaurus"—is the latest highlight in this surprisingly interesting small museum. Found by a local prospector, it is one of the things you will discover more about by taking the free "Golden Treasures" 20-minute guided tour of the museum, run daily at 4:30pm. As well as a large collection of gold nuggets found at Ballarat, the museum has displays of alluvial deposits, gold ornaments, coins, and the history of gold mining in the area.

Bradshaw St. (opposite Sovereign Hill). ℭ **03/5337 1107.** Admission A$11 adults, A$5.90 children 5–15, A$30 family of 6. Admission free with entry to Sovereign Hill (see below). Daily 9:30am–5:30pm (except Christmas Day).

Museum of Australian Democracy at Eureka ★★   The highlight of a visit to Australia's newest museum—especially after you've learned the story of the Eureka Uprising (see "A Eureka Moment," p. 124)—is the sight of the original Eureka flag, made from petticoat fabric by the women of the uprising and now enshrined here. Opened in May 2013, the museum features an evocative, dimly lit purpose-built display gallery for the beautiful, fragile blue-and-white Eureka Flag. Interactive exhibitions look at the evolution and future of democracy and associated issues such as culture, civics, history, and citizenship. It also has a cafe, gift shop, and gardens.

102 Stawell St. S. (at Eureka St.). ℭ **1800 287 113** in Australia. www.made.org. Admission A$12 adults, free for children 15 and under. Daily 10am–5pm. Closed Christmas Day. Bus: 9 from Ballarat Station (Bus 8 for the return trip).

Sovereign Hill ★★★   Living in the gold-rush times wasn't all beer and skittles, and the latest multimillion-dollar underground exhibit at this colonial-era "living museum" tells the story of a mining disaster that struck in 1882. "Trapped" is a multisensory experience that tells a story of bravery, love, and loss. Ballarat's history comes to life at Sovereign Hill, long described as Australia's best outdoor museum, which transports you back to the 1850s and the heady days of the gold rush. More than 40 reproduction buildings, including shops and businesses on Main Street, sit on the 25-hectare (62-acre) former gold-mining site. There are also tent camps around the diggings on what would have been the outskirts of town. Sovereign Hill has a lot to see and do, so expect to spend at least 4 hours here. The township bustles with actors in period costumes going about their daily business. You can pan for real gold, ride in horse-drawn carriages, and watch potters, blacksmiths, and tanners make their wares. Don't miss the gold pour at the smelting works, or the redcoats as they parade through the streets. On top of Sovereign Hill are the mine shafts and pithead equipment. The guided tour of a typical underground gold mine takes around 45 minutes and costs A$7.50 for adults, A$4 children, and A$20 for a family of 6. A restaurant and several cafes and souvenir stores are scattered around the site.

Bradshaw St. ℭ **03/5331 1944.** www.sovereignhill.com.au. Admission A$43 adults, A$20 children 5–15, A$78–A$108 families. **Gold Pass** (including Gold Museum, unlimited coach rides, 3 mine tours, and 1 souvenir gold bottle per ticket type) A$77 adults, A$38 children, A$158–A$199 families. Daily 10am–5pm. Closed Christmas Day. Bus: 9 from Curtis St. or the railway station. A free bus meets the daily 9:07am (9:28am on Sun) train (the "Goldrush Special" from Melbourne's Southern Cross railway station) when it arrives at Ballarat Station, and takes visitors direct to Sovereign Hill. Return service connects with the 3:58pm (4:10pm on Sat–Sun) train back to Melbourne.

WHERE TO EAT

Eclectic Tastes ★★ CAFE   You might find it hard to concentrate on your breakfast, lunch, coffee or snack, as your eyes will be on the surroundings, which live up to the cafe's name—five rooms packed to the rafters with colorful trash and treasure! Your menu is pasted inside the cardboard covers of a Little Golden Book (think *The Shy Little Kitten* and other titles from your childhood) and might include a great Thai chicken curry, a seafood laksa, or something more simple, like a steak sandwich. You'll find it opposite the Ballarat Cemetery near the shores of Lake Wendouree (a bit off the beaten track but worth the effort).

2 Burbank St., Ballarat. © **03/5339 9252.** www.eclectictastes.net. Main courses A$9–A$26. Mon–Fri 9am–4pm; Sat–Sun 8am–4pm.

Oscar's ★ CONTEMPORARY   This cafe and bar inside one of Ballarat's historic old pubs is in the heart of the town, walking distance from shopping, the art gallery, and many other attractions. The former gold rush–era hotel has an appealing open-plan restaurant, with a courtyard and bar. It's open for breakfast, lunch, and dinner and you can get snacks all day. Meals include Asian, pizzas, pasta, steaks, and gluten-free dishes.

18 Doveton St. S., Ballarat. © **03/5331 1451.** www.oscarshotel.com.au. Main courses A$17–A$36. Daily 7am–10pm.

BRISBANE

Brisbane is one of those cities that seems always to be changing, without ever losing its essential heart and character. It's that most Australian of cities—big-hearted, blue-skied, and with a down-to-earth attitude that soon rubs off on you. Brisbane will most likely be your first port of call in Queensland, and you can even reach the southernmost part of the Great Barrier Reef on a day trip from here.

Brisbane (pronounced *Briz*-bun), "Brizzie" to locals, functions on a very human scale. It's a place where you can cuddle koalas, join bronzed urbanites on the beaches on the weekend, and sunbathe by the Brisbane River while gazing up at the city's gleaming skyscrapers. Take the lead of the easygoing Brisbanites because Queensland's subtropical capital is too hot to rush.

Beyond landmarks such as the 1920s **City Hall,** which reopened in 2013 after a A$215-million 3-year restoration, and the **Treasury Building**'s graceful colonnades, Brisbane's major attractions are outdoors. Cool down under a canopy of subtropical foliage at the **Brisbane Botanic Gardens.** Gaze at contemporary art at the **Gallery of Modern Art (GOMA),** dinosaurs at the **Queensland Museum,** and skyscrapers from the gently revolving **Wheel of Brisbane.** Koalas—more than 130 of them—beg a cuddle at the **Lone Pine Koala Sanctuary.**

The **city center** and surrounding suburbs represent fusion cuisine at its finest. Party and dining hotspot **Fortitude Valley** serves the world on a plate—everything from Spanish tapas to Thai—in chic lounge-style restaurants. **South Bank** goes alfresco in casual eateries dishing up fresh seafood and modern Australian fare, with glittering Brisbane River views.

ESSENTIALS

Arriving

BY PLANE About 30 international airlines serve Brisbane from Europe, North America, Asia, and New Zealand. From North America, you can fly direct from Los Angeles to Brisbane on Qantas, but from other places you will likely fly to Sydney first, then take a connecting flight to Brisbane, or come via Auckland, New Zealand.

Qantas (© **13 13 13** in Australia; www.qantas.com.au) and its subsidiary **QantasLink** (book through Qantas) operate daily flights from all state capitals, Cairns, Townsville, and several other towns. **Jetstar** (© **13 15 38** in Australia; www.jetstar.com.au) has daily service from the Queensland

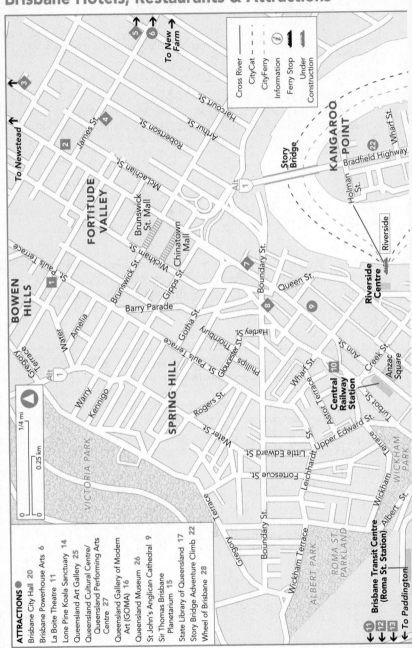

ATTRACTIONS ●

Brisbane City Hall 20
Brisbane Powerhouse Arts 6
La Boite Theatre 11
Lone Pine Koala Sanctuary 14
Queensland Art Gallery 25
Queensland Cultural Centre/
Queensland Performing Arts
Centre 27
Queensland Gallery of Modern
Art (GOMA) 16
Queensland Museum 26
St John's Anglican Cathedral 9
Sir Thomas Brisbane
Planetarium 15
State Library of Queensland 17
Story Bridge Adventure Climb 22
Wheel of Brisbane 28

FORTITUDE VALLEY
BOWEN HILLS
SPRING HILL
KANGAROO POINT

To Newstead
To New Farm
To Paddington

Story Bridge
Bradfield Highway

Central Railway Station
Brisbane Transit Centre
(Roma St. Station)

Riverside Centre
Riverside

VICTORIA PARK
ALBERT PARK
ROMA ST. PARKLAND
WICKHAM PARK

Cross River
CityCat
CityFerry
Information
Ferry Stop
Under Construction

1/4 mi
0.25 km

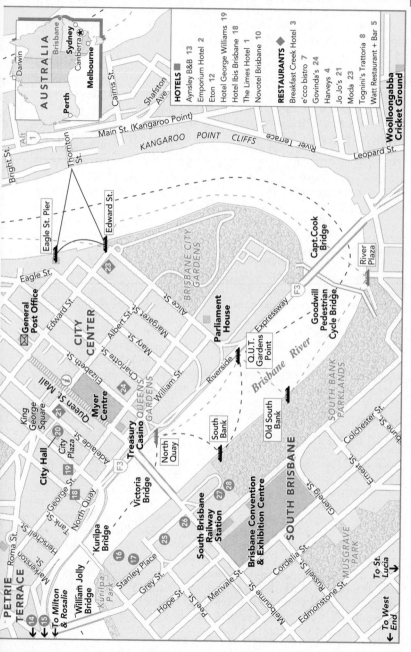

HOTELS ■
Aynsley B&B 13
Emporium Hotel 2
Eton 12
Hotel George Williams 19
Hotel Ibis Brisbane 18
The Limes Hotel 1
Novotel Brisbane 10

RESTAURANTS ◆
Breakfast Creek Hotel 3
e'cco bistro 7
Govinda's 24
Harveys 4
Jo Jo's 21
Moda 23
Tognini's Trattoria 8
Watt Restaurant + Bar 5

centers of Cairns, Townsville, Proserpine and Hamilton Island, as well as Sydney, Melbourne, and other Australian cities. **Virgin Australia** (✆ **13 67 89** in Australia; www.virginaustralia.com.au) offers direct services from all capital cities as well as Cairns, Townsville, Hamilton Island and Proserpine in the Whitsundays, and other centers. **Tigerair** (✆ **03/9335 3033;** www.tigerairways.com.au) flies from Sydney and Melbourne too.

Brisbane International Airport (www.bne.com.au) is 16km (10 miles) from the city, and the domestic terminal is 2km (1¼ miles) farther away. An inter-terminal bus costs A$5, or you can catch the train (see p. 132) for the same price. If you are traveling on Virgin Australia, the train is free upon showing your boarding pass. The arrivals floor of the international terminal, on Level 2, has a check-in counter for passengers transferring to domestic flights and an information desk to meet all flights, help with flight inquiries, dispense tourist information, and make hotel bookings. **Travelex** currency-exchange bureaus are on the departures and arrivals floors. **Avis** (✆ **07/3633 8666**), **Budget** (✆ **1300/362 848** in Australia), **Europcar** (✆ **13 13 90** in Australia), **Hertz** (✆ **07/3860 4996**) **Thrifty** (✆ **3000 8200**), and local company **Red Spot Rentals** (✆ **07/3860 5766**) have desks on Level 2. On levels 2, 3, and 4 you will find ATMs, free showers, and baby-changing rooms. The domestic terminal has a Travelex currency-exchange bureau, ATMs, showers, and the big four car-rental desks. For security reasons, luggage lockers are not available at either terminal.

Con-x-ion (✆ **07/5556 9888;** www.con-x-ion.com) runs a shuttle between the airport and city hotels and the Brisbane Transit Centre every 30 minutes from 5am to 11pm. The one-way cost is A$15 per person (or A$25 for two; cheaper the more in your group). The trip takes about 40 minutes. No public buses serve the airport. A **taxi** to the city costs around A$35, plus a A$3.30 airport fee for departing taxis.

Airtrain (✆ **1800/119 091** in Australia or 07/3216 3308; www.airtrain.com.au), a rail link between the city and Brisbane's domestic and international airport terminals, runs every 15 minutes from around 5:45am to 10pm daily. Fares from the airport to city stations are A$16 per adult one-way, A$30 round-trip; kids aged 14 and under travel free. The trip takes about 20 minutes. A taxi between terminals costs about A$12.

BY TRAIN   **Queensland Rail** (✆ **1800/872 467** in Australia; www.queenslandrail.com.au) operates several long-distance trains to Brisbane from Cairns. The high-speed Tilt Train takes about 24 hours and costs A$369 for business class. The slower Sunlander takes 32 hours and costs A$161 for a sitting berth, from A$268 for a sleeper, or A$899 for the all-inclusive Queenslander class. **NSW TrainLink** (✆ **13 22 32** in Australia; www.nswtrainlink.info) runs two daily train services to Brisbane from Sydney. The 7:15am departure arrives in the town of Casino, south of the border, at about 7pm, where passengers transfer to a bus for the rest of the trip to Brisbane, arriving at about 10:30pm. The overnight train leaves Sydney at 4:10pm and arrives in Brisbane at 6:30am the next day. Fares vary slightly but cost around A$91 for an adult economy seat or A$122 for a first-class seat. A sleeper costs A$216.

All intercity and interstate trains pull into the city center's **Brisbane Transit Centre at Roma Street,** often called the Roma Street Transit Centre. From here, most city and Spring Hill hotels are a few blocks' walk or a quick cab ride away. The station has food outlets, showers, tourist information, and lockers.

Queensland Rail CityTrain (℡ **13 12 30** in Queensland) provides daily train service from the Sunshine Coast and plentiful service from the Gold Coast.

BY BUS   All intercity and interstate coaches pull into the Brisbane Transit Centre (see "By Train," above). **Greyhound Australia** (℡ **1300/473 946** in Australia or 07/3236 3035 for the Brisbane terminal; www.greyhound.com.au) serves the city several times daily. A one-way Cairns-Brisbane ticket costs A$309; the trip takes nearly 30 hours. The Sydney-Brisbane trip takes about 17 hours and costs A$182 one-way.

BY CAR   The Bruce Highway from Cairns enters the city from the north. The Pacific Highway enters Brisbane from the south.

Visitor Information

The **Brisbane Visitor Information Centre** (℡ **07/3006 6290;** www.visitbrisbane. com.au) is in the Queen Street Mall, between Edward and Albert streets. It's open Monday through Thursday from 9am to 5:30pm, Friday 9am to 7pm, Saturday 9am to 5pm, Sunday 10am to 5pm, public holidays 9:30am to 4:30pm, and from 1:30pm on Anzac Day (Apr 25). It's closed Christmas Day and Good Friday. There are also visitor information centers at the airport, and at South Bank Parklands (see p. 142).

City Layout

The city center's office towers shimmer in the sun on the north bank of a curve of the Brisbane River. At the tip of the curve are the lush Brisbane City Gardens (sometimes called the City Botanic Gardens). The 30m (98-ft.) sandstone cliffs of Kangaroo Point rise on the eastern side of the south bank; to the west are the South Bank Parklands and the Queensland Cultural Centre, known as South Bank. Two pedestrian bridges link South Bank with the city: the **Goodwill Bridge** links South Bank with the City Gardens, while the **Kurilpa Bridge** links Tank Street, in the city center, with the Gallery of Modern Art at South Bank. To the west 5km (3 miles), Mount Coot-tha (pronounced *Coo*-tha) looms out of the flat plain.

MAIN ARTERIES & STREETS   It's easy to find your way around central Brisbane once you know that the east-west streets are named after female British royalty, and the north-south streets are named after their male counterparts. The northernmost is Ann, followed by Adelaide, Queen, Elizabeth, Charlotte, Mary, Margaret, and Alice. From east to west, the streets are Edward, Albert, George, and William, which becomes North Quay, flanking the river's northeast bank.

Queen Street, the main thoroughfare, becomes a pedestrian mall between Edward and George streets. Roma Street exits the city diagonally to the northwest. Ann Street leads all the way east into Fortitude Valley. The main street in Fortitude Valley is Brunswick Street, which runs into New Farm.

Neighborhoods in Brief

CITY CENTER   The vibrant city center is where residents eat, shop, and socialize. Queen Street Mall, in the heart of town, is popular with shoppers and moviegoers, especially on weekends and Friday night (when stores stay open until 9pm). The Eagle Street financial and legal precinct has great restaurants with river views and, on Sunday, markets by the Riverside Centre tower and the Pier. Much of Brisbane's colonial architecture is in the city center, too. Strollers, bike riders, and in-line skaters shake the summer heat in the green haven of the Brisbane City Gardens at the business district's southern end.

FORTITUDE VALLEY "The Valley," as locals call it, was once one of the sleazier parts of town. Today, it is a stamping ground for street-smart young folk who meet in restored pubs and eat in cool cafes. The lanterns, food stores, and shopping mall of Chinatown are here, too. On weekends, you'll find Brisbane's only alternative market, Valley Markets in the Brunswick Street and Chinatown malls (take Turbot Street from the city center). Venture a little farther to the trendy boutiques and cafes of James Street.

NEW FARM Always an appealing suburb, New Farm is an in-spot for cafe-hopping. Merthyr Street is where the action is, especially on Friday and Saturday nights. From the intersection of Wickham and Brunswick streets, follow Brunswick southeast for 13 blocks to Merthyr.

PADDINGTON This hilltop suburb, a couple of miles northwest of the city, is one of Brisbane's most attractive. Brightly painted Queenslander cottages line the main street, Latrobe Terrace, as it winds west along a ridge top. Many of the houses have been turned into shops and cafes, where you can browse, enjoy coffee and cake, or just admire the charming architecture.

MILTON & ROSALIE Park Road, in Milton, is not quite a little bit of Europe, but it tries hard—right down to a replica Eiffel Tower above the cafes and shops. Italian restaurants line the street, buzzing with office workers who down espressos at alfresco restaurants, scout interior-design stores for a new objet d'art, and stock up on European designer rags.

WEST END This small inner-city enclave is alive with ethnic restaurants, cafes, and the odd, interesting housewares or fashion store. Most action centers on the intersection of Vulture and Boundary streets, where Asian grocers and delis abound.

GETTING AROUND
By Public Transportation

TransLink operates a single network of buses, trains, and ferries. For timetables and route inquiries, call **TransInfo** (🕿 **13 12 30**; www.translink.com.au). It uses an integrated ticket system, and the easiest place to buy your tickets is on the buses and ferries or at the train stations. You can also buy tickets and pick up maps and timetables at the Queen Street bus station information center (in the Myer Centre, off Queen St. Mall) and the Brisbane Visitor Information Centre in the Queen Street Mall. Tickets and electronic go-cards are also sold at some inner-city newsdealers and 7-Eleven convenience stores.

A trip in a single sector or zone on the bus, train, or ferry costs A$4.80. A single ticket is good for up to 2 hours on a one-way journey on any combination of bus, train, or ferry. When traveling with a parent, kids under 5 travel free and kids 5 to 14 and students pay half fare. If you plan on using public transport a lot, it is worth investing in a go-card, which gives discounted rates (you can also buy online and just top up the card balance as you need it). This would reduce the price of a one-zone one-way trip to A$3.30. You will probably not need to travel farther than four zones on the transport system. This will cost you the princely sum of A$7.50. On weekends and public holidays, it's cheaper to buy an **off-peak ticket.** The off-peak ticket is also available on weekdays, but you must plan your sightseeing around the fact that it cannot be used before 9am or between 3:30 and 7pm. You might also like to buy a **SEEQ card,** specially designed for visitors, which offers 3 or 5 consecutive days' travel on all public transport services, including two Airtrain trips. It also includes around A$700 worth of discounts at 80 attractions in and around Brisbane. SEEQ cards cost A$79 adults and A$40 children for 3 days or A$129 adults and A$65 children for 5 days.

BY BUS Buses operate from around 5am to 11pm weekdays, with less service on weekends. On Sunday, many routes stop around 5pm. Most buses depart from City Hall at King George Square, Adelaide, or Ann Street. The Loop is a free bus service that circles the city center. The Loop's distinctive red buses run on two routes, stopping at convenient places including Central Station, Queen Street Mall, City Botanic Gardens, Riverside Centre, and King George Square. Look for the red bus stops. They run every 15 minutes from 7am to 6pm Monday through Friday.

BY FERRY The fast **CityCat** ferries run to many places of interest, including South Bank and the Queensland Cultural Centre; the restaurants and Sunday markets at the Riverside Centre; and New Farm Park, not far from the cafes of Merthyr Street. They run every half-hour between the University of Queensland to the south of the city center, and Hamilton to the north (a route of around 20km/12 miles). Slower but more frequent CityFerry service (the **Inner City** and **Cross River** ferries) has stops at points including the south end of South Bank Parklands, Kangaroo Point, and Edward Street right outside the Brisbane City Gardens. Ferries run from around 6am to 10:30pm daily. Two hours on the CityCat takes you the entire length of the run (and there's free Wi-Fi on board too!).

BY TRAIN Brisbane's suburban rail network is fast, quiet, safe, and clean. Trains run from around 5am to midnight (until about 11pm on Sun). All trains leave Central Station, between Turbot and Ann streets at Edward Street.

BY BICYCLE CityCycle (© **1300/229 253**; www.citycycle.com.au) has 150 bike parking stations across inner city Brisbane, with bright yellow bikes and helmets (compulsory by law) to hire. You can hire a bike between 5am and 10pm daily and return it to the station at any time. You can buy a subscription for A$2 a day or A$11 a week, and the first 30 minutes of hire is free. After that, usage charges start from A$2.20. Two to three hours will cost A$20, and 24 hours A$165—so unless you are only planning a short ride, it's cheaper to hire a bike elsewhere.

By Car or Taxi

Brisbane's grid of one-way streets can be confusing, so plan your route before setting out. Brisbane's biggest parking lot is at the Myer Centre (off Elizabeth St.), open 24 hours (© **07/3229 1699**). Most hotels and motels have free parking for guests.

Avis (© **13 63 33** or 07/3247 0577), **Budget** (© **1300/362 848** in Australia or 07/3220 0699), **Europcar** (© **13 13 90** in Australia or 07/3006 7440), **Hertz** (© **13 30 39** or 07/3221 6166) and **Thrifty** (© **07/3006 3255** in Australia) all have outlets in the city center.

For a taxi, call **Yellow Cabs** (© **13 19 24** in Australia) or **Black and White Taxis** (© **13 32 22** in Australia). There are taxi stands at each end of Queen Street Mall, on Edward Street and on George Street (outside the Treasury Casino).

[Fast FACTS] BRISBANE

ATMs/Banks Banks are open Monday through Thursday 9:30am to 4pm, until 5pm on Friday.

Business Hours Brisbane shops are open Monday through Thursday 9am to 6pm, Friday 9am to 9pm, Saturday 9am to 5:30pm, and Sunday 10am to 6pm. On Friday evening in the city, the Queen Street Mall is abuzz with cinemagoers and revelers; the late (until 9pm) shopping night in Paddington is Thursday. Some restaurants close Monday night, Tuesday night, or both; bars are generally open from 10 or 11am until midnight.

Dentists **Calm Dental,** 171 Moray St., New Farm (© **07/3358 1333**), is open 8am to 8pm Monday through Thursday, 8am to 5pm Friday, and 8am to 3pm weekends. For after-hours emergencies, call for recorded info on who to contact.

Doctors & Hospitals The **Royal Brisbane Hospital** is about a 15-minute drive from the city at Herston Road, Herston (© **07/3636 8111**).The **Travel Doctor** (© **07/3221 9066;** www.thetraveldoctor.com. au) is on Level 5, 247 Adelaide St., between Creek and Edward streets. It's

open Monday to Friday 8am to 4:30pm (until 5pm Mon and 7pm Wed) and Saturday 8:30am to 2pm. For after-hours emergencies, call © **0408/199 166.**

Embassies & Consulates The United States, Canada, and New Zealand have no representation in Brisbane; see chapter 4, "Sydney," for those countries' nearest offices. The **British Consulate** is at Level 9, 100 Eagle St. (© **07/ 3223 3200**). It is open weekdays from 9am to 5pm.

Emergencies Dial © **000** for fire, ambulance, or police help in an emergency. This is a free call from a private or public telephone. **Lifeline** (© **13 11 14**) is a 24-hour emotional crisis counseling service.

Internet Access The **State Library of Queensland,** Stanley Place, South Bank (© **07/3840 7666;** www.slq.qld.gov.au), has free Internet and computer access, as well as wireless, on levels 1 to 4. The library is open Monday through Thursday 10am to 8pm and Friday to Sunday 10am to 5pm.

Mail & Postage The General Post Office is at 261 Queen St., opposite

Post Office Square. It is open Monday through Friday 7am to 6pm and Saturday 10am to 1:30pm.

Newspapers & Magazines The **Courier-Mail** (Mon–Sat) and the **Sunday Mail** are Brisbane's daily newspapers. Another good news source is the online newspaper **Brisbane Times** (www.brisbanetimes.com. au). The free weekly **Brisbane News** magazine is a good guide to dining, entertainment, and shopping.

Pharmacies (Chemist Shops) The **Pharmacy on the Mall,** 141 Queen St. (© **07/3221 4585**), is open Monday through Thursday 7am to 9pm, Friday 7am to 9:30pm, Saturday 8am to 9pm, Sunday 8:30am to 6pm, and public holidays 9am to 7:30pm.

Police Dial © **000** in an emergency, or © **13 14 44** for police headquarters. Police are stationed 24 hours a day at 67 Adelaide St. (© **07/ 3224 4444**).

Safety Brisbane is relatively crime free, but as in any large city, be aware of your personal safety, especially when you're out at night. Stick to well-lit streets and busy precincts.

WHERE TO STAY

Expensive

Emporium Hotel ★★★   With its zebra-skin chairs, frangipani motifs, rich fabrics and colors, huge antique chandelier, and French stained-glass window in the cocktail bar, this is Brisbane's grooviest and most eclectic hotel. It has luxury touches such as bathrobes and slippers, a pillow menu, and a pampering menu. The whole place oozes modern elegance. Kitchens—cunningly hidden from view—are standard in all rooms and have a small dishwasher as well as a microwave. There is one suite designed for guests with disabilities, at standard room rates.

1000 Ann St., Brisbane, QLD 4006. www.emporiumhotel.com.au. 📞 **1300/883 611** in Australia, or 07/3253 6999. 102 units, 42 with spa baths. A$249–A$259 double; A$279 double King Spa suite; A$429 double Emporium suite; A$479 double Deluxe corner suite. Valet parking A$35 per day. **Amenities:** Restaurant; bar; concierge; exercise room; outdoor heated lap pool; room service; sauna; Wi-Fi (A$10/1 hr., A$20/24 hr., A$45/3 days).

The Limes Hotel ★   The first Australian hotel to be part of Design Hotels, the Limes considers itself "backstreet boutique." There are no frills or frippery, but that doesn't mean it's not stylish, interesting, and functional, designed with an eye to what travelers want. Three rooms on the ground floor have courtyards with hammocks and a table and chairs; all are practical in design, with a kitchen area that doubles as a work station. The hotel bar is also home to a popular 30-seat rooftop cinema (and an area for smokers on the mezzanine), and a guest swipe card for lift access ensures security.

142 Constance St., Fortitude Valley, Brisbane, QLD 4006. www.limeshotel.com.au. 📞 **07/3852 9000.** 21 units. A$440 double; A$550 double courtyard rooms. Train: Brunswick St. Parking A$13 per day (nearby). **Amenities:** Bar; free access to nearby health club; free Wi-Fi.

Novotel Brisbane ★★   This well-appointed contemporary hotel, a short walk from Brisbane's main shopping areas, is popular among families and business travelers. The modern, stylish rooms and suites are spacious and were refurbished in 2010. The lap pool is very inviting and has terrific city views. For dining, you can choose among **The Restaurant**, the more casual **Plan B** bistro, or an all-day menu in **The Bar.** All rooms are nonsmoking.

200 Creek St., Brisbane, QLD 4000. www.novotelbrisbane.com.au. 📞 **1300/656 565** in Australia, or 07/3309 3309. 296 units. A$199–A$599 double. Children 15 and under stay free in parent's room with existing bedding. Free crib. Parking A$25–A$35; valet parking A$40. Train: Central. **Amenities:** 2 restaurants; bar; babysitting; concierge; gymnasium; outdoor pool; room service; sauna; free Wi-Fi.

Moderate

Aynsley B&B ★★   On a quiet street just off the main shopping and restaurant strip in Paddington, this restored 1905 Queenslander house retains most of its original features, such as leadlight windows, tongue-and-groove walls, high ceilings, and polished timber floors. The two air-conditioned guest bedrooms are nicely furnished and have comfy, good-quality mattresses. Each has its own ensuite bathroom. A rear deck on both levels overlooks mango trees, busy with birdlife, and it's hard to believe you are only 3km (2 miles) from the city center. There's also a large swimming pool and a guest laundry. No smoking indoors.

14 Glanmire St., Paddington, Brisbane, QLD 4064. www.aynsley.com.au. © **07/3368 2250.** 2 units. A$155–A$195 single; $165–$195 double. Rates include full breakfast. Free off-street parking. Bus: 375 or 377; stop 200m (656 ft.) away. **Amenities:** Outdoor pool; free Wi-Fi.

Eton ★   This heritage-listed colonial cottage, not far from the Brisbane Transit Centre, has five rooms and an attic suite, all with ensuite bathrooms. The attic suite is a self-contained apartment with its own entrance and kitchen. Room no. 1, at the front of the house, is my pick—it has a claw-foot tub and king-size bed. Out in the back is a garden courtyard, where you can breakfast among the palms, ferns, and frangipani trees. It has a guest laundry and kitchen. There's no smoking indoors and children under 4 are not allowed.

436 Upper Roma St., Brisbane, QLD 4000. www.babs.com.au/eton. © **07/3236 0115.** 6 units. A$100–A$150 double; A$600 apt weekly. Extra person A$30. Limited free parking. Train: Roma St. **Amenities:** Free Wi-Fi.

Hotel George Williams ★★   This smart, great-value YMCA hotel is a good budget choice for inner-city stays. Rooms are small, but some manage to sleep up to four adults. Queen terrace rooms have a small sheltered balcony with table and chairs. Among the useful facilities are a 24-hour front desk and business center and safe-deposit boxes. Several rooms are designed for guests with disabilities (inquire when booking), and there is also easy access to the gym.

317–325 George St. (btw. Turbot and Ann sts.), Brisbane, QLD 4000. www.hgw.com.au. © **1800/064 858** in Australia, or 07/3308 0700. 106 units. A$89–A$160 double. Extra person A$30. Limited parking, A$24 per night. Train: Roma St. Bus: Downtown Loop. Ferry: North Quay (CityCat or CityFerry). **Amenities:** Restaurant; bar; health club; Wi-Fi (A$4.40/30 min. to A$22/24 hr.).

Hotel Ibis Brisbane ★★   You get what you pay for at this AAA three-and-a-half-star sister property to the Novotel Brisbane (see above). In this case, what you get is basically a comfortable room with the standard amenities you might expect in a large hotel. But the Isis Brisbane has much larger rooms than those in most hotels of this standard, furnished in contemporary style, with sizable work desks and small but smart bathrooms. If you don't mind doing without river views, porters, a pool, or other small luxuries, this could be the place for you. Guests can also use the restaurant and bar at the adjoining **Mercure Hotel.**

27–35 Turbot St. (btw. North Quay and George St.), Brisbane, QLD 4000. www.ibishotels.com.au. © **1300/656 565** in Australia or 07/3237 2333. 218 units. From A$159 double. Extra person A$38. One child 11 or under stays free in parent's room with existing bedding. Parking (at the Mercure Hotel) A$27. Train: Roma St. Bus: Downtown Loop. Ferry: North Quay (CityCat or CityFerry). **Amenities:** Restaurant; bar; babysitting; Wi-Fi (A$28/24 hr.).

WHERE TO EAT

Brisbane has a sophisticated dining scene. Stylish bistros and cafes line the riverfront at South Bank; cute cafes are plentiful in Paddington; Asian eateries are a good choice in West End; and in Fortitude Valley, you'll find Chinatown. A street full of upscale but laid-back restaurants, many with a Mediterranean flavor, sits under the kitschy replica Eiffel Tower on Park Road in Milton, and in the city center you can find slick waterfront restaurants at Eagle Street Pier and Riverside. The intersection of Albert and Charlotte streets buzzes with inexpensive, good-quality cafes.

Expensive

e'cco bistro ★★★ CONTEMPORARY   *E'cco* means "here it is" in Italian, and that's the philosophy behind the food at this award-winning bistro. It serves simple food, done exceptionally well and with passion. In a former tea warehouse on the city fringe, it's one of Australia's best. Dishes include such delights as roast pork belly with spiced eggplant relish, chilli caramel and crisp garlic; or crispy-skin salmon with Brussel sprouts, seeded mustard, bacon, and parsley. The bistro is enormously popular, so bookings are essential. Large windows, bold colors, and modern furniture make it a pleasant setting. There's an extensive wine list—many by the glass.

100 Boundary St. (at Adelaide St.). ℰ **07/3831 8344.** www.eccobistro.com. Reservations required. Main courses A$40–A$43. Tues–Fri noon–2:30pm; Tues–Sat 6–10pm. Closed Christmas Day till January 2. Metered street parking.

Moda ★★★ CONTEMPORARY   Whether you choose the more formal and private mezzanine floor or the relaxed courtyard dining area (my pick), you're sure to enjoy this Spanish-flavored restaurant. Owner-chef Javier Codina has combined his Catalan, French, and Italian influences with fresh (often organic) Queensland produce to produce some marvelous dishes. The menu changes often, but you might find something like wild hare pie with purple potatoes, persimmon, and five-spice sauce, or a simple angel-hair pasta with seafood and aioli. If you're there for Friday lunch (or order ahead), you can sample Javier's paella. It's expensive (A$35), but wonderful. ***Be warned:*** So is the wine list. A good choice is the Pica Pica lunch menu, five small courses (plus coffee and petit fours) for A$30, or Javier's three-course "table experience" for A$85 per person.

12 Edward St. ℰ **07/3221 7655.** www.modarestaurant.com.au. Main courses A$40–A$59. Thurs–Fri noon–late; Mon–Sat 6pm–late. Metered street parking or nearby parking buildings.

Watt Restaurant + Bar ★★ CONTEMPORARY   With a menu of modern fare with Asian, Middle Eastern, and European influences, Watt is one of my favorite places to eat out in Brisbane—partly because of the riverside setting in New Farm Park, and partly because of the good food. Whether it's for a leisurely weekend breakfast, lunch, or dinner before a show at the Brisbane Powerhouse, dishes are always satisfying, such as chicken breast wrapped in prosciutto with pea puree, preserved lemon, and basil risotto, or smoked lamb loin with olive and aubergine white polenta and grain-mustard dressing. Weekday specials, at lunch and before 7pm, give you a main course and drink for A$25. A bar menu offers pizza and mezze plates. There's music on Sunday afternoons.

Brisbane Powerhouse, 119 Lamington St. (near the river), New Farm. ℰ **07/3358 5464.** www.watt restaurant.com.au. Main courses A$25–A$38. Mon–Fri 9am–late; Sat–Sun 8am–late; public holidays 10am–6pm. Ample free parking.

Moderate

Breakfast Creek Hotel ★★ STEAKHOUSE   Built in 1889 and listed by the National Trust, this Renaissance-style pub is fondly known as the Brekky Creek—or simply the Creek—and is considered a Brisbane icon. The quintessentially Queensland establishment is famed for its gigantic steaks (choose your own), served with baked potato (or chips), coleslaw, salad, and a choice of mushroom, pepper, or chilli sauce, and for serving beer "off the wood" (from the keg). The pub's **Spanish Garden Steakhouse** and the **Staghorn beer garden** are always popular, and an outdoor dining area overlooks Breakfast Creek. The **Substation No. 41** bar, created in the shell of a derelict electricity substation next to the hotel, makes the most of its exposed brick walls and soaring ceilings. The 4.5m-long (15-ft.) wooden bar is just the place to sip the latest cocktail.

2 Kingsford Smith Dr. (at Breakfast Creek Rd.), Albion. ℂ **07/3262 5988.** www.breakfastcreek hotel.com. Main courses A$20–A$40. Daily 10am–late. Substation 141 daily noon–late. Bus: 300 or 322. Wickham St. becomes Breakfast Creek Rd.; the hotel is just off the route to the airport.

Harveys ★★ CONTEMPORARY   In the heart of trendy James Street, take a table under the shady white umbrellas or in the light-filled restaurant and prepare for some delectable tastes. Owner/chef PJ McMillan has a strong local following for his deceptively simple dishes, which may include offerings such as grain-fed eye filet steak with mashed Royal Blue potatoes, silverbeet pancetta, and blue cheese; or a simple beer-battered fish 'n' chips. The service is smart and friendly, and the coffee's good, too!

31 James St., Fortitude Valley (next to the Centro Cinemas). ℂ **07/3852 3700.** www.harveys.net. au. Main courses A$22–A$38; Mon–Fri 7am–3pm; Sat–Sun 7:30am–3pm; Wed–Sat 5:30pm–late. Closed public holidays. Train: Brunswick St.

Jo Jo's ★ INTERNATIONAL/CAFE FARE   A spectacular timber, limestone, and glass bar dominates the center of this casual cafe-style eating spot, housing more than 1,000 bottles of wine. The locals have dropped in here for years for a shopping pit stop or a postcinema meal. Three menus—chargrill, Oriental, and Mediterranean—are available, and the food is well priced and good. You order at the bar and meals are delivered to the table (try to get one on the balcony overlooking the Queen Street Mall). Among your options are steaks and seafood from the grill; curries and stir-fries from the Oriental menu; and Mediterranean pastas, antipasto, and wood-fired pizzas.

1st floor, Queen Street Mall, at Albert St. ℂ **07/3221 2113.** www.jojos.com.au. Main courses A$16–A$39. Daily 10:30am–late. Train or bus: Central.

Inexpensive

Govinda's ★★ VEGETARIAN   If you're on a budget, or a committed vegetarian, seek out the Hare Krishnas' chain of Govinda restaurants. This one serves vegetable curry, dal soup, pappadam, samosas, and other tasty stuff with a north-Indian influence. Everything is buffet-style, and the atmosphere is pretty spartan, but the food is very satisfying. This is a stimulant-free zone, so don't come expecting alcohol, tea, or coffee—you're likely to get something like homemade ginger-and-mint lemonade instead. There are two other locations: **Govinda's Café** (302 Logan Rd., Stone's Corner; ℂ **07/3847 4674**) and **Govinda's West End** (82 Vulture St.; ℂ **0404/173 027**).

99 Elizabeth St. (opposite Myer Centre), 1st floor. ℂ **07/3210 0255.** www.brisbanegovindas.com. au. A$13 all-you-can-eat; A$10 students. No credit cards. Mon–Thurs 11am–3pm and 5–7:30pm; Fri 11am–8:30pm; Sat–Sun 11am–3pm. Bus: Downtown Loop.

Tognini's Trattoria ★ CONTEMPORARY   Owners Mark and Narelle Tognini run this relaxed modern bistro, incorporating an extensive deli and walk-in cheese room. Popular with inner-city dwellers and business folk, it serves gourmet delights to

A teahouse of some kind has been on top of Mount Coot-tha for more than a century. Part 19th-century Queenslander house and part modern extension, the **Summit** restaurant (© **07/3369 9922;** www.brisbanelookout.com) has wrap-around covered decks with views of the city and Moreton Bay. A changing menu features local produce and wines. The sunset dinner menu—A$40 for three courses if you finish by 7pm—is available starting at 5pm. After your meal, spend some time on the observation deck—the city lights provide a glittering panorama. On Sundays, high tea is served from 3 to 5pm (A$35 per person). Reservations are recommended for Friday and Saturday night. The Summit is open daily 11:30am to midnight and Sunday brunch 8 to 10am (closed for lunch New Year's Day, Good Friday, and Boxing Day [Dec 26]; closed for dinner Christmas Day). To get there, take bus 47; if you're driving, take Upper Roma Street from the city center, then Milton Road 3.5km (2¼ miles) west to the Western Freeway roundabout at Toowong Cemetery. Veer right into Sir Samuel Griffith Drive, and follow the road about 3km (2 miles) up the mountain.

eat in or take out from breakfast through to dinner. Sit at one of the communal tables and try the penne carbonara or perhaps a chicken and mushroom risotto. There are also lots of gourmet burgers and little plates of tasty treats for sharing, if you just prefer to graze. Another Tognini's is on Baroona Road, Milton.

Turbot and Boundary sts., Spring Hill. © **07/3831 5300.** www.togninis.com. Main courses A$15–A$20. Mon–Fri 7am–6pm; Sat–Sun 8am–3pm. Closed public holidays.

EXPLORING BRISBANE

Brisbane City Hall ★★★ The imposing Brisbane City Hall reopened in 2013 after a 3-year multimillion-dollar restoration. Built in the 1920s and once the city's tallest building, City Hall is the heart of Brisbane. Free guided tours are offered daily at 10:30, 11:30am, 1:30, 2:30 and 3:30pm. Tours are hugely popular and numbers are limited, so it's essential to book your spot (© **07/3403 8463**). This is still a working civic building, so at times some of the rooms and features are not open. Separate free tours are run to the top of the **Clock Tower** every 15 minutes daily from 10am to 4:45pm. You cannot book ahead for these tours, but it pays to arrive early because the heritage elevator only holds seven passengers. You'll need to get a ticket from the **Museum of Brisbane** reception counter on Level 3, and then wait your turn. The museum is also well worth spending time in; it provides an insight into the history and essence of Brisbane. Changing exhibitions relate the stories, events, and ideas that have shaped the city. This is a beautiful building—don't miss it!

City Hall, King George Sq. © **07/3403 8888.** www.museumofbrisbane.com.au. Free admission. Daily 10am–5pm. Closed New Year's Day, Good Friday, Christmas Day and Boxing Day (Dec 26), and until 1pm Anzac Day (Apr 25). Train: Roma St. or Central. Bus: The Loop.

Brisbane Powerhouse Arts ★★ A former electricity powerhouse, this massive brick factory is now a dynamic art space for exhibitions, contemporary performance, and live art. The building retains its character, an industrial mix of metal, glass, and stark surfaces etched with 20 years of graffiti. It's a short walk from the New Farm ferry terminal along the riverfront through New Farm Park. The **Powerhouse Farmers Markets** operate on the second and fourth Saturday morning of each month, and there's a restaurant/cafe/bar overlooking the river (see Watt Restaurant + Bar, p. 137).

119 Lamington St., New Farm (*©* **07/3358 8600.** www.brisbanepowerhouse.org. CityCat to New Farm Park.

La Boite Theatre ★★ This is a well-established innovative company that performs contemporary Australian plays and some classics in the 400-seat Roundhouse Theater, ensuring an intimate theatre experience. Tickets cost A$54 (slightly more for opening nights); previews are A$28. If you are 30 or under, tickets cost A$30.

6 Musk Ave., Kelvin Grove. (*©* **07/3007 8600.** www.laboite.com.au. Take bus no. 390 from the city to Kelvin Grove Rd., and get off at stop 12.

Lone Pine Koala Sanctuary ★★ This is the best place in Australia to cuddle a koala—and one of the few places where koala cuddling is actually still allowed. Banned in New South Wales and Victoria, holding a koala is legal in Queensland under strict conditions that ensure that each animal is handled for less than 30 minutes a day—and gets every third day off! When it opened in 1927, Lone Pine had only two koalas, Jack and Jill; it is now home to more than 130. You can cuddle them anytime and have a photo taken holding one (for a fee); once you've paid, you can have some photos taken using your own camera, too. Lone Pine isn't just koalas—you can also hand-feed kangaroos and wallabies and get up close with emus, snakes, baby crocs, parrots, wombats, Tasmanian devils, skinks, lace monitors, frogs, bats, turtles, possums, and other native wildlife. There is a currency exchange, a gift shop, and a restaurant and cafe. You can also take advantage of the picnic and barbecue facilities.

The nicest way to get to Lone Pine is a cruise down the Brisbane River aboard the MV *Mirimar* (*©* **0412/749 426**; www.mirimar.com), which leaves the Cultural Centre at South Bank Parklands at 10am. The 19km (12-mile) trip to Lone Pine takes 75 minutes and includes commentary. You have 2½ hours to explore before returning, arriving in the city at 3pm. The round-trip fare is A$68 for adults, A$38 for children ages 3 to 13, and A$195 for families of five, including entry to Lone Pine. Cruises run daily except April 25 (Anzac Day) and Christmas Day.

Jesmond Rd., Fig Tree Pocket. (*©* **07/3378 1366.** www.koala.net. Admission A$33 adults, A$22 children 3–13, A$52–A$80 families. Daily 9am–5pm; Anzac Day (Apr 25) 1:30–5pm; Christmas Day 9am–4pm. By car (20 min. from city center), take Milton Rd. to the roundabout at Toowong Cemetery, and then Western Fwy. toward Ipswich. Signs point to Fig Tree Pocket and Lone Pine. Ample free parking. Bus: 430 or 445 from the city center. Bus fare A$6.70 adults, A$3.40 children. Taxi from city center about A$40.

Queen Street Mall ★ Brisbane's inner-city shopping centers on **Queen Street Mall,** which has around 500 stores. Fronting the mall at 171–209 Queen St. is the three-level **Wintergarden** shopping complex (*©* **07/3229 9755**; www.wgarden.com.au), housing upscale jewelers and Aussie fashion designers. Farther up the mall at 91 Queen St. (at Albert St.) is the **Myer Centre** (*©* **07/3223 6900**; www.myercentre shopping.com.au), which has Brisbane's biggest department store and five levels of moderately priced stores, mostly fashion. The gorgeous **Brisbane Arcade,** 160 Queen St. (𝄐 **07/3231 9777;** www.brisbanearcade.com.au), runs through to Adelaide Street, and abounds with the boutiques of local Queensland designers. Just down the mall from it is the **Broadway on the Mall** arcade (𝄐 **07/3229 9755;** www.broadway onthemall.com.au), which stocks affordable fashion, gifts, and accessories on two levels. Across from the Edward Street end of the mall is a smart fashion and lifestyle shopping precinct, **MacArthur Central** (𝄐 **07/3007 2300;** www.macarthurcentral. com), right next door to the General Post Office on the block between Queen and Elizabeth streets. This is where you'll find top-name designer labels, Swiss watches, galleries, and accessory shops. On Edward and Adelaide streets, you'll find more hot shopping at **QueensPlaza** (𝄐 **07/3234 3900;** www.queensplaza.com.au). There are also weekly farmers markets in the Queen Street Mall (at the Victoria Bridge end) on Wednesdays from 10am to 6pm.

Queen St. www.queenstreetmall.com.au.

Queensland Cultural Centre ★★★ This modern complex stretching along the south bank of the Brisbane River houses many of the city's performing-arts venues as well as the state art galleries, museum, and library. With plenty of open plazas and fountains, it is a pleasing place to wander or just sit and watch the river and the city skyline. It's a 7-minute walk from town, across the Victoria Bridge from the Queen Street Mall.

The **Queensland Performing Arts Centre** (𝄐 **13 62 46** for bookings Mon–Sat 9am–8:30pm; www.qpac.com.au) houses the 2,000-seat Lyric Theatre for musicals, ballet, and opera; the 1,800-seat Concert Hall for orchestral performances; the 850-seat Playhouse theater for plays; and the 315-seat Cremorne Theatre for theater-in-the-round, cabaret, and experimental works. The complex has a restaurant and a cafe.

This is where you will come for performances by the **Queensland Theatre Company** (www.qldtheatreco.com.au), which offers eight or nine productions a year, from the classics to new Australian works; **Opera Queensland** (www.operaqueensland. com.au), which performs a lively repertoire of traditional as well as modern works, musicals, and choral concerts; and the **Queensland Symphony Orchestra** (www. thequeenslandorchestra.com.au), which provides classical music lovers with a diverse mix of orchestral and chamber music, with the odd foray into fun material, such as movie themes, pop, and gospel music. It schedules about 30 concerts a year.

The **Queensland Art Gallery** ★★★ (𝄐 **07/3840 7303;** www.qagoma.qld.gov.au) is one of Australia's most attractive galleries, with vast light-filled spaces and interesting water features inside and out. It is a major player in the Australian art world, attracting blockbuster exhibitions of works by the likes of Renoir, Picasso, and van Gogh, and showcasing diverse modern Australian painters, sculptors, and other artists. It also has an impressive collection of Aboriginal art. The adjacent **Queensland Gallery of Modern Art (GOMA)** ★★★ houses collections of modern and contemporary Australian, indigenous Australian, Asian, and Pacific art, and also gives a stunning sense of light and space. Admission is free to both galleries, and both run regular free tours that take around 30 to 40 minutes. Tours of each gallery's collection highlights are held daily at 2pm, and at GOMA you can tour the highlights of the Indigenous Australian Art Collection at 11am and 1pm daily. The galleries are open Monday through Friday 10am to 5pm and weekends and public holidays 9am to 5pm; closed Good Friday, Christmas Day, and until noon on April 25 (Anzac Day).

Queensland Museum ★★★ Brisbane scientists are abuzz over the mid-2013 discovery of 50-million-year-old fossils—including a frog, snail, crocodile, and fish—at a local construction site. A small display is on show at this interesting museum until more work can be done on the find, adding new interest to an already eclectic museum collection ranging from natural history specimens to insects, dinosaurs—including Queensland's own *Muttaburrasaurus*—and more. Children will love the blue whale model that greets you at the entrance and the interactive Sciencentre on Level 1. The museum also has a cafe and gift shop. Admission is free, except to the Sciencentre and to any special exhibitions.

Grey St., (at Melbourne St.), adjacent to the Queensland Art Gallery. © **07/3840 7555**. www.qm.qld.gov.au. Daily 9:30am–5pm; closed Good Friday, Christmas Day and Boxing Day (Dec 26), and until 1:30pm on Anzac Day (Apr 25). Admission to Sciencentre A$15 adults, A$12 children 3–15, A$45 family of 6. Plentiful underground parking. Ferry: South Bank (CityCat) or Old South Bank (Inner City Ferry). Bus: Numerous routes from Adelaide St. (near Albert St.). Train: South Brisbane.

St. John's Anglican Cathedral ★★ Brisbane's stunning neo-Gothic Anglican cathedral took more than a century to complete, but the result has been worth the wait. Plagued by lack of funding throughout its history, the building was finally completed in 2009, making it one of the last Gothic-style cathedrals to be completed anywhere in the world, with stonemasons using traditional medieval building techniques. Volunteer guides run tours and point out some of the details that make this cathedral uniquely Queensland—such as the carved possums on the organ screen and the hand-stitched cushions.

373 Ann St. (btw. Wharf and Queen sts.). © **07/3835 2222**. www.stjohnscathedral.com.au. Daily 9:30am–4:30pm; free tours Mon–Sat 10am and 2pm and most Sun at 2pm. Closed to visitors, except for services, Anzac Day (Apr 25), Christmas Day, and some other public holidays. Train: Central Station.

Sir Thomas Brisbane Planetarium & Cosmic Skydome ★★ Digital multimedia systems that present real-time digital star shows and computer-generated images in the Cosmic Skydome theater are a popular feature of a visit here for all ages. The fascinating 40-minute astronomical show includes a re-creation of the Brisbane night sky using a Ziess star projector. Special shows designed for kids aged 9 and under are given at 11:30am and 12:30pm on weekends; the planetarium is not recommended for younger children. Kids' shows cost A$7.40 for both adults and children.

Brisbane Botanic Gardens, Mt. Coot-tha Rd., Toowong. © **07/3403 2578**. www.brisbane.qld.gov.au/planetarium. A$15 adults, A$9 children 14 and under, A$40 families of 4. Tues–Fri 10am–4pm; Sat 11am–8:15pm (last entry at 7:30pm); Sun 11am–4pm. Shows Tues–Fri 3pm; Sat 11:30am, 12:30, 2, 3, 6, and 7:30pm; Sun 11:30am, 12:30, 2, and 3pm. Extended hours during school holidays. Closed Mondays and public holidays. Bus: 471, 598, or 599.

South Bank Parklands ★★★ Follow the locals' lead and spend some time at this delightful 16-hectare (40-acre) complex of parks, restaurants, cafes, shops, playgrounds, street theater, and weekend markets. There's a manmade beach lined with palm trees, with waves and sand, where you can swim, stroll, and cycle the meandering pathways. From the parklands it's an easy walk to the museum, art gallery, and other parts of the adjacent **Queensland Cultural Centre** (see p. 141). Hop on the **Wheel of Brisbane** (© **07/3844 3464**; www.thewheelofbrisbane.com.au) for a 13-minute ride in an air-conditioned enclosed gondola, where you get a 360-degree bird's-eye view of Brisbane from 60m (197 ft.) up; it costs A$15 adults, A$10 children 4 to 12, A$2 children 1 to 3, A$42 family of four. The buzzing outdoor **South Bank Lifestyle Market** is illuminated by fairy lights at night. The market is open Friday 5 to 10pm, Saturday 10am to 5pm, and Sunday 9am to 5pm. The South Bank Parklands are a 7-minute walk from town.

South Bank. (℃) **07/3867 2170** for Visitor Centre. www.visitsouthbank.com.au. Free admission. Park daily 24 hr.; Visitor Centre daily 9am–5pm (closed Good Friday and Christmas Day, open from 1pm on Anzac Day [Apr 25]). From the Queen Street Mall, cross the Victoria Bridge to South Bank or walk across Goodwill Bridge from Gardens Point Rd. entrance to Brisbane City Gardens. Plentiful underground parking in Queensland Cultural Centre. Train: South Brisbane. Ferry: South Bank (CityCat or Cross River Ferry). Bus: Numerous routes from Adelaide St. (near Albert St.), including 100, 111, 115, and 120, stop at the Queensland Cultural Centre; walk through the Centre to South Bank Parklands.

Story Bridge Adventure Climb ★★★   Brisbane seems to have a fascination with building bridges across its wide river. There are 14 (at last count), but the most interesting is the Story Bridge, built in 1940. If you are over 12 years old and at least 130 centimeters (just over 4 ft., 3 in.) tall, you can "climb" this overgrown Meccano set. The Story Bridge Adventure Climb peaks at a viewing platform on top of the bridge, 44m (143 ft.) above the roadway and 80m (262 ft.) above the Brisbane River. This is only the third "bridge climb" in the world (after Sydney's and Auckland's), so make the most of the chance. You'll be rewarded with magnificent 360-degree views of the city, river, and Moreton Bay and its islands, not to mention interesting stories from your guide. Children must be accompanied by an adult. Do it—you'll love it!

170 Main St. (at Wharf St.), Kangaroo Point. (℃) **1300/254 627** in Australia or 07/3514 6900. www. storybridgeadventureclimb.com.au. Day climbs, night climbs and dawn climbs (Sat only) A$99 adults and A$84 children ages 12–16; Twilight climbs Mon–Thurs A$99 adults and A$84 children, Fri–Sun A$119 adults, A$101 children. Ferry: Holman St.

Treasury Casino ★   This lovely heritage building—built in 1886 as, ironically enough, the state's Treasury offices—houses a modern casino. Three levels of 100 gaming tables offer roulette, blackjack, baccarat, craps, sic-bo, and traditional Aussie two-up. Open 24 hours, the casino has more than 1,300 gaming machines, six restaurants, and five bars. DJs bring music to **The Kitty** bar Wednesday to Sunday nights, or you can relax in the clubby atmosphere of **Ryan's on the Park.** At press time for this book, plans to relocate the casino to new premises in George Street were still in the planning and approval stages, so could be some time off yet.

Queen St. btw. George and William sts. (℃) **07/3306 8888.** www.treasurybrisbane.com.au. Must be 18 years old to enter; neat casual attire required (no beachwear or thongs). Closed Good Friday, Christmas Day, and until 1pm Anzac Day (Apr 25). Train: Central or South Brisbane, and then walk across the Victoria Bridge.

ORGANIZED TOURS

RIVER CRUISES   The best way to cruise the river, in my view, is aboard the fast **CityCat ferries ★★★.** Board at Riverside and head downstream under the Story Bridge to New Farm Park, past Newstead House to the restaurant row at Brett's Wharf, or cruise upriver past the city and South Bank for only a few dollars. For more information, see "Getting Around," earlier in this chapter.

For those who'd like to dine as they cruise, the **Kookaburra River Queen** paddle-wheelers (℃ **07/3221 1300;** www.kookaburrariverqueens.com) are a good option. Lunch cruises, for around 90 minutes, cost A$42 adults on Tuesday, Thursday, and Friday, or A$59 on weekends (kids aged 4–14 pay half price). Dinner cruises run on Thursday and Sunday for A$79, and Friday and Saturday nights for A$89. The boat departs from the Eagle Street Pier (parking is available under the City Rowers tavern on Eagle St.) at 7:30pm. On Sunday lunch cruises there's live jazz. Or you can just cruise, without the food, at a cost of A$20 for adults and A$10 for children.

BUS TOURS   For a good introduction to Brisbane, look no further than a **City Sights** bus tour run by the Brisbane City Council (℃ **07/3235 7369;** www.citysights. com.au). City Sights buses stop at 19 points of interest in a continuous loop around the city center, Spring Hill, Milton, South Bank, and Fortitude Valley, including China-town. They take in various historic buildings and places of interest. The driver of the blue-and-yellow bus narrates, and you can hop on and off at any stop you like. The tour is a good value—your ticket also gives unlimited access to CityCat ferries for the day. The bus departs every 45 minutes from 9am to 5pm daily except Good Friday, April 25 (Anzac Day), and Christmas Day. The entire trip, without stopping, takes about 80 minutes. Tickets cost A$35 for adults, A$20 for children 5 to 14 or A$80 for a family of five. Buy your ticket on board. You can join anywhere along the route, but the most central stop is City Hall, stop 2, on Adelaide Street at Albert Street.

WALKING TOURS   The best walking tours in town are run by the **Brisbane Greeters** (www.brisbanegreeters.com.au)—and even better, they're free. You get your own personal tour guide (or you can join a group), often a local with a particular area of expertise or interest in some aspect of the city. So you can choose from tours that look

Whale-Watching in Moreton Bay

Gasps of delight and wonder are the norm aboard Captain Kerry Lopez's whale-watching boat, and Australia's only female whale-watching captain never tires of hearing them. Lopez's purpose-built vessel, the MV *Eye-Spy*, carries up to 320 passengers out into Moreton Bay between June and November for one of the most awesome sights you may ever see. When I traveled with them, we witnessed the antics of 17 humpback whales as they breached and displayed in the waters around the boat. It was an amazing, unforgettable experience.

Brisbane Whale Watching ★★★ (℃ **07/3880 0477;** www.brisbane whalewatching.com.au) will organize your 30-minute transfers from city hotels to the departure point in the northern suburb of Redcliffe. If you choose to drive yourself, there's free all-day parking near the jetty. Tours depart daily at 10am, returning at around 2:30 to 3pm. The trip onto the bay features excellent educational commentary about the whales while Kerry and her crew keep a lookout for these gentle giants of the deep. Prices are A$135 adults, A$125 seniors and students, A$95 children 4 to 14, or A$365 for a family of four, including lunch and morning and afternoon tea. Transfers from Brisbane hotels are an extra A$30 per person.

The best part? There's a guarantee you'll see a whale—or you can take another cruise for free.

at architecture, arts and culture, history, and more, or at a particular neighborhood or precinct. Guides are volunteers with a passion and enthusiasm for the city, and you'll learn a lot along the way. Some tours combine bicycling using the CityCycle bikes (see p. 133). But really, it's up to you to decide what to do and how long the walk will be. You'll likely see the Greeters in their bright red shirts out and about in the city. Tours start from the Visitor Information Centre in the Queen Street Mall, and last anywhere from 1 to 4 hours. Try to book at least 48 hours ahead. Book online or at the Visitor Information Centre.

Free guided walks of the **City Botanic Gardens** at Alice Street leave from the rotunda at the Albert Street entrance Monday through Saturday at 11am and 1pm (except public holidays and mid-Dec to mid-Jan). They take about 1 hour. Bookings are not necessary.

Prepare for shivers up your spine when you take one of Jack Sim's **Ghost Tours ★** (*©* **0401/666 441;** www.ghost-tours.com.au), which relive Brisbane's gruesome past. Ninety-minute "Haunted Brisbane" walking tours of the city leave from the Queen Street Mall at 7:30pm Thursday and Sunday (A$30 adults, A$20 ages 12–17). On Friday and Saturday nights, you can take a 2-hour tour of the historic and haunted Toowong cemetery (A$40 adults, A$25 teens). Or choose from a range of other spooky tours. Reservations are essential; tours are not suitable for children under 12.

A DAY TRIP TO THE GREAT BARRIER REEF

Brisbane is south of the most southern parts of the Great Barrier Reef (see chapter 7), but it is still possible to experience the Reef in a day trip to **Lady Elliot Island,** off the coast near Bundaberg (384km/238 miles north of Brisbane). If you are pressed for time before heading south or to Central Australia and Uluru, this is an excellent option.

Lady Elliot is a small coral cay ringed by a lagoon filled with coral and marine life. Reef walking, snorkeling, and diving are the main reasons people come to this coral cay, but you can snorkel and reef walk only for the 2 to 3 hours before and after high tide, so your day trip activities will be reliant on nature to some extent.

Keep in mind that you will not be able to dive and fly on the same day. But the snorkeling on Lady Elliott is a wonderful experience (and the island has accommodations if you wish to stay longer or do some diving; see p. 192). You will see beautiful corals, brightly colored fish, clams, sponges, urchins, and anemones, and with luck, green and loggerhead turtles (which nest on the beach Nov–Mar) and manta rays. Whales migrate through these waters from June through September.

Be aware that Lady Elliot is a sparse, grassy island rookery, not a sandy tropical paradise. Some find it too spartan; others relish chilling out in a beautiful, peaceful spot with reef all around. Just be prepared for the smell and constant noise of the birds.

Seair (*©* **07/5599 4509;** www.seairpacific.com.au) offers a day-trip package from Brisbane for A$699 adults and A$349 children aged 3 to 12. In addition to the flights, the price includes snorkel gear, a glass-bottom-boat ride, lunch, and guided activities (and the Reef tax).

Your day trip begins with a early pickup (around 6am) from your Brisbane hotel to drive to the northern Brisbane suburb of Redcliffe for the coastal scenic flight. The flight takes about 90 minutes. Seair is Lady Elliott Island's own airline and operates a fleet of 9- and 13-seat aircraft. All you need to take is a daypack with swimwear, camera, sunscreen, and footwear suitable for getting wet. Take some cash too, in case you decide to buy an underwater camera or a small souvenir from the resort gift shop.

You'll have around 5 hours to explore the island and Reef. You can take an island orientation tour, a guided reef walk at low tide (if possible), a snorkeling lesson in the resort pool (if you need it), and a glass-bottom-boat or guided snorkel tour, and even feed the fish in the lagoon fish pool.

All snorkel equipment (mask, snorkel, fins, and wetsuit) is provided, along with towels and reef walking shoes. Storage lockers are available, as are resort shower facilities. A hot and cold buffet lunch includes fresh prawns, champagne, wine, beer, and soft drinks.

You'll be boarding your light plane for the return trip at 2:15pm, arriving back at your Brisbane hotel at around 5pm—but you'll feel like you've been gone much longer. Such is the magic of a day on the Great Barrier Reef!

CAIRNS & THE GREAT BARRIER REEF

F ish out your flippers and prepare to dive! Or snorkel. Beneath the aqua blue waters off Queensland's northern coast lie the jewels of the deep—gardens of coral, inhabited by colorful reef fish. Welcome to what is arguably Australia's most famous attraction, the Great Barrier Reef. And while the Reef is by no means the only thing worth seeing in a state that's two and a half times the size of Texas, it is the focus of this chapter. There are many gateways to the Reef along the Queensland coast, but Cairns is the major center and where most commercial boat tours depart from. I've also included some of the smaller towns that offer easy access to this natural wonder.

White sandy beaches grace nearly every inch of coastline in Queensland, and a string of islands and coral reefs dangles just offshore. **Cairns,** set between rainforest hills, sugarcane fields and the Coral Sea, still has fewer options for direct arrivals; for most people, Brisbane or Sydney will be their first stop before heading to the far north of Australia's east coast. In Cairns, a harbor full of boats awaits to take you to the Reef. An hour north, the village of **Port Douglas** provides another for direct access to the Reef.

Another departure point is Airlie Beach on the Whitsunday Coast. Off this coast, you'll be tempted by one tropical island after another; a cluster of 74 makes up the **Whitsunday** and **Cumberland** groups. These idyllic islands are laced by coral reefs rising out of calm, blue waters teeming with colorful fish—warm enough for swimming year-round.

Townsville boasts 320 days of sunshine a year and marks the start of the Great Green Way—an area of lush natural beauty on the way to Cairns—for those who choose to drive. Townsville is also the home of the Great Barrier Reef Marine Park Authority.

EXPLORING THE QUEENSLAND COAST

VISITOR INFORMATION   The **Queensland Holidays** website at **www.queensland holidays.com.au,** is a great resource on traveling and touring the state, including the Great Barrier Reef, or call **Go Queensland** (© **13 88 33** in Australia; www. goqueensland.com.au) to book online or speak to a Queensland travel specialist. **Tourism & Events Queensland** has websites specifically designed for overseas markets; in the United States go to www.destinationqueensland.com and for the United Kingdom check out www.experiencequeensland.com.

WHEN TO GO   Winter (June–Aug) is high season in Queensland; the water can be chilly—at least to Australians—but its temperature rarely drops below 72°F (22°C). April through November is the best time to visit the Great Barrier Reef, because although southeast trade winds can sometimes make it a tad choppy at sea, this is peak visibility time for divers. December through March can be uncomfortably hot and humid, particularly as far north as the Whitsundays, Cairns, and Port Douglas. In the winter months (June–Aug), the water can be a touch chilly (Aussies think so, anyway), but it rarely drops below 72°F (22°C).

GETTING AROUND   BY CAR   The Bruce Highway travels along the coast from Brisbane to Cairns. It is mostly a narrow two-lane highway, with the scenery varying from eucalyptus bushland to sugarcane fields.

Tourism Queensland (see "Visitor Information," above) publishes regional motoring guides. All you are likely to need, however, is a state map from the **Royal Automobile Club of Queensland** (**RACQ**) (© **13 19 05** in Australia; www.racq.com.au). A large range of touring maps is available online, and the website is brimming with advice about driving in Australia. For recorded road-condition reports, call © **13 19 40.** Specialist map shop **World Wide Maps & Guides,** in the Anzac Square Arcade, 267 Edward St., Brisbane (© **07/3221 4330;** www.worldwidemaps.com.au), is open Monday to Friday 9am to 5:30pm and 10am to 3pm on Saturdays. It stocks a range of Australia maps, atlases, and street directories.

BY TRAIN   Queensland Rail (© **1800/872 467** in Australia; www.queenslandrail. com.au) operates two long-distance trains along the Brisbane-Cairns route, a 32-hour trip aboard the **Sunlander** or about 8 hours less on the high-speed **Tilt Train.** See the "Getting Around" section in chapter 9 for more details.

BY PLANE   This is the fastest way to see a lot in such a big state. **Qantas** (© **13 13 13** in Australia; www.qantas.com.au) and its subsidiaries **QantasLink** and **Jetstar** (© **13 15 38** in Australia; www.jetstar.com.au) serve most coastal towns from Brisbane, and a few from Cairns. **Virgin Australia** (© **13 67 89** in Australia; www.virgin australia.com) services Brisbane, Cairns, Townsville, Gladstone, Bundaberg, and Proserpine and Hamilton Island in the Whitsundays, as well as other centers.

EXPLORING THE GREAT BARRIER REEF

First, a few facts. It's the only living thing on earth visible from the moon; at 348,700 sq. km (135,993 sq. miles), it's bigger than the United Kingdom and more than

The Great Barrier Reef

HOTELS ■
Cairns Plaza Hotel **2**
Coral Tree Inn **3**
The Hotel Cairns **4**
Novotel Cairns Oasis Resort **5**
Pullman Reef Hotel Casino **10**
Rydges Esplanade
  Resort Cairns **1**

RESTAURANTS ◆
Caffiend **8**
Candy **9**
Ochre Restaurant **7**
Perrotta's at the Gallery **6**

Information ⓘ
Post Office ✉

2,000km (1,240 miles) long, stretching from Lady Elliot Island off Bundaberg to Papua New Guinea; it's home to 1,500 kinds of fish, 400 species of corals, 4,000 kinds of clams and snails, and who knows how many sponges, starfish, and sea urchins; the Great Barrier Reef region is listed as a World Heritage Site and contains the biggest marine park in the world.

There are three kinds of reef on the Great Barrier Reef—fringing, ribbon, and platform. **Fringing reef** is the stuff you see just off the shore of islands and along the mainland. **Ribbon reefs** create "streamers" of long, thin reef along the outer edge of the continental shelf and are only found north of Cairns.

The Reef Tax

Every passenger over 4 years old must pay a A$3.50 daily **Environmental Management Charge (EMC),** commonly called the "reef tax," every time they visit the Great Barrier Reef. This money goes toward the management and conservation of the Reef. Your tour operator will collect it from you when you pay for your trip (or it may be included in the tour price).

Coral is very sharp, and coral cuts get infected quickly and badly. If you cut yourself, ask the staff on your cruise boat for immediate first aid as soon as you come out of the water.

The sun and reflected sunlight off the water can burn you fast. Remember to put sunscreen on your back and the back of your legs, especially around your knees and the back of your neck, and even behind your ears—all places that rarely get exposed to the sun but will be exposed as you swim facedown. Apply more when you leave the water.

Platform or **patch reefs** can be up to 16 sq. km (10 sq. miles) of coral emerging off the continental shelf all the way along the Reef's length. Platform reefs, the most common kind, are what most people think of when they refer to the Great Barrier Reef. Island resorts in the Great Barrier Reef Marine Park are either "continental," meaning part of the Australian landmass, or "cays," crushed dead coral and sand amassed on the reef tops over time by water action.

The rich colors of the coral can be seen best with lots of light, so the nearer the surface, the brighter and richer the marine life. That means snorkelers are in a prime position to see it at its best. Snorkeling the Reef can be a wondrous experience. Green and purple clams, pink sponges, red starfish, purple sea urchins, and fish from electric blue to neon yellow to lime are truly magical sights.

Apart from the impressive fish life around the corals, the Reef is home to large numbers of green and loggerhead turtles, one of the biggest dugong (relative of the manatee) populations in the world, sharks, giant manta rays, and sea snakes. In winter (June–Aug) humpback whales gather in the warm waters south of the Reef around Hervey Bay and as far north as Cairns to give birth to calves. This is what you've come to see!

You can snorkel the Reef, dive, ride a semisubmersible, or fly over it. For most people, the Great Barrier Reef means the Outer Reef, the network of reefs that are an average of 65km (40 miles) off the coast (about 60–90 min. by boat from the mainland).

If your Reef cruise offers a guided snorkel tour or "snorkel safari," take it. Some include it as part of the price, but even if you pay an extra A$30 or so, it is worth it. Most safaris are suitable for beginners and advanced snorkelers and are led by guides trained by marine biologists. Snorkeling is easy to master, and crews on cruise boats are always happy to tutor you.

A day trip to the Reef also offers a great opportunity to go scuba diving—even if you have never dived before. Every major cruise boat listed in this book and many dedicated dive boats offer introductory dives ("resort dives") that allow you to dive without

Safe Swimming

All of the northern beaches have small, netted enclosures for safe swimming from October through May, when deadly stingers (box jellyfish) render all mainland beaches in north Queensland off-limits.

DIVING the Reef

Divers have a big choice: dive boats that make one-day runs to the Outer Reef, overnight stays on some boats, live-aboard dive boats making excursions that last up to a week, or staying on an island. As a general rule, on a typical 5-hour day trip to the Reef, you will fit in about two dives. The companies listed in this book give you an idea of the kinds of trips available and how much they cost. Prices quoted include full gear rental; knock off about A$20 if you have your own gear. It is recommended that you only dive with members of **Dive Queensland.** The website, **www.dive-queensland.com.au,** has a full list of member companies.

Many dive companies in Queensland offer instruction, from initial open-water certification all the way to dive-master, rescue-diver, and instructor level. To take a course, you will need to have a medical exam done by a Queensland doctor. (Your dive school will arrange it; it usually costs between A$45 and A$70). You can find out more about dive medicals on **www.divemedicals.com.au.** You will also need two passport photos for your certificate, and you must be able to swim! Courses usually begin every day or every week. Some courses take as little as 3 days, but 5 days is regarded as the best. Open-water certification usually requires 2 days of theory in a pool, followed by 2 or 3 days on the Reef, where you make four to nine dives. Prices vary but are generally around A$600 for a 4-day open-water certification course, or A$700 for the same course as a live-aboard.

Deep Sea Divers Den (⟨© 07/4046 7333;** www.diversden.com.au) has been in operation since 1974 and claims to have certified more than 55,000 divers. Courses range from 4-day open-water courses from A$640 per person, to 5-day courses on a live-aboard boat, which costs from A$855 per person, including all meals on the boat, all your gear, a wetsuit, and transfers from your city hotel. All prices include reef tax, port and administration charges, and fuel levy. New courses begin every day of the week.

Virtually every Great Barrier Reef dive operator offers dive courses. Most island resorts offer them, too. You will find dive schools in Cairns, Port Douglas, Townsville, and the Whitsundays.

certification to a depth of 6m (20 ft.) with an instructor. You will need to complete a medical questionnaire and undergo a 30-minute briefing on the boat.

Find out more about the Reef from the **Great Barrier Reef Marine Park Authority** (⟨© 07/4750 0700;** fax 07/4772 6093; www.gbrmpa.gov.au or www.reefhq.com.au).

Choosing a Gateway to the Reef

Cairns and **Port Douglas** are good places from which to visit the Reef—but the quality of the coral is just as good off any town along the coast between **Bundaberg** and Cairns. The Reef is about 90 minutes away by high-speed catamaran. From **Townsville,** it is farther, about 2½ hours away.

Think carefully about where to base yourself. The main gateways, north to south, are **Port Douglas, Cairns, Townsville, the Whitsunday Islands, Gladstone** (for Heron Island), and **Bundaberg** (for Lady Elliot Island). The Whitsundays have the added attractions of dazzling islands to sail among; beautiful island resorts offering a wealth of watersports and other activities; and a large array of diving, fishing, and day cruises. You can snorkel every day off your island or join a sailing or cruise day trip to a number of magnificent fringing or inner shelf reefs much nearer than the main Outer Reef. Many people stay in Cairns simply because of its easy international airport access.

Diving Reminders

Don't forget your "C" certification card. Bringing along your dive log is also a good idea. Remember not to fly for 24 hours after diving.

If you are a nonswimmer, choose a Reef cruise that visits a coral cay, because a cay slopes gradually into shallow water and the surrounding coral. The **Low Isles** at Port Douglas; **Green Island, Michaelmas Cay,** or **Upolu Cay** off Cairns; and **Heron Island,** off Gladstone, are all good locations. Swimmer supports are available so nonswimmers can snorkel, too.

The major launching points for day trips to the Reef are Port Douglas, Cairns, Townsville, and the Whitsundays. Day-trip options for each are outlined in their dedicated sections of this chapter.

CAIRNS

346km (215 miles) N of Townsville; 1,807km (1,120 miles) N of Brisbane

Cairns is the only place on earth where two World Heritage-listed sites—the Wet Tropics Rainforest and Great Barrier Reef—are side by side. Explore the reef and offshore islands and slip into the distinctive pace, heat, and style of a truly tropical city.

This is the departure point for the large-scale Reef boats, taking hundreds of people out every day. Many smaller operators offer a more intimate experience, some on sailing boats. Offshore, **Michaelmas Cay** and **Upolu Cay** are two pretty coral sand blips in the ocean, 30km (19 miles) and 25km (16 miles) off Cairns, surrounded by reefs. Michaelmas is vegetated and is home to 27,000 seabirds; you may spot dugongs (cousins of manatees) off Upolu. Michaelmas and Upolu are great for snorkelers and introductory divers.

Cairns Esplanade offers top-to-bottom-dollar shopping plus an array of food halls, but its sparkling jewel is the manmade **lagoon** on the Esplanade, where you can cool off from the heat. There's plenty to do on days when the Reef's not on your radar.

Essentials

ARRIVING

BY PLANE   Qantas (© 13 13 13 in Australia) has direct flights throughout the day to Cairns from Sydney, Brisbane and Melbourne, and at least one flight a day from Uluru and Alice Springs. **QantasLink** also flies from Townsville. **Virgin Australia** (© 13 67 89 in Australia) flies to Cairns direct from Townsville, Brisbane, Sydney, and Melbourne. **Jetstar** (© 13 15 38 in Australia) flies from Brisbane. **Tigerair** (© 03/ 9034 3733) flies from Melbourne and Sydney. Some international carriers serve Cairns from various Asian cities and New Zealand.

Cairns Airport (© 1800/177 748; www.cairnsairport.com.au) is 8km (5 miles) north of downtown. A 5-minute walk along a covered walkway connects the international terminal with the domestic terminal. **Airport Connections** (© 07/4099 5950;

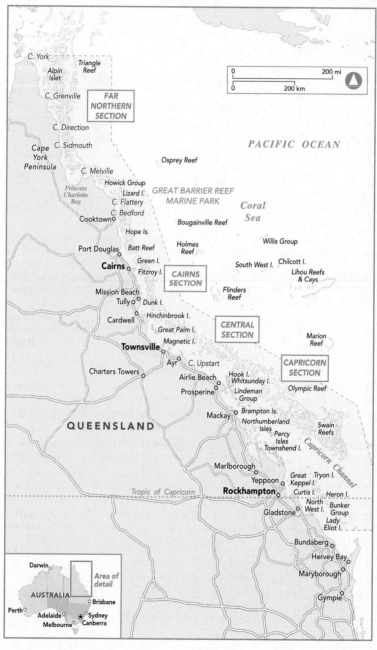

www.tnqshuttle.com) will meet all flights at both terminals. Transfers to the city cost A$14 adults and A$7 children 2 to 12, and it also runs transfers to the northern beaches and Port Douglas. Bookings are essential. **Sun Palm Australia Coach** (℃ 07/4087 2900; www.sunpalmtransport.com) provides transfers from the airport to the city and northern beaches. The one-way fare is A$14 adults and A$7.50 children 2 to 11 to the city, and A$23 adults and A$12.50 children to Palm Cove.

A taxi from the airport costs around A$29 to the city, A$55 to Trinity Beach, and A$68 to Palm Cove. There is a set fee of A$190 to Port Douglas. Call **Cairns Taxis** (℃ 13 10 08 in Australia).

Avis, Budget, Europcar, Hertz, Redspot, and **Thrifty** all have car-rental offices at the domestic and international terminals (see "By Car," below).

BY TRAIN   Long-distance trains operated by **Queensland Rail** (℃ 1800/872 467 in Queensland; www.queenslandrail.com.au) run from Brisbane several times a week. The 160kmph (100-mph) **Tilt Train** takes about 24 hours and costs from A$221 for business class. Northbound trains leave Brisbane at 6:25pm on Monday and Friday; southbound runs depart Cairns at 9:15am on Wednesday and Sunday. The train features luxury business-class seating, with an entertainment system for each seat, including multiple movie and audio channels.

The **Sunlander,** which runs three times a week between Brisbane and Cairns, takes 31 hours and costs from A$161 for a sitting berth, A$268 for a sleeper, or A$899 for all-inclusive Queenslander class (only available twice a week). Trains pull into the Cairns Central terminal (℃ 07/4036 9250) on Bunda Street in the center of town.

BY BUS   **Greyhound Australia** (℃ 1300/473 946 in Australia, or 07/4051 5899 in Cairns; www.greyhound.com.au) buses pull into Trinity Wharf Centre in the center of town. Buses travel from the south via all towns and cities on the Bruce Highway; they also run from the west, from Alice Springs and Darwin, via Tennant Creek on the Stuart Highway, and the Outback mining town of Mount Isa to Townsville, where they join the Bruce Highway and head north. The 48-hour Sydney–Cairns trip costs A$484; the 29-hour trip from Brisbane is A$302.

BY CAR   From Brisbane and all major towns in the south, you'll enter Cairns on the Bruce Highway. To reach the northern beaches or Port Douglas, take Sheridan Street in the city center, which becomes the Captain Cook Highway.

VISITOR INFORMATION   Tourism Tropical North Queensland's **Cairns & Tropical North Visitor Information Centre,** 51 The Esplanade (℃ 1800/093 300 in Australia or 07/4051 3588; www.cairnsgreatbarrierreef.org.au), has information on Cairns and the surrounding area. It's open daily from 10am to 6:30pm and 10am to 6pm on public holidays; closed Christmas Day, New Year's Day, and Good Friday. The center also has a little stall of secondhand books for a couple of dollars each and claims to sell the cheapest bottled water in town!

CITY LAYOUT   The focal point of the city is the **Esplanade,** which has a 4,000-sq.-m (43,000-sq.-ft.) man-made saltwater swimming lagoon, with a wide sandy beach, and surrounding parkland, with public artworks and picnic areas. Suspended over the mud flats and providing a platform for birding, a timber boardwalk runs 600m (1,968 ft.) along the waterfront and is lit at night. A walkway links the Esplanade to the Reef Fleet Terminal, the departure point for Great Barrier Reef boats.

Downtown Cairns is on a grid 5 blocks deep, bounded in the east by the Esplanade and in the west by McLeod Street, where the train station and the Cairns Central shopping mall are situated.

Heading 15 minutes north from the city along the Captain Cook Highway, you come to the **northern beaches:** Holloway's Beach, Yorkey's Knob, Trinity Beach, Kewarra Beach, Clifton Beach, Palm Cove, and Ellis Beach.

GETTING AROUND   **By Bus**   **Sunbus** (✆ **07/4057 7411;** www.sunbus.com.au) buses depart Cairns City Mall at the intersection of Lake and Shields streets. Buy all tickets and passes on board, and try to have correct change. Bus nos. 110 and 111 travel to Trinity Beach and Palm Cove. Routes and timetables change, so check with the driver. Most buses run from around 7am until almost midnight.

Croc Alert!
Dangerous crocodiles inhabit Cairns' waterways. Do not swim in or stand on the bank of any river or stream.

BY CAR   **Avis** (✆ **07/4048 0522**), **Budget** (✆ **07/4048 8166**), **Europcar** (✆ **13 13 90** in Australia or 07/4034 9088), **Hertz** (✆ **07/4051 6399**), and **Thrifty** (✆ **1300/367 227** in Australia or 07/4051 8099) have offices in Cairns city and at the airport. **Redspot Car Rentals** (✆ **07/4034 9045**) has an airport office. One long-established local outfit, **Sugarland Car Rentals** (✆ **07/4052 1300**), has reasonable rates. **Britz Campervan Rentals** (✆ **1800/331 454** in Australia or 07/4032 2611) and **Maui Rentals** (✆ **1300/363 800** in Australia) rent motor homes.

BY TAXI   Call **Cairns Taxis** (✆ **13 10 08**).

Cairns & Northern Beaches Hotels

High season in Cairns includes 2 weeks at Easter, the period from early July to early October, and the Christmas holiday through January. Book ahead in those periods. In low season (Nov–June), many hotels offer discounts or negotiate fees. Cairns has a good supply of affordable accommodations, both in the heart of the city and along the northern beaches. You don't have to stay in Cairns city if you don't have a car; most tour and cruise operators do transfers.

EXPENSIVE

Pullman Reef Hotel Casino ★★   This stylish seven-story hotel is a block from the water, with Trinity Inlet views from some rooms, and city/hinterland outlooks from others. All the rooms have lots of natural light, high-quality amenities, bathrobes, and small balconies with smart timber furniture. The **Cairns Wildlife Dome** (p. 160) and **Reef Casino** are attached to the hotel. Be aware that there are two Pullman hotels in Cairns (the other is in the next street), which can be confusing (even to your taxi driver!). The **Tamarind** restaurant does a great breakfast!

35–41 Wharf St., Cairns, QLD 4870. www.pullmanhotels.com/2901. ✆ **07/4030 8888.** 128 units. A$199–A$319 double; A$599–$2,750 suite. Valet parking A$15, free self-parking. **Amenities:** 3 restaurants, 3 bars; babysitting; concierge; health club; Jacuzzi; small rooftop pool; room service; sauna; Wi-Fi (A$10/2 hr., A$28/24 hr.).

Reef House Boutique Hotel & Spa ★★★   The old colonial-style Reef House has a romantic feel about it—the white walls are swathed in bougainvillea, the beds are draped in mosquito netting, and rooms have white wicker chairs. Verandah Spa rooms have a Jacuzzi on the balcony, overlook the pool, waterfalls, and lush gardens, and have extra touches, such as bathrobes and balconies within earshot of the ocean. Improvements over the past 2 years include the addition of one-, two- and four-bedroom apartments. Every night at sunset, all the candles throughout the resort are lit and Brigadier's Punch is served to guests in an old tradition. The beachfront restaurant, on a covered wooden deck beneath towering Paperbarks, is a favorite for locals and tourists alike for its ocean views and gentle breezes.

99 Williams Esplanade, Palm Cove, Cairns, QLD 4879. www.reefhouse.com.au. © **07/4080 2600.** 69 units. A$271–A$451 double. Free limited covered parking; ample street parking. Bus: 110 or 111. **Amenities:** 2 restaurants; bar; babysitting; concierge; 3 small heated outdoor pools; room service; spa; free Wi-Fi.

MODERATE

Cairns Plaza Hotel ★★ The harbor views at this five-story complex are better than those at most of the more luxurious hotels in Cairns. Two blocks from town, the accommodations are a good size, with fresh, appealing furnishings and modern bathrooms, all refurbished in 2012. Suites and studios have kitchenettes. If your balcony does not have a water vista, you overlook a nice aspect of the city or mountains instead. This is a great place for families, as most rooms sleep three or four, and if you need more space and privacy, you can book a connecting suite and standard room. A children's playground is located just across the street.

145 The Esplanade (at Minnie St.), Cairns, QLD 4870. www.cairnsplaza.com.au. © **07/4051 4688.** 60 units. A$180 double; A$210 suite. Limited free parking. **Amenities:** Restaurant (only open for breakfast); bar; babysitting; Jacuzzi; small outdoor pool; room service; free Wi-Fi (restaurant/lobby and 6th floor only).

Novotel Cairns Oasis Resort ★ The large pool, complete with swim-up bar and a little sandy beach, is the focus of this attractive six-story resort. All the contemporary-style rooms have balconies with views over the tropical gardens, the mountains, or the pool. The suites, with a large Jacuzzi bathtub, could well be the best-value suites in town.

122 Lake St., Cairns, QLD 4870. www.novotelcairnsresort.com.au. © **1300/656 565** in Australia or 07/4080 1888. 314 units. A$139–A$310 double; A$289–A$440 suite. Children 15 and under stay free in parent's room with existing bedding. Free crib. Free valet and self-parking. **Amenities:** Restaurant; 2 bars; babysitting; concierge; gymnasium; outdoor lagoon pool (with kids pool); room service; spa; Internet (A$12/hr.; A$25/24 hr.).

The Reef Retreat ★★ Tucked back one row of buildings from the beach is this little gem—a collection of contemporary studios and suites built around a swimming pool in a grove of palms and silver Paperbarks. All the rooms have cool tile floors and smart teak and cane furniture. The studios are a terrific value and much larger than the average hotel room. Some suites have two rooms; others have a Jacuzzi and a kitchenette outside on the balcony. Rooms also have iPod docks. There's a barbecue and a Jacuzzi on the grounds, but no elevator.

10–14 Harpa St., Palm Cove, Cairns, QLD 4879. www.reefretreat.com.au. © **07/4059 1744.** 36 units. A$199 studio double; A$215 suite; A$335 2-bedroom suite or villa for up to 4; A$310–A$435 3-bedroom villa or townhouse (sleeps up to 7). Extra person A$30. Children 2 and under stay free in parent's room with existing bedding. Crib A$10. Free parking. Bus: 110 or 111. **Amenities:** Jacuzzi; outdoor heated saltwater pool; Wi-Fi (A$3/hr.; A$10/8 hr.).

Rydges Esplanade Resort Cairns ★★   Despite its lack of glitz, this 14-story hotel has been the lodging of choice for a number of movie stars on location in Cairns. A 20-minute waterfront walk from downtown, the hotel offers a range of units, from hotel rooms to penthouse apartments. The one- and two-bedroom apartments face the sea; hotel rooms have sea or mountain views. Kitchenettes are in studios and apartments only. Rooms are spacious, but bathrooms are not. Out back are cheaper studios and apartments, with upgraded furnishings; in front is a pool and sun deck. On-site are a convenience store, a hairdresser, and a masseuse.

The Esplanade (at Kerwin St.), Cairns, QLD 4870. www.rydges.com. ℰ **07/4044 9000.** 240 units. A$149–A$195 double; A$189–A$205 double 1-bedroom apt; A$259–A$275 double 2-bedroom apt. Free covered parking. Bus stop about 100m (328 ft.) from the hotel. **Amenities:** 2 restaurants; 3 bars; airport transfers; babysitting; bikes; concierge; health club; Jacuzzi; 3 outdoor pools; room service; sauna; 2 lit tennis courts; Wi-Fi in lobby and restaurant, broadband Internet in guest rooms (A$29/24 hr.).

The Hotel Cairns ★★   Stay at this hotel, and you get a free car to drive around in! All guests at the Hotel Cairns have free access to five Mercedes Smart Cars—or one Cabriolet Smart Car for those who like the wind in their hair. The cars are available on a first-come, first-served basis, include unlimited mileage and a full tank of petrol. This plantation-style hotel, with its white shutters, verandas, and latticework screens, is very Queensland. Family-owned and -operated, the hotel is in tropical gardens just 5 minutes' walk from the city center. Rooms are modern, with bright splashes of color, marble floors, and large bathrooms, and some have balconies. Even the Plantation Rooms, on the lower two levels, are spacious, but for more luxury, each Tower Room is 33 sq. m (355 sq. ft.), with a generous balcony. The three Tower Suites are even bigger.

Abbott and Florence sts., Cairns, QLD 4870. www.thehotelcairns.com. ℰ **07/4051 6188.** 92 units. A$195 double; A$225 double Tower Room; A$265 double suite. Extra person A$30. Crib A$10. Free covered parking. **Amenities:** Restaurant; bar; bikes; exercise room; Jacuzzi; outdoor pool; room service; free Wi-Fi.

INEXPENSIVE

Coral Tree Inn ★   The focal point of this airy, modern resort-style motel a 5-minute walk from the city center is the friendly communal kitchen that overlooks the palm-lined saltwater pool and paved sun deck. It's a great spot to cook a steak or reef fish on the free barbecue and join other guests at the big shared tables. The smallish, basic-but-neat motel rooms have painted brick walls, terra-cotta tile or carpeted floors, and new bathrooms with marble-look laminate countertops. In contrast, the eight suites, which have kitchenettes, are huge and stylish—and some of the best-value rooms in town. All rooms have a balcony or patio; some overlook the commercial buildings next door, but most face the pool. Ask about packages that include cruises and other tours.

166–172 Grafton St., Cairns, QLD 4870. www.coraltreeinn.com.au. ℰ **07/4031 3744.** 58 units. A$129 double; A$159 suite. Extra person A$14. Limited free parking; ample street parking. **Amenities:** Bar; airport shuttle; babysitting; bike rental; outdoor saltwater pool; Wi-Fi ($15/day).

Ellis Beach Oceanfront Bungalows ★★   On arguably the loveliest of the northern beaches, about 30 minutes from Cairns, these bungalows and cabins sit under palm trees between the Coral Sea and a backdrop of mountainous rainforest. Lifeguards patrol the beach, and there are stinger nets in season as well as a shady pool and

7

Cairns

CAIRNS & THE GREAT BARRIER REEF

The **Spirit of Freedom** (☎ **07/4047 9150;** www.spiritoffreedom.com.au) in Cairns offers a chance to "sleep on the Reef" aboard the 36m (120-ft.) *Spirit of Freedom*, a sleek, modern motor yacht with electronic stabilizers, a widescreen TV with DVD player, comfortable lounge areas, sun decks, and 11 luxury double or quad shared cabins, each with an ensuite bathroom. You will visit the popular Cod Hole and Ribbon Reef and on longer trips venture into the Coral Sea.

A 3-day, 3-night trip will cost A$1,575 to A$2,375 depending on your choice of cabin and ends with a 193km (120-mile) one-way 1-hour low-level flight from Lizard Island back to Cairns. You will fit in up to 11 dives. Prices include meals and pickup from your Cairns accommodations. Allow A$120 to A$245 extra for equipment rental. There are also 4-day and 7-day cruises to choose from (the latter a combination of both shorter trips).

a toddlers' wading pool. You'll have plenty of privacy, and rooms are basic but pleasant. As you sit on your veranda and gaze at the ocean, keep an eye out for dolphins. Each bungalow and cabin sleeps four and has full kitchen facilities (with microwave, fridge, and freezer), but cabins have no ensuite bathrooms (they have use of the communal facilities at the campground in the same complex). The property has a laundry, coin-operated barbecues, and phone and fax facilities (but no phone in your room).

Captain Cook Hwy., Ellis Beach, QLD 4879. www.ellisbeach.com. ☎ **1800/637 036** in Australia, or 07/4055 3538. 15 units. A$95–A$115 double cabin; A$155–A$210 double bungalow. Extra person A$20 cabin, A$30 bungalow. 2-night minimum stay; 3-night minimum June–Sept. **Amenities:** Restaurant; 2 outdoor pools.

Where to Eat

For cheap eats, head to the Esplanade along the seafront; it's lined with cafes, pizzerias, fish-and-chips places, food courts, and ice-cream parlors. The northern beaches—particularly Palm Cove—also have some great restaurants (sometimes with prices to match!).

EXPENSIVE

NuNu ★★★ CONTEMPORARY   Your focus may be more on your plate than on the view outside at this stylish but still laid-back eatery. Dining fare includes some bold choices, such as "bunny a bunch of ways," or the pricey Queensland mud crab with a chili tamarind sauce. Other options include a whole duck, a 1.2kg Angus T-bone steak, or, on the less expensive side, some kind of curry. The menu changes seasonally, but it's always going to offer you something surprising. If you choose one of the banquette-style seats at breakfast or lunch, you could easily settle in for hours. The six-course tasting menu, at A$110 per person, is an event in itself.

123 Williams Esplanade, Palm Cove. ☎ **07/4059 1880.** www.nunu.com.au. Main courses A$22–A$80. Thurs–Mon 11:30am–late. Closed Tues–Wed. Bus: 110 or 111.

MODERATE

L'Unico ★★ ITALIAN   Ask for a table on the veranda, overlooking Trinity Beach's esplanade and the sea. This smart but relaxed Italian restaurant has a great vibe and terrific staff. The wood-fired oven produces pizzas with interesting toppings (prawns, chorizo, red onion, and paprika, for example), and the kitchen makes good use of local ingredients in all dishes (angel hair pasta with Moreton Bay bugs—that would be seafood—is one of my favorite dishes here). There's a cocktail bar and a bar menu available throughout the day—and a kids' menu too.

75 Vasey Esplanade, Trinity Beach. © **07/4057 8855.** www.lunico.com.au. Main courses A$16–A$44. Daily noon–3:30pm and 5:30–9pm (9:30pm Fri–Sat). Bus: 110 or 111.

Ochre Restaurant ★★ GOURMET BUSH TUCKER If you've always wanted to taste crocodile or kangaroo, this is the place to come. You could accuse this restaurant/bar of using weird and wonderful Aussie ingredients as a gimmick, but the diners who have flocked here for the past decade or so know good food when they taste it. Daily specials are big on fresh local seafood, and the regular menu changes often. There may be ingredients you've never heard of—but this is the place to be adventurous! Try salt-and-native-pepper crocodile and prawns with Vietnamese pickles and lemon aspen sambal, chargrilled kangaroo sirloin with a quandong chili glaze, egg noodle cake and bok choy, or just slow-roasted wallaby. It can be very busy, and you may have to wait for a table, but the food is very good.

43 Shields St., Cairns. © **07/4051 0100.** www.ochrerestaurant.com.au. Main courses A$19–A$38. Australian game platter A$50 per person; seafood platter A$69 per person. Taste of Australia 4-course set menu A$70 per person (minimum 2 people). Mon–Fri noon–3pm; daily 5:30pm–midnight. Closed Christmas Day. Hours may vary on public holidays; call to check.

Vivo Bar and Grill ★★★ CONTEMPORARY White-painted colonial style, complete with wooden shutters and a wide veranda, this is an inviting choice, looking through the palm trees to the water. Choose from some tempting pasta dishes (such as spanner crab linguine) or a simple version of fish 'n' chips, with battered barramundi. A fixed-price dinner menu—two courses ($39) or three courses ($49), including a glass of wine—changes every week, with a choice of dishes for entrée, main, and dessert. Order ahead for the Queensland chili mud crab ($79). The restaurant is also open for breakfast. Happy hour is from 3pm to 6pm, with cocktails and tapas. There's a kids' menu too.

49 Williams Esplanade, Palm Cove. © **07/4059 0944.** www.vivo.com.au. Main courses A$25–A$46. Daily 7am–10pm. Bus: 110 or 111.

INEXPENSIVE

Caffiend ★★ CAFE Tucked away between an alley full of street art and an arcade, this atmospheric little cafe is easy to miss. Tipped off by a friend, I headed here for what I'd been told was the best coffee in Cairns—and ended up staying for lunch! Terrines, salads, soups, a big BLT, croque monsieur, and other delicious eats are on a menu that changes monthly. And don't forget to check the specials board. You order and pay for your meals at the counter. There's live music at lunchtimes on Sundays.

Shop 5, 78 Grafton St., Cairns. © **07/4051 5522.** www.caffiend.com.au. Main courses A$12–A$19. Tues–Sat 7:30am–3pm, Sun 8am–2pm. Closed Mon.

Candy ★★ CAFE Green plastic hedges mark the outdoor area at Candy, but head inside for the full impact of this quirky little cafe/bar. Huge murals and dangling chandeliers give the place an offbeat but sophisticated feel. Another tip from a local—and yes, the coffee here is good—led me to this standout on the Grafton Street cafe strip.

The menu offers some unusual (for Cairns, anyway) choices, such as black pudding, and each item has a fun name attached to it. "Duck Duck Goose," for example, is shredded duck-leg confit on zucchini fritters, topped with a poached egg and beetroot jam. It also offers a range of interesting sandwiches. The cafe is a popular breakfast spot.

70 Grafton St., Cairns. © **07/4031 8816.** Main courses A$14–A$19. Mon–Fri 7am–3pm, Sat 8am–3pm, Sun 8am–noon.

Perrotta's at the Gallery ★★ CONTEMPORARY

The locals flock here for brunch and lunch, particularly on weekends, and you can team a meal here with a visit to the Cairns Regional Art Gallery next door. Breakfast differs from the usual eggs or pancakes, offering delights such as smoked salmon, sweet-potato hash browns with sour cream, and French toast with baked pears and raspberry coulis. For lunch, choose from bruschettas, focaccia, panini, and pasta, or mains such as barbecued Cajun Spanish mackerel with tomato and basil salad. At dinner, try wild barramundi, braised duck leg, or lamb shanks—and perhaps a sticky date pudding for dessert. Remember to check out the specials board.

Abbott and Shields sts., Cairns. © **07/4031 5899.** Breakfast A$3–A$8; lunch A$7–A$12; main courses at dinner A$15–A$25. Daily 8:30am–11pm.

Exploring Cairns

Many of the Cairns region's attractions lie outside the city center. Apart from the Reef, there is a string of white sandy beaches just 15 minutes north of the city center. Trinity Beach, 15 minutes from the airport or 25 minutes from the city center, is secluded, elegant, and scenic. The most upscale is Palm Cove, 20 minutes from the airport or 30 minutes from the city. If you're staying in Cairns, also check out activities in and around Port Douglas (p. 168). Many tour operators in Port Douglas offer transfers from Cairns. Ask about packages that include discounted entry when you visit several of Cairns' attractions, such as Tjapukai Aboriginal Cultural Park, Cairns Tropical Zoo, Skyrail, and Kuranda Scenic Rail.

Cairns Wildlife Dome ★★

Here, 200 animals—including a large saltwater crocodile named Goliath—are housed in a 20m-high (66-ft.) glass dome on the rooftop of the Pullman Reef Hotel Casino (see p. 155). Birds soar overhead and you can get up close with koalas, lizards, frogs, pademelons, turtles, and snakes. There are wildlife presentations and free guided tours throughout the day. Koala photos are A$15 (pay when you buy your entry ticket).

35–41 Wharf St., Cairns. © **07/4031 7250.** www.cairnsdome.com.au. Admission A$22 adults, A$11 children 4–14. Tickets are valid for reentry for up to 4 days. Daily 9am–8pm. Closed Christmas Day.

Skyrail Rainforest Cableway ★★★

This magnificent feat of engineering is one of Australia's top tourism attractions. Six-person gondolas leave every few seconds for the 7.5km (4½-mile) journey to the rainforest village of Kuranda (see p. 166). The view of the coast as you ascend is so breathtaking that even those afraid of heights will find it worthwhile. As you rise over the foothills of the coastal range, watch the lush green of the rainforest take over beneath you. Looking back, you have spectacular views over Cairns and north toward Trinity Bay. On a clear day, you can see . . . if not forever, then at least to Green Island. There are two stops during the 90-minute trip, at

Red Peak and Barron Falls. After about 10 minutes, you reach Red Peak. You are now 545m (1,788 ft.) above sea level, and massive kauri pines dominate the view. You must change gondolas at each station, so take the time to stroll around the boardwalks for the ground view of the rainforest. Free guided walks are run regularly through the day.

On board again, you continue on to Barron Falls station, built on the site of an old construction camp for workers on the first hydroelectric power station on the Barron River in the 1930s. A rainforest information center is here, as well as boardwalks to the lookouts for wonderful views of the Barron Gorge and Falls. From Barron Falls station, the gondola travels over the thick rainforest of the range. As you reach the end of the trip, the gondola passes over the Barron River and across the Kuranda railway line into the station. Don't worry if it rains on the day you go—one of the best trips I've made on Skyrail was in a misty rain, which added a new dimension to the rainforest.

I strongly recommend that you combine Skyrail with a trip on the Kuranda Scenic Rail (see p. 166) for a wonderful day trip from Cairns. The best way is to take the train from Cairns in the morning and return on Skyrail in the afternoon—for the views going down the range.

Cairns Western Arterial Rd. and Captain Cook Hwy., Smithfield. ✆ **07/4038 5555.** www.skyrail. com.au. Round-trip ticket A$94 adults, A$47 children, A$235 families, including transfers from Cairns or northern beaches hotels. Daily 9am–5:15pm. Closed Christmas Day. You must make a reservation to travel within a 15-minute time frame. The last boardings are at 2:45pm for a return trip or 3:30pm for a one-way journey. Free parking. Bus: 123. Round-trip shuttle transfers to and through the park from Cairns hotels A$25 adults and A$15 children.

Tjapukai Aboriginal Cultural Park ★

Whether you choose the day or night experience, the Tjapukai (pronounced Jab-*oo*-guy) Aboriginal Cultural Park is essentially a theme park. It's a slick, sophisticated production that has won multiple international awards, and it will give you an introduction to local Aboriginal history and culture.

Allow 2 to 3 hours to see everything. Start in the Creation Theatre, where performers use the latest in illusion, theatrics, and technology to tell the story of the creation of the world according to the spiritual beliefs of Tjapukai people. Move on through the Magic Space museum and gallery section of the complex to the History Theatre, where a 20-minute film relates the history of the Tjapukai people since the arrival of white settlers 120 years ago.

Outside, there's a cultural village where you can try fire-making, didgeridoo playing, and boomerang and spear throwing and learn about bush foods and medicines and hunting techniques. A gallery stocks the work of Aboriginal artists and crafts workers.

Tjapukai by Night tours include interactive time in the Magic Space museum, a Creation Show performance, and an outdoor Serpent Circle—a show featuring tap sticks for each guest to use, a join-in corroboree (an Aboriginal nighttime dance), and a ceremony involving fire and water. A buffet dinner and dance show follow, where you get the chance to meet the dancers.

Captain Cook Hwy. (beside the Skyrail terminal), Smithfield. ✆ **07/4042 9999.** www.tjapukai.com. au. Admission A$36 adults, A$18 children 5–14, A$90 families. Daily 9am–5pm. Tjapukai by Night tours run daily from 7:30pm-9:30pm and cost A$121 adults, A$61 children or A$305 family of four, including transfers to and from Cairns. Closed Christmas Day. Free parking. Bus: 123. Round-trip shuttle transfers to and through the park from Cairns hotels A$25 adults and A$15 children.

Packaging Your Day Trip

A package combining one-way travel on Skyrail and a trip back on the **Kuranda Scenic Railway** is A$119 for adults, A$60 for children, and A$298 for families of four with round-trip transfers from Cairns or the northern beaches. A package including the Skyrail, the Scenic Railway, and entry to the **Tjapukai Aboriginal Cultural Park** is A$155 for adults, A$78 for kids, and A$388 for families of four, including transfers. An option including the Skyrail, Scenic Railway, and **Rainforestation** (see p. 168) is A$173 for adults, A$87 for kids, and A$433 for families of four, including transfers. There are other packages too, and some can upgrade to Gold Class train service for A$48 extra per person. In most cases, these packages represent convenience rather than savings. Book them through Skyrail, Queensland Rail, or Tjapukai.

Outlying Attractions

Cairns Tropical Zoo ★   Get a dose of your favorite Aussie wildlife here—some kind of talk or show takes place about every 15 or 30 minutes throughout the day, including koala cuddling and snake handling (have your photo taken for an extra A$18) and saltwater crocodile and lorikeet feedings. Other animals on show are kangaroos (which you can hand-feed for A$1 a bag), emus, cassowaries, dingoes, and native birds in a walk-through aviary. The park also runs a nocturnal tour, during which you can see many of the more elusive creatures. The park's 3-hour **Cairns Night Zoo** tour (Mon–Thurs and Sat; www.cairnsnightzoo.com) starts at 7pm and includes a wildlife spotlighting walk, during which you can pat a koala and a possum and feed kangaroos; a stargazing interlude; a barbecue dinner with beer and wine, billy tea, and damper; and dancing to an Aussie bush band.

Captain Cook Hwy. (22km/14 miles north of the city center), Palm Cove. © **07/4055 3669.** www.cairnstropicalzoo.com. Admission A$33 adults, A$17 children 4–15 (valid for 3 days). Combination tickets with Hartley's Crocodile Adventures (see below) A$62 adults, A$31 children. Cairns Night Zoo tour A$99 adults, A$50 children 4–15 (more if you want transfers from Cairns or the northern beaches). Daily 8:30am–4pm. Closed Christmas Day; open 1:30–5pm Anzac Day (Apr 25). Free parking. Bus: 110 or 111. Transfers from Cairns through Beaches Meet and Greet (© **07/4059 2713**).

Hartley's Crocodile Adventures ★★★   Hartley's is the original Australian croc show and quite possibly the best. Its fantastic natural setting is a 2-hectare (5-acre) lagoon surrounded by melaluca (Paperbark) and bloodwood trees that are home to 23 estuarine crocs. The best time to visit is for the 3pm "croc attack" show, when you can witness the saltwater crocodile "death roll" during the 45-minute performance. At 11am you can see these monsters being hand-fed or hear an eye-opening talk on the less-aggressive freshwater crocodiles. If you are really brave (braver than me!), you can also have a **"Big Croc Experience,"** where you get to pole-feed a large crocodile yourself. Available twice a day at 10:30am and 1pm (bookings essential), you'll be one of six adults (16 and over) to take part in each group (but your friends and family can come along to watch). The cost is $125 per person. There are tours of the croc farm at 10am and 1:30pm; at 2pm there is a snake show; 4:30pm is koala-feeding time.

Cassowaries are fed at 9:30am and 4:15pm. There are also croc- and snake-handling opportunities and heaps of other interesting things to see and do.

Captain Cook Hwy. (40km/24 miles north of Cairns; about 100m off the highway). © **07/4055 3576.** www.crocodileadventures.com. Admission (good for 3 days) A$35 adults, A$18 children 4–15, A$88 families of 4. Daily 8:30am–5pm; 1:30pm–5pm Anzac Day (Apr 25). Closed Christmas Day. Free parking.

Day Trips to the Reef

For an introduction to the Great Barrier Reef, most visitors take one of the large-scale tour boats. These motorized catamarans can carry up to 300 passengers each and tie up at their own private permanent pontoons anchored to a platform reef. The boats are air-conditioned and have a bar, videos, and educational material, as well as a marine biologist who gives a talk on the Reef's ecology en route. The pontoons have glass-bottom boats for passengers who don't want to get wet, dry underwater viewing chambers, sun decks, shaded seats, and often showers. But be aware that you will be in a crowded environment. And if you are prone to seasickness, make sure you take some preventive measures before you set out!

An alternative is to go on one of the many smaller boats. These typically visit two or three Reef sites rather than just one. There are usually no more than 20 passengers on board, so you get more personal attention. Another advantage is that you will have the coral pretty much all to yourself. The drawbacks of a small boat are that you have only the cramped deck to sit on when you get out of the water, and your traveling time to the Reef may be longer. If you're a nervous snorkeler, you may feel safer on a boat where you will be swimming with 300 other people.

Most day-trip fares include snorkel gear—fins, mask, and snorkel (plus wetsuits in winter, if you want one)—free use of the underwater viewing chambers and glass-bottom-boat rides, a plentiful buffet or barbecue lunch, and morning and afternoon refreshments. Diving is an optional activity for which you pay extra. The big boats post snorkeling scouts to keep a lookout for anyone in trouble and count heads periodically. If you wear glasses, ask whether your boat offers prescription masks—this will make a big difference to the quality of your experience! Don't forget that you can travel as a snorkel-only passenger on most dive boats, too.

Wildife Passes

Wildlife enthusiasts who plan to visit several of the attractions in the Cairns region can save a few dollars by buying a **Four Park Pass,** which gives entry to the Cairns Wildlife Dome and three Kuranda attractions (see "Day Trips from Cairns" later in this chapter): the Rainforestation Nature Park, the Australian Butterfly Sanctuary, and The Wildlife Habitat (all owned by the same local family). The discounted price of A$80 adults, A$40 children, and A$200 for a family of four is a savings of A$29 per adult or A$73 per family. The pass is valid for six months and doesn't have to be used on consecutive days. Buy it at any of the participating parks. A **Kuranda Wildlife Experience** pass offers discounted admission to Bird-world, the Kuranda Koala Gardens, and the Australian Butterfly Sanctuary (p. 167). It can be bought on arrival at any of the three sanctuaries for A$46 adults, half-price for children.

Great Adventures ★ (𝒞 **07/4044 9944**; www.greatadventures.com.au) does daily cruises from Cairns in fast, air-conditioned catamarans to a three-level pontoon on the Outer Reef. The pontoon has a kids' swimming area, a semisubmersible, and an underwater observatory. The cost for the day is A$214 for adults, A$110 for children 4 to 14, and A$544 for families. You spend at least 3 hours on the Reef. Hotel transfers are available from Cairns, the northern beaches, and Port Douglas for an extra cost. The boat departs the Reef Fleet Terminal at 10:30am.

You can also depart Cairns with Great Adventures at 8:30am and spend 2 hours on Green Island en route. This gives you time to walk nature trails, rent snorkel gear and watersports equipment, or laze on the beach before continuing to the Outer Reef. This cruise costs an extra A$20 per adult and A$10 per child, or A$50 per family.

Sunlover Cruises ★ (𝒞 **1800/810 512** in Australia, or 07/4050 1333; www.sunlover.com.au) motors large, fast catamarans to Moore Reef on the Outer Reef. The day costs A$209 for adults, A$99 for children 4 to 14, and A$536 for families of four, including transfers from city hotels and about 4 hours on the Reef. This trip includes a glass-bottom-boat ride and semisubmersible viewing. Introductory dives cost A$125 for one dive or A$190 for two. Certified divers pay A$80 for one dive or A$125 for two, including all gear. The cruise includes lunch and leaves from the Reef Fleet Terminal in Cairns at 10am daily.

For a more intimate experience, **Ocean Freedom** ★★★ (𝒞 **07/4052 1111**; www.oceanfreedom.com.au) gives you the option of a motor cruise or a sailing tour—in both cases with limited numbers to ensure you don't feel crowded. Ocean Freedom is a high-speed launch that gives you 6 hours on the reef with no more than 75 passengers and takes you to two Reef sites including Upolu Cay. The day starts at 7:30am at the Reef Fleet Terminal, returning at about 4:30pm. The cost is A$185 adults, A$100 children, and A$517 for a family of four and includes glass-bottom-boat rides, all snorkeling gear, and lunch. You can do an introductory dive for A$105 or, if you are certified, dive for A$70. This is a really great way to see the Reef. On the sailing trip aboard Ocean Free (www.oceanfree.com.au) you'll be one of only 35 passengers. Ocean Free sails at 7:30am, bound for Pinnacle Reef, an exclusive mooring on the eastern lee of Green Island. The cruise costs A$140 adults, A$90 children, and A$418 for a family of four. Introductory dives cost A$85 and certified dives A$65. The friendly crew give you all the help you need.

Ocean Spirit Cruises ★★ (𝒞 **1300/858 141** in Australia, or 02/8296 7377; www.oceanspirit.com.au) operates two sailing catamarans that take no more than 150 passengers to Michaelmas Cay, a lovely white-sand cay on the Outer Reef surrounded by rich reefs. This trip includes a 2-hour sail to the cay, a guided snorkeling safari, and a guided beach walk—plus the usual reef ecology talks, semisubmersible rides, lunch, and transfers from your Cairns or northern beaches hotel. You also spend your out-of-water time on a beautiful beach, not on a boat. You get about 4 hours on the Reef. The cost is A$207 for adults, A$132 for children 4 to 14, and A$550 for families of four (but check online for specials). Introductory dives cost A$110, all gear included. The trip departs Reef Fleet Terminal at 8:30am daily. Transfers from Cairns, the northern beaches, and Port Douglas cost $14.

You can also take a coach transfer from Cairns or Palm Cove to join the **Quicksilver Wavepiercer** (𝒞 **07/4087 2100**; www.quicksilver-cruises.com), based in Port Douglas, for a day trip to the Outer Reef (p. 170). Transfers cost A$26 per adult or A$13 per child, A$65 for families of four.

Can't swim? Don't want to get your hair wet? Don't worry—you can still get underwater and see the wonders of the Reef. Several companies offer travelers the chance to don a dive helmet and "walk" underwater. Similar to old-style diving helmets, which allow you to breathe underwater, the helmet has air pumped into it by a hose. You walk into the water to a depth of about 4m (13 ft.), accompanied by instructors, and the Reef is right before you. **Quicksilver Cruises** calls it "Ocean Walker"; with **Sunlover Cruises** and at **Green Island Resort** it's called "Sea Walker." You must be at least 10 years old (at Green Island Resort) or 12 years old (with Quicksilver and Sunlover cruises). The cost is about A$140 to A$150 for 20 minutes.

Great Adventures, Quicksilver, and Sunlover also all offer helicopter flights over the Reef from their pontoons—a spectacular experience! There are fly-and-cruise trips as well.

FOR DIVERS   Tusa Dive ★★ (✆ **07/4047 9100;** www.tusadive.com) runs a custom-built 24m (72-ft.) dive boat daily to two dive sites from a choice of 15 locations on the Outer Reef. The day costs A$235 for divers and A$185 adult or A$105 child ages 4 to 14 for snorkelers, with wetsuits, guided snorkel tours, lunch, and transfers from your Cairns or northern beaches hotel. If you want to be shown the best spots, you can take a guided dive for an extra A$10. Day trips for introductory divers cost A$245 for one dive or A$285 for two. The boat takes a maximum of 60 people, with a staff-to-passenger ratio of one to five, so you get a good level of personal attention.

Day Trips to the Islands

Cairns has several coral cays and reef-fringed islands within the **Great Barrier Reef Marine Park.** Less than an hour from the city wharf, **Fitzroy Island** is a rainforest-covered national park, with a coral beach and great snorkeling right off the shore. **Green Island** is a coral cay with snorkeling equal to that of most other places on the Great Barrier Reef. It is also a popular diving spot. You can visit it in half a day if time is short.

FITZROY ISLAND ★★★   Scenic Fitzroy Island is 45 minutes from Cairns. Day-trippers visit the island for snorkeling and diving, glass-bottom-boat rides, watersports, rainforest walks, or hikes to the lighthouse at the top of the hill. A day trip can cost as little as the round-trip ferry fare: A$74 adults or A$47 for kids 4 to 14 (for a little extra you can order a picnic lunch pack too). A kiosk on the beach hires snorkeling gear, coral viewing boards, paddle skis, and stand-up paddling boards, or you can book a glass-bottom-boat tour. Check the website for packages that might save you a few dollars. Departure from Cairns is at 9am, returning at 4:30pm daily. Make reservations through **Raging Thunder Adventures** (✆ **07/4030 7990;** www.ragingthunder.com. au). Raging Thunder also runs daily guided sea-kayak expeditions around the island. These include snorkeling gear, lunch, and stinger suits (Nov–May), the return ferry trip, 3 hours of kayaking, and then you can stay on the island for the rest of the day. Tours cost A$134, but you must be at least 14 years old.

GREEN ISLAND ★★   This 15-hectare (37-acre) coral cay is just 27km (17 miles) east of Cairns. You can rent snorkel gear, windsurfers, and paddle skis; take glass-bottom-boat trips; go parasailing; take an introductory or certified dive; walk vine-forest trails; or laze on the beach. The beach is coral sand, so it's a little rough underfoot. Day visitors have access to one of the Green Island Resort pools, its main bar, the casual or upscale restaurants there, and lockers and showers. Ask the beach staff to recommend the best snorkeling spots. The island has a small attraction called **Marineland Melanesia** (✆ **07/4051 4032;** www.marinelandgreenisland.com), where you can see old nautical artifacts, a Melanesian artifacts collection, a turtle and reef aquarium, and live crocodiles, including Cassius, at 5.5 meters reputed to be the largest croc in captivity in the world. Admission is A$18 adults, A$8 kids 5 to 14; croc shows are at 10:30am and 1:30pm.

Great Adventures (✆ **07/4044 9944;** www.greatadventures.com.au) and **Big Cat Green Island Reef Cruises** (✆ **07/4051 0444;** www.greenisland.com.au) run to Green Island from Cairns. Both offer a range of half-day and full-day trips with lots of options. Half-day trips with snorkel gear or a glass-bottom-boat cruise with both companies cost from A$84 adults and A$42 children 4 to 14. Both pick up from hotels in Cairns, the northern beaches, and Port Douglas for an extra cost.

DAY TRIPS FROM CAIRNS

Kuranda

34km (21 miles) NW of Cairns

Few travelers visit Cairns without making a trip to the mountain village of **Kuranda,** near the Barron Gorge National Park. Although it's undeniably touristy, the cool mountain air and mist-wrapped rainforest refuse to be spoiled, no matter how many tourists clutter the streets. The shopping in Kuranda—for leather goods, Australian-wool sweaters, opals, crafts, and more—is more unusual than in Cairns, and the handful of cafes and restaurants are much more atmospheric. The town is easy to negotiate on foot; pick up a visitors' guide and map at the Skyrail gondola station or train station. Aside from the village, you can explore the rainforest, the river esplanade, or Barron Falls along a number of easy walking trails.

ESSENTIALS

GETTING THERE   Getting to Kuranda is part of the fun. Some people drive up the winding 25km (16-mile) mountain road, but the most popular approaches are to chuff up the mountainside in a scenic train, or to glide silently over the rainforest canopy in the world's longest gondola cableway, the Skyrail Rainforest Cableway. The most popular round-trip is one-way on the Skyrail and the other way on the train. Mornings are best for photography on Skyrail, but the view is spectacular coming down in the afternoon; make up your own mind, both are wonderful!

BY SKYRAIL   The **Skyrail Rainforest Cableway** (see p. 160) takes you up the Kuranda Range in a six-person gondola suspended over the rainforest.

BY TRAIN   The 34km (21-mile) **Kuranda Scenic Railway** (✆ **1800/577 245** in Australia or 07/4036 9333; www.ksr.com.au) is one of the most scenic rail journeys in the world. The train snakes through the magnificent vistas of the Barron Gorge

National Park, past gorges and waterfalls on the 90-minute trip from Cairns to Kuranda. It rises 328m (1,076 ft.) and goes through 15 tunnels before emerging at the pretty Kuranda station, which is smothered in ferns. Built by hand over 5 years in the late 1880s, the railway track is today a monument to the 1,500 men who toiled to link the two towns. The train departs Cairns Central at 8:30 and 9:30am daily (except Christmas Day) and leaves Kuranda at 2 and 3:30pm. The one-way fare is A$49 for adults, A$25 for children 4 to 14, and A$123 for families of four.

BY BUS **Trans North Bus & Coach Service** (✆ **07/4095 8644;** www.transnorth bus.com) operates a bus to Kuranda from Cairns five times a day. The fare is A$8 one-way. *Tip:* Buying a return ticket will give you priority if the bus is full at the end of the day. Catch it at the Cairns Transit Mall in Lake Street, at the railway station, or at the Cairns Central Shopping Centre on Spence Street.

VISITOR INFORMATION The **Kuranda Visitor Information Centre** (✆ **07/4093 9311;** www.kuranda.org) is in Centenary Park, at the top end of Coondoo Street. It is open 10am to 4pm daily, except Christmas Day.

EXPLORING KURANDA

Kuranda is known for its markets. The **Kuranda Original Rainforest Markets**, at 7 Therwine St., entry through the Kuranda Market Mall (✆ **07/4093 9440;** daily 9:30am–3pm), are devoted exclusively to local artisans who vend fashion, jewelry, leather work, and indigenous art, as well as local produce including honey, coffee, fruit, sugarcane juice, coconuts, and macadamias.

The 90-stall **Heritage Market** (✆ **07/4093 8060;** www.kurandamarkets.com.au) is open daily from 9:30am to 3:30pm on Rob Veivers Drive, with a range of souvenirs, food, produce, and crafts.

A group of about 50 local artisans sell their work in the **Kuranda Arts Co-Operative** gallery, Coondoo Street (opposite the church) (✆ **07/4093 9026;** www. artskuranda.asn.au). It's open from 10am to 4pm daily. The gallery sells quality furniture crafted from recycled Australian hardwoods, jewelry, photography, glasswork, and more.

Australian Butterfly Sanctuary ★★ A rainbow-hued array of 1,500 tropical butterflies—including the electric-blue Ulysses and Australia's largest species, the Cairns bird wing—occupies a lush walk-through enclosure here. Take the free 30-minute guided tour and learn about the butterfly's fascinating life cycle. The butterflies will land on you if you wear pink, red, and other bright colors.

8 Rob Veivers Dr. ✆ **07/4093 7575.** www.australianbutterflies.com. Admission A$19 adults, A$9.50 children 4–15, A$48 families of 4. Daily 9:45am–4pm. Closed Christmas Day. Street parking.

Birdworld ★ Behind the markets off Rob Veivers Drive, Birdworld has eye-catching macaws, a pair of cassowaries, and Australia's largest collection of free-flying birds—about 500 of them, representing 75 worldwide species. Two lakes are home to waterbirds including stilts, herons, and Australia's Black Swan.

Rob Veivers Dr. ✆ **07/4093 9188.** www.birdworldkuranda.com. Admission A$17 adults, A$9 children 4–15. Daily 9am–4pm. Closed Christmas Day. Street parking.

Kuranda Koala Gardens ★ You can cuddle a koala and have your photo taken at this small wildlife park next to the Heritage Markets. Other animals include freshwater crocodiles, wombats, lizards, and wallabies. Or take a stroll through the walk-through snake enclosure while they slither at your feet—not for the fainthearted.

Rob Veivers Dr. ☎ **07/4093 9953.** www.koalagardens.com. Admission A$17 adults, A$9 children 4–15. Daily 9am–4pm. Closed Christmas Day. Street parking.

Kuranda Riverboat Tours ★★   If you want to learn about the rainforest, take one of these informative 45-minute river cruises. The cruises depart from the riverside landing across the footbridge, near the train station. A team of local naturalists headed by former crocodile hunter Brian Clarke, who has lived in the rainforest for more than 30 years, will answer your questions and point out some of the rainforest secrets. Buy your tickets on board (cash only).

Rob Veivers Dr. ☎ **07/4093 7476.** www.kurandariverboat.com. A$15 adults, A$7 children 5–15, A$37 families of four. Cruises depart hourly from 10:45am–2:30pm.

Rainforestation Nature Park ★★   At this 40-hectare (99-acre) nature and cultural complex, you can take a 45-minute ride into the rainforest in a World War II amphibious Army Duck. You'll hear commentary on orchids and other rainforest wild-life along the way. You can also see a performance by Aboriginal dancers; learn about Aboriginal legends and throw a boomerang on the Dreamtime Walk; or have your photo taken cuddling a koala in the wildlife park (photos extra). The Army Duck runs on the hour, beginning at 10am; the Aboriginal dancers perform at 10:30am, noon, and 2pm; and the 30-minute Dreamtime Walk leaves at 10, 11, and 11:30am, and 12:30, 1:30, and 2:30pm.

Kennedy Hwy., a 5-min. drive from the center of Kuranda. ☎ **07/4085 5008.** www.rainforest.com. au. A$44 adults, A$22 children 4–14, A$110 families of 4 (or you can buy tickets to each attraction separately). Daily 9am–4pm. Closed Christmas Day. Free parking. Shuttle from the Butterfly Sanctuary, Rob Veivers Dr., every 30 min. 10:45am–2:45pm for A$10 adults, A$5 children, A$24 families, round-trip.

WHERE TO EAT IN KURANDA

Frogs Restaurant ★ CAFE   This is a good place to stop for lunch, tucked into the wildlife attractions and Heritage Markets just off the main street. Simple offerings like wraps, pizzas, and salads dominate, but you can also get a hearty steak, seafood, or a bush tasting platter (kangaroo, emu, and crocodile) if you want something bigger. Or try the Curry of the Day, a bargain at only A$7. Be on the lookout for the water dragons (they're harmless) on the deck overlooking the rainforest. It also has free Wi-Fi.

2/4 Rob Veivers Dr., Kuranda. ☎ **07/4093 8952.** www.frogsrestaurant.com.au. Main courses A$7–A$27. Daily 9am–3:30pm. Closed Christmas Day.

PORT DOUGLAS

Port Douglas: 67km (42 miles) N of Cairns; Mossman: 19km (12 miles) N of Port Douglas

The fishing village of Port Douglas is where the rainforest meets the Reef. Just over an hour's drive from Cairns, through rainforest and along a winding (sometimes treacherously so) road beside the sea, Port Douglas may be small, but stylish shops and seriously trendy restaurants line the main street, and beautiful Four Mile Beach is not to be missed. This is a favorite spot with celebrities big and small. Travelers often base themselves in "Port," as the locals call it, because they like the rural surroundings, the uncrowded beach, and the absence of tacky development (so far, anyway). Many Reef tours originate in Port, and many of the tours in the Cairns section pick up here.

The waters off Port Douglas boast just as many wonderful reefs and marine life forms as the waters around Cairns; the reefs are equally close to shore and equally colorful and varied. The closest Reef site off Port Douglas, the **Low Isles,** is only 15km (9 miles) northeast. Coral sand and 22 hectares (55 acres) of coral surround these two coral cays; the smaller is a sand cay covered in rich vegetation and the larger is a shingle/rubble cay covered in mangroves and home to thousands of nesting Torresian Imperial pigeons. If you visit the Low Isles, wear old shoes that you can get wet, because the coral sand can be rough underfoot.

The coral is not quite as dazzling as the Outer Reef's—which is where you should head if you have only one day to spend on the Great Barrier Reef—but the fish life here is rich, and you may spot sea turtles. Because you can wade out to the coral right from the beach, the Low Isles are a good choice for nervous snorkelers. A half-day or day trip to the Low Isles makes for a more relaxing day than a visit to Outer Reef sites, because in addition to exploring the coral, you can walk or sunbathe on the sand or laze under palm-thatched beach umbrellas.

Essentials

GETTING THERE   There is no train to Port Douglas, and no scheduled air service. A small airport handles light aircraft and helicopter charters.

BY CAR   Port Douglas is a scenic 65-minute drive from Cairns, in part along a narrow winding road that skirts the coast. Take Sheridan Street north out of the city as it becomes the Captain Cook Highway; follow the signs to Mossman and Mareeba until you reach the Port Douglas turnoff on your right. A **taxi** fare from Cairns to Port Douglas is a set price of A$173; call **Cairns Taxis** (℗ **13 10 08** in Cairns).

BY BUS   A one-way ticket with **Sun Palm Transport** (℗ **07/4087 2900;** www.sunpalmtransport.com) to Port Douglas hotels from Cairns airport is A$43 adults, A$23 children 2 to 11.

VISITOR INFORMATION   The biggest and most central information center in town is the privately run **Port Douglas Tourist Information Centre,** 23 Macrossan St. (℗ **07/4099 4540;** www.tourismportdouglas.com.au), open from 7:30am to 6pm daily. There is no official visitor information office in Port Douglas, but the official tourism information website of **Tourism Port Douglas and Daintree** (℗ **07/4099 4588;** www.visitportdouglasdaintree.com.au) is a good source.

GETTING AROUND   Avis (℗ **07/4099 4331**), **Budget** (℗ **07/4099 5702**), and **Thrifty** (℗ **07/4099 5555**) have offices in Port Douglas. All rent regular vehicles as well as four-wheel-drives, which you need if you plan to drive to Cape Tribulation. For a taxi, call **Port Douglas Taxis** (℗ **13 10 08**).

A good way to get around the town's flat streets is by bike. **Holiday Bike Hire,** 46 Macrossan St. (℗ **07/4099 6144;** www.pdbikeworks.com), or **Port Douglas Bike Hire,** 3 Warner St. (℗ **07/4099 5799**), rent bikes for around A$15 for 6 hours or A$20 for a full day.

Exploring the Great Barrier Reef

The waters off Port Douglas are home to dramatic coral spires and swim-throughs at the Cathedrals; giant clams at Barracuda Pass; a village of parrot fish, anemone fish, unicorn fish, and two moray eels at the pinnacle of Nursery Bommie; fan corals at Split-Bommie; and many other wonderful sites.

Without a doubt, the most popular large vessels visiting the Outer Reef are the **Quicksilver Wavepiercers** (© 07/4087 2100; www.quicksilver-cruises.com), based out of Port Douglas. These ultrasleek, high-speed, air-conditioned 37m (121-ft.) and 46m (151-ft.) catamarans carry 300 or 440 passengers to Agincourt Reef, a ribbon reef 39 nautical miles (72km/45 miles) from shore on the outer edge of the Reef. After the 90-minute trip to the Reef, you tie up at a two-story pontoon, where you spend 3½ hours.

Quicksilver departs Marina Mirage at 10am daily except on December 25. The cost for the day is A$225 for adults, A$115 for kids 4 to 14, and A$572 for families of four. Guided snorkel safaris cost A$54 per adult, half-price for kids; introductory dives cost A$155 per person. Qualified divers take a dive-tender boat to make one dive for A$110 or two dives for A$155 per person, all gear included. Booking in advance is a good idea.

The dive boat **Poseidon** (© 1800/085 674 in Australia or 07/4099 4772; www.poseidon-cruises.com.au) welcomes snorkelers. It presents a Reef ecology talk and takes you on a guided snorkel safari. The price of A$180 for adults, A$125 for children 4 to 14, and A$549 for a family of four includes lunch and transfers from Port Douglas hotels. The Poseidon is a fast 24m (79-ft.) vessel that visits three Outer Reef sites. The day-trip price of A$220 for adults, A$152 for kids 4 to 14, and A$670 for families of four includes snorkel gear, a marine-biology talk, snorkel safaris, lunch, and pickups from Port Douglas hotels. Certified divers pay an extra A$20 for one dive, A$40 for two dives or A$55 for three, plus A$20 gear rental. Guides will accompany you, free of charge, to show you great locations. Introductory divers pay A$60 extra for one dive, A$100 for two, or A$140 for three, including all gear and tuition. The vessel gets you to the Reef in just over an hour, giving you 5 hours on the coral. The boat departs Marina Mirage daily at 8:30am. Among the 15-plus dive sites visited by Poseidon are **Turtle Bay,** where you may meet a friendly Maori wrasse; the **Cathedrals,** a collection of coral pinnacles and swim-throughs; and **Barracuda Pass,** home to coral gardens, giant clams, and schooling barracuda.

The snorkeling specialist boat *Wavelength* (© 07/4099 5031; www.wavelength.com.au) does a full-day trip to the Outer Reef for A$220 for adults, A$165 for children 14 and under, and A$699 for families of four. The trip visits three different snorkel sites each day and incorporates a guided snorkel tour and a reef presentation by a marine biologist. It carries only 30 passengers and includes snorkel gear, sunsuits, lunch, and transfers from your hotel. Both beginners and experienced snorkelers will like this trip, which departs daily at 8:30am.

Another way to spend a pleasant day—closer to shore—on the Great Barrier Reef is to visit the **Low Isles,** 15km (9½ miles) northeast of Port Douglas. The isles are 1.5-hectare (3¾-acre) coral-cay specks of lush vegetation surrounded by white sand and 22 hectares (54 acres) of coral—which is what makes them so appealing. The coral is not quite as good as the Outer Reef's, but the fish life is rich, and the proximity makes for a relaxing day.

The trip aboard the 30m (98-ft.) luxury sailing catamaran **Wavedancer**, operated by Quicksilver (© 07/4087 2100; www.quicksilver-cruises.com), is A$173 for adults, A$90 for kids 4 to 14, and A$442 for families. Once there, you can snorkel, take a glass-bottom-boat ride or do a guided beach walk with a marine biologist. Coach transfers are available through Quicksilver from your Port Douglas accommodations for A$10 adults, A$5 kids, or A$25 for a family.

Exploring Port Douglas

Some companies in Cairns that offer outdoor activities will pick up from Port Douglas hotels.

The best outdoor activity in Port Douglas, however, is to do absolutely nothing on spectacular **Four Mile Beach.** From May through September, the water is stinger-free. From October through April, swim in the stinger safety net.

Every Sunday from 7:30am to 1pm, a colorful **handicrafts and food market** is held on the lawn under the mango trees by Dickson Inlet, at the end of Macrossan Street. Stalls offer everything from foot massages to fresh coconut milk.

The Secret of the Seasons

High season in Port Douglas is roughly June 1 through October 31. Low-season holiday periods run from approximately November to May (excluding Christmas and New Year's).

Kuku Yalanji Cultural Habitat Tours ★★★ Brothers Linc and Brandon Walker will take you on the walk of a lifetime, on the beach opposite their parents' house. This is the traditional fishing ground of the Kubirri Warra people, when the mudflats and mangroves are exposed at low tide and the place where you will spend 2 hours learning to throw a spear, hunt and stalk, and use coastal resources wisely. If you are lucky, you may spear a crab (not so lucky for the crab!), and when enough has been foraged to make a small meal, you'll take it back to the house where Linc and Brandon's mother will cook it up for you to eat on the veranda. The brothers also run a night tour, for a maximum of three people. It's an authentic and unforgettable experience. Don't forget to take insect repellent (just in case), especially for the night tour, and wear shoes you don't mind getting wet (bare feet are best!).

Bougainvilia St., Cooyah Beach (north of Port Douglas; take Bonnie Doon Rd., off the Captain Cook Highway). ☏ **07/4098 3437.** www.bamaway.com.au. A$75 adults, A$45 kids 5–15; night tour A$150 per person (no children under 5). Daily at 9:30am, 1:30pm, 7:30pm. Free parking. Transfers from Port Douglas area A$30 per person.

Mossman Gorge Centre ★★★ Opened in 2012, this centre is the gateway to wonderful Mossman Gorge, where the gushing Mossman River tumbles over massive boulders through the rainforest. You can visit the gorge on your own and take the short boardwalks along the river, but I highly recommend joining one of the guided **Ngadiku Dreamtime Walks,** with a member of the local KuKu-Yalanji tribe. You will learn about Aboriginal bush medicines and food, Dreamtime legends, and the sacred sites their families have called home for thousands of years. There are two tours to choose from, starting from A$50 adults, A$25 children or A$125 for a family of four. The centre has a gift shop, art gallery and cafe. You can only access the gorge by taking the shuttle bus which leaves every 15 minutes between 8am and 6pm daily. The cost is A$6 adults, A$3 children 5 to 15, or A$15 family of four.

Mossman Gorge Rd., Mossman (20km North of Port Douglas). ☏ **07/4099 7000.** www.mossman gorge.com.au. Daily 8am–6pm. Closed Christmas Day. Free parking. Bus transfers from Port Douglas through BTS Tours (☏ **07/4099 5665**) depart 49 Macrossan St. at 8:15am and 11:30am, returning at 12:15pm and 2:30pm, and cost A$22 adults, A$15 children 4–14 and A$69 families.

Wildlife Habitat ★★★ This is a really great place to see animals that are too shy to be spotted in the wild. Here, 180 animal species from the Wet Tropics are in one place for you to see up close. You can see saltwater and freshwater crocodiles, hand-feed kangaroos, and have your photo taken with a koala. The highlight is the walk-through aviary that houses more than 100 Wet Tropics bird species, including cassowaries. Between 8 and 10:30am, the park serves "breakfast with the birds," and between noon and 2pm "lunch with the lorikeets." Each costs A$47 for adults, A$24 for kids, and A$118 families, including admission. Don't miss one of the excellent free guided tours that run regularly from 9:30am to 3:15pm. You can also do a "behind the scenes" tour for an extra A$20 adults, A$10 children or A$50 families. Allow at least 2 hours here.

Port Douglas Rd. (corner Captain Cook Hwy). ☎ **07/4099 3235.** www.wildlifehabitat.com.au. A$32 adults, A$16 kids 4–14, A$80 families of 4. Daily 8am–5pm. Closed Christmas Day. Free parking.

Where to Eat
EXPENSIVE

Sassi Cucina e Bar ★★ ITALIAN Presided over by gregarious Italian owner/chef Tony Sassi—who's something of a local celebrity—this traditional Italian cucina offers fresh seasonal flavors done simply and well. Start with some *spuntini* (small plates) of delicacies such as crispy fried small local prawns with garlic and chili, then move on to a pasta or risotto. If you're really hungry (and price is no object), the house specialty, *piatto del pescatore* (seafood platter), is piled with reef fish, prawns, bugs, calamari, mussels and clams, at A$140 for two to share. Sit inside in the air-conditioning, on the pavement outside, or in the garden out the back. Prices are lower at lunch!

Macrossan St. (at Wharf St.), Port Douglas. ☎ **07/4099 6744.** www.sassi.com.au. Main courses A$20–A$49. Daily noon–10pm.

MODERATE

Salsa Bar & Grill ★★★ CONTEMPORARY This trendy restaurant, in a timber Queenslander with wraparound verandas, has seriously good food, great prices, and lively, fun service. Little wonder you need to book well ahead—sometimes up to 2 weeks in advance—and it's the restaurant of choice for everyone from presidents to pop stars! Choose simple fare such as gnocchi or Caesar salad or such mouthwatering delights as a jambalaya with tiger prawns, squid, yabbie, smoked chicken, and crocodile sausages or a king rib pork cutlet with pomme puree, cider beurre blanc, and red cabbage relish. There's a kids' menu too.

26 Wharf St. (at Warner St.), Port Douglas. ☎ **07/4099 4922.** www.salsaportdouglas.com.au. Main courses A$18–A$37. Daily noon–midnight.

Zinc ★★ CONTEMPORARY If you're like me, you may find yourself coming back more than once to this casual but very smart restaurant during your Port Douglas stay. The food is very good (think pan-fried barramundi with citrus-scented crushed potatoes and a caper and champagne butter sauce, or maybe a prawn and mussel laksa). It offers service with a smile, and kids are welcomed with a children's menu. Make sure you check out the restrooms, which have floor-to-ceiling aquariums. Reservations are recommended for dinner.

Macrossan St. (at Davidson St.), Port Douglas. ☎ **07/4099 6260.** www.zincportdouglas.com. Main courses A$26–A$35. Daily 10am–late.

INEXPENSIVE

Port O'Call Bistro ★ CAFE/BISTRO   This poolside bistro and bar at the Port O'Call Eco Lodge (p. 174) offers good, honest food, such as lamb shanks and steaks, in hearty portions at painless prices. The atmosphere is fun and friendly. There are pasta and curry dishes, and every night you can try one of the chef's blackboard surprises, including local seafood. It has kids' meals, as well as burgers, chicken, and Asian stir-fries.

In the Port O'Call Lodge, Port St. at Craven Close. ⓒ **07/4099 5422.** Main courses A$17–A$26. Tues–Sun 6pm–midnight. Closed Mon.

Where to Stay

Port Douglas Accommodation Holiday Rentals (ⓒ **07/4099 5355;** www.portdoug lasaccom.com.au) rents a wide range of apartments and homes.

EXPENSIVE

QT Resort ★★   One of the most stylish resorts in Port Douglas, QT is a magnet for the hip crowd, who jam the bar on weekends, dying to be seen. The rooms are hip and colorful too, with a slightly retro feel (and in case you fall in love with any of the *objets* scattered around, there is—rather strangely, I thought—a price list for everything from the coat hangers to the armchairs). There are also one- and two-bedroom villas to rent. It's too far to walk to town, but it offers free bikes to use and a regular shuttle. From June to October the QT Moonlight Cinema shows classic and new release films.

87–109 Port Douglas Rd., Port Douglas, QLD 4877. www.qtportdouglas.com.au. ⓒ **07/4099 8900.** 170 units. A$209–A$229 double; A$259–A$279 1-bedroom villa; A$349–A$369 2-bedroom villa. Free parking. Shuttle bus operates to town every 15 minutes from 7:30am–11:30pm daily (A$5 one-way or A$9 return). **Amenities:** Restaurant; bar; babysitting; bikes; concierge; health club; 2 outdoor swimming pools; room service; spa; 2 tennis courts; free Wi-Fi.

MODERATE

By the Sea ★   You won't find a friendlier or more convenient place to stay in Port Douglas than these apartments, 10 seconds from the beach and less than 10 minutes' walk from town. There are also heaps of "extras" such as bikes, iPads, laptops, and beach towels on loan. Some of the apartments are on the small side (most suit only three people), but all are well cared for. You can opt for a tiny Garden apartment with a patio; Balcony and Seaview apartments are a bit larger and have private balconies. Seaview apartments are quite roomy and have side views of Four Mile Beach. Towels are changed daily and linen weekly, and rooms are serviced every 4 days (or you can pay A$15 per day extra for daily service). It has no elevator and no porter, so be prepared to carry your luggage upstairs.

72 Macrossan St., Port Douglas, QLD 4877. www.bytheseaportdouglas.com.au. ⓒ **07/4099 5387.** 21 units. A$75–A$275 double studio; A$325 1-bedroom apt; A$165–A$375 2-bedroom apt. Additional person A$25. Free crib. Free covered parking. **Amenities:** Bikes; Jacuzzi; outdoor heated pool; free Wi-Fi.

Marae ★★   John and Pam Burden's architecturally stunning timber home, on a hillside 15km (9½ miles) or 10 minutes' drive north of Port Douglas, is a glamorous and restful bush retreat. The contemporary bedrooms have white mosquito nets and smart linens on king-size beds, not to mention elegant bathrooms. The garden room overlooks the valley and the pool. Wallabies and bandicoots (small marsupials) feed in the garden, kingfishers and honeyeaters use the two birdbaths, and butterflies are everywhere. A delicious tropical breakfast is served on the deck in the company of a flock of red-browed finches and peaceful doves. Mossman Gorge is just a few minutes' drive away.

Chook's Ridge, Shannonvale, QLD 4877. www.marae.com.au. ℂ **07/4098 4900.** 2 units. A$145 single; A$195 double. 2-night minimum. Rates include full breakfast. Covered parking. Children 12 and under not accepted. **Amenities:** Outdoor swimming pool.

INEXPENSIVE

Port Douglas Retreat ★   This well-kept two-story studio apartment complex on a quiet street, featuring white-battened balconies in the Queenslander architectural style, is a good value. Even some of the ritzier places in town can't boast its lagoonlike saltwater pool, surrounded by dense jungle and wrapped by an ample shady sun deck that cries out to be lounged on with a good book and a cool drink. The apartments are not enormous, but they're fashionably furnished with terra-cotta tile floors, wrought-iron beds, cane seating, and colorful bedcovers. All have large furnished balconies or patios looking onto tropical gardens; some on the ground floor open onto the common-area boardwalk, so you might want to ask for a first-floor (second-story) unit. The town and beach are a 5-minute walk away.

31–33 Mowbray St. (at Mudlo St.), Port Douglas, QLD 4877. www.portdouglasretreat.com.au. ℂ **07/4099 5053.** 36 units. A$119–A$169 double. Extra person A$50. Crib A$10 per night. Minimum 3-night stay. Secure covered parking. **Amenities:** Free airport transfers; outdoor saltwater pool; free Wi-Fi.

Port O'Call Eco Lodge ★   This modest lodge on a suburban street a 10-minute walk from town is popular with backpackers, families, and travelers on a budget. With 100% of its hot water provided by solar power, Port O'Call has a three-and-a-half-green-star rating for ecological sustainability from Australia's AAA Tourism rating system. You can swap stories with other guests as you cook and eat in the communal kitchen and dining room or join the lively crowd at the poolside **Port O'Call Bistro** (p. 173). The rooms are light, cool, and fresh, with small patios.

Port St. at Craven Close, Port Douglas, QLD 4877. www.portocall.com.au. ℂ **1800/892 800** in Australia or 07/4099 5422. 34 units. A$110–A$129 double for budget and deluxe motel rooms. Backpacker double rooms A$107 YHA members, A$119 non-members; quad rooms A$33 per person YHA members, A$38 nonmembers. Free parking. Bus: 110 or 111 (stop at front door). **Amenities:** Restaurant; free airport transfers (if staying 2 nights); bikes; outdoor pool; free Wi-Fi.

TOWNSVILLE & MAGNETIC ISLAND

346km (215 miles) S of Cairns; 1,371km (850 miles) N of Brisbane

With a population of 140,000, Townsville is Australia's largest tropical city. With an economy based on mining, manufacturing, education, and tourism, it is sometimes —rather unjustly, I think—overlooked as a holiday destination. The people are friendly, the city is pleasant, and there's plenty to do. The town nestles by the sea below the pink face of Castle Rock, which looms 300m (about 1,000 ft.) directly above. The focus is The Strand, a waterfront parkland (p. 176).

Cruises depart from the harbor for the Great Barrier Reef, about 2½ hours away, and just 8km (5 miles) offshore is Magnetic Island—"Maggie" to the locals—a popular place for watersports, hiking, and spotting koalas in the wild.

Townsville's waters boast hundreds of large patch reefs, some miles long, with excellent coral and marine life, including mantas, rays, turtles, and sharks, and sometimes canyons and swim-throughs in generally good visibility. One of the best reef complexes is **Flinders Reef,** which is actually in the Coral Sea, beyond the Great Barrier Reef Marine Park boundaries. At 240km (149 miles) offshore, it has 30m (100-ft.) visibility, plenty of coral, and big walls and pinnacles with big fish to match, such as whaler shark and barracuda.

What draws most divers to Townsville, though, is one of Australia's best wreck dives, the **SS *Yongala*.** Still largely intact, the sunken remains of this steamer lie in 15m to 30m (50–98 ft.) of water, with visibility of 9m to 18m (approximately 30–60 ft.). Divint the Yongala is not for beginners—most dive companies require their customers to have advanced certification or to have logged a minimum of 15 dives with open-water certification. The boat is usually visited on a live-aboard trip of at least 2 days, but some companies run day trips.

Although Townsville can be hot and humid in the summer—and sometimes in the path of cyclones—it is generally spared the worst of the Wet-season rains and boasts 300 days of sunshine a year.

ESSENTIALS
Getting There
BY CAR   Townsville is on the Bruce Highway, a 3-hour drive north of Airlie Beach and 4½ hours south of Cairns. The Bruce Highway breaks temporarily in the city. From the south, take Bruce Highway Alt. 1 route into the city. From the north, the highway leads into the city. The drive from Cairns to Townsville through sugar-cane fields, cloud-topped hills, and lush bushland is a pretty one—one of the most picturesque stretches in Queensland.

BY PLANE   Qantas (© **13 13 13** in Australia; www.qantas.com.au) flies direct from Brisbane. **QantasLink** flies from Cairns and Brisbane. **Jetstar** (© **13 15 38** in Australia) flies direct from Brisbane, Sydney, and Melbourne's Tullamarine airport; and **Virgin Australia** (© **13 67 89** in Australia) flies direct from Brisbane, Cairns, Rockhampton, the Gold Coast, and Sydney daily. **Con-X-ion** (© **1300/266 9466** in Australia; www.con-X-ion.com) runs an airport shuttle. A trip into town is A$10 one-way. A **taxi** from the airport to most central hotels costs about A$22.

BY TRAIN   Seven **Queensland Rail** (© **1300 131 722** in Queensland, or 07/3235 1122; www.queenslandrail.com.au) long-distance trains stop at Townsville each week. The 19-hour Tilt Train journey from Brisbane costs A$189. The 24-hour Sunlander journey costs A$141 for an economy seat, A$245 to A$386 for a sleeper, and A$825 in the luxury Queenslander Class.

BY BUS   Greyhound Australia (© **1300/473 946** in Australia or 07/4772 5100 in Townsville) coaches stop at Townsville several times a day on their Cairns-Brisbane-Cairns routes. The fare from Cairns is A$60; trip time is around 5 to 6 hours. The fare from Brisbane is A$264; trip time is 23 hours.

VISITOR INFORMATION   There are three official information centers in town. One is in the heart of the city on Flinders Street (© **1800/801 902** in Australia or

07/4721 3660; www.townsvilleholidays.info); it's open Monday through Friday from 9am to 5pm, and weekends from 9am to 1pm. The other is on the Bruce Highway 10km (6¼ miles) south of the city (© **07/4778 3555**); it's open daily from 9am to 5pm. There's also an information center in the Museum of Tropical Queensland (see "Exploring Townsville," below).

GETTING AROUND Local **Sunbus** (© **07/4771 9800**) buses depart Flinders Street. Car-rental chains include **Avis** (© **07/4799 2022**), **Budget** (© **07/4762 7433**), **Europcar** (© **07/4762 7050**), **Hertz** (© **07/4775 4821**), and **Thrifty** (© **07/4725 4600**).

Detour Coaches (© **07/4728 5311**) runs tours to most attractions in and around Townsville. For a taxi, call © **13 10 08**.

DAY TRIPS TO THE REEF

Most boats visiting the Reef from Townsville are live-aboard vessels that make trips of 2 or more days, designed for serious divers. **Adrenalin Dive** (© **1300/664 600** in Australia or 07/4724 0600; www.adrenalindive.com.au) operates day trips on which you can make introductory dives for A$80 for the first one and A$120 for two; certified divers can make two dives for A$70, all gear included. The cruise costs A$196 for adults and A$146 for children 6 to 12. The price includes lunch and morning and afternoon tea, and snorkel gear. Cruises depart Townsville at 6:30am, with a pickup at Magnetic Island en route at 7:25am. They also run trips to the **Yongala** wreck. day trips in which you will do two dives on the *Yongala*. The cost is A$266, including all gear, and A$10 per dive for a guide, if you have logged fewer than 15 dives.

EXPLORING TOWNSVILLE

Don't miss the views of the city, Cleveland Bay and Magnetic Island from **Castle Hill;** it's a 2.5km (1½-mile) drive or a shorter, steep walk up from town (make sure to do it in the cool part of the day). To drive to the top, follow Stanley Street west from Flinders Street to Castle Hill Drive; the walking trails up are posted en route.

The Strand is a 2.5km (1½-mile) strip with safe swimming beaches, a fitness circuit, a great water park for the kids, and plenty of covered picnic areas and free gas barbecues. Stroll along the promenade or relax at one of the many cafes, restaurants, and bars while you gaze across the Coral Sea to Magnetic Island. For the more active, there are areas to in-line skate, cycle, walk, fish, or play half-court basketball. Four rocky headlands and a picturesque jetty adjacent to Strand Park provide good fishing spots, and two surf lifesaving clubs service the three swimming areas along the Strand. Cool off in the Olympic-size Tobruk Pool or the seawater Rockpool or at the beach itself. During summer (Nov–Mar), three swimming enclosures operate to keep swimmers safe from marine stingers. If watersports are on your agenda, try a jetski, hire a canoe, or take to the latest in pedal skis. A state-of-the-art water park has waterfalls, hydrants, water slides, and water cannons, plus a huge bucket of water that continually fills until it overturns and drenches laughing children.

Billabong Sanctuary ★★★ You could easily spend 2 or 3 hours here, seeing Aussie wildlife in a natural setting and hand-feeding kangaroos and emus. You can also be photographed (starting at A$16) holding a koala, a (baby) crocodile, a python, or a wombat. Interesting interactive talks and shows run continuously starting at 10am; one of the most popular is the saltwater-crocodile feeding at 1:15pm (for an extra

A$99, you can also personally feed the croc). It also has gas barbecues, a cafe, and a pool.

Bruce Hwy. (17km/11 miles S of Townsville). ℘ **07/4778 8344.** www.billabongsanctuary.com.au. A$30 adults, A$27 students, A$19 children 4–16, A$85 families of 5. Daily 9am–4pm. Closed Christmas Day.

Museum of Tropical Queensland ★★ If you're lucky enough to be here on the second Tuesday of the month, you'll have the chance to hear a museum expert give an hour-long lunchtime talk as part of the museum's "Discover More" lecture series. Subjects cover everything from underwater robotic research to frogs to the history of Townsville. With its curved roof, shaped like a ship under sail, this interesting museum holds the treasures salvaged from the wreck of the HMS *Pandora,* which sank in 1792 and lies 33m (108 ft.) underwater on the edge of the Great Barrier Reef. This is the highlight of the museum, and the exhibit's centerpiece is a full-scale replica of a section of the ship's bow and its 17m-high (56-ft.) foremast, crafted by local shipwrights. The exhibition traces the ship's voyage and the retrieval of the sunken treasure—make sure you watch the film about the salvage. The museum has five other galleries, including a hands-on science center; a natural history display; one dedicated to north Queensland's indigenous heritage, with items from Torres Strait and the South Sea Islands; and stories from people of different cultures about the settlement of north Queensland. Another is devoted to touring exhibitions, which change every 3 months. Allow 2 to 3 hours.

70–102 Flinders St. (next to Reef HQ). ℘ **07/4726 0600.** www.mtq.qm.qld.gov.au. Admission A$15 adults, A$11 students, A$8.80 children 4–16, A$38 families of 5. Daily 9:30am–5pm. Closed Good Friday, Christmas Day, and until 1pm Anzac Day (Apr 25).

Reef HQ Aquarium ★★★ Reef HQ is the education center for the Great Barrier Reef Marine Park Authority's headquarters and the largest living coral reef aquarium in the world. The highlight is walking through a 20m-long (66-ft.) transparent acrylic tunnel, gazing into a giant predator tank where sharks cruise silently. A replica of the wreck of the SS *Yongala* provides an eerie backdrop for blacktip and whitetip reef sharks, leopard sharks, and nurse sharks, sharing their 750,000-liter (195,000-gal.) home with stingrays, giant trevally, and a green turtle. Watching them feed is quite a spectacle. The tunnel also reveals the 2.5-million-liter (650,000-gal.) coral-reef exhibit, with its hard and soft corals providing a home for thousands of fish, giant clams, sea cucumbers, sea stars, and other creatures. During the scuba show, the divers speak to you over an intercom while they swim with the sharks and feed the fish. Other highlights include a touch tank and a wild-sea-turtle rehabilitation center, plus interactive activities for children. Reef HQ is an easy walk from the city center.

2–68 Flinders St. ℘ **07/4750 0800.** www.reefhq.com.au. Admission A$27 adults, A$20 students, A$13 children 5–16, A$39–A$67 families. Daily 9:30am–5pm. Closed Christmas Day. Public parking lot opposite Reef HQ. All buses from the City Mall stop nearby.

WHERE TO EAT

There are many restaurants and cafes on **Palmer Street,** an easy stroll across the river from Flinders Street, and on the Strand.

C Bar ★★ CONTEMPORARY Right on the waterfront, this is a great place for casual seaside dining any time of day. It offers healthy choices for breakfast and an interesting all-day menu (from 11:30am), and is a lovely spot for sundowners or dinner. At lunch or dinner, try a pot of chili mussels with sourdough, a simple fish 'n' chips, or maybe a chicken and peanut curry. It's all good.

Gregory Street Headland, The Strand. (C) **07/4724 0333.** www.cbar.com.au. Main courses A$16–A$28. Daily 6am–10pm.

Michel's Cafe and Bar ★ CONTEMPORARY/FRENCH   This big contemporary space is popular with the Townsville in crowd—and has prices to reflect that. Choose a table on the sidewalk or opt for air-conditioning inside where you can watch the chefs working in the open kitchen. You might choose a char-grilled rib filet with roasted garlic mash, pancetta-wrapped beans, braised shallots, and French mustard jus, or something more casual like a classic French bouillabaisse (with garlic croutons). The wine list is mostly Australian.

7 Palmer St. (C) **07/4724 1460.** www.michelsrestaurant.com. Main courses A$36–A$40. Tues–Fri 11:30am–2:30pm; Tues–Sat 5:30pm–late.

TOWNSVILLE HOTELS

Holiday Inn Townsville ★   Just a stroll from all the city's major attractions and the Magnetic Island ferries, this 20-story hotel is fairly standard but a good choice for its heart-of-the-city location. The locals call it the "Sugar Shaker" because of its distinctive circular shape (which gives every room a view of the city, the bay, or Castle Hill). Suites have kitchenettes. The star attractions are the rooftop pool and sundeck with barbecues. Parking is in a separate building, which can be inconvenient at times.

334 Flinders St., Townsville, QLD 4810. www.holidayinn.com. (C) **13 83 88** in Australia or 07/4729 2000. 230 units. A$170–A$214 double; A$227–A$243 double suite. Parking A$13 per day. **Amenities:** Restaurant; 2 bars; babysitting; bikes; concierge; gymnasium; rooftop pool; room service; Wi-Fi (A$9–A$28).

Mercure Townsville ★★   Set in tropical gardens on the shores of a large lake, this resort-style hotel is a pleasant surprise. It's a bit out of town (on the main road north), right next to a big shopping center, but once you're there you may not want to travel far. The free-form swimming pool is Townsville's largest (it also has a Jacuzzi); take a dip or go for a stroll around the lake and watch the birds. Rooms are a good size, and family suites sleep four and have kitchenettes.

Woolcock and Attlee sts, Townsville, QLD 4810. www.accorhotels.com. (C) **07/4759 4900.** 144 units. A$119–A$159 double; A$169 double suite. Free outdoor parking. **Amenities:** Restaurant; bar; babysitting; swimming pool; room service; 2 lit tennis courts; Internet (A$28/24 hr.).

Seagulls Resort ★★   This popular, low-key resort, a 5-minute drive from the city, is built around an inviting free-form saltwater pool in 1.2 hectares (3 acres) of tropical gardens. Despite the Esplanade location, the motel-style rooms do not boast waterfront views, but they are comfortable and a good size. The larger deluxe rooms have painted brick walls, sofas, dining furniture, and kitchen sinks. Studios and family rooms have kitchenettes; executive suites have Jacuzzis. Apartments have a main bedroom and a bunk bedroom (sleeps three), a kitchenette, dining furniture, and a roomy balcony. The entire resort is wheelchair-friendly, with bathroom facilities for people with disabilities. The accommodations wings surround the pool and its pretty open-sided restaurant, which is popular with locals. It's a 10-minute walk to the Strand, and most tour companies pick up at the door.

74 The Esplanade, Belgian Gardens, QLD 4810. www.seagulls.com.au. © **1800/079 929** in Australia, or 07/4721 3111. 70 units. A$125–A$184 double; A$191 family rooms; A$210 2-bedroom apt; A$241 executive suite. Free parking. Bus: 7. **Amenities:** Restaurant; bar; airport shuttle (A$7 one-way or A$12 round-trip); children's playground; 2 large outdoor saltwater pools and children's wading pool; room service; small tennis court; free Wi-Fi.

Day Trips from Townsville

MAGNETIC ISLAND

Magnetic Island—or just "Maggie"—is a delightful 51-sq.-km (20-sq.-mile) national-park island 20 minutes from Townsville by ferry. About 2,500 people live here, and it's popular with Aussies, who love its holiday atmosphere. Small settlements dot the coastline and there's a good range of restaurants and laid-back cafes. Most people come for the 20 or so pristine and uncrowded bays and white beaches, but hikers, botanists, and birders may want to explore the eucalyptus woods, patches of gully rainforest, and granite tors. The island got its name when Captain Cook thought the "magnetic" rocks were interfering with his compass readings. It is famous for koalas, easily spotted in roadside gum trees; ask a local to point you to the nearest colony. Rock wallabies are often seen in the early morning.

The island is not on the Great Barrier Reef, but surrounding waters are part of the Great Barrier Reef Marine Park. There is good reef snorkeling at Florence Bay on the southern edge, Arthur Bay on the northern edge, and Geoffrey Bay, where you can even reef-walk at low tide. (Wear sturdy shoes and do not walk directly on coral to avoid damaging it.) First-time snorkelers will have an easy time of it in Maggie's weak currents and softly sloping beaches. Outside the stinger season, there is good swimming at any number of bays all around the island. Reef-free Alma Bay, with its shady lawns and playground, is a good choice for families; Rocky Bay is a small, secluded cove.

Essentials

GETTING THERE   Sealink (© **07/4726 0800;** www.sealinkqld.com.au) runs 19 round-trip ferry services a day from the Breakwater terminal on Sir Leslie Thiess Drive. Round-trip tickets are A$32 for adults, A$16 for children 5 to 14, and A$74 for families of five. The trip takes about 20 minutes.

VISITOR INFORMATION   There is no information center on Magnetic Island. Stop off at the **Flinders Street Visitor Information Centre** (© **1800/801 902** in Australia, or 07/4721 3660) in Townsville before you cross to the island. It's open Monday through Friday from 9am to 5pm, and weekends from 9am to 1pm. For information on Magnetic Island, also check **www.magneticinformer.com.au, www.magnetic-island. com.au, or www.magneticisland.info.**

GETTING AROUND   You can take your car on the ferry, but most people get around by renting an open-sided minimoke (similar to a golf cart) from the many rental outfits on the island. Minimokes are unlikely to go much over 60kmph (36 mph). **MI Wheels** (© **07/4758 1111;** www.miwheels.com.au) rents them—and other vehicles—from around A$65 to A$80 a day. Local **Sun Bus** (© **07/4778 5130;** www.sunbus.com. au) will get you anywhere on the island for a daily fare of A$7.20 adults and A$3.60 children aged 5 to 15.

Exploring Magnetic Island

There is no end to the things you can do on Maggie—snorkeling, swimming in one of a dozen or more bays, catamaran sailing, waterskiing, paraflying, horseback riding on the beach, biking, tennis or golf, scuba diving, sea kayaking, sailing or cruising around the island, taking a Harley-Davidson tour, fishing, and more. Equipment for all these activities is for rent on the island.

One of the best, and most popular, of the island's 20km (13 miles) of hiking trails is the **Nelly Bay–Arcadia trail,** a one-way journey of 5km (3 miles) that takes 2½ hours. The first 45 minutes, starting in rainforest and climbing to a saddle between Nelly Bay and Horseshoe, are the most interesting. Another excellent walk is the 2km (1¼-mile) trail to the **Forts,** remnants of World War II defenses, which, not surprisingly, have great 360-degree sea views. The best koala spotting is on the track up to the Forts off Horseshoe Bay Road. Carry water when walking—some bays and hiking trails are not near shops.

If you feel like splurging, consider a jet-ski circumnavigation of the island with **Adrenalin Jet Ski Tours & Hire** (✆ 07/4778 5533). The 3-hour tour on a two-seat jet ski costs A$385 per ski, which includes your wetsuits, life jackets, and tinted goggles. Tours depart from Horseshoe Bay at 9am daily. Keep your eyes peeled for dolphins, dugongs (manatees), sea turtles, and humpback whales in season. A 90-minute tour of the northern side of the island costs A$185 per ski and runs daily at 9am, 11:30am and 1:30pm.

Bungalow Bay Koala Village (✆ 1800/285 577 in Australia or 07/4778 5577; www.bungalowbay.com.au), on Horseshoe Bay Road, Horseshoe Bay, is a backpacker hostel that has a wildlife sanctuary on its 6.5 hectares (16 acres) of bushland, home to rock wallabies, curlews, lorikeets, and koalas. Two-hour tours of the koala park are run at 10am, noon, and 2:30pm, starting at reception. The first hour is within the wildlife park, where you can wrap yourself in a python, pet a lizard, hold a small saltwater crocodile, and get up close with a koala. The second hour is a guided bush walk to explore nearby habitats of eucalyptus forest, wetlands, mangroves, or coastal dunes, and to learn about the history of the traditional owners, the Wulgurukaba people. Entry to the park costs A$21 adults, A$19 backpackers or students, A$12 children 4 to 16, or A$62 for families of five. Koala holding costs A$15 including two souvenir photos, with proceeds supporting Magnetic Island wildlife care groups.

THE WHITSUNDAYS

Airlie Beach: 640km (397 miles) S of Cairns; 1,146km (711 miles) N of Brisbane

A day's drive or a 1-hour flight south of Cairns brings you to the dazzling collection of 74 islands known as the Whitsundays. No more than 3 nautical miles (3.4km/2 miles) separate most of the islands, and altogether they represent countless bays, beaches, dazzling coral reefs, and fishing spots that make up one fabulous Great Barrier Reef playground. Sharing the same latitude as Rio de Janeiro and Hawaii, the water is at least 72°F (22°C) year-round, the sun shines most of the year, and in winter you'll require only a light jacket at night.

Most of the islands consist of densely rainforested national park land. The surrounding waters belong to the Great Barrier Reef Marine Park. But don't expect palm trees and coconuts—these islands are covered with dry-looking pine and eucalyptus forests full of dense undergrowth, and rocky coral coves far outnumber the few sandy beaches. Only eight islands have resorts, but all offer just about every activity you could ever want—snorkeling, scuba diving, sailing, reef fishing, water-skiing, jet-skiing, parasailing, sea kayaking, hiking, rides over the coral in semisubmersibles, fish feeding, putt-putting around in dinghies to secluded beaches, tennis, and more! Accommodations range from small, low-key wilderness retreats to midrange family havens to one of Australia's most luxurious resorts, Hayman.

The village of **Airlie Beach** is the center of the action on the mainland. But the islands themselves are just as good a stepping stone to the outer Great Barrier Reef as Cairns, and some people consider them better, because you don't have to make the 90-minute trip to the Reef before you hit coral. Just about any Whitsunday island has fringing reef around its shores, and there are good snorkeling reefs between the islands, a quick boat ride away from your island or mainland accommodations.

The reef here is just as good as off Cairns, with many drop-offs and drift dives, a dazzling range of corals, and a rich array of marine life, including whales, mantas, shark, reef fish, morays, turtles, and pelagics. Visibility is usually around 15 to 23m (49–75 ft.).

A popular reef for both snorkeling and diving is **Blue Pearl Bay** off Hayman Island, which has loads of corals and some gorgonian fans in its gullies, and heaps of reef fish, including Maori wrasse and sometimes manta rays. It's a good place to make an introductory dive, walking right in off the beach. A little island commonly called **Bali Hai Island,** between Hayman and Hook islands, is a great place to be left to your own devices. You'll see soft-shelf and wall coral, tame Maori wrasse, octopus, turtles, reef shark, various kinds of rays including mantas, eagles and cow-tails, plus loads of fish.

Essentials

GETTING THERE BY CAR The Bruce Highway leads south from Cairns or north from Brisbane to Proserpine, 26km (16 miles) inland from Airlie Beach. Take the Whitsunday turnoff to reach Airlie Beach and Shute Harbour. Allow a good 8 hours to drive from Cairns. There are several car-storage facilities at Shute Harbour when you want to go to the islands.

BY PLANE There are two air routes into the Whitsundays: Great Barrier Reef Airport on Hamilton Island and Whitsunday Coast Airport at Proserpine on the mainland. **QantasLink** (℧ 13 13 13 in Australia; www.qantas.com.au) flies direct to Hamilton Island from Cairns. **Virgin Australia** (℧ 13 67 89 in Australia; www.virginaustralia.com) flies to Proserpine direct from Brisbane, with connections from other capitals, and direct from Brisbane, Melbourne and Sydney to Hamilton Island. **Jetstar** (℧ 13 15 38 in Australia; www.jetstar.com.au) flies from Brisbane and Sydney to Proserpine and from Brisbane, Melbourne, and Sydney to Hamilton Island. If you stay on an island, the resort may book your launch transfers automatically. These may appear on your airline ticket, in which case your luggage will be checked through to the island.

BY TRAIN Several **Queensland Rail** (℧ 1300 131 722 in Australia; www.queenslandrail.com.au) long-distance trains stop at Proserpine every week. The one-way fare from Brisbane on the Tilt Train is A$173, or you can book a sleeper on the Sunlander for A$226 or in the luxury all-inclusive Queenslander Class for A$755. There is a bus link to Airlie Beach for A$17.

BY BUS **Greyhound Australia** (✆ **1300/473 946** in Australia; www.greyhound.com.au) operates plentiful daily services to Airlie Beach from Brisbane (trip time: around 18 hr.) and Cairns (trip time: 11 hr.). The fare is A$230 from Brisbane and A$93 from Cairns.

VISITOR INFORMATION The **Whitsundays Information Centre** (✆ **1300/717 407** in Australia, or 07/4945 3711; www.whitsundaytourism.com) is at 192 Main St., Proserpine (on the Bruce Highway in the town's south). It's run by Tourism Whitsundays and is open weekdays from 9am (9:30am on Tues) to 5pm and weekends and public holidays (except Good Friday and Christmas Day) from 10am to 4pm. It's also easy to pick up information from the private booking agents lining the main street of Airlie Beach. All stock a vast range of cruise, tour, and hotel information, and make bookings free of charge. All have similar material, but because some represent certain boats exclusively, and because prices can vary a little from one to the next, it pays to shop around.

GETTING AROUND **BY BOAT** **Cruise Whitsundays** (✆ **07/4946 4662**; www.cruisewhitsundays.com.au) operates Resort Connections, providing transfer services between Hamilton Island Airport and Whitsunday Coast Airport at Proserpine and Daydream Island and Long Island, as well as all Airlie Beach properties.

Island ferries and Great Barrier Reef cruises leave from Shute Harbour, a 10-minute drive south of Airlie Beach on Shute Harbour Road. Most other tour-boat operators and bareboat charters anchor at Abell Point Marina, a 15-minute walk west from Airlie Beach. A new marina, Port of Airlie, is under development and is expected to be open by 2015. Most tour-boat operators pick up guests free from Airlie Beach hotels and at some or all island resorts.

BY BUS **Whitsunday Transit** (✆ **07/4946 1800;** www.whitsundaytransit.com.au) meets all flights and trains at Proserpine and provides door-to-door transfers to Airlie Beach hotels or to Shute Harbour. The fare from the airport is A$15 adults and A$9 children to Airlie Beach or Shute Harbour. From the train station, it is A$8.20 adults and A$4.20 children to Airlie Beach or A$11 adults and A$5.50 children to Shute Harbour. Bookings are essential, and should be made 48 hours in advance if possible. It also runs buses every half-hour between Airlie Beach and Shute Harbour.

> ## Safety in the Water
>
> Deadly **marine stingers** may frequent the shorelines of the Whitsundays from October through April. The best place to swim is in the beachfront Airlie Beach lagoon. The rivers in these parts are home to dangerous **saltwater crocodiles** (which mostly live in fresh water, contrary to their name), so don't swim in streams, rivers, or water holes.

BY CAR **Avis** (✆ **07/4967 7188**), **Europcar** (✆ **07/4946 4133**), and **Hertz** (✆ **07/4946 4687**) have outlets in Airlie Beach and Proserpine Airport (telephone numbers serve both locations). **Budget** (✆ **07/4945 1024**) has an office at Proserpine Airport.

Exploring the Whitsundays

The little town of Airlie Beach, perched on the edge of the Coral Sea with views across Pioneer Bay and the Whitsunday Passage, is the focal point of activity on the

Whitsunday mainland. Cruises and yachts depart from Shute Harbour, a 10-minute drive south on Shute Harbour Road, and Abell Point Marina, a 10-minute walk west along the foreshore or a quick drive over the hill on Shute Harbour Road. For a bird's-eye view of it all, head to the Lions Lookout.

Airlie Beach has a massive beachfront artificial lagoon, with sandy beaches and landscaped parkland, which solves the problem of where to swim in stinger season. The lagoon is the size of about six full-size Olympic swimming pools, set in 4 hectares (10 acres) of botanic gardens, with a children's pool, plenty of shade, barbecues, picnic shelters, toilets, showers, and parking.

Getting out on the water is the most important thing here. Countless opportunities are offered, with the focus firmly on sailing, snorkeling and diving.

REEF CRUISES

Cruise Whitsundays (☏ **07/4946 4662;** www.cruisewhitsundays.com.au) makes daily trips to Hardy Reef in a high-speed, air-conditioned catamaran. The boat has a bar, and a biologist gives a marine ecology talk en route. You anchor at the massive Reefworld pontoon, which was built to hold up to 600 people, and spend up to 3½ hours on the Reef. The day trip costs A$210 for adults, A$95 for children 5 to 15. Guided snorkel safaris cost A$45 extra for adults and A$30 for children. You can book dives on board for A$119 for first-time divers and A$99 for certified divers. Cruises depart at 8am from Airlie Beach, picking up at Hamilton Island at 9am. Passengers from Daydream and Long islands take the ferry to Hamilton to board there.

A unique experience is Cruise Whitsundays' **ReefSleep,** during which you spend the night on the pontoon. You travel with the day-trippers, but when they leave you will be with a maximum of 16 people. This gives you a fabulous chance to snorkel at night when the coral is luminescent in the moonlight and nocturnal sea creatures get busy. The trip includes 2 full days on the Reef, all meals, and the chance to sleep under the stars (or in the one double cabin that's available). The cost is A$449 per person for the double room, or A$399 per person for a "swag" (a type of outdoor sleeping bag) on the deck under the stars (which may have never seemed closer).

In and around the Whitsunday islands, you can visit and explore the many excellent dive sites close to shore. **Mantaray Charters** (☏ **07/4948 1117;** www.mantaray charters.com), based at Abell Point Marina, runs day tours to Whitehaven Beach and gives you the chance to dive near Hayman Island or Hook Island. Tours are limited to 36 passengers and leave at 8am, returning at around 4:30pm. The cost is A$148 adults, A$80 kids ages 4 to 14, and A$435 for a family of four. The cost includes lunch, snacks and all equipment, whether you are diving or snorkeling. You'll pay A$80 for an introductory dive.

SAILING & SNORKELING TRIPS

A journey on one of the many yachts offering 3-day, 2-night sailing adventures is a great way to see the islands. You can learn to sail or get involved with sailing the boat as much or as little as you want, snorkel to your heart's content over one dazzling reef after another, beachcomb, explore national park trails, stop at secluded bays, swim, sunbathe, and generally have a laid-back good time. A few companies offer introductory and qualified scuba diving for an extra cost per dive. Most boats carry a maximum of 12 passengers, so the atmosphere is always friendly and fun. The food is generally good, the showers are usually hot, and you sleep in comfortable but small berths off the galley. Some have small private twin or double cabins.

Prices usually include all meals, Marine Park entrance fees, snorkel gear, and transfers to the departure point (Abel Point Marina or Shute Harbour). In the off season, the boats compete fiercely for passengers; you'll see signboards on the main street in Airlie Beach advertising standby deals.

Prosail (© **1800/810 116** in Australia or 07/4946 7533; www.prosail.com.au) runs sailing trips through the Great Barrier Reef Marine Park. All trips include sailing, snorkeling, scuba diving, and bushwalking, and you can sail on megayachts such as the *Condor, Broomstick,* and *Hammer.* A 2-day overnight trip costs A\$349 per person.

These kind of trips are a cheaper alternative to "bareboating" (skippering your own yacht)—which is a hugely popular thing to do, despite the cost. If you are confident about sailing yourself—and most yacht-charter companies in the islands will want one person on the boat to have a little experience—you do not need a license, and sailing is surprisingly easy in these uncrowded waters, where the channels are deep and hazard-free and the seas are protected from big swells by the Great Barrier Reef. The 74 islands are so close to one another that one is always in sight, and safe anchorages are everywhere. But for extra reassurance, the company may require you to take a skipper along at an extra cost of around A\$40 per hour or A\$355 overnight. Before departure, the company provides a thorough 2- to 3-hour briefing and easy-to-read maps marking channels, anchorage points, and the very few dangerous reefs. Your charter company will radio in once or twice a day to check that you're still afloat, and you can contact them anytime for advice.

You can buy your own provisions or have the charter company stock the boat at an extra cost of about A\$30 per person per day. Most operators will load a windsurfer, fishing tackle, and scuba-diving equipment on request, for an extra fee if they are not standard.

In peak season, you may have to charter the boat for a week. At other times, most companies impose a minimum of 5 days, but many will rent for 3 nights if you ask, rather than let a vessel sit idle. In peak season, expect to pay A\$600 to A\$750 per night for a standard four- to six-berth yacht, more if you want something luxurious. Rates in the off season, and even in the Whitsundays' busiest time, June through August, will be anywhere from A\$100 to A\$200 less. If you are prepared to book within 14 days of when you want to sail, the deals can be even better; you should be able to find a boat that late in the off season. You may be asked to post a credit card bond of around A\$2,000. Fuel and park fees are extra, and mooring fees apply if you want to stop at one of the island resorts overnight. A number of bareboat-charter companies offer "sail-'n'-stay" packages that combine a few days of sailing with a few days at an island resort.

The Secret of the Seasons

High season in the Whitsundays coincides with school vacations, which occur in January, in mid-April, from late June to early July, from late September to early October, and in late December. The Aussie winter, June through August, is popular, too. You have to book months ahead to get high-season accommodations, but any other time you can indeed find some good deals: Specials on accommodations, sailing trips, day cruises, and diving excursions fairly leap off the blackboards outside the tour-booking agents in Airlie Beach.

Hitting the Sand at Whitehaven Beach

The 6km (3¾-mile) stretch of pure-white silica sand on **Whitehaven Beach** ★★ will leave you in rapture. The beach, on uninhabited Whitsunday Island, does not boast a lot of coral, but the swimming is good and the forested shore is beautiful. Take a book and chill out. Some sailboat day trips visit it, as do some motorized vessels. A half-day trip with **Cruise Whitsundays** (© 07/4946 4662; www.cruisewhitsundays.com) costs A$95 for adults and A$45 for children ages 5 to 15, and gives you around 2 hours on the beach. You can travel in the morning (leaving Airlie Beach at 7am) or in the afternoon (departing at 1:15pm). It offers full day trips too, and combines Whitehaven Beach with other islands on some tours.

Most bareboat charter companies will make complete holiday arrangements for you in the islands, including accommodations, transfers, tours, and sporting activities. Most companies operate out of Airlie Beach, Hamilton Island, or both. Well-known operators include **Whitsunday Rent-A-Yacht** (© **1800/075 000** in Australia or 07/ 4946 9232; www.rentayacht.com.au); **Queensland Yacht Charters** (© **1800/075 013** in Australia or 07/4946 7400; www.yachtcharters.com.au); and **Sunsail** (© **1800/803 988** in Australia or 02/8912 7055; www.sunsail.com.au).

ISLAND HOPPING

Day-trippers to the resorts on Hamilton, Daydream, Long Island, and Hook Island can rent the hotels' watersports equipment, laze by the beaches and pools, scuba dive, join the resorts' activities programs, hike their trails, and eat at some or all of their restaurants. **Cruise Whitsundays** (© **07/4946 4662;** www.cruisewhitsundays.com) has an Island Hopper day pass that allows you to hop-on, hop-off at the islands for A$110 adults or A$55 children 5 to 15. They also offer day-trip packages (including lunch) to each of the islands.

Where to Eat

Mangrove Jack's Café Bar ★★ PIZZA/CAFE FARE   Bareboat sailors, local sugar farmers, Sydney yuppies, and European backpackers all flock to this big, open-fronted sports bar and restaurant. The mood is upbeat and pleasantly casual, the surroundings are spick-and-span, and the food passes muster. Wood-fired pizzas with trendy toppings are the specialty. There is no table service; place your order at the bar and collect your food when your number is called.

In the Airlie Beach Hotel, 16 The Esplanade (enter from Shute Harbour Rd.), Airlie Beach. © **07/4964 1888.** Main courses A$15–A$35. Mon–Fri 11:30am–2:30pm and 5:30–9:30pm (to 10pm on Fri); Sat 11:30am–9:30pm.

Whitsunday Sailing Club ★★ CONTEMPORARY   This casual club is a popular hangout for locals, with one of the best views in the Whitsundays, overlooking Pioneer Bay and the islands. The menu includes light meals such as tortillas or a steak sandwich; for something heartier go for roast duck, lamb rogan josh, or a veal filet. If you're feeling really hungry, go for the A$95 "Grand Catch," a platter of oysters, crispy soft-shell crab, prawns, salt 'n' pepper calamari, scallop-and-prawn stir-fry, French fries, salad, and a piece of both the daily fish of the day and and the house battered fish.

Airlie Point (enter from The Esplanade), Airlie Beach. ✆ **07/4946 6138.** www.whitsundaysailing club.com.au. Main courses A$18–A$28. Daily noon–late.

Whitsunday Hotels & Resorts

The advantages of staying on the mainland are cheaper accommodations, a choice of restaurants, and the freedom to visit a different island each day, and plenty of activities such as jet-skiing, kayaking, parasailing, catamaran rental, and windsurfing.

But if you are here it would be a shame not to spend at least a couple of days soaking up the island life. The main advantage of staying on an island is that swimming, snorkeling, bushwalking, and a huge range of watersports, many of them free, are right outside your door. You won't be isolated if you stay on an island, because most Great Barrier Reef cruise boats, sail-and-snorkel yacht excursions, Whitehaven Beach cruises, dive boats, fishing tour vessels, and so on stop at the island resorts every day or on a frequent basis. Be warned, however, that once you're "captive" on an island, you may be slugged with high food and drink prices. And although most island resorts offer nonmotorized watersports, such as windsurfing and sailing, free of charge, you will pay for activities that use fuel, such as parasailing, water-skiing, and dinghy rental.

AIRLIE BEACH

Airlie Beach Hotel ★   In the heart of Airlie Beach, this large hotel complex offers fairly standard accommodations but is ideal if you like to be in the thick of things. The hotel straddles an entire block, giving it frontage on both the Esplanade and the main street. Rooms are spacious and well appointed, with views over the inlet. There are standard motel rooms, as well as newer hotel rooms and executive-style suites with kitchens. My pick would be any of the rooms at the front, which have small balconies and overlook the Esplanade and the inlet.

16 The Esplanade (at Coconut Grove), Airlie Beach, QLD 4802. www.airliebeachhotel.com.au. ✆ **1800/466 233** in Australia or 07/4964 1999. 80 units. A$145 double standard motel room; A$189–A$239 double hotel room; A$289 double suite. Extra person A$49 (children 14 and under free using existing bedding). Free crib. Free covered parking. **Amenities:** 3 restaurants; 3 bars; heated outdoor saltwater pool; free Wi-Fi.

Coral Sea Resort ★★★   In Airlie Beach's best location, on the edge of Paradise Point, this resort is one of the best places to stay on the Whitsunday mainland. It suits everyone from honeymooners to families, and although it's relatively sprawling, the design is such that you can easily feel you're alone. The Coral Sea suites are divine, complete with a Jacuzzi and double hammock on the balcony. There are four styles of suites, apartments, and family units. Bayview suites have a Jacuzzi inside. It's a 3-minute walk along the waterfront to Airlie Beach village.

25 Oceanview Ave., Airlie Beach, QLD 4802. www.coralsearesort.com. ✆ **1800/075 061** in Australia or 07/4964 1300. 78 units. A$245–A$395 double; A$330 double 1-bedroom apt; A$380–A$440 2-bedroom apt; A$500 3-bedroom apt; A$440 1-bedroom penthouse; A$570 double 2-bedroom penthouse; A$740 double 3-bedroom penthouse. Extra person A$30–A$40. Crib A$15. Free parking. **Amenities:** Restaurant; bar; babysitting; bikes; exercise room; 25m (82-ft.) outdoor pool; room service; spa; watersports rental; Wi-Fi in restaurant/lobby A$10 for 2 hr.; Internet in rooms A$6/30min, $12/2 hr., A$23/24 hr.

ISLAND RESORTS

Daydream Island Resort ★★ One of the Whitsundays' oldest resorts is now one of Australia's most extensive and modern spa resorts. Features such as the outdoor cinema and the kids' club have always made it popular with families, but the 16 therapy rooms at the **Rejuvenation Spa** appeal to those who are seeking one of the most sophisticated and well-equipped health resorts in Australia. At the entrance to the resort, the "Living Reef" is a large man-made coral reef lagoon, with more than 115 species of marine fish and 80 species of coral. During guided tours, guests can hand-feed resident stingrays, sharks, and other fish. Rooms are large, smart, and comfortable, with uninterrupted ocean views. The "village" at the southern end of the island, a short stroll along the boardwalk from the resort, has shops, cafes, a pool and bar, and a tavern serving bistro-style meals. A rainforest walk stretches almost the entire length of the kilometer-long (just over half a mile) island; other activities include snorkeling, sailboarding, jet-skiing, parasailing, reef fishing, diving, tennis, volleyball, and minigolf.

Daydream Island (40km/25 miles northeast of Shute Harbour), Whitsunday Islands (P.M.B. 22), Mackay, QLD 4741. www.daydreamisland.com. ☏ **1800/075 040** in Australia or 07/4948 8488. 296 units. A$299–A$460 double; A$475–A$1004 suite. Rates include breakfast. (☏ **07/4946 4662**) provides launch transfers from Abel Point Marina and Hamilton Island Airport. **Amenities:** 3 restaurants; 3 bars; gymnasium; 3 Jacuzzis; kids club; 3 freshwater outdoor pools (1 heated); sauna; spa; 2 lit tennis courts; watersports; free Wi-Fi.

Hamilton Island ★★ More a vacation village than a single resort, Hamilton has the widest range of activities, accommodations styles, and restaurants of any Great Barrier Reef island resort and is a great place for families.

The accommodations choices are extra-large rooms and suites in the high-rise hotel; high-rise one-bedroom apartments; Polynesian-style bungalows in tropical gardens (ask for one away from the road for real privacy); and glamorous rooms in the two-story, adults-only **Beach Club** (with a personal "host" to cater to every whim, and private restaurant, lounge, and pool for exclusive use of Beach Club guests); as well as one-, two-, three-, and four-bedroom apartments and villas, including villas at the waterfront Yacht Club. The best sea views are from the second-floor Beach Club rooms, from floors 5 to 18 of the **Reef View Hotel,** and from most apartments and villas. If your budget is huge, the poshest part of the resort is the ultraluxe **qualia,** an exclusive, adults-only retreat on the northern part of the island. It has 60 one-bedroom pavilions, each with a private swimming pool and a guest pavilion. There's a spa and two restaurants, and none of these facilities are available to other Hamilton Island guests.

A marina village with cafes, restaurants, shops, and a yacht club is set apart from the accommodations, most of which are set around a large free-form pool and swim-up bar and the curve of Catseye Beach. Hamilton offers a huge range of watersports, fishing trips, cruises, speedboat rides, go-karts, a "wire flyer" flying-fox hang glider, a shooting range, minigolf, an aquatic driving range, beach barbecue safaris, hiking trails, a wildlife sanctuary (you may have seen Oprah here, cuddling a koala), and an extensive daily activities program.

There are no cars on the island, and because a steep hill splits the resort, the best way to get around is on the free bus service, which operates on three loops around the island from 7am to 11pm, or by rented golf buggy (A$45/1 hr.; A$85/24 hr). The

Heart Reef

The iconic image of the Great Barrier Reef is the stunning heart-shaped reef called—yes, **Heart Reef.** But Heart Reef is not a place you can visit; it is protected by law, and you cannot swim or snorkel here. In any case, the best way to see this tiny reef's perfect shape is from the air. There are many helicopter or seaplane options available for that perfect photographic opportunity (or, of course, if you are planning a mid-air proposal). A 1-hour seaplaner flight over the Great Barrier Reef costs A$290 per person with **Air Whitsunday** (✆ **07/4946 9111;** www.airwhitsunday. com.au), which offers a large range of tours, including seaplane flights to a Reef pontoon to snorkel for a couple of hours.

biggest drawback is that just about every activity costs extra, so you are constantly adding to your bill. To get away from the main resort area, hit the beach or the hiking trails—most of the 750-hectare (1,853-acre) island is virgin bushland.

Hamilton Island (16km/10 miles SE of Shute Harbour), Whitsunday Islands, QLD 4803. www. hamiltonisland.com.au or www.qualiaresort.com.au. ✆ **13 73 33** in Australia, 02/9433 3333 (Sydney reservations office), or 07/4946 9999 (the island). 880 units. A$280–A$410 Palm Bungalow; A$370–A$535 hotel double; A$650–A$1,345 hotel suite; A$570–A$699 Beach Club double; A$855–A$1,700 Yacht Club villas; A$975–A$2,125 qualia; A$3,500–A$4,800 qualia house. Rates at qualia and Beach Club include breakfast. Ask about packages and special deals. **Amenities:** 12 restaurants, 7 bars; babysitting; child-care center for kids from 6 weeks to 14 years (in 3 groups); minigolf and driving range; health club; 7 outdoor pools; room service; lit tennis courts; free Wi-Fi.

THE CAPRICORN COAST

Taking its name from the Tropic of Capricorn, which cuts through it, this stretch of the Queensland coast is the southernmost part of the Great Barrier Reef. It is here that you will find the most spectacular of the Great Barrier Reef islands, Heron Island, off the coast from Gladstone. Heron's reefs are a source of enchantment for divers and snorkelers; its waters boast 21 dive sites. In summer, large turtles lumber ashore to nest on its beaches, and in winter humpback whales cruise by.

To the south of Gladstone, off the small town of Bundaberg, is another tiny coral cay, Lady Elliot Island, a nesting site for tens of thousands of seabirds and home to a first-rate fringing reef. Two little-known attractions in Bundaberg are its good shore scuba diving and a loggerhead turtle rookery that is a major drawcard in summer.

Gladstone: Gateway to Heron Island

Gladstone: 550km (341 miles) N of Brisbane; 1,162km (720 miles) S of Cairns

The industrial port town of Gladstone is the departure point for beautiful Heron Island. Gladstone is on the coast 21km (13 miles) off the Bruce Highway. Most flights to Gladstone arrive in time to connect with the ferry to Heron Island, but if you need to stay overnight a couple of good, centrally located options are **Mercure Gladstone** (✆ **07/4979 8200;** www.accorhotels.com) and **Rydges Gladstone** (✆ **07/4970 0000;** www.rydges.com/gladstone).

ESSENTIALS
Getting There

BY PLANE QantasLink (book through Qantas © 13 13 13 in Australia; www.qantas.com.au) and **Virgin Australia** (© 13 67 89 in Australia; www.virginaustalia.com.au) both have daily flights from Brisbane and Sydney. A courtesy coach meets flights from Brisbane (with connections from other cities) at Gladstone airport at 10am to take guests to Gladstone Marina for the **launch transfer** to the island (see p. 190).

BY TRAIN Queensland Rail (© 1800/872 467 in Queensland; www.queenslandrail.com.au) operates trains to Gladstone from Brisbane and Cairns most days. The economy fare from Brisbane is A$89 on the high-speed Tilt Train (trip time: 6 hr.) or A$119 on the Sunlander (trip time: 9½ hr.).

BY BUS Greyhound Australia (© 1300/473 946 in Australia; www.greyhound.com.au) operates daily coaches to Gladstone on the Brisbane-Cairns run. The fare is A$143 from Brisbane (trip time: 10½ hr.), A$201 from Cairns (trip time: 20 hr.).

GETTING AROUND Avis (© 07/4978 2633), **Budget** (© 07/4972 8488), **Hertz** (© 07/4978 6899), and **Thrifty** (© 07/4972 5999) have offices in Gladstone.

VISITOR INFORMATION The **Gladstone Visitor Information Centre** is in the ferry terminal at Gladstone Marina, 72 Bryan Jordan Drive, Gladstone (© 07/4972 9000; www.gladstoneregion.info). It's open 8:30am to 4:30pm Monday through Friday and 9:30am to 4:30pm Saturday and Sunday. Closed Christmas Day.

Heron Island

72km (45 miles) NE of Gladstone

Heron Island is often referred to as "the jewel of the Reef." And rightly so. The difference between Heron and other islands is that once there, you are right on the Reef. Step off the beach and you enter magnificent fields of coral that seem to stretch for miles. And the myriad life forms that abound here are accessible to everyone through diving, snorkeling, or reef walks at low tide.

There has been a resort on Heron since 1932, and in 1943 the island became a national park. It is a haven for wildlife and people, and an experience of a lifetime is almost guaranteed at any time of year, particularly if you love turtles—Heron is a haven for giant green and loggerhead turtles. Resort guests gather on the beach from late November to February to watch the female turtles lay eggs, and from February to mid-April to see the hatched babies scuttle down the sand to the water. Every night during the season, volunteer guides from the island's University of Queensland research station tag and measure the turtles before they return to the water. Only one in 5,000 hatchlings will live to return in about 50 years to lay its own eggs. Humpback whales also pass through from June through September.

Three days on Heron will give you plenty of time. The island is so small that you can walk around it at a leisurely pace in about half an hour. One of the first things to do is to take advantage of the organized activities that operate several times a day and are designed so guests can plan their own days. Snorkeling and reef walking are major occupations for visitors—if they're not diving, that is. The island is home to 21 of the world's most stunning dive sites.

Guided walks provide another way to explore the island. Walks include a visit to the island's research station. As for the reef walk, just borrow a pair of sand shoes, a balance pole, and a viewing bucket, and head off with a guide at low tide. The walk can take up to 90 minutes.

Heron is also home to colonies of mutton birds; be warned, they can be particularly noisy during their breeding and mating season, from November to January. They also create a fairly . . . shall I say…distinctive smell (you get used to it, but some people find it highly offensive). That's nature for you.

GETTING THERE A **170-seater launch** departs Gladstone Marina, Bryan Jordan Drive, at 11am daily (except Christmas Day). Transfers cost A$100 one-way for adults, half-price for kids 2 to 12. Trip time is around 2 hours. Helicopter transfers can also be arranged.

Heron Island Resort ★★★ This is a lovely, low-key resort, with no daytrippers and a focus very much on the outdoors. The colors of the island's surrounding water and Reef are reflected in the interiors, and everything is light-filled and breezy. Heron's central complex is equal parts grand Queenslander home and sophisticated beach house, with bar and lounge areas open to ocean views and sunsets. Duplex-style Turtle rooms are designed for couples or families, or you can go for greater luxury in the Wistari suites or the private Beach House (the only rooms with air-conditioning).

The property has a lounge with TVs and public phones (only the four Point suites and the Beach House have private phones). There is no mobile phone coverage, and the only Internet access is through two computers in the bar (which also has Wi-Fi access) for A$3 for 15 minutes. The **Aqua Soul Spa** offers double treatment rooms and all the usual spa treatments and pampering.

Heron Island, off Gladstone, QLD 4680. www.heronisland.com. ✆ **1300/863 248** in Australia or 03/9426 7550 (reservations office), or 07/4972 9055 (resort). 109 units. A$419 Turtle Room double or A$439 for families; A$529 Reef Room double or A$549 families; A$669 Beachside Suite double; A$869 Point Suite or Wistari Suite; A$909 Beach House double. Free crib. Rates include breakfast and some activities. No children allowed in Point and Wistari suites or Beach House. **Amenities:** Restaurant; bar; children's program (ages 7–12) during Australian school vacations; Jacuzzi; outdoor pool; spa; 2 lit tennis courts; limited watersports equipment rental.

Bundaberg: Gateway to Lady Elliot Island

384km (238 miles) N of Brisbane; 1,439km (892 miles) S of Cairns

The small sugar town of Bundaberg is the closest to the southernmost point of the Great Barrier Reef. If you visit the area between November and March, allow an evening to visit the Mon Repos Turtle Rookery. Divers may want to take in some of Australia's best shore diving right off Bundaberg's beaches.The southern reefs of the Great Barrier Reef are just as prolific, varied, and colorful as the reefs farther north off Cairns. However, because this part of the coast is less accessible by visitors and the reefs farther offshore, fewer snorkel and dive boats visit them.

There are two islands to be visited in this area, both part of the **Bunker Group,** which are around 80km (50 miles) due north of Bundaberg. The islands are due east of Gladstone and closer to that town, but only live-aboard boats visit them from there. The only one visited by snorkelers and divers on a daily basis is pretty **Lady Musgrave Island,** a vegetated 14-hectare (35-acre) national-park coral cay, 52 nautical miles off the coast. It is surrounded by a lagoon 8km (5 miles) in circumference, filled with hundreds of corals and some 1,200 of the 1,500 species of fish and other marine creatures found on the Great Barrier Reef. The other is **Lady Elliot Island,** which is accessed by air and has a resort on it.

ESSENTIALS

Getting There

BY CAR   Bundaberg is on the Isis Highway, about 50km (31 miles) off the Bruce Highway from Gin Gin in the north and 53km (33 miles) off the Bruce Highway from just north of Childers in the south.

BY PLANE   Jetstar (© 13 15 38 in Australia; www.jetstar.com.au) flies from Brisbane daily.

BY TRAIN   Queensland Rail (© 1800 872 467 in Queensland; www.queensland rail.com.au) trains stop in Bundaberg every day en route between Brisbane and Cairns. The fare is A$58 from Brisbane in economy class or A$87 business class on the Tilt Train; the trip takes about 4½ hours.

BY BUS   Greyhound Australia (© 1300/473 946 in Australia; www.greyhound. com.au) stops here many times a day on runs between Brisbane and Cairns. The 7½-hour trip from Brisbane costs A$88.

Getting Around

BY CAR   Avis (© 07/4131 4533), **Budget** (© 07/4151 1355), **Europcar** (© 07/4128 2100), **Hertz** (© 07/4155 0884), and **Thrifty** (© 07/4151 6222) all have offices in Bundaberg.

BY BUS   Duffy's City Buses (© 1300 383 397 or 07/4151 4226; www.duffysbuses. com.au) operates the town bus service. There are no public buses on Sundays.

VISITOR INFORMATION   The **Bundaberg Tourism Visitor Information Centre** (© 1300/722 099 in Australia; www.bundabergregion.org), at 271 Bourbong Street, Bundaberg West (next to the hospital), is open daily 9am to 5pm, public holidays 10am to 3pm. Closed Good Friday and Christmas Day.

EXPLORING BUNDABERG

The best shore diving in Queensland is in Bundaberg's **Woongarra Marine Park.** It has soft and hard corals, urchins, rays, sea snakes, and 60 fish species, plus a World War II Beaufort bomber wreck.

Dive Musgrave (© 1800/552 614 in Australia; www.divemusgrave.com.au) runs 3-day, 3-night dive cruises to Lady Musgrave Island twice a week for a maximum of 13 passengers. The cruise costs A$698, including all meals and 8 to 10 dives. Equipment rental, including a dive computer, is A$80 per person.

By far the most popular attraction in Bundaberg is the annual turtle nesting season on Mon Repos Beach, about 14km (8¾ miles) from the city center. **Mon Repos Conservation Park** is one of the two largest loggerhead-turtle rookeries in the South Pacific. The visitor center by the beach has a great display on the turtle life cycle and shows films at 7:30pm daily in summer. There is a strict booking system for turtle-watching tours, to help cope with the crowds. Access to the beach is by ticket only, and you must book your visit to Mon Repos during the turtle season. Tickets are sold through the **Bundaberg Visitor Information Centre** at 271 Bourbong St., Bundaberg (© 1300/722 099 in Australia), or you can book online at www.bookbundabergregion. com.au from September 1. The website has a lot of very useful information on how to get to the rookery and what to expect from your turtle-watching experience. Tours start at 7pm, but you may have to wait up to 2 hours or more, depending on when the turtles appear. Nesting happens around high tide; hatching usually occurs between 8pm and midnight. Take a sweater, as it can get quite cool.

The Conservation Park **information center** (www.nprsr.qld.gov.au/parks/mon-repos) is at 141 Mon Repos Road and is well signposted. During turtle-nesting season (Nov to late Mar), the park and information center are open 24 hours a day. Public access to the beach is closed from 6pm to 6am. Turtle viewing tours run from 7pm until midnight daily (except for Dec 24, 25, and 31). From April to early November (when no turtles are around), the information center is open Monday to Friday from 8am to 3:30pm, but the park is still open 24 hours. Admission to the visitor center is free from April through November; but when the turtles start nesting, you pay A$11 for adults, A$5.55 for children ages 5 to 14 and seniors, and A$25 for families, including your tour. It's the best value anywhere!

WHERE TO EAT

Café 1928 ★ CAFE   Set in the leafy surrounds of the Bundaberg Botanic Gardens, this casual cafe is a solid spot for brunch or lunch. Apart from good coffee, it offers quite an extensive menu, everything from muffins and sandwiches to home-cooked lasagne, quiche and salads, chicken schnitzel, and a range of burgers and pizzas.

Bundaberg Botanic Gardens, Young St., Bundaberg. © **07/4153 1928.** www.bundabergcafe.com. au. Main courses A$7.50–A$16. Daily 9am–4pm (kitchen closes at 2:30pm); public holidays 10am–3pm.

WHERE TO STAY

Kellys Beach Resort ★   This family-run resort is a great base for families. All the accommodations are in stand-alone two-bedroom villas, each with its own private veranda. Each self-contained unit has a queen-size bedroom downstairs and a loft bedroom upstairs and can sleep up to five. Larger villas also have a set of bunk beds downstairs, sleeping up to six. The whole resort was given a makeover in 2012–13, right down to repainting the swimming pool. You can rent snorkels and bikes, and you can walk to the beach, which is just a block away.

6 Trevors Rd., Bargara Beach, Bundaberg, QLD 4670. www.kellysbeachresort.com.au. © **1800/246 141** in Australia or 07/4154 7200. 41 units. A$155–A$182 double. Extra person A$15. 3-night minimum in peak Christmas season. Free undercover parking. **Amenities:** Restaurant; Jacuzzi; kids' club during Queensland school holidays; outdoor pool (heated in winter); sauna; tennis court; Wi-Fi (A$7.50/day), available in public areas such as lobby and pool, but only in a few villas (ask when booking if it's important to you!).

Lady Elliot Island

80km (50 miles) NE of Bundaberg

Lady Elliot is a 42-hectare (104-acre) coral cay ringed by a wide, shallow lagoon filled with dazzling coral life. Reef walking, snorkeling, and diving are the main reasons people come to this coral cay, which is so small you can walk across it in 15 minutes. You may snorkel and reef walk during only the 2 to 3 hours before and after high tide, so plan your day accordingly. You will see dazzling corals and brilliantly colored fish, clams, sponges, urchins, and anemones. Divers will see a good range of marine life, including green and loggerhead turtles (which nest on the beach Nov–Mar). Whales pass by from June through September.

Lady Elliot is a sparse, grassy island rookery, not a sandy tropical paradise. Some find it too spartan; others relish chilling out in a beautiful, peaceful spot with reef all around. Just be prepared for the smell and constant noise of the birds.

GETTING THERE   The 30-minute flight with **Seair** (✆ **07/5599 4509;** www.seair pacific.com.au) from Bundaberg runs three times a day. You can also do a day-trip flight from Brisbane or the Gold Coast. From Bundaberg, it costs A$269 adults and A$148 children 3 to 12, round-trip. Book your airfare with your accommodations. There is a 10-kilogram (22-lb.) luggage limit.

Lady Elliot Island Eco Resort ★★★   Accommodations here are fairly basic, but visitors come for the Reef, not the room. The top-of-the-range rooms are Island suites (the only rooms with air-conditioning), which have one or two separate bedrooms and great sea views from the deck. Most Reef rooms sleep four and have decks with views through the trees to the sea. The cool, spacious safari-tent "eco-huts" have four bunks, electric lighting, and timber floors but share the public toilets and showers used by day guests. The limited facilities include a boutique, an education center, and a dive shop, which runs shore and boat dives, introductory dives, and rents equipment. The resort has no TVs, no radio, no mobile phone reception, and no phones in the rooms (but there is a public telephone). A program of mostly free activities includes glass-bottom-boat rides, badminton, guided walks, and beach volleyball.

Great Barrier Reef, off Bundaberg (P.O. Box 348), Runaway Bay, QLD 4216. ✆ **1800/072 200** in Australia, or 07/4156 4444. www.ladyelliot.com.au. 40 units. A$326–A$360 eco-hut double; A$492–A$524 double garden unit; A$548–A$590 double reef unit; A$674–A$716 suite double. A$63–A$71 children 3–12 years. Crib A$20 per stay. 3-night minimum Christmas/New Year; 2-night minimum for suites. Rates include breakfast, dinner, and some guided tours. **Amenities:** Restaurant; bar; children's program (ages 3–12) during Queensland school holidays; saltwater pool.

ULURU & THE RED CENTRE

8

The Red Centre is the landscape most closely associated with Australia's Outback—endless horizons, vast deserts of red sand, a mysterious monolith, and cloudless blue skies. If there is a soundtrack, it is the rhythmic, haunting tones of the didgeridoo. At its heart is the magnificent monolith called Uluru—the "Rock"—that is the reason every visitor is drawn to this arid land.

The Centre is home to sprawling cattle ranches, ancient mountain ranges, "living fossil" palm trees that survived the Ice Age, cockatoos and kangaroos, ochre gorges, lush water holes, and intriguing tracks leading to heart-stopping landscapes.

Aboriginal people have lived here for tens of thousands of years, but the Centre is still largely unexplored by non-Aboriginal Australians. One highway cuts from Adelaide in the south to Darwin in the north, and a few roads and four-wheel-drive tracks make a lonely spider web across it; in many other areas, non-Aborigines have never set foot.

Alice Springs is the only big town in Central Australia, which together with the Top End makes up the Northern Territory. And let's get one thing straight from the start: Alice Springs and Uluru are *not* side by side. Uluru is 462km (286 miles) away. You can get there and see it in a day from Alice Springs, but it's an effort, and in doing so you will miss much of what is on offer, for visiting Uluru is much more than just a quick photo opportunity. It may well be the most meaningful and memorable part of your trip to Australia.

"The Alice" is a gateway to Uluru, but you can also fly there direct to Ayers Rock Airport, which takes its name from the European name given to Uluru by early explorers but seldom used today.

Give yourself a few days to experience all there is in the Centre—visiting the magnificent domes of Kata Tjuta ("the Olgas") near Uluru, walking the rim of Kings Canyon, riding a camel down a dry riverbed, exploring the intricacies of Aboriginal paintings (either on rock or canvas), swimming in water holes, or staying at an Outback homestead. A few days in Alice will give you the chance to see beautiful surrounding attractions such as Palm Valley, Ormiston Gorge, and Trephina Gorge Nature Park, each is an easy day trip. Too many visitors jet in, snap a photo of Uluru, and head home, only to miss the essence of the desert.

EXPLORING THE RED CENTRE

VISITOR INFORMATION   The **Central Australian Tourism Industry Association** (see "Visitor Information" under "Alice Springs," p. 198) is your best one-stop source of information.

Most of the Red Centre lies within the Northern Territory. **Tourism NT** has a great website (www.travelnt.com) with special sections tailored for international travelers (choose your country) and for the self-drive market. It can help you find a travel agent who specializes in the Northern Territory and details many hotels, tour operators, car-rental companies, and attractions, as well as lots of information on local Aboriginal culture and Aboriginal tours. Tourism NT's **Territory Discoveries division** (www.holidaysnt.com) offers package deals.

WHEN TO GO   April, May, September, and October have sunny days (coolish in May, hot in Oct). Winter (June–Aug) means mild temperatures with cold nights. Summer (Nov–Mar) is ferociously hot and best avoided. In summer, limit exertions to early morning and late afternoon, and choose air-conditioned accommodations. Rain is rare but can come at any time of year.

DRIVING TIPS   The **Automobile Association of the Northern Territory**, 14 Knuckey St., Darwin, NT 0800 (✆ **08/8925 5901;** www.aant.com.au), offers emergency-breakdown service to members of affiliated overseas automobile associations and dispenses maps and advice. It has no office in the Red Centre. For a recorded report of **road conditions,** call ✆ **1800/246 199** in Australia.

Only a handful of highways and arterial roads in the Northern Territory are sealed (paved) roads. A conventional two-wheel-drive car will get you to most of what you want to see, but consider renting a four-wheel-drive for complete freedom. All the big car-rental chains have them. Some attractions are on unpaved roads good enough for a two-wheel-drive car, but your car-rental company will not insure a two-wheel-drive for driving on them.

Normal restricted speed limits apply in all urban areas, but speed limits on Northern Territory highways (introduced only in 2006) are considerably higher than in other states. The speed limit is set at 130kmph (81 mph) on the Stuart, Arnhem, Barkly, and Victoria highways, while rural roads are designated 110kmph (68 mph) speed limits unless otherwise signposted. However, drivers should be careful to keep to a reasonable speed and leave enough distance to stop safely. The road fatality toll in the Northern Territory is high: 27 fatalities per 100,000 people each year, compared with the Australian average of 8 per 100,000.

> ### Buzz Off!
>
> Uluru is notorious for plagues of flies in summer. Don't be embarrassed to cover your head with the fly nets sold in souvenir stores—there will be "no flies on you, mate," an Aussie way of saying you are clever.

Another considerable risk while driving is that of hitting wildlife: camels, kangaroos, and other protected native species. Avoid driving at night, early morning, and late afternoon, when 'roos are more active; beware of cattle lying down on the warm bitumen at night.

Road trains (trucks hauling more than one container) and fatigue caused by driving long distances are two other major threats. For details on safe driving, review the tips in the "By Car" section of "Getting Around" in chapter 9.

OTHER TRAVEL TIPS   **Always carry drinking water.** When hiking, carry 4 liters (about a gallon) per person per day in winter and a liter (¼ gal.) per person per hour in summer. Wear a broad-brimmed hat, high-factor sunscreen, and insect repellant.

Bring warm clothing for chilly evenings in winter. Make sure you have a full tank of gas before setting out and check distances between places you can fill up.

TOUR OPERATORS   Numerous coach, minicoach, and four-wheel-drive tour operators run tours that take in Alice Springs, Kings Canyon, and Uluru. These depart from Alice Springs or Uluru, offering accommodations ranging from spiffy resorts, comfortable motels, and basic cabins to shared bunkhouses, tents, or swags (sleeping bags) under the stars. Most pack the highlights into a 2- or 3-day trip, though leisurely trips of 6 days or more are available. Many offer one-way itineraries between Alice and the Rock (via Kings Canyon if you like), or vice versa, which will allow you to avoid backtracking.

Among the reputable companies are **AAT Kings** (𝄐 **1300/228 546** in Australia, or 08/8952 1700 for the Alice Springs office; www.aatkings.com), which specializes in coach tours but also has four-wheel-drive camping itineraries; **Alice Springs Holidays** (𝄐 **1800/801 401** in Australia or 08/8631 1331; www.alicespringsholidays.com.au), which does upscale soft-adventure tours for groups; and **Intrepid Connections** (𝄐 **1300/018 871** in Australia; www.intrepidtravel.com), which conducts camping safaris (or if you prefer, hotel, motel, or lodge accommodation) in small groups for all ages. **Tailormade Tours** (𝄐 **08/8952 1731**; www.tailormadetours.com.au) offers public tours as well as customized luxury charters.

ALICE SPRINGS

462km (286 miles) NE of Uluru; 1,491km (924 miles) S of Darwin; 1,544km (957 miles) N of Adelaide; 2,954km (1,831 miles) NW of Sydney

"Alice" or "The Alice," as Australians fondly call it, is the unofficial capital of the Red Centre and a gateway to Uluru.

Many tourists visit Alice only to get to Uluru, but you might like to spend a few days here exploring its indigenous culture and outlying natural attractions. Home to about 27,000 people, it's a rambling, unsophisticated place that is the heart of the Aboriginal Arrernte people's country. Alice is a rich source of tours, shops, and galleries for those interested in Aboriginal culture, art, or souvenirs. However, parts of this region are also evidence that ancient Aboriginal civilization has not always meshed well with the 21st century, which has resulted in fractured riverbed communities plagued by alcohol and other social problems. And it is likely that you will see evidence of this on the streets.

No matter what direction you come from to get here, you will fly for hours over a vast, flat landscape. On arrival, you will see that in fact it is close to a low, dramatic range of rippling red mountains, the **MacDonnell Ranges.** Many visitors excitedly expect to see Uluru, but that marvel is about 462km (286 miles) down the road.

The red folds of the MacDonnell Ranges hide lovely gorges with shady picnic grounds. The area has an old gold-rush town to poke around in, quirky little museums,

Alice Springs

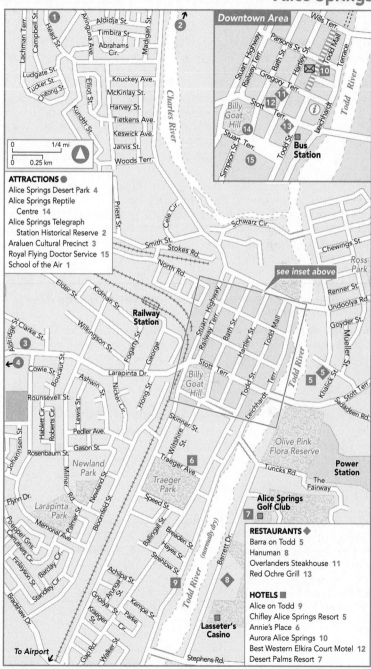

ATTRACTIONS ●
Alice Springs Desert Park 4
Alice Springs Reptile
  Centre 14
Alice Springs Telegraph
  Station Historical Reserve 2
Araluen Cultural Precinct 3
Royal Flying Doctor Service 15
School of the Air 1

RESTAURANTS ◆
Barra on Todd 5
Hanuman 8
Overlanders Steakhouse 11
Red Ochre Grill 13

HOTELS ■
Alice on Todd 9
Chifley Alice Springs Resort 5
Annie's Place 6
Aurora Alice Springs 10
Best Western Elkira Court Motel 12
Desert Palms Resort 7

wildlife parks, a couple of cattle stations (ranches) that welcome visitors, hiking trails to put red dust on your boots, and one of the world's top 10 desert golf courses.

Essentials

GETTING THERE   By Plane   Qantas (ⓒ **13 13 13** in Australia) flies direct from Sydney, Adelaide, Darwin, Perth, Melbourne, Brisbane, Cairns, and Uluru. Low-cost carrier **Tigerair** (ⓒ **02/8073 3421;** www.tigerair.com) has direct flights from Melbourne and Sydney.

Alice Springs Airport (www.alicespringsairport.com.au) is about 15km (9⅓ miles) out of town. The airport shuttle operated by **Alice Wanderer Airport Transfers** (ⓒ **1800/722 111** in Australia or 08/8952 2111; www.alicewanderer.com.au) meets all flights and transfers you to your Alice hotel door for A$15 per passenger for the first two passengers and then A$10 for each subsequent passenger in your group. A taxi from the airport to town is around A$35.

BY TRAIN   If you are a train buff, you may want to plan a trip that takes in two of Australia's great train journeys. From Sydney, you can get to Alice Springs by train using the **Indian Pacific** and **Ghan** trains. First take the Indian Pacific (which travels across the continent from Sydney to Perth) from Sydney to Adelaide, then change direction (and trains) to head north to Alice. Named after Afghan camel-train drivers who carried supplies in the Red Centre during the 19th century, the Ghan makes the trip from Adelaide to Alice every week, continuing to Darwin. The twice-weekly Adelaide–Alice service takes roughly 24 hours. It promises to be a very long—but memorable—journey. For information, contact **Great Southern Railway** (ⓒ **1800/703 357** in Australia or 08/8213 4401; www.gsr.com.au).

BY BUS   Greyhound (ⓒ **1300/473 946** in Australia or 08/8952 7888 in Alice Springs; www.greyhound.com.au) runs from Sydney via Adelaide. It's a monster 45-hour trip, and the fare is around A$445. Unless you really love bus travel, there are better ways to get there!

BY CAR   Alice Springs is on the Stuart Highway linking Adelaide and Darwin. Allow a very long 2 days or a more comfortable 3 days to drive from Adelaide, the same from Darwin. From Sydney, connect to the Stuart Highway via Broken Hill and Port Augusta north of Adelaide; from Cairns, head south to Townsville, then west via the town of Mount Isa to join the Stuart Highway at Tennant Creek. Both routes are long and dull. From Perth, it is even longer; drive across the Nullarbor Plain to connect with the Stuart Highway at Port Augusta. If you fancy a driving holiday of the area, check out **www.travelnt.com** for specific advice on routes, accommodations, and everything else you'll need to know, including things like locations of fuel stops.

VISITOR INFORMATION   The **Tourism Central Australia Visitor Information Centre,** Todd Mall, (ⓒ **1800/645 199** in Australia or 08/8952 5800; www.central australiantourism.com), is the official one-stop shop for bookings and touring information for the Red Centre, including Alice Springs, Kings Canyon, and Uluru–Kata Tjuta National Park. It also acts as the visitor center for the Parks & Wildlife Commission of the Northern Territory. It's open Monday through Friday from 8am to 5pm and weekends and public holidays from 9:30am to 4pm. It also has desks at the airport and train station.

GETTING AROUND Virtually all tours pick you up at your hotel. If your itinerary traverses unpaved roads, as it may in outlying areas, you will need to rent a four-wheel-drive vehicle, because regular cars will not be insured on an unpaved surface. However, a regular car will get you to most attractions. **Avis,** Gregory Terrace (at Bath St.; ✆ 08/8952 3694); **Budget,** 113 Todd Mall (✆ 08/8952 8899); **Hertz,** 34 Stott Terrace (✆ 08/8952 2644); and **Thrifty,** corner of Stott Terrace and Hartley St. (✆ 08/8952 9999), all rent conventional and four-wheel-drive vehicles. **Europcar** (✆ 08/8953 3799) has a desk at the airport, as do all the other companies. You may get a better deal on car rental by going through the **Outback Travel Shop** (www.outbacktravelshop.com.au) in Alice Springs, a booking agent that negotiates bulk rates with most Alice car-rental companies.

Many rental outfits for motor homes (camper vans) have Alice offices. They include **Apollo Campers,** 40 Stuart Hwy., corner of Smith Street (✆ 1800/777 779 in Australia), and **Britz Campervan Rental,** corner of Stuart Highway and Power Street (✆ 08/8952 8814). Renting a camper van can be significantly cheaper than staying in hotels and going on tours, but it pays to do your math first.

The best way to get around town without your own transport is aboard the **Alice Wanderer** bus (see "Organized Tours," p. 204). Public buses (✆ 08/8924 7066) run around town; the main bus stop is at the corner of Gregory Terrace and Railway Terrace. A A$3 fare gives you unlimited bus travel for 3 hours from the time of purchase. A **Show & Go** daily ticket costs A$7 and provides unlimited bus travel on that day. A weekly Show & Go costs A$20 for 7 days from the date of purchase. Tickets can be bought on the bus. There are no public bus services on Sundays or public holidays.

For a taxi, call **Alice Springs Taxis** (✆ 13 10 08 or 08/8952 1877) or find one at the rank (stand) on the corner of Todd Street and Gregory Terrace. Taxi fares here are high.

CITY LAYOUT **Todd Mall** is the heart of town. Most shops, businesses, and restaurants are here or within a few blocks' walk. Most hotels, the casino, the golf course, and many of the town's attractions are a few kilometers outside of town. The dry Todd River "flows" through the city east of Todd Mall.

Where to Stay in Alice Springs

Alice's hotel stock is not grand. Many properties have dated rooms and modest facilities; they're no match for the gleaming **Ayers Rock Resort** (described later in this chapter). You may pay lower rates than those listed in the summer off-season

---

Behold the Bizarre

Alice Springs hosts a couple of bizarre events. The **Camel Cup** camel race (www.camelcup.com.au) takes place on the second Saturday in July. In mid- to late August, people from hundreds of miles around come out to cheer the **Henley-on-Todd Regatta** (www.henleyontodd.com.au), during which gaudily decorated, homemade bottomless "boats" race down the dry Todd River bed. Well, what else do you do on a river that rarely flows? See "Australia Calendar of Events" in chapter 3 for more details.

(Dec–Mar) and even as late as June. Peak season typically runs from July through October or November.

Several backpacker resorts offer dorm rooms and doubles. One of the best is **Annie's Place,** 4 Traegar Ave., Alice Springs, NT 0870 (📞 **1800/359 089** in Australia, or 08/8952 1545; www.mulgas.com.au/annies). Doubles cost between A$60 for a room with shared bathroom and A$75 for one with your own bathroom. Dorm rooms (single sex or mixed) sleep 4 to 6 and cost A$23 per person. Annie's Place runs **Mulga's Adventures** (www.mulgas.com.au), which operates a 3-day backpackers' tour of the area, including Uluru, for A$355.

If you've rented a camper van, the **Stuart Tourist and Caravan Park,** Larapinta Drive, Alice Springs (📞 **1300/823 404** in Australia or 08/8952 2547; www.stuartcaravan park.com.au), has powered sites costing A$35 a night. Cabins here cost between A$85 and A$175 per night, depending on the cabin and the season.

Alice on Todd ★★ This contemporary complex has nice studio, one-bedroom, and two-bedroom apartments, about half of which are one-bedroom deluxe apartments opened in 2010. It's a very good option, particularly if you have kids. The apartments are very large, and some have two bathrooms. The hotel overlooks the Todd River and is just a short stroll from town. All but the studios have balconies. The two luxury two-bedroom apartments each have an extra sofa bed. There is a washing machine in each unit and other amenities such as free storage lockers.

Strehlow St. and South Terrace (P.O. Box 8454), Alice Springs, NT 0870. www.aliceontodd.com. 📞 **08/8953 8033.** 57 units. A$128 studio apt; A$156–A$170 1-bedroom apt (sleeps 4); A$195–A$210 2-bedroom apt (sleeps 4). Additional person A$20. Undercover parking. **Amenities:** Babysitting; bikes; children's playground; Jacuzzi; pool, free Wi-Fi.

Aurora Alice Springs ★★ This pleasant hotel is smack in the center of town. Rooms in the newer wing are standard motel-style lodgings, all large and nicely decorated. Those in the original wing are small and a little dark; they have a heritage theme, with floral bedcovers and lace curtains. Executive rooms have a king-size bed and private balconies facing the Todd River. Deluxe and standard rooms have one double bed and one single bed. Family rooms have a double bed and two bunk beds. The courtyard has a barbecue. The tiny pool and Jacuzzi are tucked away in a corner, so this is not the place for chilling out poolside; stay here to be within walking distance of shops and restaurants.

11 Leichhardt Terrace (backing onto Todd Mall), Alice Springs, NT 0870. www.auroraresorts.com. au. 📞 **1800/089 644** in Australia or 08/8950 6666. 109 units. A$210 double standard room; A$230 deluxe room; A$299 executive room; A$299 family room. Extra adult A$22–A$30. Free parking. **Amenities:** Restaurant (Red Ochre Grill; see review, p. 202); airport shuttle; babysitting; Jacuzzi; small outdoor pool; room service; free Internet (executive rooms only; free 1 hr./per stay in standard, deluxe, and family rooms).

Best Western Elkira Court Motel ★ The cheapest rooms in the heart of town—decent ones, that is—are at this unpretentious motel, which has been revamped and refurbished. The rooms are basic, but you won't get better value. Deluxe rooms have kitchenettes, and some have queen-size beds. Deluxe Spa rooms have two-person Jacuzzis. Ask for a room away from the road; the traffic is noisy during the day.

65 Bath St. (opposite Kmart), Alice Springs, NT 0870. www.bestwestern.com.au. 📞 **131 779** in Australia or 08/8952 1222. 58 units. A$110 double standard room; A$130 double deluxe room;

A$155 double Executive Spa Room. Extra person A$20. Free parking. **Amenities:** Restaurant; airport shuttle; nearby golf course; Jacuzzi; outdoor pool; room service; free Wi-Fi.

Chifley Alice Springs Resort ★★ This friendly, well-run, low-rise property is a 3-minute walk from town over the Todd River. Standard and superior rooms are quite pleasant, and the hotel was fully renovated in 2010. Deluxe rooms are a bit plusher, with bathtubs and bathrobes, and have a balcony or veranda overlooking the Todd River or the gardens. In summer, it's nice to repair to the pool under a couple of desert palms for a drink at the poolside bar after a hot day's sightseeing.

34 Stott Terrace, Alice Springs, NT 0870. www.chifleyhotels.com.au. ✆ **1300/272 132** in Australia or 08/8951 4545 (resort). 139 units. A$205–A$305 double. Extra person A$40. Children 11 and under stay free in parent's room with existing bedding. Free parking. **Amenities:** Restaurant; 2 bars; free airport shuttle; babysitting; bikes; concierge; solar-heated outdoor pool; room service; free Wi-Fi.

> ### Taking Care at Night
>
> Incidents of violence and crime in Alice Springs, including attacks on tourists by groups of young people—fueled by alcohol and substance abuse—have made headlines in Australia in recent years. Much of the trouble is centered around the drybed of the Todd River and Aboriginal "town camps." Visitors are advised not to wander around the streets at night.

Desert Palms Resort ★ A large swimming pool with its own palm-studded island is the focal point at this complex of bright cabins. Privacy from your neighbors is ensured by trailing pink bougainvillea and palm trees, making this one of the nicest places to stay in Alice. Don't be deterred by the prefab appearance; inside the cabins are surprisingly large, well kept, and inviting, with pine-pitched ceilings, kitchenettes, a tiny bathroom, and furnished front decks. Four rooms are suitable for travelers with disabilities. The pleasant staff at the front desk sells basic grocery and liquor supplies and books tours. You are also right next door to Lasseter's Casino (a debatable advantage) and the Alice Springs Golf Club.

74 Barrett Dr. (1km/½ mile from town), Alice Springs, NT 0870. www.desertpalms.com.au. ✆ **1800/678 037** in Australia, or 08/8952 5977. 80 units. A$140 double; A$155 triple; A$170 quad; A$185 family. Free crib. Free secure parking. **Amenities:** Large pool; half-size tennis court; free Wi-Fi.

Where to Eat

Barra on Todd ★★ CONTEMPORARY Part of the Chifley Alice Springs Resort, this restaurant serves up barramundi 10 different ways! You can try this freshwater fish simply char-grilled with a lemon and dill risotto, topped with asparagus, green beans, beurre blanc and king prawns, or served in a variety of ways with nods to Chinese, Indian, Thai, and Greek tastes. If you're not a fan of fish, don't worry; the menu offers plenty of other dishes including chicken, steaks, lamb, and duck. Barra on Todd does a good breakfast menu and has all-day (well, 11:30am–9pm) dining by the pool. It's popular for dinner, so book a table.

At the Alice Springs Resort, 34 Stott Terrace. ✆ **08/8951 4545.** www.chifleyhotels.com.au. Main courses A$29–A$42. Daily 6am–10pm.

Hanuman ★★★ CONTEMPORARY ASIAN   This is one of the most exotic restaurants in Alice Springs. The "Nonya"-style cuisine is a fusion of Chinese- and Malaysian-style cooking, and the decor is created with use of Asian artifacts and moody lighting. You are very unlikely to be disappointed by dishes such as red duck curry with coconut, lychees, kaffir lime, Thai basil, and fresh pineapple; or wok-tossed prawns in a coconut, wild ginger, and curry sauce.

82 Barrett Dr. (in the Crowne Plaza hotel). ✆ **08/8953 7188.** www.hanuman.com.au. Main courses A$15–A$36. Mon–Fri noon–2:30pm (except public holidays); daily 6:30–11pm. Closed Christmas Day, Boxing Day (Dec 26), and New Year's Day.

Overlanders Steakhouse ★ STEAK/BUSH TUCKER   This landmark on the Alice dining scene is famous for its "Drover's Blowout" menu, which assaults the mega-hungry with soup and damper, then a tasting platter of crocodile, camel, kangaroo filets, and emu—these are just the appetizers—followed by rump steak or barramundi and dessert (apple pie or Pavlova). There's a regular menu with a 700-gram (1½-lb.) steak, plus some lighter fare. The barnlike interior is Outback throughout, from the rustic bar to the saddlebags hanging from the roof beams. Vegetarians, take heart: There's actually a reasonable menu for you too.

72 Hartley St. ✆ **08/8952 2159.** www.overlanders.com.au. Reservations required in peak season. Main courses A$18–A$55. Daily 6–10pm.

Red Ochre Grill ★ GOURMET BUSH TUCKER   The chef at this upscale restaurant fuses native Aussie ingredients with dishes from around the world. If you've never tried kangaroo filet, rubbed with *dukkah* (an Egyptian spice blend) and served with pumpkin and wattleseed bake, sautéed baby spinach, and a port wine jus, then this is your chance. Maybe start your meal with a gumnut-smoked emu salad. A "game medley" plate combines kangaroo with camel, barramundi, and emu dishes. Although it might seem a touristy formula, the food is delicious. Dine in the contemporary interior fronting Todd Mall or outside in the attractive courtyard. Reservations recommended at dinner.

Todd Mall. ✆ **08/8952 9614.** www.redochrealice.com.au. Main courses A$13–A$18 at lunch (10am–5pm) and A$26–A$50 at dinner. "Early Bird" dinner, prebooked before 6pm and ordered before 7pm, gives 20% off your food bill (not available for specials or on Sun or public holidays). Daily 6:30am–9pm (closed Christmas Day).

Exploring Alice Springs

All the major attractions in Alice Springs are within easy reach of the city center.

Alice Springs Desert Park ★★★   By means of an easy 1.6km (1-mile) trail through three reconstructed natural habitats, this impressive wildlife and flora park shows you 120 or so of the animal species that live in the desert around Alice but that you won't spot too easily in the wild (including kangaroos you can walk among). Most of the creatures are small mammals (like the rare bilby), reptiles (cute thorny devil lizards), and birds. Don't miss the excellent **Birds of Prey** show at 10am and 3:30pm. There's a cafe here, too. Allow 2 to 3 hours to see it all.

Larapinta Dr., 6km (3¾ miles) west of town. ✆ **08/8951 8788.** www.alicespringsdesertpark. au. Admission A$25 adults, A$13 children 5–16, A$43-A$68 families. Daily 7:30am–6pm (last suggested entry 4:30pm). Closed Christmas Day. Tailormade Tours operates **Desert Park Transfers** (✆ **08/8952 1731**), with four to five bus transfers from accommodations a day in each direction.

The cost is A$48 adults, A$33 children 5–15, A$96–A$143 for families, including return transfers and park entry fee. The **Alice Wanderer** bus (© **1800/722 111** in Australia, or 08/8952 2111; www. alicewanderer.com.au) offers a service to the park as an add-on to its town tour (see "Organized Tours," below).

Alice Springs Reptile Centre ★★   Kids love this place, where they can drape a python around their neck or have a bearded dragon (lizard) perch on their shoulders. Rex, the easygoing proprietor, helps you get the best photos and lets kids hand-feed bugs to the animals at feeding time. More than 50 species are on display, including the world's deadliest land snake (the taipan) and big goannas. Also here are brown snakes, death adders, and mulga, otherwise known as king brown snakes. Don't miss the salt-water croc exhibit featuring underwater viewing. The best time to visit is between 11am and 3pm, when the reptiles are at their most active. There are talks at 11am and 1 and 3:30pm. Allow an hour or so.

9 Stuart Terrace (opposite the Royal Flying Doctor Service). © **08/8952 8900.** www.reptilecentre. com.au. Admission A$16 adults, A$8 children 4–16, A$40 families of 4. Daily 9:30am–5pm. Closed Christmas Day and New Year's Day.

Alice Springs Telegraph Station Historical Reserve ★★   This oasis marks the first European settlement of Alice Springs, which takes its name from the water hole nearby. Alice Springs began life here in 1872 as a telegraph repeater station, against a backdrop of red hills and sprawling gum trees. Arm yourself with the free map or join a free 45-minute tour. You can wander around the old stationmaster's residence; the telegraph office, with its Morse-code machine tap-tapping away; the shoeing yard, packed with blacksmithing equipment; and the stables, housing vintage buggies and saddlery. From the on-site computer, you can "telegraph" e-mails to your friends or be really old-fashioned and send mail through the Telegraph/Post Office, which will be stamped with a special franking stamp. It's a charming and much-underrated place. Allow a good hour—more to walk one of the several hiking trails—or bring a picnic and stay longer. You are also likely to see kangaroos and rock wallabies. It has a gift shop and offers coffee and snacks for sale.

Stuart Hwy., 4km (2½ miles) north of town (past the School of the Air turnoff). © **08/8952 3993.** Free admission to picnic grounds and trails; station A$8.50 adults, A$4.50 children 5–15, A$23 family of 4. Daily 8am–5pm (picnic grounds and trails till 9pm). Station closed Christmas Day. To get there, take a cab or Alice Wanderer bus (see "Organized Tours," p. 204) or the 4km (2½-mile) riverside pedestrian/bike track that starts near the corner of Wills Terrace and Undoolya Road.

Araluen Cultural Precinct ★★   Take several hours to explore the many facets of this interesting grouping of attractions, all within walking distance of one another. The **Museum of Central Australia** mostly shows local fossils, natural history displays, and meteorites. Some impressive Aboriginal and contemporary Aussie art is on display at the **Araluen Arts Centre** (© **08/8951 1122;** www.araluenartscentre.nt.gov. au), the town's performing-arts hub, which incorporates the Albert Namatjira Gallery, with works by this famous Aboriginal artist, as well as a display of the Papunya Community School Collection, a group of 14 paintings from the early 1970s. Check out the "Honey Ant Dreaming" stained-glass window in the foyer. Aviation buffs may want to browse the old radios, aircraft, and wreckage in the **Central Australian Aviation Museum,** which preserves the territory's aerial history. You can buy stylish crafts, and sometimes catch artists at work, in the **Central Craft** gallery. You may also want to amble among the fabulous outdoor sculptures, including the 15m (49-ft.) Yeperenye caterpillar, or among the gravestones in the cemetery, where "Afghani" camel herders (from what is now Pakistan) are buried facing Mecca.

Larapinta Dr., at Memorial Ave., 2km (1¼ miles) west of town. © **08/8951 1120.** Admission A$15 adults; A$10 children 5–16; A$40 families of 4. Mon–Fri 10am–4pm; Sat–Sun 11am–4pm. Closed Good Friday and for 2 weeks from Christmas Day.

Royal Flying Doctor Service Tourist Facility ★★   Alice is a major base for this airborne medical service that treats people living and traveling in the vast Outback. After a A$3 million redevelopment in 2012, the visitor center now provides great insight into the work the RFDS does. Guided tours run every half-hour from 9am to 4pm; allow another 30 minutes or so to browse the museum and listen to some of the recorded conversations between doctors and patients. You can explore a replica fuselage of a Pilatus PC12 or test your hand at the throttle in a flight simulator. It also has a cafe, gift shop, and art gallery.

8–10 Stuart Terrace (at end of Hartley St.). © **08/8958 8411.** www.rfdsalicesprings.com.au. Admission A$12 adults, A$6 children 6–15, A$30 family of 4. Mon–Sat 9am–5pm; Sun and public holidays 1–5pm. Closed New Year's Day and Christmas Day.

School of the Air ★★★   Sitting in on school lessons may not be your idea of a vacation, but this school is different—it broadcasts by radio to a 1.3-million-sq.-km (507,000-sq.-mile) "schoolroom" of 140 children on Outback stations. That area's as big as Germany, Great Britain, Ireland, New Zealand, and Japan combined—or twice the size of Texas. Visitors watch and listen in when classes are in session; outside class hours, you may hear taped classes. You can browse the kids' artwork, photos, video, and other displays in the well-organized visitor center.

80 Head St. (2.5km/1½ miles from town). © **08/8951 6834.** www.assoa.nt.edu.au. Admission A$7.50 adults; A$4.80 children 5–16; A$19 families of 4. Mon–Sat 8:30am–4:30pm; Sun and public holidays 1:30–4:30pm. Closed Christmas Day–Jan 1 and Good Friday. Bus: 3 or Alice Wanderer (see "Organized Tours," below).

Organized Tours

AROUND TOWN & OUT IN THE DESERT   The **Alice Wanderer** bus (© **1800/ 722 111** in Australia or 08/8952 2111; www.alicewanderer.com.au) does a running loop of 14 town attractions every 70 minutes, starting at 9am, with the last departure at 4pm. Hop on and off as you please and enjoy the commentary from the driver. The bus departs daily from the south end of Todd Mall. Tickets are sold on board and cost A$44 for adults, and A$28 for kids 4 to 14. Call for free pickup from your hotel. For A$10 more, you can buy extra days. It's well worth checking out the Alice Wanderer website to help you plan your time before you visit. The company also runs full- and half-day tours to outlying areas, including to Palm Valley in the West MacDonnell Ranges, costing A$117 for adults and A$72 for kids (p. 206).

Many Alice-based companies offer minicoach or four-wheel-drive day trips and extended tours of Alice and of outlying areas including the East and West Macs, Hermannsburg, and Finke Gorge National Park. Among the well-regarded ones is **Alice Springs Holidays** (© **1800/801 401** in Australia or 08/8953 1331; www.alicesprings holidays.com.au).

CAMEL SAFARIS The camel's ability to get by without water was key to opening the arid inland parts of Australia to European settlement in the 1800s. With the advent of cars, they were released into the wild, and today more than 200,000 roam Central Australia. Australia even exports them to the Middle East! **Pyndan Camel Tracks** (© **0416/170 164;** www.cameltracks.com) runs camel rides daily, with pickup from your hotel. A 1-hour tour, at noon, 2:30pm, or sunset, costs A$50 adults and A$30 for kids 14 and under. Kids under 3 must ride with an adult. A half-day ride, leaving at 9am and returning about noon, costs A$110 per person. Make sure you wear comfortable, casual clothes, and sensible shoes—you are likely to get a bit dirty.

HOT-AIR BALLOON FLIGHTS Dawn balloon flights above the desert are popular in central Australia. You have to get up 90 minutes before dawn, though. **Outback Ballooning** (© **1800/809 790** in Australia or 08/8952 8723; www.outbackballooning. com.au) offers a 1-hour flight followed by champagne breakfast in the bush for A$385 adults, A$313 for kids 6 to 16. A 30-minute breakfast flight costs A$290 adults, A$237 for children. Kids under 6 are discouraged from participating because they cannot see over the basket. Don't make any other morning plans—you probably won't get back to your hotel until close to noon.

Outdoor Activities

BUSHWALKING The 223km (138-mile) **Larapinta Trail** winds west from Alice through the sparse red ranges, picturesque semidesert scenery, and rich bird life of the West MacDonnell National Park (p. 206). This long-distance walking track is divided into 12 sections, each a 1- to 2-day walk. Sections range from easy to hard. The shortest is 8km (5 miles), all the way up to 29km (18 miles). The Larapinta Trail begins at the old Alice Springs Telegraph Station and meanders through many gaps and sheltered gorges and climbs steeply over rugged ranges. Each section is accessible to vehicles (some by high-clearance four-wheel-drive only), so you can join or leave the trail at any of the trail heads. Camping out under a sea of stars in the Outback is a highlight of the experience. Although they vary, most campsites offer picnic tables and hardened tent sites—all trail heads have a water supply and some have free gas barbecues. The Parks & Wildlife Commission of the Northern Territory strongly recommends any individual or group walking the Larapinta Trail to carry a communication device— a satellite phone or a location device such as a PLB/EPIRBS or SpotMessenger. Trail maps and information can be obtained from the **Visitor Information Centre** (see "Visitor Information," earlier in this chapter). Check **www.nt.gov.au/nreta/parks/ walks/larapinta** for detailed information on the trail. It also has details of companies that provide transfers to access points along the trail, food drops, camping equipment, or fully guided and supported treks. *Warning: Always* carry drinking water. The trail may close in extremely hot summer periods.

GOLF The **Alice Springs Golf Club,** 1km (just over a half mile) from town on Cromwell Drive (© **08/8952 1921;** www.alicespringsgolfclub.com.au), boasts a Thomson-Wolveridge course rated among the world's top desert courses by touring pros. The course is open from sunup to sundown. Nine holes cost A$42; 18 holes, A$80. Club rental costs A$38, and a motorized cart, which many locals don't bother with, goes for A$35 for 18 holes.

Shopping for Aboriginal Art

Alice Springs is one of the best places in Australia to buy Aboriginal art and crafts. You will find no shortage of paintings, didgeridoos, spears, clapping sticks, *coolamons* (dishes used by women to carry anything from water to babies), animal carvings, baskets, and jewelry, as well as books, CDs, and all kinds of merchandise printed with Aboriginal designs. Prices can soar to many thousands for large canvases by world-renowned painters, but you'll also find plenty of smaller, more affordable works. Most galleries arrange shipment. Store hours can vary with the seasons and the crowds, so it pays to check ahead.

Mbantua Aboriginal Art Gallery, 71 Gregory Terrace (*℗* **08/8952 5571;** www. mbantua.com.au), is a highly respected and reliable source of authentic Aboriginal art, with a dazzling selection to choose from. The art comes from a harsh desert region called Utopia, home to several Aboriginal communities. Mbantua owner Tim Jennings began supplying locals with paints and canvas during food deliveries to Utopia, first as sheriff, then as the general-store owner. Every 2 weeks, the Mbantua gallery team drops off new materials and pays the artists for finished works. Some of the 200 Utopia residents who paint have been recognized internationally, including Barbara Weir, Gloria Petyarre, the late Emily Kame Kngwarreye, and Minnie Pwerle. Jennings authenticates every piece of art; he and his team photograph the artist with the work and record the traditional meaning behind it. Works by established artists can be priced up to tens of thousands of dollars, but a much smaller investment can get you work by lesser-known but talented painters. Mbantua Gallery is a member of Art.Trade, an organization that operates to promote the ethical trade of indigenous art.

Papunya Tula Artists, 63 Todd Mall (*℗* **08/8952 4731;** www.papunyatula.com.au), sells paintings on canvas and linen from Papunya, a settlement 240km (150 miles) northwest of Alice Springs, and work by other artists living in the Western Desert, as far as 700km (434 miles) from Alice Springs.

The **Aboriginal Australia Art & Culture Centre,** 125 Todd St. (*℗* **08/8952 3408;** www.aboriginalaustralia.com), is a community-based, Aboriginal-owned and -operated business that runs painting classes, has a retail gallery, and is a community arts base. It is open 9am to 5pm weekdays; weekends by appointment for serious collectors.

DAY TRIPS FROM ALICE SPRINGS

The key attraction of a day trip to the MacDonnell Ranges is unspoiled natural scenery and few crowds. Many companies run coach or four-wheel-drive tours—half- or full-day, sometimes overnight—to the West and East Macs. Some options appear in "Organized Tours" in the "Alice Springs" section, earlier in this chapter.

The West MacDonnell Ranges

WEST MACDONNELL NATIONAL PARK The 300km (186-mile) round-trip drive west from Alice Springs into West MacDonnell National Park (www.nt.gov.au/west macs) is a stark but picturesque expedition to a series of red gorges, semidesert country, and the occasional peaceful swimming hole. The 12-stage, 223km (138-mile)

Larapinta Walking Trail takes you along the backbone of the West MacDonnell Ranges through some of the most unique and isolated country in the world. The hills, colors, birds, water holes, gorges, and the never-ending diversity of this trail will leave you spellbound by the beauty of Central Australia. The track stretches from the Telegraph Station in Alice Springs to Mount Sonder, past Glen Helen Gorge. Detailed track notes are on the website of the **Parks & Wildlife Commission** (www.nt.gov.au/nreta/parks/walks/larapinta) and at the visitor information center in Alice Springs. Don't attempt the walk in the height of summer unless you are very well prepared. For great tips, and other information, look up the **Alice Wanderer** website (www.alicewanderer.com.au).

From Alice, take Larapinta Drive west for 18km (11 miles) to the 8km (5-mile) turnoff to **Simpson's Gap,** a water hole lined with ghost gums. Black-footed rock wallabies hop out on the cliffs in the late afternoon (so you may want to time a visit here on your way back to Alice). There are a couple of short trails here, including a .5km (.3-mile) Ghost Gum circuit and a 17km (11-mile) round-trip trail to Bond Gap. Swimming is not permitted. The place has an information center/ranger station and free use of barbecues.

Twenty-three kilometers (14 miles) farther down Larapinta Road, 9km (5½ miles) down a turnoff, is **Standley Chasm** (✆ **08/8956 7440;** www.standleychasm.com.au). This rock cleft is only a few meters wide but 80m (262 ft.) high, reached by a 10-minute creek-side trail. Aim to be here at midday, when the walls glow orange in the overhead sun. A kiosk sells snacks and drinks. Admission is A$7 for adults and A$6.50 for children 5 to 14. The chasm is open daily from 8am to 6pm (last entry at 5pm; closed Christmas Day).

Six kilometers (3¾ miles) past Standley Chasm, you can branch right onto Namatjira Drive or continue to Hermannsburg Historical Precinct (see below). If you take Namatjira Drive, you'll go 42km (26 miles) to picturesque **Ellery Creek Big Hole.** *Be warned:* The spring-fed water is icy cold. A 3km (2-mile) walking trail explains the area's geological history.

Eleven kilometers (7 miles) farther along Namatjira Drive is **Serpentine Gorge,** where a trail leads up to a lookout for a lovely view of the ranges through the gorge walls. Another 12km (7½ miles) on are **ocher pits,** which Aboriginal people quarried for body paint and for decorating objects used in ceremonial performances. Twenty-six kilometers (16 miles) farther west, 8km (5 miles) from the main road, is **Ormiston Gorge and Pound** (✆ **08/8956 7799** for the ranger station/visitor center). This is a good spot to picnic, swim in the wide, deep pool below red cliffs, and walk a choice of trails, such as the 30-minute Ghost Gum Lookout trail or the easy 7km (4⅓-mile) scenic loop (allow 3–4 hr.). The water is warm enough for swimming in the summer.

Farther on is **Glen Helen Gorge,** where the Finke River cuts through the ranges, with more gorge swimming, a walking trail, guided hikes, and helicopter flights. **Glen Helen Resort** (✆ **08/8956 7489;** www.glenhelen.com.au) has a restaurant and offers scenic helicopter flights on demand (minimum two people) from A$55 per person.

GETTING THERE If you are not driving yourself, you can arrange to be dropped off by **Larapinta Transfers** (✆ **08/8952 2111;** www.larapintatransfers.com.au) at several stops in the Ranges. It costs around A$200 for two people for the return trip to Simpson's Gap or Standley Chasm; A$290 to Serpentine Gorge, Ormiston Gorge or Glen Helen Gorge. The Alice Wanderer (p. 204) also does group tours.

Facilities are scarce outside Alice, so bring food, drinking water, and a full gas tank. Leaded, unleaded, and diesel fuel are for sale at Glen Helen Resort and Hermannsburg. Wear walking shoes.

Many of the water holes dry up too much to be good for swimming—those at Ellery Creek, Ormiston Gorge, and Glen Helen are the most permanent. They can be intensely cold, so take only short dips to avoid cramping and hypothermia, don't swim alone, and be careful of underwater snags. Don't wear sunscreen, because it pollutes drinking water for native animals.

Two-wheel-drive rental cars will not be insured on unsealed (unpaved) roads—that means the last few miles into Trephina Gorge Nature Park and the 11km

(7-mile) road into N'Dhala Gorge Nature Park, both in the East Macs. If you are prepared to risk it, you can probably get into Trephina in a two-wheel-drive car, but you will need a four-wheel-drive for N'Dhala and Arltunga. The West MacDonnell road is paved to Glen Helen Gorge; a few points of interest may require driving for short lengths on unpaved road. Before setting off, drop into the Tourism Central Australia **Visitor Information Centre** (see "Visitor Information," earlier in this chapter) for tips on road conditions and details on the free ranger talks, walks, and slideshows that take place in the West and East Macs from April through October. Entry to all sights, parks, and reserves (except Standley Chasm) is free.

HERMANNSBURG HISTORICAL PRECINCT An alternative to visiting the West Mac gorges is to stay on Larapinta Drive all 128km (79 miles) from Alice Springs to the old **Lutheran Mission** at the **Hermannsburg Historical Precinct** (© **08/8956 7402;** www.hermannsburg.com.au). Some maps show this route as an unpaved road, but it is paved. Settled by German missionaries in the 1870s, this is a cluster of 16 National Trust–listed farmhouse-style mission buildings and a historic cemetery. There is a museum, a gallery housing landscapes by Aussie artist Albert Namatjira, and tearooms serving light snacks and apple strudel from an old German recipe. The mission is open daily from 9am to 4pm. Admission to the precinct is A$10 for adults, A$5 for school-age kids, or A$25 for families of four. The precinct is closed for 5 weeks in December and January.

FINKE GORGE NATIONAL PARK Just west of Hermannsburg is the turnoff to the 46,000-hectare (113,620-acre) **Finke Gorge National Park,** 16km (10 miles) to the south on an unpaved road (or about a 2-hr. drive west of Alice Springs). Turn south off Larapinta Drive just west of Hermannsburg. Access along the last 16km (10 miles) of road, which follows the sandy bed of the Finke River, is limited to four-wheel-drive vehicles only. Heavy rains may cause this section of the road to be impassable. The park is most famous for **Palm Valley,** where groves of rare Livistona mariae cabbage palms have survived since Central Australia was a jungle millions of years ago. You will need to have a four-wheel-drive vehicle or take a tour to explore this park. Four walking trails between 1.5km (1 mile) and 5km (3 miles) take you among the palms or up to a lookout over cliffs; one is a signposted trail exploring Aboriginal culture. For information, call the Visitor Information Centre in Alice Springs before you leave; there is no visitor center in the park.

The East MacDonnell Ranges

Not as many tourists tread the path on the Ross Highway into the East Macs, but if you do, you'll be rewarded with lush walking trails, fewer crowds, traces of Aboriginal history, and possibly even the sight of wild camels.

The first points of interest are **Emily Gap,** 10km (6 miles) from Alice, and **Jessie Gap,** an additional 7km (4⅓ miles), a pretty picnic spot. You can cool off in the Emily Gap swimming hole if there is any water. Don't miss the *Caterpillar Dreaming* Aboriginal painting art on the wall, on your right as you walk through.

At **Corroboree Rock,** 37km (23 miles) farther, you can make a short climb up the outcrop, which was important to local Aborigines. The polished rock "seat" high up in the hole means Aboriginal people must have used this rock for eons.

Twenty-two kilometers (14 miles) farther is the turnoff to **Trephina Gorge Nature Park,** an 18-sq.-km (7-sq.-mile) beauty spot with peaceful walking trails that can take from 45 minutes to 4½ hours. The last 5km (3 miles) of the 9km (5½-mile) road into the park are unpaved, but you can make it in a two-wheel-drive car.

N'Dhala Gorge Nature Park, 10km (6 miles) past Trephina Gorge Nature Park, houses an "open-air art gallery" of rock carvings, or petroglyphs, left by the Eastern Arrernte Aboriginal people. An interesting 1.5km (1-mile) signposted trail explains the Dreamtime meanings of a few of the 6,000 rock carvings, hundreds or thousands of years old, that are thought to be in this eerily quiet gorge. A four-wheel-drive vehicle is a must to traverse the 11km (7-mile) access road.

The Ross Highway is paved all the way to Ross River Resort, 86km (53 miles) from Alice Springs.

ULURU–KATA TJUTA NATIONAL PARK

462km (286 miles) SW of Alice Springs; 1,934km (1,199 miles) S of Darwin; 1,571km (974 miles) N of Adelaide; 2,841km (1,761 miles) NW of Sydney

Why travel so far to look at a large red rock? Because it will send a shiver up your spine. Because it may move you to tears. Because there is something indefinable and indescribable but definitely spiritual about this place. Up close, Uluru is more magnificent than you can imagine. It is immense and overwhelming and mysterious. Photographs never do it justice. There is what is described as a "spirit of place" here. It is unforgettable and irresistible (and you may well want to come back again, just for another look). It will not disappoint you. On my first visit—yes, I am one who will keep coming back—a stranger whispered to me: "Even when you are not looking at it, it is always just *there,* waiting to tap you on the shoulder." A rock with a presence.

"The Rock" has a circumference of 9.4km (6 miles), and two-thirds of it is thought to be underground. In photos, it looks smooth and even, but the reality is much more interesting—dappled with holes and overhangs, with curtains of stone draping its sides, creating little coves hiding water holes and Aboriginal rock art. It also changes color from pink to a deep wine red depending on the angle and intensity of the sun. And if you are lucky enough to be visiting when it rains, you will see a sight like no other. Here, rain brings everyone outside to see the spectacle of the waterfalls created off the massive rock formed by sediments laid down 600 to 700 million years ago in an inland sea and thrust up aboveground 348m (1,141 ft.) by geological forces.

In 1985, **Uluru–Kata Tjuta National Park** was returned to its Aboriginal owners, the Pitjantjatjara and Yankunytjatjara people, known as the Anangu, who manage the property jointly with the Australian government. Don't think a visit to Uluru is just about snapping a few photos and going home. There are many ways of exploring it, and one of the best is to join Aboriginal people on guided walks. You can walk around the Rock, climb it (we'll talk about *that* later), fly over it, ride a camel to it, circle it on a Harley-Davidson, trek through the nearby Olgas, and dine under the stars while you learn about them.

Just do yourself one favor: Plan to spend at least 2 days here, if not 3.

Isolation (and a lack of competition) makes such things as accommodations, meals, and transfers relatively expensive. A coach tour or four-wheel-drive camping safari is often the cheapest way to see the place. See "Exploring the Red Centre," at the beginning of this chapter, for recommended tour companies.

Essentials

ARRIVING   By Plane   Qantas (© 13 13 13 in Australia) flies to Ayers Rock (Connellan) Airport direct from Alice Springs and Cairns. Flights from other airports go via Alice Springs. **Jetstar** (© **13 15 38** in Australia) and **Virgin Blue** (© **13 67 89** in Australia) fly direct from Sydney. The airport is 6km (3¾ miles) from Ayers Rock Resort. A free shuttle ferries all resort guests, including campers, to their door.

By Car   Take the Stuart Highway south from Alice Springs 199km (123 miles), turn right onto the Lasseter Highway, and go 244km (151 miles) to Ayers Rock Resort. The Rock is 18km (11 miles) farther on. It is about a 4½-hour drive in total.

If you are renting a car in Alice Springs and want to drop it at Uluru and fly out from there, be prepared for a one-way penalty. Only Avis, Hertz, and Thrifty have Uluru depots ("Getting Around," p. 211).

The Rock in a Day?

It's a *loooong* day to visit Uluru in a day from Alice by road. Many organized coach tours pack a lot—perhaps a Rock-base walk or climb, Kata Tjuta (the Olgas), the Uluru–Kata Tjuta Cultural Centre, and a champagne sunset at the Rock—into a busy trip that leaves Alice around 5:30 or 6am and gets you back late at night. You should consider a day trip only between May and September. At other times, it's too hot to do much from early morning to late afternoon.

VISITOR INFORMATION   For online information before you arrive, check out the Uluru-Kata Tjuta National Park website, www.environment.gov.au/parks/uluru. Tourism Central Australia has a **Visitor Information Centre** at 60 Gregory Terrace, Alice Springs (© **1800/645 199** in Australia or 08/8952 5800; www.centralaustraliantourism. com). Another good source of online information is Ayers Rock Resort's site (www. ayersrockresort.com.au).

One kilometer (a half mile) from the base of the Rock is the **Uluru–Kata Tjuta Cultural Centre** (© **08/8956 1128**), owned and run by the Anangu, the Aboriginal owners of Uluru. It uses eye-catching wall displays, frescoes, interactive recordings, and videos to tell about Aboriginal Dreamtime myths and laws. It's worth spending some time here to understand a little about Aboriginal culture. A National Park desk (© **08/8956 1100**) has information on ranger-guided activities and animal, plant, and bird-watching checklists. The center also has a cafe, a souvenir shop, and two Aboriginal arts and crafts galleries. It's open daily from early in the morning to after sundown; exact hours vary from month to month.

Cultural Etiquette

The Anangu ask you not to photograph sacred sites or Aboriginal people without permission and to approach quietly and respectfully. For more information on climbing Uluru, see p. 215.

The **Ayers Rock Resort Visitor Centre,** next to the Desert Gardens Hotel (© **08/8957 7377**), has displays on the area's geology, wildlife, and Aboriginal heritage, plus a souvenir store. It's open daily from 9:30am to 4:30pm. You can book tours at the **tour desk** in every hotel at Ayers Rock Resort, or visit the **Ayers Rock Resort Tour & Information Centre** (© **08/8957 7324**) at the shopping center in the resort complex.

PARK ENTRANCE FEES Entry to the Uluru–Kata Tjuta National Park is A$25 per adult, free for children under 16, and valid for 3 days. Some tours include this fee but others do not, so it pays to check. National Park tickets can only be purchased from the National Park Entry Station. The park is open from between 5am and 6:30am (depending on the time of year) and closes between 7:30pm and 9pm.

Getting Around

Ayers Rock Resort runs a **free shuttle** every 20 minutes or so around the resort complex from 10:30am to after midnight, but to get to the Rock or Kata Tjuta (the Olgas), you will need to take transfers, join a tour, or have your own wheels. The shuttle also meets all flights. There are no taxis at Yulara.

BY SHUTTLE **Uluru Express** (© **08/8956 2019;** www.uluruexpress.com.au) provides a shuttle from Ayers Rock Resort to and from the Rock about every 50 minutes from before sunrise to sundown, and four times a day to Kata Tjuta. The basic round-trip fare is A$55 for adults and A$30 for kids 1 to 14. To Kata Tjuta, it costs A$85 for adults and A$45 for children. A 2-day pass that enables you to explore Uluru and Kata Tjuta as many times as you wish costs A$195 adults and A$100 children; a 3-day pass costs A$225 for adults and A$115 for kids. A National Park entry pass, if you don't already have one, is A$25 extra.

BY CAR If there are two of you, the easiest and cheapest way to get around is likely to be a rental car. All roads in the area are paved, so a four-wheel-drive is unnecessary. Expect to pay around A$120 to A$140 per day for a medium-size car. Rates drop a little in low season. Most car-rental companies give you the first 100 or 200km (63–126 miles) free and charge between A17¢ and A25¢ per kilometer after that. Take this into account, because the round-trip from the resort to the Olgas is just over 100km (63 miles), and that's without driving about 20km (13 miles) to the Rock and back. Hire periods of under 3 days incur a one-way fee based on kilometers traveled, up to about A$330. **Avis** (© **08/8956 2266**), **Hertz** (© **08/8956 2244**), and **Thrifty** (© **08/8956 2030**) all rent regular cars and four-wheel-drives.

The **Outback Travel Shop** (© 08/ 8955 5288; www.outbacktravelshop. com.au), in Alice Springs, often has better deals on car-rental rates than you'll get by booking direct.

BY ORGANIZED TOUR Several tour companies run a range of daily sunrise and sunset viewings, circum-navigations of the Rock by coach or on foot, guided walks at the Rock or the Olgas, camel rides, observatory evenings, visits to the Uluru–Kata Tjuta Cultural Centre, and innumerable combinations of all of these. Some offer "passes" containing the most popular activities. Virtually every company picks you up at your hotel. Among the most reputable are AAT Kings and Tailormade Tours (see "Exploring the Red Centre," p. 195).

Where to Stay & Eat

Ayers Rock Resort is not only in the township of Yulara—it *is* the township. Located about 30km (19 miles) from Uluru, outside the national park boundary, it is the only place to stay. It is an impressive contemporary complex, built to a high standard, effi-ciently run, and attractive—all things you can end up paying an arm and a leg for. Because everyone either is a tourist or lives and works here, it has a village atmo-sphere—with a supermarket, bank, post office, newsdealer, a medical center, beauty salon, several gift, clothing, and souvenir shops, and a gas station.

You have a choice of seven places to stay within the complex, from luxury hotel rooms and apartments to campsites. In keeping with this village feel, no matter where you stay, even in the campground, you are free to use all the pools, restaurants, and other facilities of every hostelry, except the exclusive Sails in the Desert pool, which is reserved for Sails guests, and Longitude 131˚.

You can book any of the accommodations through a central reservations office in Sydney (© **1300/134 044** in Australia or 02/8296 8010; www.ayersrockresort.com.au). High season is July through November. Book well ahead, and shop around for special deals on the Internet and with travel agencies. Ask about special packages for 2- or 3-night stays.

In addition to the resort dining options, the small shopping center has the pleasant **Gecko's Café,** which offers gourmet pizzas, pastas, and burgers (as well as take-out); a bakery; and a deli. Several of the resort restaurants offer kids' menus.

Ayers Rock Campground ★ Instead of red dust, you get green lawns at this campground, which has barbecues, a playground, swimming pool, a small general store, and clean communal bathrooms and kitchen. If you don't want to camp but want to travel cheap, consider the modern two-bedroom cabins. They're a great value; each has air-conditioning, a TV, a kitchenette with a fridge, dining furniture, a double bed, and four bunks (but no phone). They book up quickly in winter. Bookings must be made directly through the campground.

Yulara Dr., Yulara, NT 0872. www.ayersrockresort.com.au/arrcamp. © **08/8957 7001.** 220 tent sites, 198 powered sites, 14 cabins, none with bathroom. A$155 cabin for up to 6; A$36 double tent site or A$45 family of 4; A$41–A$46 double-powered motor-home site or A$50 family of 4. Extra adult A$17, extra child 6–15 A$9.50. **Amenities:** Free airport shuttle; children's playground; outdoor pool; no Wi-Fi.

DINNER IN THE desert

Why sit in a restaurant when you can eat outside and soak up the desert air? Ayers Rock Resort's **Sounds of Silence** dinner is not just a meal, it's an event. In an outdoor clearing, you sip champagne and nibble canapés as the sun sets over the Rock to the strains of a didgeridoo. Then head to communal white-clothed, candlelit tables and a buffet meal that will include kangaroo, emu, crocodile, and barramundi. The food is not exceptional, but you're really here for the atmosphere. After dinner, the lanterns fade and you're left with stillness. For some city folk, it's the first time they have ever heard complete silence. Look up into the usually clear skies, and (if it's a clear night) an astronomer will point out the constellations of the Southern Hemisphere. You can also look at the stars through telescopes. Sounds of Silence is held nightly, weather permitting, and costs A$185 for adults and A$93 for children 10 to 12, including transfers from Ayers Rock Resort. Surcharges apply for Christmas Day. It's mighty popular, so book as far ahead as you can, even up to 3 months ahead in peak season. Book through the Ayers Rock Resort office in Sydney (☏ **1300/134 044** in Australia or 02/8296 8010) or online (www.ayersrock resort.com.au).

Desert Gardens Hotel ★★ This is the only hotel with views of Uluru (albeit rather distant ones) from some of the rooms. It is set amid wonderful ghost gum trees and the flowering native shrubs that give it its name. The accommodations are not as lavish as Sails in the Desert, but they're equally comfortable and have elegant furnishings. The **Arnquli Grill** serves à la carte flame-grilled meals.

Yulara Dr., Yulara, NT 0872. www.ayersrockresort.com.au/desert. ☏ **08/8957 7714.** 218 units. A$340–A$398 double standard room; A$398–A$440 double deluxe room; A$440–A$498 double deluxe Rock-view room. Extra person A$50. Children 12 years and under stay free in parent's room using existing bedding. **Amenities:** Restaurant, bar; free airport shuttle; outdoor pool; room service.

Emu Walk Apartments ★★ These bright, contemporary apartments have full kitchens, separate bedrooms, and roomy living areas. They have daily maid service, and sleep 4 or 6 people, so they're great for families or groups of friends. There's no restaurant or pool, but Gecko's Café and the market are close, and you can cool off in the Desert Gardens Hotel pool.

Yulara Dr., Yulara, NT 0872. ☏ **08/8957 7714.** 60 apts. A$340–A$398 double 1-bedroom apt; A$440–A$498 double 2-bedroom apt. Extra person A$50. **Amenities:** Free airport shuttle.

Longitude 131° ★★★ When you wake in your luxury "tent" here, you can reach out from your king-size bed and press a button to raise the blinds on your window for a view unmatched anywhere in the world: Uluru as dawn strikes its ochre walls. Your bed, under a softly draped romantic white canopy, is in one of 15 five-star eco-sensitive "tents" set among isolated sand dunes a mile or two from the main resort complex. Each room is decorated in tribute to the European explorers and pioneers of this region. There's a CD player and MP3 docking station but no TV (and who needs one?). The central area, the **Dune House,** has a restaurant with superb food, a 24-hour bar, and a library. Settle in for some after-dinner chess or chat. For a special dining experience, book your place at **Table 131°**, where dinner is set up in style under the stars among gently rolling sand dunes. No children under 13.

Yulara Dr., Yulara, NT 0872. www.longitude131.com.au. ✆ **08/8957 7131.** 15 units. A$2,200 double. Rates include walking and bus tours, entry to the national park, meals, selected drinks. 2-night minimum. **Amenities:** Restaurant; bar; free airport shuttle; outdoor pool; no Wi-Fi or mobile phone access.

Outback Pioneer Hotel and Lodge ★ An all-ages crowd congregates at this midrange collection of hotel rooms, budget rooms, shared bunkrooms, and dorms. Standard hotel rooms offer clean, simple accommodations with private bathrooms, a queen-size bed, and a single; these have TVs with pay movies, a fridge, a minibar, and a phone. Budget rooms have access to a common room with a TV and Internet access, as well as a communal kitchen and laundry. Each quad bunkroom holds two sets of bunk beds; these are coed and share bathrooms. The single-sex dorms sleep 20. Plenty of lounge chairs sit by the pool. The **Bough House Restaurant** offers à la carte meals, and the **Outback Pioneer Kitchen** sells burgers, pizza, wraps, and sandwiches. What seems like the entire resort gathers nightly at the **Pioneer BBQ & Bar.** This barn with big tables, lots of beer, and live music is the place to join the throngs throwing a steak or sausage on the cook-it-yourself barbie (buy your meat at the bar).

Yulara Dr., Yulara, NT 0872. www.ayersrockresort.com.au/outback. ✆ **08/8957 7605.** 125 units, all with private bathroom; 12 budget rooms without bathroom; 30 budget rooms with bathroom; 32 quad bunkrooms; 20-bed male-only dorm without bathroom, 20-bed female-only dorm without bathroom. A$298–A$328 double standard room; A$240–A$260 budget room with bathroom; A$198–A$220 budget room without bathroom; A$46 quad share bed; A$38 dorm bed; A$184 budget quad room per room. **Amenities:** 2 restaurants; bar; free airport shuttle; Internet (A$2 for 10 min.); outdoor pool.

Sails in the Desert ★★★ This top-of-the-range hotel offers expensive, contemporary-style rooms with private balconies, many overlooking the pool, some with Jacuzzis. You can't see the Rock from your room, but most guests are too busy sipping cocktails by the pool to care. The pool area is shaded by white shade "sails" and surrounded by sun lounges. The lobby art gallery has artists in residence. The **Mayu** restaurant serves elegant à la carte fine-dining fare with bush-tucker ingredients, and **Ilkari** is a smart brasserie. The hotel's **Red Ochre Spa** is the only day spa at Yulara. It has four therapy rooms offering a range of treatments and therapies, with two rooms offering "dry" massage therapies and two "wet" rooms that have tubs on the veranda.

Yulara Dr., Yulara, NT 0872. www.ayersrockresort.com.au/sails. ✆ **08/8957 7417.** 228 units. A$440–A$498 double standard room; A$540–A$598 double terrace room; A$900–A$950 double deluxe suite. Extra person A$50. Children 12 and under stay free using existing bedding. **Amenities:** 2 restaurants, 2 bars; free airport shuttle; large outdoor pool; room service; 2 outdoor lighted tennis courts; Wi-Fi (A$10 /hr.; A$25 for 3 days).

Exploring Uluru

AT SUNRISE & SUNSET The peak time to catch the Rock's beauty is sunset, when oranges, peaches, pinks, reds, and then indigo and deep violet creep across its face. Some days it's fiery; other days the colors are muted. A sunset-viewing car park is on the Rock's western side. Plenty of sunset and sunrise tours operate from the resort, and many throw in a glass of wine to toast the end of the day as you watch. At sunrise, the colors are less dramatic, but many people enjoy the spectacle of Uluru unveiled by the

TO climb OR NOT TO CLIMB?

The Pitjantjatjara people refer to tourists as *minga*—little ants—because that's what they look like crawling up Uluru. Climbing this sacred rock is a fraught subject, one which Australians fall into two camps over: Those who have or want to and those who never will. I fall into the latter category. Climbing Uluru is against the wishes of the traditional owners, the Anangu ("the people," a term used by Aboriginal people from the Western Desert to refer to themselves), because of its deep spiritual significance to them. The climb follows the trail the ancestral Dreamtime Mala (rufous hare-wallaby) men took when they first came to Uluru, something you will hear about when you visit. While tourists are still allowed to climb, the traditional owners strongly prefer that they don't, and you will see signs and information to this effect.

Apart from respecting Uluru as a sacred place, there are several good practical reasons for resisting the temptation to undertake the 348m (1,142-ft.) hike. "The Rock" is dangerously steep and rutted with ravines about 2.5m (8¼ ft.) deep; and 36 people have died while climbing—either from heart attacks or falls—in the past five decades. The Anangu feel a duty to safeguard visitors to their land, and feel great sorrow and responsibility when visitors are killed or injured. The climb, by all accounts, is tough. There are sometimes strong winds, the walls are almost vertical in places (you have to hold onto a chain), and it can be freezing cold or maddeningly hot. Heat stress is a real danger. If you're unfit, have breathing difficulties, heart trouble, high or low blood pressure, or are scared of heights, don't do it. The climb takes at least 1 hour up for the fit, and 1 hour down. The less sure-footed should allow 3 to 4 hours. The Rock is closed to climbers during bad weather; when temperatures exceed 97°F (36°C), which they often do from November to March; and when wind speed exceeds 25 knots. It is closed at 8am daily in January and February because of the extreme heat.

The Australian government recognized the existence of the traditional Aboriginal owners in 1979 and created a national park to protect Uluru and Kata Tjuta. In 1983, the traditional owners were granted ownership of the land and the park was leased to the Australian National Parks and Wildlife Service for 99 years, with the agreement that the public could continue to climb it. The Australian government's 10-year management plan for Uluru decrees that the climb will close permanently if climber numbers drop to below 20% of all visitors to Uluru—and that target is close to being met, with an estimated 40,000 people climbing in 2012. In any case, visitors will be given 18 months' warning of any planned closure.

dawn to birdsong. You'll need an early start—most tours leave about 90 minutes before sunup. A typical sunrise tour is offered by **AAT Kings** (© **08/8956 2171;** ww.aatkings. com). It includes morning tea and costs A$59 for adults, A$30 for children 5 to 15. AAT Kings offers several other tours around the area, so if large-group touring is what you want, check out its website.

WALKING, DRIVING, OR BUSING AROUND IT A paved road runs around the Rock. The easy 9.4km (6-mile) **Base Walk** circumnavigating Uluru takes about 2 hours (the best time is early morning), but allow extra time to linger around the water holes, caves, folds, and overhangs that make up its walls. A shorter walk is the easy 1km (.6-mile) round-trip trail from the **Mutitjulu** parking lot to the pretty water hole near the Rock's base, where there is some rock art. The **Liru Track** is another easy trail; it runs 2km (1.2 miles) from the Cultural Centre to Uluru, where it links with the Base Walk.

Before setting off on any walk, it's a good idea to arm yourself with the self-guided walking notes available from the Cultural Centre (see "Visitor Information," above).

FLYING OVER IT   Several companies do scenic flights by light aircraft or helicopter over Uluru, Kata Tjuta (the Olgas), nearby Mount Conner, the vast white saltpan of Lake Amadeus, and as far as Kings Canyon. **Professional Helicopter Services** (✆ 08/ 8956 2003; www.phs.com.au), for example, does a 15-minute flight over Uluru for A$145 per person, and a 30-minute flight, which includes Kata Tjuta, for A$275, among others. Helicopters don't land on top of the Rock.

MOTORCYCLING AROUND IT   Harley-Davidson tours are available as sunrise or sunset rides, laps of the Rock, and various other Uluru and Kata Tjuta tours with time for walks. A blast out to the Rock at sunset with **Uluru Motorcycle Tours** (✆ 08/8956 2019; www.ulurucycles.com) will set you back A$170; it includes a glass of champagne. The guide drives the bike, and you sit behind and hang on.

VIEWING IT ON CAMELBACK   Legend has it that a soul travels at the same pace as a camel; it's certainly a peaceful way to see the Rock. **Uluru Camel Tours** (✆ 08/8956 3333; www.ulurucamel tours.com.au) makes daily forays aboard "ships of the desert" to view Uluru. Amble through red-sand dunes with great views of the Rock, dismount to watch the sun rise or sink over it, and ride back to the depot for billy tea and beer bread in the morning, or champagne in the evening. The 1-hour rides depart Ayers Rock Resort 1 hour before sunrise or 1½ hours before sunset and cost A$119 per person, including transfers from your hotel. All tours leave from the Camel Depot at the Ayers Rock Resort. Shorter rides are also available.

> ### Timing Your Trip
>
> Most tourists visit Uluru in the mornings and Kata Tjuta (the Olgas) in the afternoon. Reverse the order (do the Valley of the Winds walk in the morning and Uluru in the afternoon), and you'll likely find both spots a little more silent and spiritual.

Exploring Kata Tjuta

While it would be worth coming all the way to Central Australia just to see Uluru, there is a second unique natural wonder to see, just a 50km (31-mile) drive away. Kata Tjuta, or the Olgas, consists of 36 immense ochre rock domes rising from the desert, rivaling Uluru for spectacular beauty. Some visitors find it lovelier and more mysterious than Uluru. Known to the Aborigines as Kata Tjuta, or "many heads," the tallest dome is 200m (656 ft.) higher than Uluru, and Kata Tjuta figures more prominently in Aboriginal legend than Uluru.

This part of Australia's red heart was first discovered in the 1870s by English explorers. Ernest Giles named part of Kata Tjuta "Mount Olga" after the reigning

Queen Olga of Wurttemberg, while William Gosse gave Uluru the name "Ayers Rock" after Sir Henry Ayers, the Chief Secretary of South Australia.

Two walking trails take you in among the domes: the 7.4km (4.6-mile) **Valley of the Winds** ★★ walk, which is fairly challenging and takes 3 to 5 hours, and the easy 2.6km (1.6-mile) **Gorge** walk, which takes about an hour. The Valley of the Winds trail is the more rewarding in terms of scenery. Both have lookout points and shady stretches. The Valley of the Winds trail closes when temperatures rise above 97°F (36°C).

PLANNING YOUR TRIP TO AUSTRALIA

A little preparation is essential before you start your journey to Australia, especially if you plan to do any special-interest activities, such as diving the Great Barrier Reef. This chapter provides a variety of planning tools, including information on how to get there, and on-the-ground resources.

GETTING THERE

By Plane

Australia is a very long haul from anywhere except New Zealand. Sydney is a nearly 15-hour nonstop flight from Los Angeles, longer if you come via Honolulu. From the East Coast of the U.S., add 5½ hours. If you're coming from the States via Auckland, add transit time in New Zealand plus another three hours for the Auckland–Sydney leg. If you are coming from the United Kingdom, brace yourself for a flight of 12 hours, more or less, from London to Asia; then possibly a long day in transit, because flights to Australia have a habit of arriving in Asia early in the morning and departing around midnight; and finally the 8- to 9-hour flight to Australia.

Sydney (SYD), Cairns (CNS), Melbourne (MEL), and Brisbane (BNE) are all international gateways. Sydney is the major entry point into Australia, but you may also fly through another port first, depending where you're coming from.

By Boat

Sydney Harbour is Australia's main port for cruise ships and the only port in Australia with two dedicated cruise-passenger terminals—the Overseas Passenger Terminal at Circular Quay (in the heart of the city, close to major tourist attractions) and the recently opened White Bay Cruise Terminal in the suburb of Rozelle, about 5km from the city center. Melbourne and Brisbane are also major ports.

GETTING AROUND

By Plane

Australia is a big country with a small population to support its air routes, so airfares may be higher than you are used to paying. Don't assume there is a direct flight to your chosen destination, or that there is a flight every hour or even every day.

Most domestic air travel is operated by **Qantas** (ℰ **800/227-4500** in the U.S. and Canada, 13 13 13 in Australia, 208/600 4300 in the U.K., 1/407 3278 in Ireland, 09/357 8900 in Auckland, 0800/808 767 in New Zealand; www.qantas.com.au), **Virgin Australia** (ℰ **1855/253-8021** in the U.S., 13 67 89 or 07/3295 2296 in Australia, 0800/051-1281 in the U.K.; www.virginaustralia.com), or Qantas-owned **Jetstar** (ℰ **1866/397 8170** in the U.S., 13 15 38 in Australia, or 03/9645 5999; 0800/800 995 in New Zealand; www.jetstar.com.au). **Regional Express** (ℰ **13 17 13** or 02/6393 5550 in Australia; www.regionalexpress.com.au) serves regional New South Wales and Victoria.

Between them, Virgin Australia and Qantas and its subsidiaries, QantasLink and Jetstar, service every capital city, as well as most major regional towns on the east coast. Melbourne has two airports: the main international and domestic terminals at Tullamarine, and Avalon Airport, about 50km (31 miles) from the city, which is used by some Jetstar flights. Make sure you check which one your flight leaves from before you book.

Low-cost carrier **Tigerair** (ℰ **03/9034 3733** or 02/8073 3421; www.tigerairways.com) flies the all-important route between Melbourne and Sydney, as well as linking both cities with Alice Springs and Cairns. It also flies to the Queensland ports of Brisbane, Sunshine Coast, and Gold Coast, as well as other ports around the country.

Competition is hot, so it's likely that all airlines will have added to their route networks by the time you read this.

FARES FOR INTERNATIONAL TRAVELERS Qantas offers international travelers discounts off the full fares that Australians pay for domestic flights bought within Australia. To qualify, quote your passport number and international ticket number when reserving. Don't assume the fare for international travelers is the best deal, though—the latest deal in the market that day (or even better, perhaps, a package deal with accommodations thrown in) may be cheaper still.

AIR PASSES If you are visiting from the U.S. and plan on visiting more than one city, purchasing a Qantas **Walkabout AirPass** is much cheaper than buying regular fares. The pass is for economy-class travel only and must be purchased along with your Qantas or American Airlines fare from the U.S. to Australia. Prices vary according to which "zone" you are traveling to, offering more than 75 domestic Australia city pairs to choose from, but the deals will get you to all major destinations covered in this book.

By Car

Australia's roads sometimes leave a bit to be desired. The taxes of 21 million people get spread pretty thin when it comes to maintaining roads across a continent. Some "highways" are two-lane affairs with the occasional rut and pothole, often no outside line markings, and sometimes no shoulders to speak of. You will strike these if you plan to drive in the Red Centre.

If you plan long-distance driving, get a road map (see "Maps" below for sources) that marks paved and unpaved roads.

You can use your current driver's license or an international driver's permit in every state of Australia. By law, you must carry your license with you when driving. The minimum driving age is 16 or 17, depending on which state you visit, but some car-rental companies require you to be 21, or sometimes 26, if you want to rent a four-wheel-drive vehicle.

CAR RENTALS

Think twice about renting a car in tourist hot spots such as Cairns. In these areas most tour operators pick you up and drop you back at your hotel door, so having a car may not be worth the expense.

The "big four" car-rental companies–Avis, Budget, Hertz, and Thrifty—all have networks across Australia. Other major car-rental companies are Europcar, which has the third largest fleet in Australia, and Red Spot Car Rentals, which has depots in Sydney, Melbourne, Brisbane, Cairns, and some other major centers.

A small sedan for zipping around a city will cost about A$45 to A$80 a day. A feistier vehicle with enough grunt to get you from state to state will cost around A$70 to A$100 a day. Rentals of a week or longer usually reduce the price by A$5 a day or so.

A regular car will get you to most places in this book, except for some parts of the Red Centre, where you will need a four-wheel-drive vehicle. All the major car-rental companies rent them. Four-wheel-drives are more expensive than a regular car, but you can get them for as little as A$75 per day if you shop around (cheaper for rentals of a week or longer).

The rates quoted here are only a guide. Many smaller local companies—and the big guys, too—offer competitive specials, especially in tourist areas with distinct off-seasons. Advance purchase rates, usually 7 to 21 days ahead, can offer significant savings.

If you are concerned about reducing your carbon emissions, consider hiring a **hybrid car.** In Australia, all the "big five" major car-hire companies have the hybrid Toyota Prius available. Ask when making your bookings.

INSURANCE Insurance for loss of or damage to the car and third-party property insurance are usually included, but read the agreement carefully because the fine print contains information the front-desk staff may not tell you. For example, damage to the

Insurance Alert

Damage to a rental car caused by an animal (hitting a kangaroo, for instance) may not be covered by your car-rental company's insurance policies. Different car-rental companies have very different rules and restrictions, so make sure you check each one's coverage. For example, some will not cover animal damage incurred at night, while others don't have such limits. The same applies to the rules about driving on unpaved roads, of which Australia has many. Avis and Budget say you may only drive on roads "properly formed and constructed as a sealed, metalled, or gravel road," while the others limit you largely to sealed roads. Check the fine print.

car body may be covered, but not damage to the windshield or tires, or damage caused by water or driving too close to a bushfire.

The deductible, known as "excess" in Australia, on insurance may be as high as A$2,000 for regular cars and up to A$5,500 on four-wheel-drives and motor homes. You can reduce it, or avoid it altogether, by paying a premium of between about A$20 to A$50 per day on a car or four-wheel-drive, and around A$25 to A$50 per day on a motor home. The amount of the excess reduction premium depends on the vehicle type and the extent of reduction you choose. Your rental company may bundle personal accident insurance and baggage insurance into this premium. And again, check the conditions; some excess reduction payments do not reduce excesses on single-vehicle accidents, for example.

ONE-WAY RENTALS Australia's long distances often make one-way rentals a necessity, for which car-rental companies can charge a hefty penalty amounting to hundreds of dollars. A one-way fee usually applies to motor-home rentals, too—usually around A$260 to A$360. An extra A$650 remote-location fee can apply for Outback areas such as Alice Springs. And there are minimum rental periods of between 7 and 21 days.

MOTOR HOMES Motor homes (Aussies call them camper vans) are popular in Australia. Generally smaller than the RVs in the United States, they come in two-, three-, four-, or six-berth versions and usually have everything you need, such as a minifridge and/or freezer (icebox in the smaller versions), microwave, gas stove, cooking and cleaning utensils, linens, and touring information, including maps and campground guides. All have showers and toilets, except some two-berthers. Most have air-conditioned driver's cabins, but not all have air-conditioned living quarters, a necessity in most parts of the country from November through March. Four-wheel-drive campers are available, but they tend to be small, and some lack hot water, toilet, shower, and air-conditioning. Minimum driver age for motor homes is usually 21.

Australia's biggest national motor-home-rental companies are **Apollo Motorhome Holidays** (© **1800/777 779** in Australia, or 07/3265 9200; www.apollocamper.com), **Britz Campervan Rentals** (© **1800/331 454** in Australia or 800/2008 0801 from outside Australia; www.britz.com), and **Maui** (© **800/2008 0801** from anywhere in the world, or 1300/363 800 within Australia; www.maui.com.au).

Rates vary with the seasons and your choice of vehicle. May and June are the slowest months; December and January are the busiest. It's sometimes possible to get better rates by booking in your home country before departure. Renting for longer than 3 weeks knocks a few dollars off the daily rate. Most companies will demand a minimum 4- or 5-day rental. Give the company your itinerary before booking, because some routes may need the company's permission.

Most local councils take a dim view of "free camping," the practice of pulling over by the roadside to camp for the night. Instead, in most places you will have to stay in a campground—and pay for it.

ON THE ROAD

GAS The price of petrol (gasoline) will probably elicit a cry of dismay from Americans and a whoop of delight from Brits. Prices go up and down, but at press time you were looking at around A$1.58 a liter for unleaded petrol in Sydney, and A$1.72 a liter, or more, in the Outback. Most rental cars take unleaded gas, and motor homes run on diesel.

DRIVING RULES   Australians drive on the left, which means you give way to the right. Left turns on a red light are not permitted unless a sign says so.

Roundabouts (traffic circles) are common at intersections; approach these slowly enough to stop if you have to, and give way to all traffic on the roundabout. Flash your indicator as you leave the roundabout (even if you're going straight, because technically that's a left turn).

The only strange driving rule is Melbourne's requirement that drivers turn right from the left lane at certain intersections in the city center and in South Melbourne. This allows the city's trams to carry on uninterrupted in the right lane. Pull into the left lane opposite the street you are turning into, and make the turn when the traffic light in the street you are turning into becomes green. These intersections are signposted.

The maximum permitted blood alcohol level when driving is .05 percent, which equals approximately two 200-milliliter (6.6-oz.) drinks in the first hour for men, one for women, and one drink per hour for both sexes after that. The police set up random breath-testing units (RBTs) in cunningly disguised and unlikely places all the time, so getting caught is easy. You will face a court appearance if you do.

The speed limit is 50kmph (31 mph) or 60kmph (37 mph) in urban areas, 100kmph (62 mph) in most country areas, and sometimes 110kmph (68 mph) on freeways. In the Northern Territory, the speed limit is set at 130kmph (81 mph) on the Stuart, Arnhem, Barkly, and Victoria highways, while rural roads are designated 110kmph (68 mph) unless otherwise signposted. *Be warned:* The Territory has a high death toll. Speed-limit signs show black numbers circled in red on a white background.

Drivers and passengers, including taxi passengers, must wear a seatbelt at all times when the vehicle is moving forward, if the car is equipped with a belt. Young children are required to sit in the rear seat in a child-safety seat or harness; car-rental companies will rent these to you, but be sure to book them. Tell the taxi company you have a child when you book a cab so that it can send a car with the right restraints.

MAPS   The maps published by the state automobile clubs listed below in "Auto Clubs" will likely be free if you are a member of an affiliated auto club in your home country. None will mail them to you overseas; pick them up on arrival. Remember to bring your auto-club membership card to qualify for discounts or free maps.

Two of the biggest map publishers in Australia are **HEMA Maps** (✆ 07/3340 0000; www.hemamaps.com.au) and **UBD Gregory's** (✆ 02/9857 3700; www.hardiegrant. com.au). Both publish an extensive range of national (including road atlases), state, regional, and city maps. HEMA has a strong list of regional maps, while UBD Gregory's produces a complete range of street directories by city, region, or state. HEMA produces four-wheel-drive and motorbike road atlases and many regional four-wheel-drive maps—good if you plan to go off the trails. Many of its maps are also available as Apps.

TOLL ROADS   Electronic "beeper" or e-tags are used on all major Australian toll roads, including Melbourne's City Link motorways, Brisbane's Logan and Gateway motorways, the Sydney Harbour Bridge and tunnel and all Sydney's major tunnels and motorways. The tag is a small device attached to the front windscreen of the vehicle, which transmits signals to the toll points on the road. This deducts the toll amount from your toll account. The same e-tag can be used on all Australian toll roads. While some toll roads still have physical collection points at which you can pay the toll, others—such as Melbourne's freeways—don't. If you are likely to need an e-tag, your car-rental company can arrange one for you.

ROAD SIGNS   Australians navigate by road name, not road number. The easiest way to get where you're going is to familiarize yourself with the major towns along your route and follow the signs toward them.

AUTO CLUBS   Every state and territory in Australia has its own auto club. Your auto association back home probably has a reciprocal agreement with Australian clubs, which may entitle you to free maps, accommodations guides, and emergency roadside assistance. Don't forget to bring your membership card.

Even if you're not a member, the clubs are a good source of advice on local traffic regulations, touring advice, road conditions, traveling in remote areas, and any other motoring questions you may have. The clubs sell maps, accommodations guides, and camping guides to nonmembers at reasonable prices. They even share a website: **www.aaa.asn.au,** which lists numerous regional offices.

ROAD CONDITIONS & SAFETY

Here are some common motoring dangers and ways to avoid them:

FATIGUE   Fatigue is a killer on Australia's roads. The rule is to take a 20-minute break every 2 hours, even if you don't feel tired. In some states, "driver reviver" stations operate on major roads during holiday periods. They serve free tea, coffee, and cookies and are often found at roadside picnic areas that have restrooms.

KANGAROOS & OTHER WILDLIFE   It's a sad fact, but kangaroos are a road hazard. Avoid driving in country areas between dusk and dawn, when 'roos are most active. If you hit one, always stop and check its pouch for live joeys (baby kangaroos), because females usually have one in the pouch. Wrap the joey tightly in a towel or old sweater, don't feed or overhandle it, and take it to a vet in the nearest town or call one of the following wildlife care groups: **Wildlife Information & Rescue Service (WIRES)** in New South Wales (✆ **1300/094 737**); **Wildlife Victoria** (✆ **1300/094 535**); **Wildcare Australia** in Queensland (✆ **07/5527 2444**); **Wildcare** in Alice Springs (✆ **0419/221 128**). Most vets will treat native wildlife for free.

Some highways run through unfenced stations (ranches), where sheep and cattle pose a threat. Cattle like to rest on the warm bitumen road at night, so put your lights on high to spot them. If an animal does loom up, slow down—but never swerve, or you may roll. If you have to, hit it. Tell farmers within 24 hours if you have hit their livestock.

Car-rental companies will not insure for animal damage to the car, which should give you an inkling of how common an occurrence this is.

ROAD TRAINS   Road trains consist of as many as three big truck carriages linked together to make a "train" up to 54m (177 ft.) long. If you're in front of one, give the driver plenty of warning when you brake, because the trains need a lot of distance to slow down. Allow at least 1 clear kilometer (over a half mile) before you pass one, but don't expect the driver to make it easy—"truckies" are notorious for their lack of concern for motorists.

UNPAVED ROADS   Many country roads are unsealed (unpaved). They are usually bone-dry, which makes them more slippery than they look, so travel at a moderate speed—35kmph (22 mph) is not too cautious, and anything over 60kmph (37 mph) is dangerous. That said, when you are on a heavily corrugated or rutted road (which many are), you may need to keep to a higher speed (60kmph/37 mph) just to stay on top of them. Don't overcorrect if you veer to one side. Keep well behind any vehicles, because the dust they throw up can block your vision.

FLOODS   Floods are common north of Cairns from November or December through March or April (the "Wet" season). Never cross a flooded road unless you are sure of its depth. Crocodiles may be in the water, so do not wade in to test it! Fast-flowing water is dangerous, even if it's very shallow. When in doubt, stay where you are and wait for the water to drop; most flash floods subside in 24 hours. Check the road conditions ahead at least once a day in the Wet season.

RUNNING OUT OF GAS   Gas stations (also called "roadhouses" in rural areas) can be few and far between in the Outback, so fill up at every opportunity.

WHAT IF YOUR VEHICLE BREAKS DOWN?

Warning: If you break down or get lost, never leave your vehicle. Many a motorist—often an Aussie who should have known better—has died wandering off on a crazy quest for help or water, knowing full well that neither is to be found for maybe hundreds of miles. Most people who get lost do so in Outback spots; if that happens to you, conserve your body moisture by doing as little as possible and staying in the shade of your car.

EMERGENCY ASSISTANCE

The emergency breakdown assistance telephone number for every Australian auto club is © **13 11 11** from anywhere in Australia. It is billed as a local call. If you are not a member of an auto club at home that has a reciprocal agreement with the Australian clubs, you'll have to join the Australian club on the spot before the club will tow or repair your car. This usually costs around A$80, not a big price to pay when you're stranded—although in the Outback, the charge may be considerably higher. Most car-rental companies also have emergency assistance numbers.

TIPS FOR FOUR-WHEEL DRIVERS

Always keep to the four-wheel-drive track. Going off-road causes soil erosion, a significant environmental problem in Australia. Leave gates as you found them. Obtain permission from the owners before venturing onto private station (ranch) roads. On an extended trip or in remote areas, carry 5 liters (1⅓ gallons) of drinking water per person per day (dehydration occurs fast in the Australian heat); enough food to last 3 or 4 days more than you think you will need; a first-aid kit; spare fuel; a jack and two spare tires; spare fan belts, radiator hoses, and air-conditioner hoses; a tow rope; and a good map that marks all gas stations. In seriously remote areas outside the scope of this book, carry a high-frequency and a CB radio. (A mobile phone may not work in the Outback.) Advise a friend, your hotel manager, the local tourist bureau, or a police station of your route and your expected time of return or arrival at your destination.

By Train

Australia's trains are clean, comfortable, and safe, and for the most part service standards and facilities are perfectly adequate. The rail network in Australia links Perth to Adelaide and continues on to Melbourne and north to Sydney, Brisbane, and Cairns. There's also a line from Adelaide to Alice Springs and Darwin. Trains generally cost more than buses but are still reasonably priced.

Most long-distance trains have sleepers with big windows, air-conditioning, electric outlets, wardrobes, sinks, and fresh sheets and blankets. First-class sleepers have ensuite (attached private) bathrooms, and fares often include meals. Second-class sleepers use shared shower facilities, and meals are not included. Some second-class sleepers are private cabins; on other trains you share with strangers. Single cabins are usually of broom-closet dimensions but surprisingly comfy, with their own toilet and basin. The food ranges from mediocre to pretty good. Smoking is banned on all Australian rail networks.

Different entities manage Australia's rail routes. They include the government-owned **Queensland Rail** (✆ **131 617** in Australia or 07/3072 2222; www.queenslandrail.com.au), which handles rail within that state and **NSW TrainLink** (✆ **13 22 32** in Australia or 02/4907 7501; www.nswtrainlink.info), which manages travel within New South Wales and from Sydney to south to Melbourne and north to Brisbane. **Great Southern Rail**'s *Southern Spirit* (✆ **13 21 47** in Australia or 08/8213 4592; www.gsr.com.au) links Adelaide, Melbourne and Brisbane seasonally, in January and February, and has a range of other fabulous Outback train journeys.

Queensland Rail operates two trains on the Brisbane-Cairns route: The *Sunlander* runs three times a week from Brisbane to Cairns, offering a choice of the premium, all-inclusive Queenslander Class; single-, double-, or triple-berth sleepers; or economy seats. The high-speed **Tilt Train** operates twice-weekly trips on the same route in less time—by about 5 hours—with business-class-style seating. All Queensland and New South Wales long-distance trains stop at most towns en route, so they're useful for exploring the eastern states.

RAIL PASSES NSW TrainLink's **Backtracker** pass gives you unlimited economy class trips on all its train and coach services in both directions between Melbourne and Brisbane (and some NSW inland cities) for up to 6 months. A 14-day pass costs A$232, a 1-month pass A$275, a 3-month pass A$298, and a 6-month pass A$420. Prices are about 10 percent cheaper if you buy before arriving in Australia. Backtracker passes are available only to overseas visitors holding non-Australian passports and return airline tickets.

The **East Coast Discovery** rail pass covers travel between Melbourne and Brisbane. It provides 6 months of unlimited one-way travel in economy seating on coastal trains between Brisbane, Sydney, and Melbourne. Fares range from A$130 for Sydney–Brisbane or Sydney–Melbourne services to A$220 for Melbourne–Brisbane.

The **Queensland Explorer** pass offers unlimited economy seat travel for 3 or 6 months across the Queensland Rail network, from Cairns in the north to the Gold Coast in the south, and in the Queensland outback. It costs A$409 for 3 months or A$579 for 6 months.

By Bus

Bus travel in Australia is as comfortable as it can be, given the nature of coach travel. Terminals are centrally located and well lit, the buses—called "coaches" Down Under—are clean and air-conditioned, you sit in adjustable seats, videos play onboard, and drivers are polite and sometimes even point out places of interest along the way. Buses are all nonsmoking and some have restrooms. The extensive bus network will take you almost everywhere.

Australia has one national coach operator: **Greyhound Australia** (📞 **1300/473 946** in Australia or 07/3236 3035; www.greyhound.com.au; no relation to Greyhound in the U.S.). In addition to point-to-point services, Greyhound Australia also offers a limited range of tours at popular locations on its networks, including Uluru and the Great Ocean Road in Victoria.

Fares and some passes are considerably cheaper for students, backpacker cardholders, and Hostelling International/YHA members.

BUS PASSES Bus passes are a great value. There are several kinds: hop-on-hop-off passes, mini passes, and kilometer passes. Note that even with a pass, you may still need to book the next leg of your trip 12 or 24 hours ahead as a condition of the pass; during school vacation periods, which are always busy, booking as much as a week ahead is smart.

Greyhound Australia's **Micro Passes** let you travel between two destinations, with limited stops over 10 to 14 days, as long as you don't backtrack.

Hop-on-hop-off **Mini Traveller Passes** are valid for 90 days and link most of the popular destinations. Travel from Melbourne to Cairns costs A$472. Mini passes can be bought for a range of destinations around Australia.

The **Kilometre Pass,** valid for 12 months, allows unlimited stops in any direction within the mileage you buy. Passes are available for 1,000km (620 miles) for A$188, and then in increments of 1,000km (620 miles). A 2,000km (1,240 miles) pass—enough to get you from Brisbane to Cairns—will cost A$377, and from there you can go up to A$2,777 for a whopping 25,000km (15,535 miles).

[FastFACTS] AUSTRALIA

ATMs/Banks The easiest and best way to get cash away from home is from an **ATM (automated teller machine),** sometimes referred to as a "cash machine" or a "cashpoint." The **Cirrus** (www.mastercard.com) and **PLUS** (www.visa.com) networks span the globe. Go to your bank card's website to find ATM locations at your destination. Be sure you know your daily withdrawal limit before you depart. Australian ATMs use a four-digit code, so check with your bank and make sure you change yours before you leave. **Note:** Many banks impose a fee every time you use a card at another bank's ATM, and that fee can be higher for international transactions (A$5 or more) than for domestic ones (usually A$2 or A$2.50). In addition, the bank from which you withdraw cash may charge its own fee. For international withdrawal fees, ask your bank.

Customs The duty-free allowance in Australia is A$900 or, for those under 18, A$450. Anyone over 18 can bring in up to 50 cigarettes or 50 grams of cigars or other tobacco products, 2.25 liters (41 fluid oz.) of alcohol, and "dutiable goods" to the value of A$900 or A$450 if you are under 18. "Dutiable goods" are luxury items such as perfume, watches, jewelry, furs, plus gifts of any kind. Keep this in mind if you intend to bring presents for family and friends in Australia; gifts given to you also count toward the dutiable limit. Personal goods that you're taking with you are usually exempt from duty, but if you are returning with valuable goods that you already own, file form B263. Customs officers do not collect duty—less than A$50—as long as you declared the goods in the first place.

A helpful brochure, available from Australian consulates or Customs offices, as well as online, is *Know Before You Go*. For more information, contact the **Customs Information and Support Centre** (℅ **1300/ 363 263** in Australia, or 02/9313 3010), or check out **www.customs.gov.au.**

You need not declare cash in any currency, and other currency instruments, such as traveler's checks, under a value of A$10,000.

Australia is a signatory to the **Convention on International Trade in Endangered Species** (CITES), which restricts or bans the import of products made from protected wildlife. Banned items include ivory, tortoise (marine turtle) shell, rhinoceros or tiger products, and sturgeon caviar. Bear

this in mind if you stop in other countries en route to Australia, where souvenirs made from items like these may be sold. Australian authorities may seize these items.

Because Australia is an island, it is free of many agricultural and livestock diseases. To keep it that way, **strict quarantine** applies to importing plants, animals, and their products, including food. "Sniffer" dogs at airports detect these products (as well as drugs). Some items may be confiscated, and others may be held over for you to take with you when you leave the country. Heavy fines apply to breaches of the laws. Amnesty trash bins are available before you reach the immigration counters in airport arrivals halls for items such as fruit. Don't be alarmed if, just before landing, the flight attendants spray the aircraft cabin (with products approved by the World Health Organization) to kill potentially disease-bearing insects. For more information on what is and is not allowed, contact the nearest Australian embassy or consulate, or Australia's Department of Agriculture, Fisheries, and Forestry (℅ **02/6272 3933;** www. daff.gov.au/biosecurity), which is in charge of biosecurity in Australia.

For information on what you're allowed to bring home, contact one of the following agencies:

U.S. Citizens: U.S. Customs & Border Protection (CBP), 1300 Pennsylvania Ave., NW, Washington, DC 20229 (℅ **877/CBP 5111;** www. cbp.gov).

Canadian Citizens: Canada Border Services Agency, Ottawa, Ontario, K1A 0L8 (℅ **800/461-9999** in Canada, or 204/983-3500; www. cbsa-asfc.gc.ca).

U.K. Citizens: Border Force, Lunar House, 11th floor Long Corridor, 40 Wellesley Rd, Croydon, CR9 2BY (www.ukba.homeoffice. gov.uk).

New Zealand Citizens: Auckland City Customhouse, 50 Anzac Ave., Auckland, (℅ **09/927-8036** or 0800/428-786 in New Zealand; www.customs.govt.nz).

Disabled Travelers

Most disabilities shouldn't stop anyone from traveling to Australia. There are more options and resources than ever before. Most hotels, major stores, attractions, and public restrooms in Australia have wheelchair access. Many smaller lodges and even B&Bs are starting to cater to guests with disabilities, and some diving companies cater to scuba divers with disabilities. National parks make an effort to include wheelchair-friendly pathways. Taxi companies in bigger cities can usually supply a cab equipped for wheelchairs.

TTY facilities are still limited largely to government services. For information on all kinds of facilities and services (not just travel-related organizations) for people with disabilities, contact **National Information Communication Awareness Network,** Unit 5, 48 Brookes St., Mitchell ACT 2911 (✆ **1800/806 769** voice and TTY in Australia, or 02/6241 1220; www. nican.com.au). This free service can put you in touch with accessible accommodations and attractions throughout Australia, as well as with travel agents and tour operators who understand your needs.

Doctors & Hospitals

Doctors are listed under "M," for "Medical Practitioners," in the Yellow Pages, and most large towns and cities have 24-hour clinics. Your hotel may be able to help you find a local doctor. Failing that, go to the local emergency room. See "Fast Facts" in other chapters of this book for local details.

Drinking Laws

Hours vary from pub to pub, but most are open daily from around 10am or noon to 10pm or midnight. The minimum drinking age is 18. Random breath tests to catch drunk drivers are common, and drunk-driving laws are strictly enforced. Getting caught drunk behind the wheel will mean a court appearance, not just a fine. The maximum permitted blood-alcohol level is .05 percent. Alcohol is sold in liquor stores, in the "bottle shops" attached to every

pub, and in some states in supermarkets.

Electricity

The current is 240 volts AC, 50 hertz. Sockets take two or three flat, not rounded, prongs. Bring a connection kit of the right power and phone adapters, a spare phone cord, and a spare Ethernet network cable—or find out whether your hotel supplies them to guests. North Americans and Europeans will need to buy a converter before they leave home. (Don't wait until you get to Australia, because Australian stores are likely to stock only converters for Aussie appliances to fit American and European outlets.) Some large hotels have 110V outlets for electric shavers (or dual voltage), and some will lend converters, but don't count on it in smaller, less expensive hotels, motels, or B&Bs. Power does not start automatically when you plug in an appliance; you need to flick the switch beside the socket to the "on" position.

Embassies & Consulates

Most diplomatic posts are in Canberra. **Canada:** High Commission of Canada, Commonwealth Avenue, Yarralumla, ACT 2600 (✆ **02/6270 4000**); **Ireland:** Consulate General of Ireland, Level 26, 1 Market St., Sydney, NSW 2000 (✆ **02/9264 9635**); **New Zealand:** New Zealand High Commission, Commonwealth Avenue, Canberra, ACT 2601 (✆ **02/6270**

4211); **United Kingdom:** British High Commission, Commonwealth Avenue, Canberra, ACT 2601 (✆ **02/ 6270 6666**); **United States:** United States Embassy, 21 Moonah Place, Yarralumla, ACT 2600 (✆ **02/6214 5600**).

Emergencies

Dial ✆ **000** anywhere in Australia for police, ambulance, or the fire department. This is a free call from public and private telephones and needs no coins. The TTY emergency number is ✆ **106.**

Family Travel

Australians travel widely with their own kids, so facilities for families, including family passes to attractions, are common.

A great accommodations option for families is Australia's huge stock of serviced or unserviced apartments (with or without daily maid service). Often less expensive than a hotel room, they offer a living room, a kitchen, a bathroom or two, and the privacy of a separate bedroom for adults. Most Australian hotels will arrange babysitting when given a day's notice.

International airlines and domestic airlines in Australia charge 75% of the adult fare for kids under 12. Most charge 10% for infants under 2 not occupying a seat. Australian transport companies, attractions, and tour operators typically charge half-price for kids under 12 or 14 years.

Many Australian resorts have "kids' clubs" with extensive programs designed for children under 12 and, in some cases, teenagers. Others resorts have "kids stay, eat, and play free" offers, particularly during holiday periods. Many hotels will offer connecting units or "family rooms." Ask when booking.

Don't forget that children entering Australia on their parent's passport still need their own visa.

Resources for Family Travel: Rascals in Paradise (𝒞 **415/273-2224;** www.rascalsinparadise.com) is a San Francisco–based company specializing in family vacation packages to Australia. The Australian travel magazine **Holidays with Kids** has a comprehensive website listing great options for family travel in Australia (www.holidayswithkids.com.au). **Family Travel Forum** is also a good resource; see **www.myfamilytravels.com** for destinations, ideas, and more.

Health No vaccinations are needed to enter Australia unless you have been in a yellow fever danger zone—that is, South America or Africa—in the 6 days prior to entering.

Australian pharmacists may only fill prescriptions written by Australian doctors, so carry enough medication with you for your trip. Doctors are listed under "M," for "Medical Practitioners," in the yellow pages,

and most large towns and cities have 24-hour clinics. Failing that, go to the local hospital emergency room.

Generally, you don't have to worry much about health issues on a trip to Australia. Hygiene standards are high, hospitals are modern, and doctors and dentists are well qualified. Because of the continent's size, however, you can sometimes be a long way from a hospital or a doctor. Remote areas are served by the Royal Flying Doctor Service. But it may be advisable to purchase standard medical travel insurance.

○ **Tropical Illnesses** Some parts of tropical far-north Queensland have sporadic outbreaks of the mosquito-borne dengue fever. The areas affected include Cairns, Port Douglas, and Townsville. But as dengue-fever mosquitoes breed in urban environments, tourist activities in north Queensland such as reef and rainforest trips carry a low risk. The risk can be further minimized by staying in screened or air-conditioned accommodations, using insect repellent at all times, and wearing long, loose, light-colored clothing that covers arms and legs.

○ **Bugs, Bites & Other Wildlife Concerns** Snake and spider bites may not be as common as the hair-raising stories you will hear would suggest, but it pays to be wary. Your other concerns should be marine life, including jellyfish, and saltwater crocodiles. For more information and background on the fauna of Australia, and how to avoid dangerous encounters with them (see p. 31).

○ **Sun/Elements** Australians have the world's highest death rate from skin cancer because of the country's intense sunlight. Limit your exposure to the sun, especially during the first few days of your trip, and from 11am to 3pm in summer and 10am to 2pm in winter. Remember that UV rays reflected off walls, water, and the ground can burn you even when you're not in direct sunlight. Use a broad-spectrum sunscreen with a high protection factor (SPF 30 or higher). Wear a broad-brimmed hat that covers the back of your neck, ears, and face (a baseball cap won't do it), and a long-sleeved shirt. Remember that children need more protection than adults do. Don't even think about traveling without sunglasses, or you'll spend your entire vacation squinting against Australia's "diamond light."

o **Extreme Weather Exposure** Cyclones sometimes affect tropical areas, such as Queensland's coastal regions, from about Gladstone north, during January and February. Serious damage is normally rare.

Insurance Standard medical and travel insurance is advisable for travel to Australia. Divers should also ensure they have the appropriate insurance. For information on traveler's insurance, trip cancelation insurance, and medical insurance while traveling, please visit www.frommers.com/tips.

Internet Access Most hotels throughout Australia offer dataports for laptop modems, high-speed Internet access, and Wi-Fi. Check the list of hotel amenities in each hotel listing to see what kind of Internet service your hotel offers.

Aside from cybercafes, most **youth hostels** and **public libraries** have Internet access. Avoid **hotel business centers** unless

you're willing to pay exorbitant rates. Cybercafes (called Internet cafes in Australia) can be found almost everywhere. In major tourist cities there are entire streets full of them. Most major airports have **Internet kiosks** that provide basic Web access for a per-minute fee that's usually higher than cybercafe prices. To find cybercafes in your destination, check **www.cybercafe.com.** For help locating cybercafes and other establishments where you can go for Internet access, please see the "Fast Facts" sections in other chapters of this book.

Legal Aid If you find yourself in trouble with the long arm of the law while visiting Australia, the first thing you should do is contact your country's embassy or nearest consulate in Australia. See contact details for Canberra diplomatic posts under "Embassies & Consulates" above. Embassies or consulates with posts in state capitals are listed in "Fast Facts," in the relevant state chapters of this book. The U.S. Embassy considers an "emergency" to be either your arrest or the loss of your passport. If arrested in Australia, you will have to go through the Australian legal process for being charged, prosecuted, possibly convicted and sentenced, and for any appeals process. However, U.S. consular officers (and those of other countries) provide a

wide variety of services to their citizens arrested abroad and their families. These may include providing a list of local attorneys to help you get legal representation, providing information about judicial procedures, and notifying your family and/or friends, if you wish. However, they cannot demand your release, represent you at your trial, give you legal advice, or pay your fees or fines.

LGBT Travelers Sydney is one of the most gay-friendly cities in the world, and across most of Australia the gay community has a high profile and lots of support services. There are plenty of gay and lesbian bars, and most Saturday nights see a privately operated gay dance party taking place in an inner-city warehouse somewhere. The cafes and pubs of Oxford Street in Darlinghurst, a short cab ride or long stroll from Sydney's downtown area, are the liveliest gay spots. The annual **Sydney Gay & Lesbian Mardi Gras,** culminating in a huge street parade and party in late February or early March, is a high point on the city's calendar.

In rural areas of Australia, you may still encounter a little conservative resistance to gays and lesbians, but Australians everywhere are generally open-minded. Noosa, on Queensland's Sunshine Coast, is a favored destination for revelers after Mardi Gras, and a couple of resorts in north Queensland cater to gay and lesbian travelers. One of the best known is **Turtle Cove Beach Resort** (𝄞 **1300/727 979** in Australia, or 07/4059 1800; www.turtlecove.com), on a private beach between Cairns and Port Douglas.

LGBT Resources: Some services you may find useful are the **Gay & Lesbian Counselling Service of NSW** (𝄞 **02/8594 9596**), which runs a national hotline (𝄞 **1800/184 527** in Australia) from 5:30 to 9:30pm daily. Its website, **www.glcsnsw.org.au,** has lots of useful information. In Sydney, the **Albion Street Centre** (𝄞 **02/9332 9600** for administration or 02/9332 9700 for the information line) is a HIV clinic and information service. **The International Gay and Lesbian Travel Association** (**IGLTA;** 𝄞 **954/630-1637** in the U.S.; www.iglta.org) is the trade association for the gay and lesbian travel industry and offers an online directory of gay- and lesbian-friendly travel businesses and tour operators. **Gay & Lesbian Tourism Australia** (www.galta. com.au) has listings of businesses in each state.

Mail & Postage A postcard costs A$1.70 to send anywhere in the world. A letter (up to 50g in weight) will cost A$1.75 to send to New Zealand, or A$2.60 to the U.S., Canada or U.K. A card or letter will take 4 to 6 working days to reach North America or Europe. A parcel of up to 20kg will cost A$13.70 to send to the United States by airmail.

Mobile Phones The three letters that define much of the world's wireless capabilities are **GSM** (Global System for Mobile Communications), a big, seamless network that makes for easy cross-border cellphone use throughout Europe and dozens of other countries worldwide. In the U.S., T-Mobile and AT&T Wireless use this quasi-universal system; in Canada, Microcell and some Rogers customers are GSM; and all Europeans and most Australians use GSM. GSM phones function with a removable plastic SIM card, encoded with your phone number and account information. If your cellphone is on a GSM system, and you have a world-capable multiband phone, you can make and receive calls around much of the globe. Just call your wireless operator and ask for "international roaming" to be activated on your account. But be sure to check the cost of "data roaming" on smart phones, because the cost can be astronomical, and you do not want a nasty (and I mean *really* nasty!) surprise on your return home when you get the bill. Unless you turn off your data roaming, it will activate automatically.

For many, **renting** a phone is a good idea. While you can rent a phone from any number of overseas sites, including kiosks at airports and at car-rental agencies, we suggest renting the phone before you leave home. North Americans can rent one before leaving home from **InTouch U.S.A.** (𝄞 **800/872-7626;** www. intouchglobal.com) or **RoadPost** (𝄞 **888/290-1616** or 905/272-5665; www.roadpost.com). InTouch will also, for free, advise you on whether your existing phone will work overseas; simply call 𝄞 **703/ 222-7161** between 9am and 4pm EST, or go to **http://intouchglobal.com/ travel.htm.**

In Australia—reputed to have one of the world's highest per-capita rates of ownership of "mobile" telephones, as they are known here—the cell network is digital, not analog. Calls to or from a mobile telephone are generally more expensive than calls to or from a fixed telephone. The price varies depending on the telephone company, the time of day, the distance between caller and recipient, and the telephone's pricing plan.

Buying a prepaid phone can be economically attractive. Once you arrive in Australia, stop by a local cellphone shop and get the cheapest package; you'll probably pay less than A$100 for a phone and a starter calling card with a significant amount of free credit.

In Australia, the mobile phone company **Vodafone** (© **1300/300 404** in Australia; www.vodafone.com.au) has outlets at Brisbane international airport and at both international and domestic terminals in Sydney selling SIMs, handsets, and mobile broadband. **Optus** (© **1300/768 453** in Australia; www.optus.com.au) has stores at Sydney and Melbourne airports. Charges vary depending on the kind of phone and coverage you want, but some of the benefits include one low call rate throughout Australia, free incoming calls, international direct-dialing access, text messaging and voicemail. Alternatively, you are able to rent a mobile phone or SIM card for your existing mobile phone to stay in touch while you're traveling.

Money & Costs The Australian dollar is divided into A100¢. Coins are A5¢, A10¢, A20¢, and A50¢ pieces (silver) and A$1 and A$2 pieces (gold). Prices often end in a variant of A1¢ and A2¢ (for example, A78¢ or A$2.71), a relic from the days before 1-cent and 2-cent pieces were phased out. Prices are rounded to the nearest A5¢—so A77¢ rounds down to A75¢, and A78¢ rounds up to A80¢. Bank notes come in denominations of A$5, A$10, A$20, A$50, and A$100.

Frommer's lists exact prices in the local currency. However, rates fluctuate, so before departing consult a currency exchange website such as **www.oanda.com/currency/converter** to check up-to-the-minute rates.

You should consider changing a small amount of money into Australian currency before you leave (though don't expect the exchange rate to be ideal), so you can avoid lines at airport ATMs or exchange desks. You can exchange money at your local American Express or Thomas Cook office or your bank.

If you're using a **credit card,** note that Visa and MasterCard are universally accepted in Australia; American Express and Diners Club are less common; and Discover is not used. Always carry a little cash, because many merchants will not take cards for purchases under A$10 or so.

Beware of hidden credit-card **fees** while traveling. Check with your credit or debit card issuer to see what fees, if any, will be charged for overseas transactions. Fees can amount to 3% or more of the purchase price. Check with your bank before departing to avoid any surprise charges on your statement.

For help with currency conversions, tip calculations, and more, download Frommer's convenient **Travel Tools app** for your mobile

device. Go to www.frommers.com/go/mobile and click on the Travel Tools icon.

Newspapers & Magazines The national daily newspaper is *The Australian,* which publishes an expanded edition with a color magazine on Saturday. All capital cities have their own daily papers. Newspapers and magazines can be bought at a wide range of places including newsagents, supermarkets, gas stations, and convenience stores.

Packing Tips Dressing in layers (and packing layers) is the best way of kitting yourself out for Australia. Depending on where you are going in Australia—and the season—you will need different gear. For example, if you are visiting Queensland or central Australia in the summer, pack only light clothing (but always throw in a little something warm just in case!). But if you're heading for Victoria in winter you'll need full cold-weather outfits. Wherever and whenever you go, take a light rain jacket: Summer in the tropics can often be quite wet! Most restaurants in Australia accept "smart casual" dress; in the cities you will need proper shoes (no thongs/flip-flops) and often (for men) a shirt with a collar to dine in most places. For more helpful information on packing for your trip, download our convenient Travel

Tools app for your mobile device. Go to www.frommers.com/go/mobile and click on the Travel Tools icon.

Police Dial 🕐 **000** anywhere in Australia. This is a free call from public and private telephones and requires no coins.

Safety Travelers to Australia should follow the same precautions against petty theft and potential identity theft as they would at home or in any other country. Violent crime is, of course, not uncommon, but you are not likely to become a target in the normal course of your travels.

Driving probably poses one of the greatest risks to visitors to Australia. Australians drive on the left, something that North American and European visitors often have difficulty remembering. Drivers and passengers, including taxi passengers, must wear a seatbelt at all times, by law. Avoid driving between dusk and dawn in country areas, because this is when kangaroos and other wildlife are most active, and a collision with a 'roo is something to be avoided at all costs, for both party's sakes. Road trains—as many as three big truck carriages linked together, which can be up to 54m (177 ft.) long—are another danger to look out for, particularly when you are in the Outback.

Warning: If you break down or get lost, *never*

leave your vehicle. Most people who get lost do so in Outback spots, and those who wander off to look for help or water usually die in the attempt. If it happens to you, stay with your car. See "By Car" in the "Getting Around" section, p. 219.

Senior Travel Seniors—often called "pensioners" in Australia—from other countries don't always qualify for the discounted entry prices to tours, attractions, and events that Australian seniors enjoy, but it is always worth asking. Inquire about discounts when booking hotels, flights, and train or bus tickets. The best ID to bring is something that shows your date of birth or that marks you as an "official" senior, such as a membership card from AARP.

Senior Resources: Many reliable agencies and organizations target the 50-plus market. **Road Scholar** (formerly Elderhostel; 🕐 **800/454-5768** in the U.S.; www.roadscholar.org) arranges worldwide study programs—including to Australia—for those ages 55 and over. In Australia, pick up a copy of **Get Up & Go** (www.getupandgo.com.au), the only national travel magazine for the over-50 crowd and the official Seniors Card travel magazine. It's a glossy quarterly, available at most newsstands, with an extensive section called "Destination Australia," which covers a

region in each state/territory in every issue.

Smoking Smoking is banned in most indoor public places throughout the country, including government buildings, museums, cinemas, theaters, restaurants and airports (and on all aircraft). In Queensland you are not allowed to smoke on a patrolled beach or near children's playgrounds; in Victoria you may find that some pubs have outdoor (or rooftop) smoking areas. Laws vary from state to state, so the safest thing is to ask before you light up.

Student Travel Australia has agreements with many countries, including the U.S., Canada, and the U.K., that give students between 18 and 30 years old the right to apply for a "working holiday" visa to stay in Australia for up to 12 months. You must apply for your visa outside of Australia, show evidence of your student or recent graduate status, and hold a return ticket as well as sufficient funds for the first part of your stay. For more information, check the website **www.immi.gov.au/visitors.**

Check out the **ISIC Association** (www.isic.org) website for comprehensive travel-services information and details on how to get an **International Student Identity Card (ISIC),** which qualifies students for substantial savings on rail passes, plane tickets, entrance fees, and more. It also provides students with basic health and life insurance and a 24-hour helpline. The card is valid for a maximum of 16 months. You can apply for the card online or in person at **STA Travel,** the biggest student travel agency in the world; check out the website (www.statravel.com) to locate STA Travel offices worldwide. If you're no longer a student but are still under 26, you can get an **International Youth Travel Card (IYTC),** which entitles you to some discounts. **Travel CUTS** (☎ **800/667-2887;** www.travelcuts.com) offers similar services for Canadians and U.S. residents. Irish students may prefer to turn to **USIT** (☎ **01/602-1906;** www.usit.ie), an Ireland-based specialist in student, youth, and independent travel.

Taxes   Australia applies a 10 percent Goods and Services Tax (GST) on most products and services. Your international airline tickets to Australia are not taxed, nor are domestic airline tickets for travel within Australia *if you bought them outside Australia.* If you buy Australian airline tickets once you arrive in Australia, you will pay GST on them. Items bought in duty-free stores will not be charged GST. Nor will items you export—such as an Aboriginal painting that you buy in a gallery in Alice Springs and have shipped straight to your home outside Australia.

Basic groceries are not GST-taxed, but restaurant meals are.

Through the **Tourist Refund Scheme** (TRS), Australians and international visitors can claim a refund of the GST (and of a 14½% wine tax called the Wine Equalisation Tax, or WET) paid on a purchase of more than A$300 from a single outlet, within the last 60 days before you leave. More than one item may be included in that A$300. For example, you can claim the GST you paid on 10 T-shirts, each worth A$30, as long as they were bought from a single store. Do this as you leave by presenting your receipt or "tax invoice" to the Australian Customs Service's TRS booths, in the International Terminal departure areas at most airports. Items must be taken as carry-on baggage, because you must show them to Customs. You can use the goods before you leave Australia and still claim the refund, but you cannot claim a refund on things you have consumed (film you use, say, or food). You cannot claim a refund on alcohol other than wine. Claims at airports are available up to 30 minutes before your flight's scheduled departure.

You can also claim a refund if you leave Australia as a cruise passenger from Sydney, Melbourne, Brisbane, Cairns, Darwin, Hobart, or Fremantle

(Perth). Claims at seaports should be made no later than 1 hour before the scheduled departure time of the ship. If your cruise departs from elsewhere in Australia, or if you are flying out from an airport other than Sydney, Melbourne, Brisbane, Adelaide, Cairns, Perth, Darwin, or the Gold Coast, telephone the **Australian Customs Service** (☎ **1300/363 263** in Australia, or 02/9313 3010) to see if you can still claim the refund.

Other taxes include a "reef tax," officially dubbed the **Environmental Management Charge,** of A$3.50 per day for every person over the age of 4 every time he or she enters the Great Barrier Reef Marine Park on a commercial tour. This charge goes toward park upkeep, and is sometimes (but not always) included in the ticket price.

Most airlines and an increasing number of tour operators, such as cruise companies and long-distance trains, also impose a "fuel surcharge" to help them combat rising fuel costs. This is usually added to the price of your ticket.

Tipping   Tipping is not expected in Australia, but it is always appreciated. It is usual to tip around 10% or round up to the nearest A$10 for a substantial meal in a family restaurant. Some passengers round up to the nearest dollar in a cab, but it's okay to insist on every bit of change back. Tipping bellboys and porters is sometimes done, but no one tips bar staff, barbers, or hairdressers.

Toilets Public toilets are easy to find—and free—in most Australian cities and towns. If you are driving, most towns have "restrooms" on the main street (although the cleanliness may vary wildly). In some remote areas, public toilets are "composting," meaning there is no flush, just a drop into a pit beneath you. If you really want to plan ahead, consult the **National Public Toilet Map** (www.toiletmap.gov.au) (there's an App for it as well!).

Index

See also Accommodations and Restaurant indexes, below.

RESTAURANT INDEX